Mel Bay Presents

The ENCYCLOPEDIA

of the Harmonica

By Peter Krampert

1 2 3 4 5 6 7 8 9 0

Visit us on the Web at www.melbay.com — E-mail us at email@melbay.com

Table of Contents

Dedication

This book is dedicated to my high school American Folklore teacher, Mr. Jim Wright, who not only introduced me to the harmonica and set me on my life's path, but also instilled in me a desire to look beyond the stories of conventional history; to strive to dig deeper, to seek the many layers of truths that lay beneath the surface and to never accept any single source as the final answer to anything.

The world is extraordinarily fortunate to have teachers who possess his commitment to quality in education and drive for excellence.

Introduction

I will always remember that moment over twenty years ago as if it just happened. I was a sophomore in high school and it was the first day of my American Folklore class. The teacher, Jim Wright, walked up to the podium, pulled a Hohner Marine Band harmonica out of his pocket, played a tune and announced, "Anybody who learns to play one of these by the end of the semester gets 100 extra credit points." I thought it would be easy, (and I did it,) but I had no idea at the time that the harmonica would lead me into an odyssey which has spanned more than two decades and shows no signs of abating.

The harmonica is the instrument that plays America's soundtrack. It has been played everywhere by every kind of person. It's been played by paupers, popes and presidents, by con men, crap-shooters, cowboys and astronauts for every kind of music from Beethoven to the Blues. A million and a half Americans play the harmonica and more than ten million are sold worldwide each year. It is, in fact, the world's most popular instrument.

The harmonica is everywhere; on the concert stage, records, radio, television, movies and commercials. It's woven into the fabric of our musical beings. John Steinbeck, Robert Service and Carl Sandburg all wrote about it. Seven U.S. Presidents and at least one Pope played the harmonica when they weren't too busy being world leaders. It made its first trip into outer space in 1965 and appeared with the Beatles on the Ed Sullivan Show. It is affordable and portable. It is the instrument of the people.

The harmonica, however, has been generally disregarded as a serious musical instrument. Go to your local library and you'll find dozens of books on everything from hand bells to horns but almost nothing on the harmonica. Go to your local newsstand and chances are that you'll find several guitar magazines, but not a single one on the humble mouth organ. Local schools spend hundreds of thousands of dollars each year on band instruments, but not a cent on the tin sandwich. At this time there is only one school in the entire United States that offers college accredited courses in harmonica.

Perhaps the harmonica itself brings on this disrespect. It's small, fitting into any pocket. In the movies you'll never see a hobo playing a piano or a trombone. Most of the instruction books you'll see at your local music store have the words "easy" or "simple" in their titles. Almost anyone can pick out a tune on the instrument after only a matter of minutes. Even the Musician's Union classified the harmonica as a "toy" until 1948 and they changed that classification only after The Harmonicats' "Peg O' My Heart" became the number one best-selling song of the previous year.

In 1995 I started to design an all-inclusive course on harmonica that would not only include instruction on how to play the instrument, but also give a comprehensive background on it's history and players. I was dumbfounded to find that the world's most popular instrument was totally lacking any reference materials on the subject. No discographies, no player indexes and only one brief history of the harmonica could be found. Over a million and a half players in the U.S. and they were left to their own devices. I immediately set out to compile an encyclopedic work that would ensure that harmonica players would have at least one source for most of their questions on the instrument.

What you see here is the end result of several years of collecting facts, conducting interviews, surfing the internet and compiling an exhaustive list of recordings that feature the harmonica. There are over 900 articles about the players, the groups they played with and many other facets of harmonica lore. You'll find over 5,000 recordings listed in these pages that feature harmonica players. There are articles on techniques, history, terminology, interesting harmonica trivia and most importantly, resources that will help anybody who is curious with finding out more about the harmonica.

In this new edition I present dozens of new articles on players and bands as well as over 1,500 new recordings. Information from the previous edition has been updated, thanks to the hundreds of letters, calls and E-mails I have received since the first edition came out. I've also had the opportunity to meet and interview dozens of the best harmonica players in the business. This new edition is lavishly illustrated, containing over 100 photographs of your favorite players.

Unfortunately, not everyone was included in this volume. Over the course of its nearly 200 years of existence, the harmonica has boasted millions of players and not every one was included into the pages of history. There are no definitive reference works on the Vaudeville harmonica bands. Most of my research in that area had to come from personal interviews and from looking at the scrapbooks that were kept by the few surviving veterans of that golden age of entertainment. Many of the early Blues and Country music players were left uncredited or unrecorded. Many of today's up and coming players haven't come to my notice yet and foreign players have been more difficult to find. I've attempted to be as thorough as possible and I apologize to anyone who feels excluded. I hope to include them in future editions of this work.

As always, this is a work in progress. New players emerge on the scene, players pass away. New recordings come out almost every day. While I have done my best to take a long, hard look at players outside the U.S., I'm certain that I've managed to miss a few. That is where the readers take over. If there is someone who deserves my attention, write me and let me know about them. If there is a recording I should hear, send it to me and I will listen. If I should make a mistake, please let me know so I can rectify it. This book is really the property of the community of harmonica players and I am the caretaker. With your help, we can make it prosper and bloom.

Overall, I think that you will find this book to be an excellent reference in your search to find more information on the harmonica. Enjoy yourself! I hope the Encyclopedia will help guide you on your quest to learn more about this wonderful instrument.

Peter Krampert, 2000

Acknowledgements

"If I have seen further, it is because I have stood on the shoulders of giants"
-Sir Isaac Newton

It would be impossible to attempt anything of the magnitude of an encyclopedic work without the contributions of a vast number of wonderfully gifted and dedicated people. Just as it is not possible to include every single person who has ever played the harmonica for an audience, it is every bit as difficult to express my gratitude to everyone who helped this project along, but I will try, never the less.

In no particular order, I would like to thank the harmonica players who got me started on the instrument. Without their guidance, I would never have come as far as I have. They include Jim Wright, my American Folklore teacher, who motivated me to start playing. My father, Bill Krampert, who bought me my first harmonica and taught me my first valuable lesson, "Don't ever let anyone else play your harmonica; it's like borrowing a toothbrush." My cousin, Paul Krampert, who took the time to teach me the secrets of note bending. And most of all, to harmonica virtuoso Larry Adler, who took the time to talk to me when I was a sixteen year old novice on the instrument.

Over the years I've benefited greatly from the time, knowledge and advice of many of the world's greatest harmonica players including: Jerry Adler, Larry Adler, Billy Boy Arnold, Richard Bain, Steve Baker, Robert Bonfiglio, Billy Branch, James Cotton, Lou Delin, George Fields, Al Fiore, Joe Filisko, William Galison, Dick Gardner, Dennis Gruenling, Adam Gussow, Cham-Ber Huang, Jelly Roll Johnson, Mindy Jostyn, Leon LaFell, Howard Levy, Larry Logan, Charlie McCoy, Paul Messinger, Chris Michalek, Tommy Morgan, Paul Oscher, Lee Oskar, George Ross, Corky Siegel, Al & Judy Smith, Manny Smith, Douglas Tate, Sonny Terry, and a host of others who were patient enough to spend some time telling me about themselves, their experiences and their secrets for playing the thing like a pro.

This book could never have been written without the help of the staffs at the public libraries in Chicago, Niles, Des Plaines, Arlington Heights and Park Ridge, Illinois. I would especially like to express my most profound gratitude to the Reader's Services staff at the Park Ridge Public Library. Their assistance as I learned the necessary word processing and typesetting programs, their patience in teaching me the various aspects of using the computer for writing and research and most of all, their enthusiasm made it a pleasure to devote so many hours to this project.

The internet has turned out to be an extremely valuable resource for information about the harmonica and I'd strongly recommend it to anyone who would like to find out more. I'd like to thank Buzz Krantz, acting president of the Windy City Harmonica Club, for turning me on to the internet's awesome potential as a research tool. I would also like to thank John Bracich whose help, in my early days of web surfing, gave me unbelievable guidance through the various search engines. Without his help in locating useful harmonica web sites, this book would not have been as complete. I'd especially like to thank the countless people who have taken the time to publish some truly remarkable web pages. Among these would be the Diatonic Reference Page by Mike Will, the Chromatic Reference Page by "G" in New Zealand, Planet Harmonica by Benoit Felten, any of the multiple pages by Danny Wilson and countless others too numerous to list here. They were and will always be a great place for anyone to go for information. I wish I had space to thank each one individually, but that would be a book unto itself.

Many thanks go out to my employers, managers and colleagues at the Movie Facts and Citation Limousine companies who accommodated my hectic work schedule, lent their moral support, gave wonderful suggestions that improved the overall character of this book and endured my seemingly endless stream of harmonica trivia.

I'd like to thank the Lee Oskar, Hering, Huang, ILUS, 101, Suzuki, and Hohner harmonica companies for the information they provided. I'd especially like to thank Toni Radler at Hohner for her support and enthusiasm for this project. It's editors like her that make writers like me look better. I'd also like to tip my hat to the fine people at Kevin's Harps, F&R Farrell, Coast-to-Coast Music and Joe's Virtual Music store. Selling harmonicas by mail order has to be a tough business, but they really come through with outstanding customer service, answers to most on my questions and great technical support. Many thanks to Johnna Cossaboon at Hohner for providing me with amany of the photos for this edition.

Dozens of the world's greatest harmonica players provided photographs, CD's and biographical information for this book. It has

3

been great receiving these packages and getting to hear the work of these master players. You will find their pictures throughout the book.

My undying gratitude goes out to the folks at SPAH, H.O.O.T., the Windy City, Milwaukee, Woodstock and Buckeye State harmonica clubs for their help and support, especially in helping me to track down some of the surviving players from the Vaudeville-era harmonica bands. Their leads led to many interviews and opportunities to play with these harmonica giants.

The cover and design of the first edition was conceived by Carol Knox and rendered by Deanna Budnick, two ladies who made that first time around all the more successful. A former teacher, my mother, Jane Krampert, did an outstanding job of proofreading the manuscript of this edition and made it an easier book to read. I'd also like to single out my sister Jennifer Moore a talented visionary in her own right whose last minute generosity made the publication of the first edition possible. Her act of faith did more for my self-confidence than I will ever be able to repay.

This work would not have been as comprehensive or concise if it hadn't been for the love and support of my family and friends, all of whom made this task a little less lonely to perform. I'd especially like to single out my wife Donna. The process of putting together a work of this depth is a long and lonely ordeal, but her encouragement and patience really kept me going through the entire process of researching and writing this book. Her insights and support helped to make this volume much easier to write.

Most of all I'd like to thank all of the harmonica players, past and present, who have given so much to the instrument. The big names and the unknowns, the great virtuosos and the little guys who were simply content to pick out a tune. They are the ones who actually wrote this history, and my life would not have been as rich without them. For those of you who are going to add to the wondrous tapestry that the harmonica has woven, my hat is off to you and I hope to see you in future editions of this book.

A Brief Chronological History of the Harmonica

Circa 3,000 B.C. - The first free-reeded instruments are developed in China. Over the next several thousand years, free-reeded instruments will evolve and spread all over Southeast Asia.

1636 - Marin Mersènne describes in his letters the Sheng, an Asian free-reed wind instrument, thus introducing the principle of the free-reed to Europe.

1776 - French Jesuit Missionary Père Amiot ships several Shengs from China to Paris.

Circa 1780's - European instrument makers begin experimenting with free-reeds.

1816 - Johann Buschmann, a German organ builder, introduces his Terpodion, a free-reeded keyboard instrument that would serve as a predecessor to both the harmonica and the harmonium.

1821 - Christian Friedrich Buschmann, son of organ builder Johann Buschmann, registers the first European patent for a free-reeded mouth organ. He calls his invention the "Aura".

1825 - The first 20 note / 10 hole, Blow-draw free-reed mouth organ configuration is developed by a Bohemian named Richter. This is the basic configuration still used in most harmonicas today.

1827 - Christian Messner, a clockmaker from Trossingen, Germany, starts building harmonicas with his cousin, Christian Weiss.

1829 - The first mass production of harmonicas begins in Vienna, Austria.

1857 - After visiting the harmonica factory of Messner and Weiss, Matthias Hohner, a fellow clockmaker from Trossingen, starts to manufacture harmonicas in his kitchen with the help of his family and one or two workmen. During their first year they produced 700 harmonicas.

1862 - At the urging of relatives who had already immigrated to the United States, Matthias Hohner begins to export harmonicas to America with great success.

1867 - The M. Hohner Company produces 22,000 harmonicas.

1878 - Machinery developed by Julius Berthold enables metal reeds to be stamped out by machines, rather than by hand. Though the reeds are stamped out by machine, the M. Hohner Company still tunes most of its harmonicas by hand to this day.

1879 - The Richter note configuration is introduced to ten-hole harmonicas. This note layout would become the leading configuration for diatonic harmonicas.

1887 - M. Hohner produces 1 million harmonicas annually.

1893 - An American depression causes M. Hohner to cease exports to the U.S. and to start marketing to other countries, thus expanding the range of influence of the harmonica.

1896 - M. Hohner introduces and later patents its Marine Band model harmonica. Sporting revolutionary raised ornate metal covers and excellent construction features, it becomes the world's number one best-selling harmonica.

1897 - M. Hohner is producing 3 million harmonicas a year.

1900 - Matthias Hohner hands over control of his company to his five sons.

Dec. 11, 1902 - Matthias Hohner dies.

1911 - The M. Hohner Company produces 8 Million harmonicas a year.

Circa 1920's - The beginning of the golden age of the harmonica. Recording allows Blues, Country, Jazz and Jug Band artists to be heard for the first time by a mass audience. Vernon Dalhart's "Wreck of The Old 97" becomes Country music's first million-selling record. Deford Bailey stars in the Grand Old Opry and cuts the first Country records in Nashville. Blues artists are recorded, first in New York and by the end of the decade, hundreds from all over the country have been recorded. Harmonica bands spring up all over the country and become the rage in Vaudeville.

1923 - Albert Hoxie, a philanthropist from Philadelphia, starts to organize harmonica contests and harmonica bands, complete with full marching band uniforms. This kicks off a national craze for harmonica bands.

1924 - M. Hohner starts producing chromatic harmonicas. It is also during the 1920's that Hohner creates bass, chord and polyphonia models in order to meet the musical needs of harmonica bands.

1927 - Entertainer and harmonica instructor Borrah Minevitch meets Johnny Puleo and The Harmonica Rascals are born. Combining harmonica music with slapstick comedy, The Harmonica Rascals quickly become one of the top-drawing acts in vaudeville and they attract thousands of players to the harmonica.

Circa 1930's - Harmonica bands are all the rage in America. Harmonica instruction is a part of the regular curriculum in many public schools. Harmonica bands starts appearing in movies. Larry Adler emerges as the first major soloist on the harmonica, playing Classical and Jazz pieces on the instrument. The Jug Band craze dies out until the Folk revival of the 1960's.

1930 - M. Hohner's annual sales reach 25 million harmonicas worldwide.

Circa 1940's - The outbreak of World War II temporarily halts the import of harmonicas from Germany to the U.S. Harmonica bands dissolves as many players enlist in the armed forces. A labor shortage in the north causes hundreds of Blues players to migrate north to Chicago and other industrial cities. Electric Blues begins as many players like Snooky Pryor experiment with amplifying their instruments.

1947 - The Harmonicats' recording of "Peg O' My Heart" is the number one best-selling record of the year. It would go on to become one of the best-selling single records of all time, topping over 20 million in sales. Its success also convinced the Musician's Union to change the classification of the harmonica from a "toy" to that of a legitimate instrument, thus allowing harmonica players to join the union.

Circa 1950's - While the larger harmonica bands virtually disappear, harmonica trios, spurred on by the success of The Harmonicats, grow in popularity. Amplified harmonica players, led by Chicago's Little Walter, dominate the Chicago Blues scene. Rock and Roll emerges as a new musical style. Guitar players dominate the new style and harmonicas are almost unheard of in Rock until the next decade. In England, Blues fans like John Mayall and Cyril Davies lay the foundation for the British Invasion of the 1960's. Jean "Toots" Thielemans becomes a major instrumentalist in Jazz.

1951 - According to legend, Little Walter becomes one of the very first to play Chicago-style amplified harmonica. While recording with Muddy Waters, Walter plugged his harmonica mike directly into a guitar amplifier, thus overdriving the sound and creating a new style of playing.

Circa 1960's - The Folk music craze, led by Bob Dylan, leads thousands to explore playing the harmonica. Jug bands make a resurgence as part of the renewed interest in Folk music. The Beatles lead the British invasion. John Lennon is often featured with his harmonica. Several British bands, such as The Rolling Stones and The Yardbirds are fronted by singer / harmonica players. By the late 1960's there is a re-birth in the popularity of Blues music led by three harmonica players from Chicago: Paul Butterfield, Charlie Musselwhite and Corky Siegel.

1962 - SPAH, (The Society for the Preservation and Advancement of the Harmonica), is formed in the Detroit area. Over the next few years dozens of smaller clubs are formed that will provide a regular meeting place for harmonica enthusiasts.

December 16, 1965 - The harmonica becomes the first musical instrument in outer space when astronaut Wally Schirra plays "Jingle Bells" on a Hohner Little Lady model that he smuggled aboard the Gemini 4 spacecraft.

Circa 1970's - The harmonica experiences a decline in popularity as guitarists continue to dominate both Rock and Blues music, and country music shifts to an over-produced Nashville sound. The J. Geils Band and its harmonica player, Magic Dick, stands on the forefront of Rock harmonica. Blues music suffers from one of its periodic declines in popularity.

Circa 1980's - The success of The Blues Brothers helps to kick off another revival of interest in Blues harmonica. The Cham-Ber Huang and Lee Oskar Harmonica Companies open up new frontiers in harmonica design by introducing innovations such as new tunings and replaceable reed plates to the instrument.

1986 - The M. Hohner Company produces it's one billionth harmonica.

Circa 1990's - The emergence of Howard Levy, Sugar Blue and John Popper of the band Blues Traveler, push the frontiers of Jazz, Blues and Rock harmonica playing. A return to traditionalist Country music sparks a renewed interest in harmonica in Country music.

Alphabetical Listings

– A –

An Accordion with Soul

A nickname for the harmonica.

The Aces

Formed: Late 1940's - Chicago, IL

Chicago Blues band

Originally Junior Wells' band, *The Aces* were taken over by Little Walter when he left the *Muddy Waters Band* and Junior Wells took his place. On some recordings, they are referred to as *The Jukes.*

The Aces included brothers Dave and Louis Myers on guitars and Fred Below on drums. They went on to become leading players on a large number of Chess and other Blues recordings during the 1950's, 60's and 70's.

Discography:

1971 - **Kings of Chicago Blues,** *Vogue* // 1971 - **Dust My Broom,** *Vogue* // 1975 - **The Aces with their Guest,** *MCM* // 1976 - **Chicago Beat,** *Black & Blue.*

Adams, Derroll

Real name: Derroll Lewis Thompson
Born: November 25, 1925 - Portland, OR
Died: February 18, 2000 - Belgium

Folk singer-songwriter, banjo, harmonica

Though known primarily as a banjo player, Derroll Adams learned to play harmonica as a teenager. During his career he accompanied Woody Guthrie, Ramblin' Jack Elliott and Donovan. He toured Europe with Elliott throughout the late 50's and early 60's.

After his career was curtailed due to severe alcoholism, he made a comeback in 1972 and continued performing until his death in 2000.

Discography:

1950's - **Portland Town** // 1957 - **The Ramblin' Boy,** (with Ramblin' Jack Elliott), *Topic UK* // 1957 - **Roll On Buddy,** (with Ramblin' Jack Elliott), *Topic* // 1970's - **Feelin' Fine,** *Village Things* // 1984 - **Songs of the Banjoman** // 1991 - **Derroll Adams' 65th Birthday Party** // 1997 - **America,** (with Ramblin' Jack Elliott) // 1999 - **Early Sessions,** (with Ramblin' Jack Elliott), *Tradition.*

Movies:

1957 - **Durango.**

Adams, Woodrow Wilson

Born: April 9, 1917 - Tchula, MS

Blues guitar, harmonica

During the 1940's, Woodrow Wilson Adams lived in the Robinsonville area where he worked with Robert Jr. Lockwood, Robert Nighthawk and Sonny Boy Williamson II. He played with *Howlin' Wolf Band* from the late 1940's until 1952 and start making radio appearances in the early 1950's. He began recording for the Checker label with the Three B's in 1952.

Adams recorded on his own for the Charly label in 1952, recorded with *The Boogie Blues Blasters* in 1955 and for the Home of the Blues label in 1961. He worked sporadically through the 1960's, recording for the Flyright label in 1967.

Discography:

1976 - **Lowdown Memphis Harmonica Jam.**

Adegbalola, Gaye

Born: March 21, 1944 - Fredricksburg, VA

Blues vocals, guitar, harmonica

Best known as a member of the Blues trio *Saffire: The Uppity Blues Women,* Gaye Adegbalola has been playing music for most of her life. After spending several years as an award-winning science teacher, she began taking guitar lessons from Ann Rabson in 1977. The two started performing together in 1984, later incorporating a third member to become *Saffire.*

A W.C. Handy Award winner, Ms. Adegbalola plays the harmonica in addition to her singing and guitar playing.

Discography: (also see: Saffire)
1999 - **Bittersweet Blues,** *Alligator*

On Video:
1997 - **Learn to Sing the Blues,** *Homespun Tapes.*

Adler, Jerry

Born: October 30, 1918 - Baltimore, MD

Pop / Classical harmonica soloist

Jerry Adler is the younger brother of harmonica legend Larry Adler. He won a statewide harmonica contest sponsored by the Baltimore Sun newspaper when he was thirteen years old. By the time he was seventeen, he had played a British Royal Command Performance.

He began working in Hollywood in 1937 and worked with *The Cappy Barra Harmonica Ensemble* on the movie "Pot O' Gold." He also coached the star, Jimmy Stewart, on how to play the harmonica for the film. Later he gave lessons to future studio harmonica player Tommy Morgan. Adler played at the White House in 1954, including a duet with President Harry Truman on the piano.

He has appeared on TV, with numerous symphony orchestras and has worked as a guest entertainer on several cruise ships.

Discography:
1983 - **The Harmonica Artistry of Jerry Adler,** *Art Brigade* // 1995 - **The Harmonica Magic of Jerry Adler,** *USA.*

Movies:
1941 - **Pot O' Gold** // 1953 - **Shane** // 1957 - **The James Dean Story** // 1960 - **The Alamo.**

Adler, Larry

Born: February 10, 1914 - Baltimore, MD
Died: August 6, 2001 - London, England

Pop / Classical harmonica soloist

Larry Adler, who grew up in Baltimore, is the brother of harmonica soloist Jerry Adler. Larry began playing in Fred Sonnen's *Baltimore Harmonica Band* at age twelve and won the Baltimore Sun's harmonica contest in 1927 by playing Beethoven's "Minuet in G."

In 1928, Adler headed to New York City to audition for Borrah Minevitch's *Harmonica Rascals.* Minevitch responded by say, "Kid, you stink". Not disheartened, Adler embarked upon a solo career instead, playing in road shows and Vaudeville.

In 1930, Adler landed his first recording job, soloing on Ruth Etting's "If I Could Be with You." He also landed a spot in Ziegfield's "Smiles." Adler made his first film appearance in "Many Happy Returns" in 1934, backed by the Duke Ellington Orchestra. In addition, in 1934, he made his first European tour. He made his first solo records in 1935; selections included Gershwin's "Rhapsody in Blue" and Ravel's "Bolero." While on tour in Paris in 1938, he recorded four sides with the *Quintet of The Hot Club of France.* Throughout the 1940's Adler worked steadily doing USO tours, Pop and Classical concerts.

Beginning in the 1930's several composers started writing orchestral pieces around Larry Adler's harmonica playing, Including; Ralph Vaughan-Williams, Malcolm Arnold, Arthur Benjamin, Darius Milhaud, Jean Berger, Graham Whettam, Francis Chagrin, Gordon Jacob, Serge Lancen, Naresh Sohal and others. Composer Maurice Ravel left specific instructions in his will that Larry Adler would be able to perform his "Bolero" without having to pay a royalty.

He was blacklisted in the early 1950's due to his opposition to the House Un-American Activities Committee and had to move to England to work. He composed the score for the film "Genevieve," which earned the 1954 Oscar nomination for best score. Due to his blacklisting, his name was not allowed to be read at the awards ceremony. It would not be until 1986 that the Academy officially acknowledged Adler as the composer of the score.

He continued to play and record steadily ever since. Occasionally he returned to the U.S. for concert appearances. In 1994, for his 80th birthday, he recorded harmonica solos for the album "The Glory of Gershwin," which became the number two album of the year in Great Britain.

Discography:
1986 - **Live at rhe Ballroom**, *Newport Classics* // 1994 - **The Mouth Organ Virtuoso**, *EMI* // 1994 - **Various Artists: The Glory of Gershwin**, (Adler solos on every song), *Mercury* // 1995 - **Maestro of the Mouth Organ - The Thirties**, *ASV* // 1995 - **Rhapsody in Blue**, *Empress* // 1996 - **Larry Adler**, *Flapper* // 1996 - **The Great Larry Adler Plays Standards**, *Pearl* // 1997 - **Harmonica Virtuoso - Legacy** // 1999 - **The Genius of Larry Adler**, *Polygram* // 1998 - **Piano Roll Recordings**, *Prestige* // 1998 - **Volume 1: Golden Era**, *Prestige* // 1998 - **Volume 2: Golden Era**, *Prestige* // 1998 - **Goes Classical**, *Danwell* // 1998 - **Salutes Gershwin**, *Danwell* // **Best of Summertime**, *BMG* // **Live in Australia**, *EMI*.

Movies:
1934 - **Many Happy Returns** // 1936 - **The Big Broadcast of 1937** // 1937 - **The Singing Marine** // 1938 - **St. Martin's Lane** // 1945 - **Music for Millions** // 1948 - **Three Daring Daughters** // 1955 - **Genevieve** // 1955 - **Jumping for Joy** // 1958 - **A Cry from the Street** // 1961 - **The Hellions** // 1963 - **The Hook** // 1963 - **King and Country** // 1963 - **The Great Chase** // 1964 - **High Wind in Jamaica**.

Books:
1963 - **Jokes and How to Tell Them** // 1984 - **It Ain't Necessarily So** // 1994 - **Me and My Big Mouth**.

Aerosmith

Formed: 1970

Rock Band
One of the top Hard rock groups to emerge in the 1970's, *Aerosmith* has managed to maintain a high-profile presence on the record charts for more than two decades. Their lead singer, Steven Tyler, occasionally plays the harmonica on record and at live concerts.

See - Steven Tyler

Discography:
1973 - **Aerosmith**, *Columbia* // 1974 - **Get Your Wings**, *Columbia* // 1975 - **Toys in the Attic**, *Columbia* // 1976 - **Rocks**, *Columbia* // 1977 - **Draw the Line**, *Columbia* // 1978 - **Live Bootleg**, *Columbia* // 1979 - **Night in the Ruts**, *Columbia* // 1980 - **Greatest Hits**, *Columbia* // 1980 - **First Decade**, *Columbia* // 1982 - **Rock in a Hard Place**, *Columbia* // 1985 - **Done with Mirrors**, *Geffen* // 1986 - **Classics Live**, *Columbia* // 1987 - **Classics Live 2**, *Columbia* // 1987 - **Permanent Vacation**, *Geffen* // 1988 - **Gems**, *Columbia* // 1989 - **Pump**, *Geffen* // 1991 - **Pandora's Box**, *Columbia* // 1993 - **Toxic Graffiti**, *KTS* // 1993 - **Get a Grip**, *Geffen* // 1994 - **Big Ones**, *Geffen* // 1994 - **Box of Fire**, *Columbia* // 1995 - **Pandora's Toys**, *Columbia* // 1997 - **Nine Lives**, *Columbia* // 1998 - **A Little South of Sanity**, *Geffen*.

Alexander, George

Born: May 18, 1946 - San Mateo, CA

Rock bass guitar and harmonica player
George Alexander played the bass guitar and harmonica for the Pop Rock band *The Flamin' Groovies* during the mid-1980's

Discography: (see - The Flamin' Groovies)

Allison, Luther

Born: August 17, 1939 - Mayflower, AR
Died: August 12, 1997 - Madison, WI

Blues guitar, vocals, harmonica
Luther Allison began his musical career singing in his family's Gospel group in the late 1940's. They moved to Chicago in 1951. Luther dropped out of school to play with local Blues bands around 1954.

He began recording in 1967 and in addition to having a stellar solo career he played with Magic Sam, Shakey Jake Harris and many others. He passed away in 1997 after a bout with cancer.

Discography:
1973 - **Bad News is Coming**, *Motown* // 1974 - **Luther's Blues**, *Gordy* // 1976 - **Night Life**, *Gordy* // 1977 - **Love Me Papa**, *Black and Blue* // 1979 - **Live in Paris**, *Buddah* // 1979 - **Live** // 1979 - **Gonna Be a Live One Here Tonight**, *Rumble* // 1982 - **Southside Safari**, *Red Lightnin'* // 1984 - **Let's Have a Natural Ball**, *JSP* // 1985 - **Here I Come**, *Encore* // 1986 - **Powerwire Blues**, *Charly* // 1987 - **Richman**, *Charly* // 1988 - **Life is a Bitch**, *Encore* // 1988 - **Love Me Mama**, *Delmark* // 1988 - **Serious**, *Blind Pig* // 1993 - **Sweet Home Chicago**, *Charly* // 1993 - **Hand Me Down My Moonshine**, *Inakustik* // 1994 - **Soul Fixin' Man**, *Alligator* // 1995 - **Blue Streak**, *Alligator* // 1996 - **The Motown Years 1972-1976**, *Motown* // 1996 - **Rick Moon**, *RFR* // 1997 - **Reckless**, *Alligator* // 1998 - **Unplugged**, *Ruf* // 1999 - **Live in Chicago**, *Alligator*.

Movies:
1976 - **Cooley High**.

The Amazing Rhythm Aces

Formed: 1972 - Knoxville, TN
Disbanded: 1981
Re-united: 1996

Country / Rock band

The Amazing Rhythm Aces blended Country with elements of Rock and R&B into their music. Scoring several big hits in the mid-1970's, they enjoyed some chart success, including their biggest hit, "Third Rate Romance," before disbanding in 1981. Their rhythm guitarist, Russell Smith also played the harmonica.

The group re-united in 1996 with Smith and began to record once more.

See - Russell Smith

Discography:

1975 - **Stacked Deck,** *ABC* // 1976 - **Too Stuffed to Jump,** *ABC* // 1977 - **Toucan Do It Too,** *ABC* // 1978 - **Burning the Ballroom Down,** *ABC* // 1978 - **The Amazing Rhythm Aces,** *Columbia* // 1980 - **How the Hell Do You Spell Rhythm?,** *Warner Brothers* // 1981 - **Full House: Aces High,** *MSS* // 1982 - **4 You 4 Ever: The Best Of...,** *M&R* // 1997 - **Ride Again,** *Breaker Productions* // 1997 - **Out of the Blue,** *Breaker Productions* // 1999 - **Concert Classics, Vol. 3,** *Renaissance* // 1999 - **Chock Full of Country Goodness,** *Valley* // 2000 - **Absolutely Live,** *Ice House.*

Amerson, Rich

Born: 1887 - Livingston, AL

Blues harmonica player

Rich Amerson played harmonica from his youth at local dances and parties in rural Alabama. He recorded for the Library of Congress in 1937 and 1940. Some film footage was also shot of those sessions. He also recorded for the Folkways label in 1950, disappeared from the Blues scene shortly after, and hasn't been heard from since that time.

Discography:

1960 - **Negro Music of Alabama, Vol. 1: Secular,** *Folkways* // **Field Recordings, Vol. 4,** *Document.*

Amiot, Père

18th Century French missionary

Père Amiot is the Jesuit missionary who was the first to bring free-reeded musical instruments to Europe, shipping several Shengs to Paris in 1776. This launched an era of experimentation into the possibilities of creating a European free-reeded instrument, thus leading to the creation of the harmonica.

Andersen, Eric

Born: February 14, 1943 - Pittsburgh, PA

Folk singer-songwriter, guitar, harmonica

Raised in upstate New York, Eric Andersen began performing in his late teens and became a part of the Folk music scenes in Boston and Greenwich Village. Discovered by Tom Paxton in the early 1960's, he has worked with Joan Baez, Phil Ochs, Judy Collins and others.

Andersen started recording in 1964 for the Vanguard label and has remained active, playing and recording well into the new century. He augments his music by playing harmonica on a neckbrace.

Discography:

1965 - **Eric Andersen '65 (AKA: Today is the Highway),** *Vanguard* // 1966 - *'Bout Changes and Things,* *Vanguard* // 1967 - **Take 2,** *Vanguard* // 1968 - **Tin Can Alley,** *Vanguard* // 1968 - **More Hits from Tin Can Alley,** *Vanguard* // 1968 - **Country Dream '66-69,** *Vanguard* // 1969 - **Eric Andersen,** *Warner Brothers* // 1970 - **Avalanche,** *Warner Brothers* // 1971 - **The Best of Eric Andersen,** *Vanguard* // 1972 - **Blue River,** *Columbia* // 1973 - **Stage,** *CBS* // 1975 - **Be True to You,** *Arista* // 1976 - **Sweet Surprise,** *Arista* // 1977 - **The Best Songs,** *Arista* // 1989 - **Ghosts Upon the Road,** *Gold Castle* // 1991 - **Stages: The Lost Album,** *Columbia/Legacy* // 1993 - **Rick Danko, Eric Andersen and Jonas Field** // 1997 - **Ridin' the Blinds** // 1997 - **The Collection,** *Archive* // 1998 - **Memory of the Future,** *Appleseed* // 1999 - **Violets of Dawn,** *Vanguard* // 2000 - **You Can't Relive the Past,** *Appleseed* // **Midnight Sun,** *Wind & Sand* // **Istanbul (AKA: Movin' in the Wind),** *Wind & Sand.*

Anderson, Bill

Real name: James William Anderson III
Born: November 1, 1937 - Columbia, SC

Country singer-songwriter, guitar, harmonica

Bill Anderson is known mostly as a highly successful singer-songwriter and a member of the Grand Old Opry. He plays harmonica and accompanies himself on guitar.

Discography:

1962 - **Bill Anderson Sings Country Heart Songs,** *Decca* // 1963 - **Still,** *Decca* // 1964 - **Bill Anderson Showcase,** *Decca* // 1964 - **Bill Anderson Sings,** *Decca* // 1965 - **Bright Lights and Country Music,** *Decca* // 1965 - **From This Pen,** *Decca* // 1966 - **I Love You Drops,** *Decca* // 1967 - **Get While the Gettin's Good,** *Decca* // 1967 - **I Can Do Nothing Alone,** *Decca* // 1968 - **Happy State of Mind,** *Decca* // 1969 - **Wild Weekend,** *Decca* // 1969 - **For Loving You,** *MCA* // 1972 - **The Bill Anderson Story,** *MCA* // 1973 - **Bill Anderson's Greatest Hits, Vol. 2,** *MCA* // 1977 - **Billy Boy and Mary Lou,** *MCA* // 1983 - **Southern & Fried,** *Southern Tracks* // 1991 - **The Best of Bill Anderson,** *Curb* // 1993 - **Country Music Heaven,** *Capitol* // 1994 - **Out in the Country,** *Drive Archive* // 1998 - **Fine**

Wine, *Warner Brothers* // 2000 - **Best of the Best,** *Federal.*

Anderson, Ian

Born: August 10, 1947 - Edinburgh, Scotland

Rock flute, vocals, harmonica

Ian Anderson is the lead singer and flute player for the Rock band *Jethro Tull.* He played harmonica on several of the band's albums, including the song, "New Day Yesterday" on the 1969 album "Stand Up."

Anderson, John

Born: December 13, 1954 - Orlando, FL

Country singer-songwriter, guitar, harmonica

John Anderson started in music at age five, first with guitar, later with the harmonica. He began performing professionally at age fifteen and shortly thereafter moved to Nashville, where he worked in a variety of jobs until he landed a record contract in the late 1970's. He's put together an impressive string of Country hits since that time.

Discography:
1980 - **John Anderson,** *Warner Brothers* // 1981 - **John Anderson 2,** *Warner Brothers* // 1982 - **Wild & Blue,** *Warner Brothers* // 1984 - **John Anderson's Greatest Hits,** *Warner Brothers* // 1985 - **Tokyo, Oklahoma,** *Warner Brothers* // 1987 - **Blue Skies Again,** *MCA* // 1988 - **10,** *MCA* // 1990 - **Too Tough to Tame,** *Capitol* // 1992 - **Seminole Wind,** *BNA* // 1993 - **Solid Ground,** *BNA* // 1993 - **Country Comfort,** *Quicksilver* // 1994 - **You Can't Keep a Good Memory Down,** *MCA* // 1994 - **Country Till I Die,** *BNA* // 1994 - **Christmas Time,** *BNA* // 1995 - **Swingin',** *BNA* // 1997 - **Takin' Back the Country,** *Mercury* // 1998 - **The Essential,** *BNA* // 1998 - **Super Hits,** *BNA* // 1999 - **Backtracks,** *Renaissance.*

Anderson, Walter

Classical composer

Walter Anderson wrote "Fantasie for Harmonica and Orchestra" for John Sebastian, Sr. in 1947.

Anderson, "Little" Willie

Born: May 21, 1920 - West Memphis, AR
Died: June 20, 1991 - Chicago, IL

Blues harmonica player

Willie Anderson was taught to play the harmonica by his father. He moved to Chicago in 1939 and learned from Little Walter in the early 1950's, occasionally substituting at shows for Walter.

Anderson began recording in the 1970's and worked with Jimmy Johnson, Smokey Smothers, Johnny Young, Muddy Waters and others before succumbing to cancer in 1991.

Discography:
1981 - **Swinging the Blues,** *Earwig* // **Low Blows,** *Rooster Blues.*

Archibald, Red

Born: 1953 - California

Blues singer, harmonica player

Red Archibald has been playing the harmonica professionally since the 1970's, in California, New Orleans and touring in Europe for several years. He now works primarily out of the San Francisco Bay area with his band, *The Internationals.* In addition to his work as a solo artist, he has played with Elvin Bishop, Luther Tucker, Mark Hummel, Memphis Slim, Champion Jack Dupree and others.

Discography:
1995 - **It Just Won't Go Away,** *Blue Tone* // 1997 - **West Coast Soul Stew,** *Blue Tone.*

Area Code 615

Formed: 1969 - Nashville, TN
Disbanded: 1970

Country / Rock band

Made up entirely of Nashville studio musicians, including harmonica superstar Charlie McCoy, *Area Code 615* recorded two albums and played four shows at the Fillmore West in 1970. The group broke up when members decided to pursue their more lucrative careers as studio musicians.

Area Code 615 is considered to have been one of the groundbreaking groups in the Country/Rock movement. Remnants of the band went on to reform as *Barefoot Jerry.*

Discography:
1969 - **Area Code 615,** *Polydor* // 1970 - **A Trip to the Country,** *Polydor.*

Arnold, Billy Boy

Real name: William Arnold
Born: September 16, 1935 - Chicago, IL

Blues singer-songwriter, harmonica
Mostly self-taught on the harmonica, with some tutoring by John Lee "Sonny Boy" Williamson, Billy Boy Arnold started playing with *Bo Diddley and his Washboard Trio* in the early 1950's and recorded with them on the Cool label in 1953. He worked with Otis Rush, Johnny Shines and others during the early 1950's and appeared on Bo Diddley's first album for the Chess label.

He signed a solo contract and recorded for the VeeJay label from 1954 to 1955. He also played and recorded extensively throughout the 1950's with the *Earl Hooker Band*, Little Walter and others. Two of his hit songs, "I Wish You Would" and "I Ain't Got You" were covered by *The Yardbirds* and have become Blues standards.

Since the 1950's, Billy Boy Arnold has performed and recorded frequently. He signed to Alligator Records in the 1990's and produced several outstanding albums of Blues music.

Discography:
1955 - **I Wish You Would,** *Charly* // 1964 - **More Blues from the Southside,** *Prestige* // 1975 - **King of Chicago Blues, Vol. 3,** *Vogue* // 1975 - **Blow the Back Off It,** *Red Lightning* // 1976 - **Sinner's Prayer,** *Red Lightning* // 1979 - **Checkin' It Out,** *Smokestack Lightnin'* // 1980 - **Johnny Jones with Billy Boy Arnold,** *Alligator* // 1980 - **Crying and Pleading,** *Charly* // 1984 - **Ten Million Dollars,** *Blue Phoenix* // 1993 - **Back Where I Belong,** *Alligator* // 1994 - **Three Harp Boogie,** (with James Cotton and Paul Butterfield), *Rhino* // 1995 - **Goin' to Chicago,** *Testament* // 1996 - **Eldorado Cadillac,** *Alligator* // 1998 - **Blowin' the Blues Away,** *Culture Press* // 1999 - **Catfish,** *Catfish* // 2000 - **Live at the Venue** // **Charly Blues Masterworks,** *Charly.*

Arnold, Eddy

Born: May 15, 1918 - Madisonville, TN

Country singer-songwriter, guitar, harmonica
Though he was best known as a Country-Western singer, Eddy Arnold also played the guitar and harmonica.

Discography:
1967 - **The Best of Eddy Arnold,** *RCA* // 1970 - **The Best of Eddy Arnold, Vol. 2,** *RCA* // 1973 - **The Best of Eddy Arnold, Vol. 3,** *RCA.*

Arnold, Jimmy

Born: June 11, 1952 - Fries, VA
Died: December 26, 1992

Country multi-instrumentalist, including harmonica
Though never as popular as his talent warranted, Jimmy Arnold was a master of traditional Country music. He began by playing guitar as a youngster, later picking up mandolin, banjo and harmonica. By the time he was thirteen he had recorded his first record.

His drinking and erratic behavior got him kicked out of several bands and in 1985 he was jailed on a narcotics charge. Joining the church in the early 1990's, he sobered up and started to get his life straightened out, but the physical damage he had done to himself took it's toll and he died the day after Christmas in 1992.

Discography:
1974 - **Strictly Arnold,** *Rebel* // 1977 - **Jimmy Arnold Guitar,** *Rebel* // 1983 - **Southern Soul,** *Rebel* // **Rainbow Ride,** *Rebel.*

Arnold, Malcolm

Born: October 21, 1921 - England

Classical composer
Malcolm Arnold wrote "Harmonica Concerto, Op. 46" in 1954 for Larry Adler.

Recordings:
1994 - **Tommy Reilly Plays Harmonica Concertos,** *Chandos* // 1995 - **Walton, Grainger, Smetana, Borodin, Arnold,** (Tommy Reilly - soloist), *BBC Radio.*

Arthur, Emry

Born: 1900 - Wayne County, KY
Died: August 1966

Country singer, guitar, harmonica player
One of the early pioneers of Country music, Emry Arthur spent most of his life working around the Indianapolis area. He cut over 40 records between 1928 and 1935, some of them harmonica instrumentals.

Discography:
1987 - **I Am a Man of Constant Sorrow,** *Old Homestead.*

Aura

Circa - 1820's, "Aura" was the name used by Christian Friedrich Buschmann on the first European patent for a free-reed mouth organ.

Aykroyd, Dan

Born: July 1, 1952 - Ottawa, Canada

Actor, harmonica player

Dan Aykroyd portrayed Elwood Blues in *The Blues Brothers Band.* Along with fellow comedian John Belushi, Aykroyd created *The Blues Brothers* as a sketch for the television program "Saturday Night Live." Due to the popularity of the sketch, The Blues Brothers recorded several albums and made a full-length movie, "The Blues Brothers," featuring Aykroyd on the harmonica.

Aykroyd currently co-owns the "House of Blues" chain of restaurants, hosts a "House of Blues" syndicated radio show and in 1998 released the "Blues Brothers 2000" movie.

Discography: (see - The Blues Brothers)

– B –

Bailey, Deford

Born: December 14, 1899 - Bellwood, TN
Died: July 2, 1982 - Nashville, TN
Country harmonica player

The first African-American star of the Grand Old Opry, Deford Bailey took up the harmonica at age three while recuperating from a bout with polio. He learned to imitate the sounds of animals around his boyhood home, as well as trains and other sounds.

Moving to Nashville in 1918, he worked at menial jobs and played the harmonica around town until 1926 when fellow harmonica player, Dr. Humphrey Bate, brought him to WSM radio. Bailey was an instant success on the station's Grand Old Opry radio show and soon had his own regular fifteen minute spot on each week's broadcast. He recorded some of the first records to be made in Nashville, cutting a total of 18 sides for the Columbia, Brunswick and Victor labels.

His performing career with the Opry came to an abrupt end in 1941 after a publishing dispute between ASCAP and BMI. He never returned to professional music and instead, he spent his

remaining years operating a shoeshine stand in Nashville, occasionally returning to the Opry for an Old-Timer's Night.

Discography:
1994 - **Harp Blowers 1926-35** (with John Henry Howard, D.H. "Bert" Bilbro & George Clarke), *Document* // 1998 - **The Legendary Deford Bailey,** *Revenant.*

Biography:
1991 - **Deford Bailey: A Black Star in Country Music,** By David C. Morton & Charles K. Wolfe, *University of Tennessee Press.*

Bain, Richard
Vaudeville harmonica player

Richard Bain played in *The Harmonica Rascals* during the 1930's and also served as harmonica soloist with the U.S. Navy Band during the 1940's and 50's.

Baker, Steve
Born: May 1, 1953 - London, England
Blues harmonica player, writer

Steve Baker began playing the harmonica at age sixteen and began playing professionally about two years later. It was while he was playing with the band *Have Mercy* that he made his first recordings. The group traveled to Germany for work and Baker has made the country his home ever since. He has recorded and performed with Bert Jansch, Chris Jones, Abi Wallenstein, Tom Shaka and others.

In the late 1980's Baker started working with the Hohner company as a product specialist, producing new tunings for the harmonica. He wrote "The Harp Handbook" and other instructional materials for the instrument. He continues to write and perform on a regular basis.

Discography:
1977 - **Have Mercy,** *Boodlam* // 1984 - **Tough Enough,** *Coolcat Records* // 1986 - **Free Fall,** *White Gold* // 1988 - **When the Sun is Shining,** *MC* // 1992 - **Strange Move,** *Village* // 1993 - **Have Mercy,** *Crosscut* // 1994 - **Two Times 2,** *WBH* // 1995 - **Slow Roll,** (with Chris Jones), *AMR* // 1998 - **Everybody's Crying Mercy,** (with Chris Jones), *AMR* // 2000 - **In Your Face,** (with Abi Wallenstein), *Stumble.*

Bibliography:
1990 - **The Harp Handbook,** *Edition Louis/Music Sales* // 1999 - **Blues Harping 1,** *Hohner Verlag* // **Blues Harping 2,** *Hohner Verlag* // **Harmonikas: Typen, Techniken, Tonfolgen,** *Hohner/Schott* // **Interactive Blues Harp Workshop CD-Rom,** *Voggenreiter Verlag* // **Blues Harmonica Playalongs,** *Artist Ahead.*

Baldry, "Long" John

Born: January 12, 1941 - London, England

Blues vocals, harmonica
Long John Baldry began performing during the mid-1950's as a

Blues singer and harmonica player in the British Blues scene. He was a member of *Blues Incorporated* and later of the *Cyril Davies' R&B All-Stars*, taking over the group when Davies died in 1964.

His bands have featured Rod Stewart, Brian Auger and Elton John in their early years. His only chart success in the U.S. came with the song "Don't Try To Lay No Boogie Woogie on the King of Rock and Roll."

Discography:
1964 - **Long John's Blues,** *Ascot* // 1966 - **Looking At Long John,** *United Artists* // 1968 - **Let the Heartaches Begin / Wait for Me,** *Pye* // 1968 - **Let There Be Long John,** *Pye* // 1969 - **Golden Hour of Long John Baldry,** *Knight / Castle* // 1970 - **Long John Baldry & the Hoochie Coochie Men,** *Hallmark* // 1971 - **It Ain't Easy,** *Warner Brothers* // 1972 - **Everything Stops for Tea,** *Warner Brothers* // 1974 - **Heartaches,** *Pye* // 1976 - **Good to Be Alive,** *Casablanca* // 1977 - **Welcome To the Club,** *Casablanca* // 1979 - **Baldry's Out!,** *EMI* // 1980 - **Long John Baldry,** *EMI* // 1991 - **It Still Ain't Easy,** *Stony Plain* // 1994 - **On Stage Tonight,** *Stony Plain* // 1996 - **Thrill's a Thrill,** *EMI* // 1996 - **Rock with the Best,** *Hypertension* // 1996 - **Right to Sing the Blues,** *Stony Plain* // 1998 - **The Very Best Of...,** *MCI.*

The Balfa Brothers
(Les Balfa Freres)

Formed: 1946 - Louisiana

Cajun band
The Balfa Brothers began as a band in the mid-1940's. Led by multi-instrumentalist Dewey Balfa, they were enormously popular with the Cajuns of rural Louisiana. In the 1960's they expanded their audience by going national, playing at concerts and festivals across the United States, as well as recording several albums.

See - Dewey Balfa, Rodney Balfa

Discography:
1967 - **Balfa Brothers Play Traditional Cajun Music,** *Swallow* // 1976 - **Balfa Brothers Play More Traditional Cajun Music,** *Swallow* // 1972 - **The Cajuns,** *Sonet* // 1975 - **The Good Times are Killing Me,** *Swallow* // 1988 - **J'ai Vu Le Loup, Le Renard Et La Bellete,** *Swallow* // 1994 - **Balfa Brothers** // 1994 - **The New York Concerts,** *Swallow* // **Arcadian Memories,** *Ace* // **Louisiana Cajun Music,** *Arhoolie.*

Balfa, Dewey

Born: March 20, 1927 - Big Mamon, LA
Died: June 17, 1992 - Eunice , LA

Cajun music vocals, fiddle, guitar, harmonica
Founder of *The Balfa Brothers Band*, Dewey Balfa was a leading proponent of traditional rural Cajun music. He was known pri-

marily as a fiddler, but was also proficient on several instruments, including the harmonica.

Solo Discography: (also see - The Balfa Brothers)
1976 - **En Bas D'un Chene Vert,** *Arhoolie* // 1987 - **Souvenirs,** *Swallow* // 1994 - **Fait a La Main,** *Swallow* // **Cajun Fiddle Tunes,** *Folkways* // **Louisiana Cajun Music,** *Arhoolie* // **Traditional Cajun Fiddle: Instruction,** *Folkways.*

Balfa, Rodney

Born: 1934
Died: February 6, 1979

Cajun music fiddle, guitar, harmonica
Brother of Dewey Balfa, Rodney Balfa was a member of *The Balfa Brothers Band* and like his brother, played several instruments, including the harmonica.

Discography: (see -The Balfa Brothers)

Ball, Tom

Born: October 24, 1950 - Los Angeles, CA

Blues harmonica, writer

Tom Ball began playing guitar at the age of eleven and harmonica at age fourteen. He has been playing harmonica as part of an acoustic Blues duo with guitarist Kenny Sultan since 1979. He has also worked as a studio musician and has written several books on the Blues and Blues harmonica.

Discography:
1981 - **Confusion,** *Sonyatone* // 1983 - **Who Drank My Beer?,** *Kicking Mule / Fantasy* // 1986 - **Bloodshot Eyes,** *Flying Fish* // 1990 - **Too Much Fun,** *Flying Fish* // 1993 - **Filthy Rich,** *Flying Fish* // 1996 - **Double Vision,** *Flying Fish* // 2000

- **20th Anniversary-Live!,** *No Guru.*

Bibliography:
1993 - **Blues Harmonica - A Comprehensive Crash Course and Overview,** *Centerstream Publishing* // 1995 - **Sonny Terry Licks for Blues Harmonica,** *Centerstream Publishing* // 1996 - The Nasty Blues, *Centerstream Publishing* // 2000 - **A Sourcebook of Little Walter / Big Walter Licks for Blues Harmonica,** *Centerstream.*

The Band

Officially formed: 1967 - Woodstock, NY
Officially disbanded: 1978

Rock Band
Originally brought together in the late 1950's as the back-up band for Ronnie Hawkins, *The Band* spent the early 1960's backing several artists including Bob Dylan, Sonny Boy Williamson II and John Hammond Jr.

When they settled together in a house in upstate New York, they began to record their own material. Their first album was an instant critical and commercial success and they spent the next several years touring and putting out hit albums.

They officially retired the group on Thanksgiving Day in 1976 at the Winterland Ballroom in San Francisco. Martin Scorcese filmed the event and dozens of their friends showed up to play with them, including Bob Dylan, Paul Butterfield, Muddy Waters, Neil Young and Van Morrison. Since then, various members have re-grouped as *The Band* for recordings and concerts. Their drummer, Levon Helm also sings, plays the mandolin and harmonica.

See - Levon Helm

Discography:
1968 - **Music from Big Pink,** *Capitol* // 1969 - **The Band,** *Capitol* // 1970 - **Stage Fright,** *Capitol* // 1970 - **Cahoots,** *Capitol* // 1972 - **Rock of Ages,** *Capitol* // 1973 - **Moondog Matinee,** *Capitol* // 1975 - **Northern Lights, Southern Cross,** *Capitol* // 1976 - **The Best Of...,** *Capitol* // 1977 - **Islands,** *Capitol* // 1978 - **Anthology, Vol. 1 & 2,** *Capitol* // 1978 -**The Last Waltz,** *Warner Brothers* // 1989 - **To Kingdom Come,** *Capitol* // 1992 - **The Night They Drove Old Dixie Down,** *CEMA* // 1993 - **Jericho,** *Rhino* // 1994 - **Across the Great Divide,** *Capitol* // 1994 - **The Band & Friends,** *Castle* // 1995 - **Live at Watkins Glen,** *Capitol* // 1996 - **High on the Hog,** *Rhino* // 1998 - **Jubilation,** *River North.*

Movies:
1978 - **The Last Waltz.**

Barefoot Jerry

Formed: 1971 - Nashville, TN
Disbanded: 1977

Country / Rock band

Formed from the remnants of the group *Area Code 615,* Barefoot Jerry featured Terry Bearmore on guitar, bass and harmonica. Charlie McCoy guest starred on many of the group's albums

See - Terry Bearmore, Charlie McCoy

<u>Discography:</u>
1971 - **Southern Delight,** *Capitol* // 1972 - **Barefoot Jerry,** *Warner Brothers* // 1974 - **Watchin' TV,** *Monument* // 1975 - **You Can't Get Off with Your Shoes On,** *Monument* // 1976 - **Grocery,** *Monument* // 1976 - **Keys to the Country,** *Monument* // 1977 - **Barefootin',** *Monument.*

Barnes, Roosevelt "Booba"

Born: September 25, 1936 - Longwood, MS
Died: April 4, 1996 - Chicago, IL

Blues guitar, vocals, harmonica

Roosevelt "Booba" Barnes taught himself to play harmonica at age 8 and began playing in juke joints when he was thirteen years old. He started putting together his own bands in Mississippi in his twenties. He then moved to Chicago in 1964.

He worked as part of the Blues scene in Chicago until 1971, when he returned to Greenville, Mississippi to operate a Blues bar. He began recording in 1973, backing *The Jones Brothers* and recording a solo album in 1990. He returned to Chicago in 1992 and was a part of the city's Blues scene until his death from cancer in 1996.

<u>Discography:</u>
1990 - **Heartbroken Man,** *Rooster Blues.*

Baron, Paul

Real name: Irwin Levine
Born: October 14, 1926

Vaudeville harmonica player

Paul Baron took over *The Harmonica Rascals* name after Borrah Minevitch died in 1955. Baron did a copyright search and found that nobody owned the name. He has toured and recorded with his own group of *Harmonica Rascals* since then.

Barrett, David

Harmonica instructor, writer

David Barrett is a harmonica instructor who has written several books on how to play the instrument. He conducts an annual workshop, "The Harmonica Masterclass" in California, where he brings in several top harmonica players to conduct seminars on the various aspects of the harmonica.

<u>Bibliography:</u>
Building Harmonica Technique, *Mel Bay Publications* // **Masters of Chicago Blues,** *Mel Bay Publications* // **Mel Bay's Scales, Patterns & Exercises for Harmonica,** *Mel*

Bay Publications // **Classic Chicago Blues Harp Book & CD,** *Mel Bay Publications* // **Basic Blues Harmonica Method Book & CD,** *Mel Bay Publications* // **Blues Harp Pocketbook,** *Mel Bay Publications* // **Blues Harp Solo Pocketbook,** *Mel Bay Publications* // **Harmonica Masterclass Complete Blues Harmonica Lesson Series,** *Mel Bay Publications* // **Carey Bell, Deep Down Transcription,** *Mel Bay Publications* // **Masters of the Chicago Blues Harp Transcription Book & CD,** *Mel Bay Publications* // **Big Walter Horton with Carey Bell Transcription Book & CD,** *Mel Bay Publications* // **Sugar Blue, In Your Eyes Transcription Book & CD,** *Mel Bay Publications* // **William Clarke, Serious Intentions Transcription Book & CD,** *Mel Bay Publications* // **Blues Harmonica Jam Tracks & Soloing Concepts #1,** *Mel Bay Publications.*

Bass Harmonica

A harmonica built to play in the lower ranges of the musical scale; the bass harmonica was first developed in the mid-1920's by the M. Hohner Company to meet the musical demands of America's growth in harmonica bands.

The bass harmonica is usually a pair of harmonicas hinged together to give the player access to a full chromatic scale of bass notes. Normally double-reeded to provide greater volume, the bass harmonica is usually all blow notes.

Great bass harmonica players include: Don Les - *The Harmonicats* // Dick Gardner - *The Harmonicats* // Paul Steigerwald - *The Stagg McMann Trio* // Mike Chimes - *The Cappy Barra Harmonica Ensemble* and *The Harmonica Rascals* // Milton Freeman - *The Harmonica Harlequins* // Carl Friedman - *The Harmonica Hi-Hats* // Danny Wilson - *The New World*

Harmonica Trio.

Bate, Dr. Humphrey

Born: May 25, 1875 - Castallian Springs, TN
Died: June 12, 1936

Country harmonica player

Dr. Humphrey Bate learned to play the harmonica from former slaves who worked on his father's farm in Castallian springs, Tennessee. By 1917 he was managing and playing in three bands as well as maintaining his medical practice.

His main band, *The Possum Hunters*, were regulars on the WSM radio Barn dance program. He also worked extensively with the Grand Old Opry from its inception and brought harmonica wizard Deford Bailey to the show. He and *The Possum Hunters* recorded 12 sides for the Brunswick / Vocalion label in August of 1928. Bate used the harmonica to play the fiddle parts in traditional country songs.

Discography:

1976 - **Nashville: The Early String Bands, Vol. 1 & 2,** *County.*

Bauer, Bob

Born: January 4, 1937
Died: January 25, 2001 - New York

Vaudeville harmonica player

Bob Bauer played the chord harmonica in *The Harmonikings* from 1959 until the late 1960's. He took over as chord harmonica player in Jerry Murad's *Harmonicats* in 1982 after Al Fiore retired. After Jerry Murad died in 1996, Bauer continued to occasionally perform as The Harmonicats with his son, Chris on lead chromatic harmonica and Dick Gardner on bass.

Discography:

1995 - **A Harmonica Holiday Festival,** *Bauer* // 1996 - **Sentimental Love,** *Bauer* // 1997 - **The Bauers with Dick Gardner,** *Bauer* // **The Harmonikings Autumn Concerto,** *Bauer.*

The Beale Street Jug Band

Formed: 1920's - Memphis, TN

1920's Jug Band

The Beale Street Jug Band was one of the leading groups to come out of Memphis during the 1920's. Led by harmonica player Jed Davenport, They recorded several sides before slipping into obscurity.

See -Jed Davenport

Bearmore, Terry

Country / Rock harmonica, guitar, bass

Terry Bearmore played bass, guitar and harmonica in the Country / Rock group *Barefoot Jerry* from 1971 until 1977 in addition to working with Brewer & Shipley and Dennis Linde.

Discography: (see - Barefoot Jerry)

The Beatles

Formed:1959 - Liverpool, England
Disbanded: 1969

Rock Band

Originally formed in the mid-1950's as a Skiffle group, *The Beatles* were the biggest musical act to ever come from England. Crossing over the Atlantic to America in early 1964, they had an unprecedented string of number one hits.

Many of their early hits, including "Love Me Do," "Please, Please Me" and others featured harmonica playing by John Lennon, though he stopped playing the harmonica after the first few albums. There is some harmonica on the later albums on songs such as "Being for the Benefit of Mr. Kite," but due to a lack of album credits, it is unsure who the players were.

See - John Lennon

Discography:

1963 - **Please, Please Me,** *Parlaphone* // 1963 - **With The Beatles,** *Parlaphone* // 1964 - **Beatles for Sale,** *Parlaphone* // 1964 - **A Hard Day's Night,** *Parlaphone* // 1965 - **Help!,** *Parlaphone* // 1965 - **Rubber Soul,** *Parlaphone* // 1966 - **Revolver,** *Parlaphone* // 1967 - **Sgt. Pepper's Lonely Heart's Club Band,** *Parlaphone* // 1967 - **Magical Mystery Tour,** *Parlaphone* // 1968 - **The Beatles,** *Apple* // 1969 - **Yellow Submarine,** *Capitol* // 1969 - **Abbey Road,** *Apple* // 1970 - **Let It Be,** *Apple* // 1988 - **Past Masters, Vol. 1 & Vol. 2,** *EMI* // 1995 - **Anthology 1,** *Apple / Capitol* // 1996 - **Anthology 2,** *Apple / Capitol* // 1996 - **Anthology 3,** *Apple / Capitol.*

1964 - **A Hard Day's Night** // 1965 - **Help!** // 1967 - **Yellow Submarine** // 1968 - **Magical Mystery Tour** // 1970 - **Let it Be.**

Beaver, Pappy Gube

Real name: Parlin Kenneth Beaver
Born: March 17, 1919 - Newport, TN

Country singer, guitar, harmonica
Pappy Gube Beaver was a Country music singer who signed with Capitol Records in 1945 and did two recording sessions, after which he got drunk, thrown in jail, found religion, quit music and became a full-time minister.

Beck

Real name: Beck Hansen
Born: July 8, 1970 - Los Angeles, CA

Alternative Rock singer-songwriter, multi-instrumentalist including harmonica
Since the mid-1990's, Beck has been using a wide range of instruments for his eclectic music that includes every instrument he can get his hands on, including the harmonica.

Discography:
1993 - **Mellow Gold,** *Geffen* // 1994 - **Stereopathic Soul Manure,** *Flipside* // 1994 - **One Foot in the Grave,** *K* // 1996 - **Odelay,** *DGC* // 1998 - **Mutations,** *Geffen* // 1999 - **New Pollution & Other Favorites,** *Import* // 1999 - **Golden Feelings,** *Sonic Enemy* // 1999 - **Midnite Vultures,** *Interscope* // 2000 - **B Side Collection: Stray Blues,** *MCA.*

Bee, Harry

Born: July 6, 1922 - Brooklyn, NY

Pop / Classical harmonica player

Harry Bee began playing at age eleven and became the New York State Harmonica Champion by the time he was thirteen. In 1939 he played in *The Rhythm Revelers* with Stan Harper as well as making a couple of movie appearances. He also did a short stint with *The Cappy Barra Harmonica Ensemble* in 1940.

World War Two found him performing in the Special Services show "Tars and Spars" with Sid Cacsar. After the war, a movie was made of the show. Since then he has worked as a soloist with symphony orchestras and on cruise ships.

Discography:
The Musical Artistry of Harry Bee.

Movies:
1939 - **One Third of a Nation** // 1939 - **Back Door to Heaven** // 1946 - **Tars and Spars.**

Behrens, Stanley

Born: December 19, 1946

Blues singer, saxophone, harmonica player
Stanley Behrens has been recording on the harmonica the late 1970's, working with Rocky Burnette, Willie Dixon, Cash McCall, Van Dyke Parks, *War* and others as well as doing numerous studio dates.

Discography:
1992 - **The Stanley Behrens/Willie Dixon Project,** *Blue Baron.*

Bell, Carey

Real name: Carey Bell Harrington
Born: November 14, 1936 - Macon, MS

Blues harmonica player

Carey Bell taught himself to play the harmonica at age eight and worked in the area of Meridian, Mississippi during the early 1950's. He moved to Chicago in 1956 and frequently worked at the Maxwell Street Market as well as doing stints with Little Walter Jacobs, Big Walter Horton and several other Blues bands.

From the late 1960's on, he worked with Earl Hooker, Muddy Waters, John Lee Hooker, Hound Dog Taylor, Willie Dixon and many others. He is still active in Blues. His son, Lurrie Bell, is a blues guitarist and co-founder of *The Sons of The Blues*.

Discography:

1969 - **Carey Bell's Blues Harp**, *Delmark* // 1972 - **Big Walter Horton with Carey Bell**, *Alligator* // 1977 - **Heartaches and Pain**, *Delmark* // 1984 - **Son of a Gun**, *Rooster Blues* // 1991 - **Mellow Down Easy**, *Blind Pig* // 1991 - **Harp Attack!** (with Billy Branch, James Cotton and Junior Wells), *Alligator* // 1994 - **Harpmaster**, *JSP* // 1994 - **Goin' Down Main Street**, *Evidence* // 1995 - **Deep Down**, *Alligator* // 1995 - **Last Night**, *One Way* // 1996 - **Harpslinger**, *JSP* // 1997 - **Good Luck Man**, *Alligator* // 1997 - **Dynasty**, *JSP* // 1998 - **Carey Bell and Spike Ravenswood**, *Blues Encore* // 1998 - **Brought Up the Hard Way**, *JSP*.

Bellini, Dan

Born: September 5, 1965 - Oak Park, IL

Chicago Blues guitar, harmonica player, historian, illustrator

Dan Bellini plays guitar and harmonica for *Howard and The White Boys*, a Chicago-based Blues band. He also has been chronicling the history of the Blues with a series of illustrated looks at various aspects of Blues history that are published regularly in various Blues magazines.

Discography: (see - Howard and the White Boys)

Bending, Note Bending (Technique)

Note bending is the backbone of the Folk, Blues, Jazz and Country styles of harmonica playing. It enables players to slur and drop the pitch of notes. Bending occurs when the direction of the airflow the harmonica is altered. This is normally done by arching the tongue or the lips while playing. Bending usually can be done on the draw notes of holes 1 through 6 and on the blow notes of holes 7 through 10.

By mastering note bending and overblowing it is possible to play a full chromatic scale on a diatonic instrument as well as using the bending technique to shape notes to create slurring and glissando effects.

Benjamin, Arthur

Born: September 18, 1893 - Australia
Died: April 10, 1960 - London, England

Classical composer

Arthur Benjamin wrote "Concerto for Harmonica and Orchestra" in 1953 for Larry Adler.

Bennett, Duster

Real name: Anthony Bennett
Born: England
Died: March 25, 1976

Blues vocals, guitar, harmonica

Duster Bennett was a Blues / Rock singer and harmonica player whose brief career was cut short by a fatal car accident in 1976. His back-up bands included members of *Fleetwood Mac*

and *The Yardbirds*. He also spent a short time as a member of John Mayall's Bluesbreakers.

Discography:
1966 - **Out in the Blue**, *Indigo* // 1968 - **Smiling Like I'm Happy**, *Blue Horizon* // 1969 - **Bright Lights**, *Blue Horizon* // 1970 - **12 Dbs**, *Blue Horizon* // 1970 - **Bennett**, *Blue Horizon* // 1970 - **Justa Buster**, *Blue Horizon* // 1995 - **Jumpin' at Shadows**, *Indigo* // 1996 - **Blue Inside**, *Indigo* // 1998 - **I Choose to Sing the Blues**, *Indigo* // 1999 - **Comin' Home**, *Indigo*.

Bennett, Robert Russell

Born; June 15, 1894 - Kansas City, MO
Died: August 17, 1981 - New York City, NY

Classical Composer
Robert Russell Bennett wrote "Concerto for Harmonica and Orchestra" in 1974 for Cham-Ber Huang.

Berger, Jean

Born: September 27, 1909 - Germany

Classical composer
Jean Berger wrote "Carribean Concerto for Harmonica and Orchestra" in 1940 for Larry Adler.

Bergman, Nat
Vaudeville harmonica player
Nat Bergman played in *The Harmonica Scamps*, Carl Freed's *Harmonica Harlequins* and *The Cappy Barra Harmonica Ensemble* during the 1930's.

Berlin, Irving

Real name: Israel Baline
Born: May 11, 1888 - Russia
Died: September 22, 1989 - New York City, NY

Pop composer
Known as one of America's most prolific composers, Irving Berlin's first instrument was the harmonica. He endorsed Hohner harmonicas in the 1920's.

Big Shoulders

Formed: 1980's - Chicago, IL

Blues / Rock band
Big Shoulders was a major club act in the Chicago music scene during the 1980's. Their sound was greatly enhanced by the harmonica playing of Ron Sorin.

See - Ron Sorin
Discography:
1989 - **Big Shoulders**, *Rounder* // 1991 - **Nickel History**, *Rounder*.

Bilbro, D.H. "Bert"
Country / Blues harmonica player
D.H. "Bert" Bilbro played Blues harmonica in the 1920's.

Discography:
Harp Blowers, (1925-1936), *Document* // **Harmonica Showcase**, *Matchbox*.

Billy the Kid

Real name: William Bonney
Born: 1859 - New York City, NY
Died: July 14, 1881 - Fort Sumner, NM

Western outlaw
According to legend, outlaw Billy the Kid played the harmonica.

Birdhead, Blues

Real name: James Simons

Blues harmonica player
Blues Birdhead was a Blues harmonica player who recorded for the Okeh label in October of 1929.

The Birmingham Jug Band

Formed: Late 1920's - Birmingham, AL

Jug band
The Birmingham Jug Band featured harmonica player Jaybird Coleman. They played in and around Birmingham, Alabama during the 1920's and 30's.

See - Jaybird Coleman
Discography:
Jaybird Coleman and the Birmingham Jug band, Complete Works, (1927-30), *Document*.

Bizor, Billy

Born: September 3, 1913 - Centerville, TX
Died: April 4, 1969 - Houston, TX

Blues singer, harmonica player
A cousin of Lightnin' Hopkins, Billy Bizor did a few solo recordings in the late 1960's, mostly as a vocalist. He also appears on several of Hopkins' albums as a harmonica player.

Discography:
1968 - **Blowing my Blues Away**, *Collectables*.

Black, Clint

Born: February 4, 1962 - Long Beach, NJ

Country singer-songwriter, guitar, bass, harmonica
Raised near Houston, Clint Black has been performing since he was fifteen years old. He sang around the Houston area through

the mid-1980's and signed with RCA Records in 1988. He plays the harmonica on several of his own recordings, as well as playing harmonica on albums by Bill Anderson, Billy Joel and others.

Discography:
1989 - **Killin' Time,** *RCA* // 1990 - **Put Yourself in My Shoes,** *RCA* // 1992 - **The Hard Way,** *RCA* // 1993 - **No Time to Kill,** *RCA* // 1993 - **Clint Black,** *RCA* // 1994 - **One Emotion,** *RCA* // 1995 - **Looking for Christmas,** *RCA* // 1996 - **Greatest Hits,** *RCA* // 1997 - **Nothin' but the Taillights,** *RCA* // 1998 - **Super Hits,** *RCA* // 1999 - **D'Lectrified,** *RCA*.

Black, Donald

Born: April 14, 1946 - Lanark, Scotland

Celtic harmonica player

Donald Black began playing the harmonica at the age of four. Specializing in playing the traditional music of his native Scotland, he began playing professionally in 1993 and has since recorded several albums. He has toured across Europe, appearing at concerts and festivals in many countries.

Discography:
1995 - **Westwinds,** *Greentrax* // 1996 - **The Music and Song of Greentrax,** *Greentrax* // 1998 - **Heart of Scotland,** *MCI* // 1998 - **Ecosse/Scotland,** *Air Mail Music* // 2000 - **Ceol Tasci,** *Vertical* // 2000 - **Close to Home,** *Macmeanmna*.

Blanco, Sam

Vaudeville harmonica player

Sam Blanco played the chord harmonica in *The Harmonica Kings* and in *The Harmonica Hi-Hats* during the late 1930's. Alan Pogson replaced him in *The Harmonica Hi-Hats*.

Blasberg, Pete

Vaudeville harmonica player

Pete Blasberg replaced Sid Gould in *The Harmonica Lads* in 1940.

Blocking: (technique)

Blocking is the creation of the hole, (or holes) through which air is blown or drawn through the harmonica. This can be done in several ways. The first, called lip or pucker blocking, is the technique of using the lips alone to create a variable sized hole.

The second, called tongue blocking, is the technique of using the lips and tongue to direct the airflow through the harmonica. The tongue can be placed to the left, the right or the middle of the hole created by the lips, thus allowing the player to have access to a larger number of note combinations.

The third, called U-blocking, occurs when a player curves their tongue, creating a "U," blocking two notes, leaving two on either side of the tongue and one or more notes in the middle. This technique is especially handy for playing chords, but is limited to only those who have the genetic ability to curl their tongues.

Blood, Sweat and Tears

Formed: 1967 - New York City, NY
Disbanded: 1977

Jazz / Rock band
Co-founded by keyboardist Al Kooper and guitarist / harmonica player Steve Katz, *Blood, Sweat and Tears* blended Rock music with Jazz horns. After adding vocalist David Clayton-Thomas, the group had a string of hits including "Spinning Wheel,"" You Made Me So Very Happy" and "And When I Die" which featured Katz playing the harmonica.

See - Steve Katz

Discography:
1968 - **Child is the Father of Man,** *Columbia* // 1969 - **Blood, Sweat and Tears,** *Columbia* // 1970 - **Blood, Sweat and Tears 3,** *Columbia* // 1970 - **The Owl & the Pussycat,** *Columbia* // 1970 - **Blood, Sweat and Tears 4,** *Columbia* // 1972 - **Blood, Sweat and Tears Greatest Hits,** *Columbia* // 1972 - **New Blood,** *Columbia* // 1973 - **No Sweat,** *Columbia* // 1974 - **Mirror Image,** *Columbia* // 1975 - **New City,** *Columbia* // 1976 - **More Than Ever,** *Columbia* // 1976 - **In Concert,** *CBS* // 1977 - **Brand New Day,** *ABC* // 1980 - **Classic BST,** *CBS* // 1980 - **Nuclear Blues,** *LAX* // 1984 - **The Challenge,** *Astan* // 1985 - **Latin Fire,** *Platinum* // 1990 - **Found Treasures,** *Columbia* // 1991 - **Live and Improvised,** *Columbia* // 1992 - **Greatest Hits,** *Hollywood* // 1994 - **Live,** *Rhino* // 1995 - **Definitive Collection,** *Alex* // 1995 - **Collection,** *Griffin*.

The Bluebells

Formed: Early 1980's - Scotland
Disbanded: 1984

Soul music band

The Bluebells recorded several singles, an EP and an album that broke into the lower reaches of the British Pop charts in the early 1980's. The group was co-founded by singer and harmonica player Kenneth McCluskey.

See - Kenneth McCluskey

Discography:
1983 - **Bluebells,** *Sire* // 1984 - **Sisters,** *London* // 1992 - **Second.**

Blue Rodeo

Formed: 1986 - Canada

Folk / Rock band

Patterned after *The Band* and *Buffalo Springfield*, *Blue Rodeo* specializes in playing Folk / Rock music. They've been recording and performing steadily since the late 1980's. Keyboard player Bob Wiseman also plays the harmonica.

See - Bob Wiseman

Discography:
1987 - **Outskirts,** *Atlantic* // 1989 - **Diamond Mine,** *Atlantic* // 1991 - **Casino,** *East West* // 1992 - **Lost Together,** *Atlantic* // 1994 -**Five Days in July,** *Musicraft* // 1995 - **Nowhere to Here,** *Discovery* // 1997 - **Tremolo,** *Discovery* // 1999 - **Just Like a Vacation,** *Warner Brothers* // 2000 - **The Days in Between,** *Warner Brothers.*

Sugar Blue

Real name: James Whiting
Born: December 16, 1949 - New York City, NY

Blues / Rock harmonica player

Sugar Blue began playing harmonica in his teens while growing up in New York City. By the mid-1970's he had recorded with Brownie McGhee, Victoria Spivey and Roosevelt Sykes.

Moving to Paris in 1976, he was discovered by *The Rolling Stones* and featured on their "Some Girls" album, including a featured solo on their smash hit "Miss You." The Stones would also feature him on their "Emotional Rescue" and "Tattoo You" albums and take Sugar Blue along on their "Steel Wheels" tour.

Returning to America, Blue worked with *The Willie Dixon All-Stars* and even won a Grammy award in 1986 for his recording of "Another Man Done Gone." Sugar Blue has since signed on with Alligator Records and has been a fixture on the Chicago Blues scene, releasing new albums on a regular basis.

Discography:
1979 - **Crossroads,** *Blue Silver* // 1994 - **Blue Blazes,** *Alligator* // 1995 - **In Your Eyes,** *Alligator* // **Chicago to Paris,** *Blue Silver* // **Absolutely Blue,** *Seven Seas.*

The Blues Band

Formed: 1979 - London, England

British Blues band

Founded by former *Manfred Mann* harmonica player Paul Jones, *The Blues Band* has been a side project for Jones and former members of other British bands.

Discography:
1980 - **The Official Blues Band Bootleg Album,** *Blues Band* // 1980 - **Ready,** *Arista* // 1981 - **Itchy Feet,** *Arista* // 1982 - **Brand Loyalty,** *Arista* // 1983 - **Bye-Bye Blues,** *Arista* // 1986 - **These Kinds of Blues,** *Date* // 1989 - **Back for More,** *Arista* // 1991 - **Fat City,** *RCA* // 1993 - **Live** // 1993 - **Homage,** *Essential* // 1995 - **Wire Less,** *Cobalt* // 1996 - **Live at the BBC,** *Windsong* // 1999 - **The Best of The Blues Band,** *Varese.*

The Blues Brothers

Formed: 1977 - New York City, NY

Comedy / Blues band

Originally put together as a sketch for the television program "Saturday Night Live" *The Blues Brothers* went on to record several albums and produced two movies, all featuring Dan Aykroyd playing the harmonica.

See - Dan Aykroyd

Discography:
1978 - **Briefcase Full of Blues,** *Atlantic* // 1980 - **Made in America,** *Atlantic* // 1980 - **The Blues Brothers,** (Soundtrack), *Atlantic* // 1981 - **The Best of...,** *Atlantic* // 1992 - **The Definitive Collection,** *Atlantic* // 1992 - **Red, White and Blues,** *Turnstyle* // 1993 - **Blues Brothers,** *Griffin Music* // 1995 - **Montreux Live!,** *WEA* // 1997 - **Blues Brothers & Friends: Live from the House of Blues,** *A&M* // 2000 - **Blues Brothers Complete,** *WEA.*

Movies:
1980 - **The Blues Brothers** // 1998 - **Blues Brothers 2000.**

The Blues Fools

Formed: 1995 - Hungary

Blues band

The Blues Fools are a Jump Blues band from Hungary that feature Matyas Pribojszki on the harmonica and vocals.

See - Matyas Pribojszki

Discography:
1999 - **Fools in the Blues,** *Cross Roads.*

Blues Harmonica

The harmonica has served as a main component to Blues music since its emergence as a musical style around the 1900's and has figured into nearly every sub-style of the Blues ever since.

During the 1920's, Country and Blues harmonica players were virtually the same in basic technique and styles varied more by region than by skin color. At that time, the harmonica was mostly featured in group situations and duos. The harmonica didn't really emerge as a soloist's instrument until the 1930's. Very predominant in Mississippi Delta Blues, a large number of great Blues guitarists actually began as harmonica players.

In Chicago, Blues harmonica took a giant leap forward when players like Snooky Pryor and Little Walter started to play their harmonicas through amplifiers in the late 1940's.

Because of the heavy influence of the Blues, most of the groups that leapt into prominence during the British Invasion of the 1960's were led by, or featured harmonica players. Three harmonica players led a revival in Chicago Blues in the mid-1960's: Paul Butterfield, Charlie Musselwhite and Corky Siegel.

Blues has come a long way since then. A second revival in the 1980's was due, in no small part, to Dan Aykroyd of *The Blues Brothers.* Currently there are several players trying new things in the Blues, including: John Popper of *Blues Traveler* and Sugar Blue, who made his mark guest-starring on several albums by *The Rolling Stones.*

Blues Harp

A southern colloquial term for the harmonica. This term is also used to describe the cross harp or 2nd diatonic position.

Blues Incorporated

Formed: 1961 -London, England
Disbanded: 1967

English Blues band

Co-founded by Alexis Korner and harmonica player Cyril Davies, *Blues Incorporated* was one of England's first electric Blues bands. It proved to be the training ground for many of England's future Rock stars including Mick Jagger, Jack Bruce, Ginger Baker, Charlie Watts, Graham Bond, Paul Jones, Robert Plant, Steve Marriott and Long John Baldry among others.

After Cyril Davies left the group in late 1962, Korner continued the group until 1967.

See - Cyril Davies, Jack Bruce, Mick Jagger, Robert Plant, Long John Baldry, Paul Jones

Discography:
R&B from the Marquee, *Mobile Fidelity* // **Blues Incorporated,** *Line.*

Blues Project

Formed: 1965 - New York City, NY
Disbanded: 1972

Rock / Jazz / Blues band

Blues Project was founded by Danny Kalb and featured vocalist Tommy Flanders and guitarist Steve Katz, both of whom could play the harmonica. Their music blended elements of Jazz, R&B, Pop and Soul.

See - Tommy Flanders, Steve Katz

Discography:
1966 - **Live at the Café Au-Go-Go,** *Verve* // 1966 - **Projections,** *Verve* // 1967 - **Live at the Town Hall,** *Verve* // 1968 - **Planned Obsolescence,** *Verve* // 1969 - **Flanders/Kalb/Katz, Etc.,** *Verve* // 1971 - **Lazarus,** *Capitol* // 1972 - **The Blues Project,** *Capitol* // 1973 - **Reunion in Central Park,** *MGM* // 1974 - **Archetypes Blues Project,** *MGM* // 1987 - **Back Door Man,** *Capitol* // 1989 - **The Best Of...,** *Verve* // 1989 - **The Best Of...,** *Rhino* // 1989 - **Projections from the Past,** *Hablabel* // 1997 - **Anthology,** *Polygram.*

Blues Traveler

Formed: 1988 - New York City, NY

Rock band

Blues Traveler has been at the cutting edge of Blues / Rock since its inception in 1988. Led by singer and harmonica player John Popper, the group offers extended jams in concert and it's recorded output, even though shorter in length, is nothing less than phenomenal.

See - John Popper

Discography:
1990 - **Blues Traveler,** *A&M* // 1991 - **Travelers and Thieves,** *A&M* // 1991 - **On Tour Forever,** *A&M* // 1993 - **Save his Soul,** *A&M* // 1994 - **Four,** *A&M* // 1996 - **Live from the Fall,** *A&M* // 1997 - **Straight On Till Morning,** *A&M.*

Bobby and The Midnites

Formed: Early 1980's - San Francisco, CA
Disbanded: 1984

Rock band

A group formed as a solo project for *Grateful Dead* rhythm guitarist Bob Weir, *Bobby and The Midnites* featured Matt Kelly on the guitar and harmonica.

See - Matt Kelly

Discography:
1981 - **Bobby and The Midnites,** *Arista* // 1984 - **Where the Beat Meets the Street,** *Columbia.*

Boblink, Bud

Born: November 14, 1936 - Chicago, IL

Vaudeville / Pop harmonica player

Bud Boblink began performing on the harmonica when he was thirteen years old and played with trios through most of the 1950's and 60's, also working with *Johnny Puleo's Harmonica Gang,* and *The Harmonicats.* A master of the chord, bass and chromatic harmonicas, Bud continues to play with harmonica bands on a regular basis.

Bonfiglio, Robert

Born: September 6, 1956 - Fort Lewis, WA

Classical harmonica soloist

Starting on the diatonic harmonica, Robert Bonfiglio played in several Blues bands in his youth. He studied with Cham-Ber Huang during the early 1970's and also studied composition at the Mannes School of Music. He earned a Master's Degree at the Manhattan School of Music.

He has given chromatic harmonica lessons to Don Brooks and Robert Papparozzi, done soundtrack for several movies, worked as a session musician on Chaka Khan's first solo album and currently performs with symphony orchestras all over the world.

Discography:
1991 - **Romances,** *High Harmony* // 1992 - **Through the Raindrops,** *High Harmony* // 1994 - **Live at the Grand Canyon,** *High Harmony* // 1997 - **Home for the Holidays,** *Street Song* // **Harmonica Classics,** *Sine Qua Non* // **Always**

On My Mind, *Street Song* // **Every Breath I Take,** *Street Song* // **Noel,** *Street Song* // **All is Calm,** *High Harmony* // **Love Me Tender,** *Street Song* // **Bonfiglio Plays the Music of Villa-Lobos,** *BMG Classics* // **Season's Joy,** *Street Song.*

Movies:
1979 - **Kramer Vs. Kramer** // 1984 - **Places in the Heart.**

On Video:
Bonfiglio Live!, *Street Song* // **An Evening with Robert Bonfiglio,** *Harmonica Ventures* // **Home for the Holidays,** *Harmonica Ventures.*

Bibliography:
2000 - **Bona Rhythm Etudes,** *Bonfiglio* // **Learn To Play,** *Street Song.*

Bonner, "Juke Boy"

Real name: Weldon Bonner
Born: March 22, 1932 - Bellville, TX
Died: June 29, 1978 - Houston, TX

Blues vocals, drums, guitar, harmonica

Juke Boy Bonner started playing music at age six and began playing guitar at age twelve. He played at local dances and church suppers during the late 1940's and began doing radio appearances in 1948.

Bonner moved to the Oakland, California area in the mid-1950's and became a part of the local Blues scene. He recorded his first album for the Irma label in 1957 and continued playing, mostly as a one-man band, until his death from chronic alcoholism in the late 1970's. During his lifetime he made records for the Irma, Goldband, Storyville, Blues Unlimited, Flyright and Sonet labels.

Discography:
1967 - **The One Man Trio,** *Flyright* // 1968 - **I'm Going Back to the Country,** *Arhoolie* // 1969 - **Life Gave Me a Dirty Deal,** *Arhoolie* // 1969 - **They Call Me "Juke Boy,"** *Ace* // 1969 - **Things Ain't Right,** *Sequel* // 1969 - **Louisiana Blues,** *Storyville* // 1972 - **Legacy of the Blues, Vol. 5,** *GNP* // 1980 - **Adventures of Juke Boy Bonner,** *Collectables* // 1981 - **The Struggle,** *Arhoolie* // 1990 - **The Texas Blues Troubadours,** *Collectables* // 1991 - **Juke Boy Bonner, 1960-1967,** *Flyright* // 1993 - **Jumpin' with Juke Boy,** *Collectables.*

Bono

Real name: Paul Hewson
Born: May 10, 1960 - Dublin, Ireland

Rock singer, harmonica player

Bono is the lead singer for the Irish Rock band *U2*. He occasionally plays the harmonica on the group's albums.

Discography: (see - U2)

The Borrah Minevitch Harmonica Institute of America

The brainchild of *Harmonica Rascals* founder Borrah Minevitch, The Borrah Minevitch Harmonica Institute of America operated in New York City during the 1930's. It had over 125,000 enrollees during its first year in business and published an eight-page booklet entitled, "Harmonica Secrets of Borrah Minevitch - The Inside Story." One of its instructors, Dave Macklin, started the harmonica band, *The Philharmonicas,* made up from students at the school.

Borum, Willie

Also known as: Memphis Willie B.
Born: November 4, 1911 - Memphis, TN
Died: Late 1960's

Jug Band Blues guitar, harmonica player

Willie Borum learned to play the harmonica from Noah Lewis in his native city of Memphis, Tennessee. He played with *Jack Kelly's Jug Busters* and *The Memphis Jug Band* during the 1920's and 30's. During the 1930's he also performed with Sonny Boy Williamson II (Rice Miller), Robert Johnson, Willie Brown, Will Shade and Joe Hill Louis.

He recorded for the Vocalion label in 1934 and continued working in music until he joined the Army in World War Two. He returned to Memphis after the war, working occasionally working with Frank Stokes. He also appeared on the King Biscuit Time radio show in the late 1940's.

Mostly stagnant during the 1950's, he was rediscovered during the Folk revival of the early 1960's, recording for the Bluesville label as well as performing with Gus Cannon and Furry Lewis in 1963.

Discography:
1961 - **Introducing Memphis Willie B.,** *Bluesville* // 1961 - **Hard Working Man** // **The Bluesville Years, Vol. 3,** *Prestige.*

Bouchard, Byron

Vaudeville harmonica player

Byron Bouchard joined *The Harmonica Lads* in 1940 with Pete Blasberg when Mike Chimes and Sid Gould left the group.

Bovee, Ben

Folk singer-songwriter, guitar, harmonica player

Ben Bovee has been performing and recording traditional Folk and Country songs since the mid-1970's, both as a solo artist and with banjo and fiddle player Gail Heil. He works primarily in Minnesota and usually plays the harmonica on a neckbrace while playing the guitar.

Discography:
1977 - **Pop Wagner and Bob Bovee,** *Train on the Island* // 1988 - **Come All of You Waddies,** *Marimac* // 1986 - **Behind the Times,** *Marimac* // 1991 - **Come Over To See Me Sometime,** *Marimac* // 1996 - **Rural Route 2,** *Marimac* // **From the Heart,** *Bob Bovee* // **Tunes From Home,** *Bob Bovee* // **For Old Time's Sake,** *Train on the Island* // **Minnesota Minstrel,** *Train on the Island* // **The Roundup,** *Train on the Island* // **Disco on the Bayou,** *Train on the Island.*

Bradshaw, Curly

Country harmonica player

Curly Bradshaw played harmonica in *Uncle Henry's Original Kentucky Mountaineers* from 1928 until 1952.

Branch, Billy

Born: October 3, 1951 - Great Lakes, IL

Blues harmonica player

Billy Branch grew up in the Los Angeles area. He started playing the harmonica at age eleven and even performed with Paul Butterfield. He came back to Chicago in 1969 to attend college.

He started working with south side Blues bands in the 1970's, occasionally working as a sideman. During the 70's he worked with Oscar Brown, Jr., Jimmy Walker, Muddy Waters and Willie Dixon. He played for a while with *The Willie Dixon All-Stars.*

Branch currently plays with the group *The Sons of the Blues* and is very active in the "Blues in Schools" program, teaching inner-city youngsters about the harmonica and Blues music. He has appeared on albums by Buster Benton, Eddy Clearwater, *The Kinsey Report,* Koko Taylor and many others.

Discography:
1982 - **Live 82,** *Evidence* // 1990 - **Harp Attack!,** (with Carey Bell, Junior Wells and James Cotton), *Alligator* // 1992 -

Mississippi Flashback, *GBW* // 1995 - **The Blues Keep Following Me Around,** *Verve* // 1995 - **Where's My Money?,** *Evidence* // 1996 - **Satisfy Me,** *Gianes* // 1999 - **Superharps,** (with James Cotton and Charlie Musselwhite) // **Billy Branch and Hubert Sumlin,** *Wolf* // **Chicago's Young Blues Generation,** (with Lurrie Bell), *L&R.*

Movies:
1989 - **Next of Kin.**

On Video:
Beginning Blues Harp, Mountain Top Video.

Bray, Bernie

Born: October 2, 1921 - Medicine Hat, Alberta, Canada
Died: February 18, 1981 - Toronto, Canada

Pop harmonica player
Canadian harmonica soloist Bernie Bray began his career as a member of a harmonica band while he was still a teenager. He spent several years working as a soloist with The Royal Canadian Air Force Band. After leaving the service, he worked as a harmonica soloist and as a harmonica technician and customizer. SPAH's Man of the year award is named in his honor.

Discography:
The Best of the Reeds, Vol. One & Two.

Brilleaux, Lee

Real name: Lee Green
Born: 1953 - Durban, South Africa
Died: April 7, 1994 - Canvey Island, England

British R&B slide guitar and harmonica player
Lee Brilleaux played slide guitar and harmonica for the band Dr. Feelgood.

Discography: (see - Dr. Feelgood)

Brim, Grace

Born: July 10, 1923 - Briscoe, AR
Died: June 28, 1999 - Gary, IN

Blues drums, harmonica player
Grace Brim was married to Blues musician John Brim from 1947 until 1964. Originally a harmonica player, when she joined his band in 1948, she took up the drums. She also played and recorded with Roosevelt Sykes, Big Maceo and Sunnyland Slim. She continued working in music well into the 1970's.

Brim, John

Born: April 10, 1922 - Hopkinsville, KY

Blues guitar, harmonica, vocals
John Brim taught himself how to play music as a child and began playing local parties at age thirteen. He moved to Chicago in 1945 and worked with John Lee "Sonny Boy"

Williamson, Eddie Boyd, Willie Mabon, Muddy Waters and others. In 1948 he formed his own group, *John Brim and his Gary Kings,* which featured Jimmy Reed.

He began recording in 1950 and throughout the next two decades he worked as a sideman for Jimmy Reed, Roosevelt Sykes, Big Maceo and others. He has been active in music well into the 1990's, recording and performing with his group, *The Ice Cream Men.*

Discography:
1950's - **John Brim / Little Hudson,** *Flyright* // 1970 - **Whose Muddy Shoes,** (with Elmore James), *Chess* // 1989 - **Chicago Blues Sessions, Vol. 12,** *Wolf* // 1994 - **Ice Cream Man,** *Tone Cool* // **Elmore James, John Brim, Floyd Jones,** *Chess.*

Brooks, Don

Born: 1947
Died: October 26, 2000 - New York City, NY

Country harmonica player

Don Brooks grew up in Texas and started playing harmonica while in high school. He moved to New York City in 1967 and played around the Greenwich Village with Jerry Jeff Walker, David Bromberg, John Paul Hammond and others. He was the harmonica player on Jerry Jeff Walker's big hit, "Mr. Bojangles."

He started working as Waylon Jennings' full-time harmonica player in 1973 and has worked as a session musician for Judy Collins, Harry Belafonte, Carly Simon, Ringo Starr, Bette Midler, Diana Ross and Billy Joel among others. Brooks played harmonica in the Broadway production of "Big River." He studied chromatic harmonica with Robert Bonfiglio and gave harmonica lessons to Mickey Raphael.

Brooks died in October 2000 after a long bout with leukemia.

Brooks, "Big" Leon

Born: November 19, 1933 - Sunflower, MS
Died: January 22, 1982 - Chicago, IL

Blues singer, harmonica player
"Big" Leon Brooks was a Blues harmonica player who came up from Mississippi to Chicago and was able to record one album before his death, shortly after his 48th birthday.

Discography:
1983 - **Let's Go To Town**, *Blues Over Blues.*

Brown, Buster

Born: August 15, 1911 - Cordele, GA
Died: January 31, 1976 - Brooklyn, NY

Blues singer and harmonica player
Buster Brown got his start in music by playing at local parties in his native Georgia from the 1930's through the 1950's. He made his first recordings in 1943 for the Flyright label. During the late 1950's and early 60's he made several records, many of which made it onto the charts. After moving to New York City in 1956, he performed regularly until his death in 1976.

Discography:
1961 - **The New King of the Blues**, *Collectables* // 1962 - **Good News**, *Charly* // 1962 - **Get Down with Buster Brown**, *Souflec* // 1976 - **Raise a Ruckus Tonight**, *DJM.*

Brown, Clarence "Gatemouth"

Born: April 18, 1924 - Vinton, LA

Blues multi-instrumentalist including harmonica
Clarence "Gatemouth" Brown began playing music at age five and started working professionally in the early 1940's. He started recording in 1947 and was active in music well into the late 1990's. He played a variety of instruments, including the harmonica, and was well versed in several musical styles.

Discography:
1940' & 50's - **Atomic Energy**, *Bluesboy* // 1940's & 50's - **San Antonio Ball Buster**, *Red Lightnin'* // 1950's - **The Original Peacock Recordings**, *Rounder* // 1960's - **Hot Times Tonight**, *P-Vine* // 1965 - **The Nashville Sessions**, *Chess* // 1970's - **Pressure Cooker**, *Alligator* // 1972 - **The Blues Ain't Nothin'**, *Black & Blue* // 1973 - **More Stuff**, *Black & Blue* // 1973 - **Cold Storage**, *Black & Blue* // 1974 - **Sings Louis Jordan**, *Black & Blue* // 1975 - **Down South in Bayou County**, *Barclay* // 1976 - **Bogalusa Boogie Man**, *Barclay* // 1977 - **Just Got Lucky**, *Evidence* // 1978 - **Black Jack**, *Music is Medicine* // 1979 - **Just Makin' Music**, *MCA* // 1981 - **Alright Again**, *Rounder* // 1986 - **Real Life**, *Rounder* // 1983 - **One More Mile**, *Rounder* // 1986 - **Real Life (Live)**,

Rounder // 1987 - **Texas Swing**, *Rounder* // 1989 - **Standing My Ground**, *Alligator* // 1992 - **No Looking Back**, *Alligator* // 1994 - **Live 1980**, *Charly* // 1995 - **Man**, *Verve* // 1995 - **The Best Of...**, *Verve* // 1996 - **Long Way Home**, *Verve* // 1996 - **Gate's on the Heat**, *Verve* // 1997 - **Gate Swings**, *Verve* // 1999 - **American Music, Texas Style**, *Polygram* // 1999 - **Okie Dokie Stomp**, *Bullseye* // 2000 - **Guitar in My Hand** // **House of the Blues, Vol. 3**, *Blue Star* // **The Guitar According To Gatemouth**, *Homespun Tapes* // **Texas Guitarman**, *Ace* // **Sings Christmas Songs**, *King.*

Brown, Dusty

Born: March 11, 1929 - Tralake, MS

Blues singer, harmonica
Dusty Brown taught himself to play the harmonica at age thirteen. He moved to Chicago at age seventeen and was soon sitting in with Muddy Waters, Little Walter and others during the late 1940's and early 1950's. He formed his own band in 1953 and was recording in 1955. He has been playing and putting out records ever since then.

Discography:
1990 - **Hand Me Down Blues.**

Brownsville Station

Formed: 1969 - Ann Arbor, MI
Disbanded: 1979

Rock band
Brownsville Station had a hit in 1973 with the song "Smokin' in the Boys' Room," which was written by guitarist Cub Koda. The song featured a harmonica solo by Koda, who played the harmonica on several of the band's recordings.

See - Cub Koda

Discography:
1970 - **No B.S.**, *Warner Brothers* // 1971 - **Brownsville Station**, *Palladium* // 1972 - **A Night on the Town**, *Big Tree* // 1973 - **Yeah!**, *Big Tree* // 1974 - **School Punks**, *Big Tree* // 1975 - **Motor City Connection**, *Big Tree* // 1977 - **Brownsville Station**, *Private Stock* // 1980 - **Air Special**, *Epic* // 1993 - **Smoking in the Boys' Room: The Best Of...**, *Rhino.*

Bruce, Jack

Born: May 14, 1943 - Glasgow, Scotland

Rock singer, bass, harmonica player
Jack Bruce was the lead singer and bass guitar player for the British Rock band, Cream. He played harmonica on such songs as "Rollin' and Tumblin'," "Spoonful" and others. He also played in such groups as *Blues Incorporated*, *The Graham Bond Organization*, *Manfred Mann* and *John Mayall's Bluesbreakers.*

Discography: (also see - Cream)
1969 - **Songs for a Tailor,** *Atco* // 1970 - **Things We Like,** *Atco* // 1971 - **Harmony Row,** *Atco* // 1974 - **Out of the Storm,** *RSO* // 1977 - **How's Tricks,** *RSO* // 1980 - **I've Always Wanted To Do This,** *Epic* // 1982 - **Truce,** *One Way* // 1990 - **A Question of Time,** *Epic* // 1993 - **Somethin' Else,** *CMP* // 1994 - **Jack Bruce & Friends,** *ITM* // 1994 - **Cities of the Heart,** *CMP* // 1995 - **BBC Radio 1 in Concert,** *Windsong* // 1995 - **Monkjack,** *CMP* // 1997 - **Sitting on Top of the World,** *Times Square.*

Buffalo, Norton

Born: September 28, 1951 - Oakland, CA

Studio harmonica player

Norton Buffalo has worked with a large number of popular musical acts including *The Doobie Brothers,* Elvin Bishop, Bette Midler, Kenny Loggins, Bonnie Raitt, Bob Welch, Johnny Cash, Judy Collins and others. He worked extensively with Steve Miller in the early 1970's, played with *Commander Cody and his Lost Planet Airmen* in the Mid-1970's and teamed up with Blues guitarist Roy Rogers in the 1990's.

Discography: (also see - Commander Cody and his Lost Planet Airmen, Steve Miller Band)
1977 - **Lovin' in the Valley of the Moon,** (with Stampede), *Capitol* // 1978 - **Desert Horizon,** (with Stampede), *Capitol* // 1991 - **R&B,** (with Roy Rogers), *Blind Pig* // 1992 - **Travelin' Tracks,** (with Roy Rogers), *Blind Pig* // 2000 - **King of the Highway,** *Blind Pig.*

On Video:
Norton Buffalo's Bag of Tricks, *Homespun Video* // **Norton Buffalo's Blues Techniques,** *Homespun Video.*

Movies:
1974 - **The Rose** // 1975 - **Dogpound Shuffle** // 1980 - **Blood Beach** // 1981 - **Heaven's Gate** // 1982 - **Lost Frontier** // 1983 - **Eddie Macon's Run** // 1983 - **Stacy's Knights** // 1991 - **The Doors** // TV - **Twilight Zone.**

Buffalo Springfield

Formed: 1966 - Los Angeles, CA
Disbanded: May 1968

Folk / Rock band
Though together only long enough to recorded four albums, *Buffalo Springfield* was one of the leading Folk / Rock groups of the late 1960's. Most of the members went on to highly successful careers with other bands. Neil Young played harmonica in addition to guitar, singing and writing several of the band's songs.

See - Neil Young

Discography:
1967 - **Buffalo Springfield,** *Atco* // 1967 - **Buffalo Springfield Again,** *Atco* // 1968 - **Last Time Around,** *Atco* // 1970 - **Expecting To Fly,** *Atlantic* // 1969 - **Retrospective,** *Atco* // 1973 - **Buffalo Springfield,** (collection), *Atco.*

Jimmy Buffett and the Coral Reefer Band

Formed: 1970's

Rock band
Jimmy Buffett has been backed by *The Coral Reefer Band* since the mid-1970's and has featured harmonica player Greg "Fingers" Taylor from it's earliest days until Taylor left the group in 2000.

See - Greg "Fingers" Taylor

Discography:
1970 - **Down To Earth,** *Barnaby* // 1973 - **A White Sport Coat and a Pink Crustacean,** *MCA* // 1974 - **Living & Dying in 3/4 Time,** *MCA* // 1974 - **A-1-A,** *MCA* // 1975 - **Rancho Deluxe,** *United Artists* // 1976 - **Havana Day Dreamin',** **MCA** // **1976 - High Cumberland Jubilee,** *Barnaby* // 1977 - **Changes in Latitudes, Changes in Attitudes,** *MCA* // 1978 - **Son of a Son of a Sailor,** *MCA* // 1978 - **You Had to Be There,** *MCA* // 1979 - **Before the Salt,** *Barnaby* // 1979 - **Volcano,** *MCA* // 1981 - **Coconut Telegraph,** *MCA* // 1982 - **Somewhere Over China,** *MCA* // 1983 - **One Particular Harbor,** *MCA* // 1984 - **Riddles in the Sand,** *MCA* // 1985 - **Last Mango in Paris,** *MCA* // 1985 - **Songs You Know By Heart,** *MCA* // 1986 - **Floridays,** *MCA* // 1988 - **Hot Water,** *MCA* // 1989 - **Off To See the Lizard,** *MCA* // 1990 - **Feeding Frenzy,** *MCA* // 1992 - **Boats, Beaches, Bars & Ballads,** *MCA* // 1994 -

Fruitcakes, *MCA* // **Margaritaville Café Late Night Gumbo**, *Island* // 1995 - **Barometer Soup**, *Margaritaville* // 1995 - **Jimmy Buffett's Margaritaville**, *Margaritaville* // 1996 - **Banana Wind**, *Margaritaville* // 1996 - **Christmas Island**, *Margaritaville* // 1998 - **Don't Stop the Carnival**, *Polygram* // 1999 - **American Storyteller**, *Delta* // 1999 - **Beach House on the Moon**, *Polygram* // 1999 - **Live: Tuesday / Thursday / Saturday**, *Mailboat* // 2000 - **Collector's Edition**, *Madacy* // **Jolly Mon**, *Music for Little People*.

Buford, George "Mojo"

Also known as: Little George Buford, Muddy Waters Jr.
Born: November 10, 1929 - Hernando, MS

Blues harmonica player

Mojo Buford learned to play the harmonica from his father as well as singing in a local church choir as a youth. He lived in Memphis in the mid-1940's and settled in Chicago in 1953, working with local blues bands.

He began working with Muddy Waters in 1962 and started recording in 1963. He replaced George "Harmonica" Smith in the Muddy Waters Band in 1967 and stayed with Waters until the early 1970's. He has continued working well into the 1990's.

Discography:
1964 - **The Exciting Harmonica Sound of Mojo Buford**, *BlesRecordSoc* // 1981 - **Mojo Buford's Blues Summit**, *Rooster* // 1989 - **State of the Blues Harp**, *JSP* // 1996 - **Back Home To Clarksdale**, (with The Reunion Blues Band), *Icehouse* // 1996 - **Still Blowin' Strong**, *Blue Loon* // 1996 - **Harpslinger**, *Blue Loon* // 1998 - **Home is Where My Harps Is**, *Blue Loon* // 1998 - **Soul of the Blues Harp**, *JSP* // 1999 - **Champagne and Reefer**, *Fedora*.

Bunge, Jens

Born: September 24, 1963

Jazz harmonica player

Jens Bunge began playing harmonica at eighteen after hearing Stevie Wonder and Toots Thielemans. Working in Jazz, Bunge uses the chromatic harmonica and has worked with several big bands.

Discography:
1991 - **Harmonicology**, *Art-Pur* // 1994 - **It's a Beautiful World**, *Mons* // 1996 - **With All My Heart**, *Yvp Music* // 2000 - **Meet You in Chicago, Jazz4Ever**.

Burns, Eddie

Also known as: Little Eddie Guitar Burns, Big Ed, Slim Pickens, Swing Brother
Born: February 8, 1928 - Belzoni, MS

Blues guitar, harmonica player

Little Eddie "Guitar" Burns taught himself to play harmonica and guitar as a child and built his first guitar from a broom handle. He moved to Clarksdale, Mississippi in 1943 and played with Sonny Boy Williamson II (Rice Miller) and Pinetop Perkins from 1943 until 1947.

He moved to Detroit in 1947 and began recording the next year. He recorded with John Lee Hooker in 1949 and has continued playing and recording ever since.

Discography:
1948 - **Treat Me Like I Treat You**, *Moonshine* // 1972 - **Bottle Up and Go**, *Action Replay* // 1989 - **Eddie Burns**, *Blue Suit* // 1993 - **Eddie Burns Blues Band**, *Evidence* // 1993 - **Detroit**, *Evidence* // **Detroit Blues, 1950-51**, *Krazy Kat*.

Burris, JC

Born: May 15, 1928 - Kings Mountain, NC
Died: 1988 - Greensboro, NC

Blues harmonica and bones player

JC Burris learned how to play the harmonica from his uncle, Sonny Terry. He moved to New York City in 1949, performed and recorded with Sonny Terry from 1953 until 1960.

Burris moved to Los Angeles in 1960, working at the Troubador and other Folk clubs. He moved to San Francisco in 1961, working at local clubs for a few years, but was inactive due to illness from 1966 through 1973. He started playing at various Bay Area clubs in the mid-1970's and made a few movies appearances as well.

Discography:
1961 - **Sonny Terry's New Sound: The Jawharp in Blues and Folk Music,** *Folkways //* **One of These Mornings,** *Arhoolie.*

Movies:
1976 - **Leadbelly //** 1976 - **Riverboat 1988.**

Burton, Michael

Pop harmonica player

Michael Burton is a chord harmonica player who has been active since the 1960's and has worked with *Johnny Puleo's Harmonica Gang, The Harmonica Rascals, The Original Harmonica Band, The New World Harmonica Trio* and *The Dave McKelvey Trio.*

Buschmann, Christian Friedrich

Born: 1805 - Germany

Harmonica inventor

Allegedly the son of organ maker Johann Buschmann, Christian Friedrich Buschmann registered the first European patent for a free-reeded mouth organ in 1821. He named his invention the Aura. His mouth organ consisted of a horizontal arrangement of 15 metal reeds placed in small wooden channels, arranged side by side and had only blow notes.

Butler, Clarence

Born: January 21, 1942 - Florence, AL

Blues singer, harmonica player

Harmonica player Clarence Butler and his brother Curtis have been working since they were teenagers as *The Butlers Twins* in the Detroit Blues scene. He has also recorded with Ben Harper, Kenny Parker and others.

Discography:
1988 - **Live in Detroit,** *Blues Factory //* 1995 - **Not Gonna Worry About Tomorrow //** 1996 - **Pursue Your Dreams,** *JSP.*

Butler, George "Wild Child"

Born: October 1, 1936 - Autaugaville, AL

Blues singer, guitar, harmonica player

George "Wild Child" Butler started playing guitar as a child but switched to the harmonica at age six. He played local parties in Alabama from the early 1940's until he moved to Chicago in 1945. He hoboed around the U.S. through the mid-1950's.

Butler worked with Sonny Boy Williamson II, (Rice Miller), in the Detroit area in 1957 and did his first recordings in 1964. He moved around a lot, recording in Detroit, Alabama, Chicago and Texas during the 1960's and 70's. He is still very active in music to this day.

Discography:
1968 - **Open Up Baby,** *Charly //* 1976 - **Funky Butt Lover,** *TK //* 1976 - **Lickin' Gravy,** *Rooster Blues //* 1991 - **Keep On Doin' What You're Doin',** *Mercury //* 1992 - **These Mean Old Blues,** *Bullseye //* 1994 - **Stranger,** *Bullseye //* **Wild Child,** *Polydor Juke Blues //* Harp and Blues, *P-Vine.*

Movies:
1967 - **The Blues According To Lightnin' Hopkins //** 1969 - **Memphis Summer Blues.**

Butler, Lester

Born: November 12, 1959
Died: May 9, 1998

Blues singer, harmonica player

During his short, but illustrious career, Blues harmonica player Lester Butler broke new ground in the fields of Blues and Blues/Rock, playing with R.L. Burnside, Billy Boy Arnold and Mick Jagger as well as recording with his own band, *The Red*

Devils and as a solo artist.

Discography:
1992 - **King, King,** (with The Red Devils), *Warner Brothers* // 1997 - **13 Featuring Lester Butler,** *Hightone.*

Butterfield, Paul

Born: December 17, 1942 - Chicago, IL
Died: May 4, 1987 - Hollywood, CA

Blues harmonica, vocals

Developing an early interest in Blues music, Paul Butterfield taught himself to play harmonica as a youth and was sitting in with the Muddy Waters Band by 1958. He played steadily in the Chicago Blues scene in the early 1960's.

In 1964 he formed *The Paul Butterfield Blues Band,* one of the first integrated Chicago Blues bands, and they recorded their first album for the Elektra label in 1965. Also that year, they performed at the Newport Folk Festival and backed up Bob Dylan. Their popularity helped to spark a revival in Blues music.

They appeared in the movies "Festival," "You Are What You Eat" and recorded the soundtrack for "Steelyard Blues" in addition to performing at the Woodstock Festival.

In 1973 Butterfield put together a new band, *Better Days,* but failed to generate the popularity of his previous band. He performed with Muddy Waters and *The Band* in the 1978 movie "The Last Waltz." A victim of his own overindulgence in drugs and alcohol, Butterfield died of a drug overdose in 1987.

Discography:
1965 - **The Paul Butterfield Blues Band,** *Elektra* // 1966 - **East-West,** *Elektra* // 1967 - **The Resurrection of Pigboy Crenshaw,** *Elektra* // 1967 - **Paul Butterfield with John Mayall,** *Decca* // 1968 - **In My Own Dream,** *Elektra* // 1969

- **Keep On Moving,** *Elektra* // 1971 - **Sometimes I Just Feel Like Smilin',** *Elektra* // 1971 - **Live,** *Elektra* // 1972 - **An Offer You Can't Refuse,** *Red Lightning* // 1972 - **Golden Butter,** *Elektra* // 1973 - **Better Days,** *Rhino* // 1973 - **It All Comes Back,** *Rhino* // 1976 - **Put It in Your Ear,** *Bearsville* // 1981 - **North-South,** *Bearsville* // 1986 - **The Legendary Paul Butterfield Rides Again,** *Amherst* // 1995 - **The Original Lost Elektra Sessions,** *Rhino* // 1995 - **Strawberry Jam,** *Winner* // 1996 - **East-West Live,** *Winner* // 1997 - **An Anthology: The Elektra Years,** *Elektra* // 1988 - **The Paul Butterfield Blues Band Anthology,** *Rhino* // **Three Harp Boogie,** (with James Cotton and Billy Boy Arnold), *Rhino* // **Fathers and Sons,** (with Muddy Waters), *Chess.*

Movies:
1966 - **Festival** // 1968 - **You Are What You Eat** // 1973 - **Steelyard Blues** // 1978 - **The Last Waltz.**

Instruction:
Blues Harmonica, (with John B. Sebastian), *Homespun* // **Paul Butterfield Teaches Blues Harmonica,** *Homespun.*

The Byrds

Formed: 1965 - Los Angeles, CA
Disbanded: 1972

Folk / Rock band
The Byrds were one of the most influential of all the bands that came out of the Folk / Rock movement of the mid-1960's. Founded by Roger McGuinn, the group featured Gene Parsons, Gene Clark and Michael Clarke, all of who could play the harmonica.

See - Gene Clark, Michael Clarke, Gene Parsons

Discography:
1964 - **Early Byrds,** *Columbia* // 1965 - **Mr. Tambourine Man,** *Columbia* // 1966 - **Turn, Turn, Turn,** *Columbia* // 1966 - **Fifth Dimension,** *Columbia* // 1967 - **Younger Than Yesterday,** *Columbia* // 1967 - **The Byrds Greatest Hits,** *Columbia* // 1968 - **The Notorious Byrd Brothers,** *Columbia* // 1968 - **Sweetheart of the Rodeo,** *Columbia* // 1969 - **Dr. Byrd and Mr. Hyde** // 1969 - **Live at the Fillmore West - February 1969,** *Columbia* // 1970 - **Ballad of Easy Rider,** *Columbia* // 1970 - **Untitled,** *Columbia* // 1971 - **Byrdmaniax,** *Columbia* // 1972 - **Farther Along,** *Columbia* // 1972 - **Preflyte,** *Columbia* // 1973 - **History of The Byrds,** *CBS* // 1973 - **The Byrds,** *Asylum* // 1980 - **The Byrds Play Dylan,** *Columbia* // 1988 - **In the Beginning,** *Rhino* // 1989 - **Never Before,** *Murray Hill* // 1990 - **The Byrds,** (Box Set), *Columbia* // 1995 - **Star Rockets,** *Essex* // 1998 - **Full Flyte,** *Raven* // 1998 - **Byrd Parts,** *Raven* // 1999 - **Greatest Hits,** *Sony.*

Caldwell, Mike
Country harmonica player

Mike Caldwell is a Country music harmonica player who has played in Loretta Lynn's band for over twelve years. He has also played with Conway Twitty, Boxcar Willie and George Jones.

<u>Discography:</u>
1997 - **Harmonica Mike's Country Classics.**

Canned Heat
Formed: 1966 - Los Angeles, CA

Blues / Rock band
One of the top groups of the late 1960's Blues revival, *Canned Heat* was co-founded by Bob "The Bear" Hite and Al "Blind Owl" Wilson, both of whom played guitar and harmonica and both were Blues historians.

Their career got a tremendous boost after appearances at both the Monterey Pop and Woodstock music festivals. Their big hits included; "On the Road Again," "Going Up the Country" and "Let's Work Together." The band stayed together in spite of Wilson's death in 1970 and Hite's death in 1981. Guitar and harmonica player James Thornbury joined the group from 1984 until 1987.

See - Bob Hite, Al Wilson, James Thornbury

<u>Discography:</u>
1967 - **Canned Heat,** *Liberty* // 1968 - **Boogie with Canned Heat,** *Liberty* // 1968 - **Livin' the Blues,** *Liberty* // 1969 - **Hallelujah,** *Liberty* // 1969 - **The Canned Heat Cookbook,** *Liberty* // 1970 - **Canned Heat '70,** *Liberty* // 1970 - **Hooker N' Heat,** *Liberty* // 1970 - **Live at Topanga Canyon,** *Wand* // 1970 - **Future Blues,** *BGO* // 1971 - **Canned Heat Concert,** *United Artists* // 1971 - **Canned Heat Collage,** *Sunset* // 1971 - **Historical Figures and Heads,** *United Artists* // 1973 - **The New Age,** *United Artists* // 1973 - **Rollin' and Tumblin',** *Sunset* // 1974 - **One More River To Cross,** *Atlantic* // 1975 - **The Very Best Of...,** *EMI America* // 1981 - **Captured Live,** *Accord* // 1986 - **Infinite Boogie,** *Rhino* // 1989 - **Reheated,** *Chameleon* // 1994 - **Burnin' Live,** *Aim* // 1995 - **Live at Turku Rock Festival,** *Bear Tracks* // 1996 - **Vintage,** *Sundazed* // 1996 - **Gamblin' Woman,** *Mausoleum* // 1996 - **Canned Heat Blues Band,** *A&M* // 1996 - **In Concert,** *King Biscuit Flower Hour* // 1997 - **The Ties That Bind,** *Archive* // 1999 - **Boogie 2000,** *Ruf* // 2000 - **The Boogie House Tapes, 1967-1976,** *Ruf* // **Boogie Up the Country,** *Inakustik.*

Cannon's Jug Stompers
Formed: 1923 - Memphis, TN
Disbanded: 1931

Jug band
Cannon's Jug Stompers was one of the leading groups to emerge from Memphis, Tennessee during the Jug Band craze of the 1920's. The group featured Noah Lewis on the harmonica and had hits with "Viola Lee Blues," "Big Railroad Blues" and "Walk Right In," which later became a smash hit during the 1960's for *The Rooftop Singers.*

See - Noah Lewis

<u>Discography:</u>
1991 - **Cannon's Jug Stompers, The Complete Works, (1927-30),** *Yazoo* // 1994 - **Complete Recorded Works, Vol. 1&2,** *Document.*

The Cappy Barra Harmonica Ensemble
Formed: 1935 - New York City, NY
Disbanded: 1944

Vaudeville harmonica band
Assembled by promoter Maurice Duke and named after the capybara, a large South American rodent, *The Cappy Barra Harmonica Ensemble* specialized in playing big band arrangements on the harmonica.

Players in the group included; Charles Leighton, George Fields, Sam Scheckter, Don Ripps, Phil King, Sam Sperling, Joe Mullendore, Leon Lafell, Nat Bergman, Phil Solomon, Alan Greene and Pro Robbins.

They made numerous radio and movie appearances and had a

lucrative career in Vaudeville. Most of the group disbanded after the outbreak of World War Two.

Movies:
1938 - **Mad About Music** // 1941 - **Pot O' Gold** // 1945 - **Rockin' in the Rockies** // 1945 - **Radio Stars on Parade** // **Bowery Boy.**

Captain Beefheart

Real name: Don Van Vliet
Born: January 15, 1941

Rock singer, multi-instrumentalist, including harmonica

Captain Beefheart is an eclectic, avant-garde Rock songwriter who worked with his own back-up group, *The Magic Band.* He was closely associated for many years with Frank Zappa. Having the talent to play several instruments, including the harmonica, Captain Beefheart worked steadily for several years with some commercial success before dropping out of music entirely in the 1980's. He is, however, considered to be very influential among the art rockers.

Discography:
1967 - **Dropout Boogie,** *Buddah* // 1967 - **Safe as Milk,** *Buddah* // 1968 - **Strictly Personal,** *Blue Thumb* // 1969 - **Trout Mask Replica,** *Straight* // 1970 - **Lick My Medals Off, Baby,** *Buddah* // 1971 - Mirror Man, *Buddah* // 1972 - **The Spotlight Kid,** *Reprise* // 1972 - **Captain Beefheart and the Magic Band,** *Reprise* // 1972 - **Clear Spot,** *Reprise* // 1974 - **Unconditionally Guaranteed,** *Mercury* // 1974 - **Blue Jeans and Moonbeams,** *Mercury* // 1975 - **Bongo Fury,** *Discreet* // 1978 - **Shiny Beast,** *Warner Brothers* // 1980 - **Doc at the Radar Station,** *Virgin* // 1982 - **Ice Cream for Crow,** *Epic* // 1984 - **The Legendary A&M Sessions,** *A&M* // 1998 - **Zig Zag Wanderer,** *Wooded Hill* // 1998 - **A Carrot is as Close as a Rabbit Gets To a Diamond,** *EMI* // 1999 - **The Dust Blows Forward: An Anthology,** *Rhino.*

The Carolina Tarheels

Formed: 1928 - North Carolina
Disbanded: Late 1930's

Old-time Country string band
The Carolina Tarheels featured the harmonica playing of Garley Foster and Gwen Foster, (no relation to each other). The group recorded about forty sides for the Victor label during the late 1920's and early 30's.

See - Garley Foster, Gwen Foster

Discography:
1962 - **The Carolina Tarheels,** *Folk Legacy* // **Look Who's Comin': The Carolina Tarheels,** *GHP Old Homestead.*

Carp, Jeff

Died: January 1, 1973

Blues harmonica player
Jeff Carp was a Blues harmonica player who made appearances on the Muddy Waters and Howlin' Wolf London Sessions albums as well as John Lee Hooker's "If You Miss 'Im...I Got 'Im" album.

Carter, William "Bom-Bay"

Born: June 23, 1950 - Chicago, IL

Blues guitar, bass, harmonica player
"Bom-Bay" Carter probably learned to play guitar and harmonica from his father. He has played and recorded with JB Hutto, Lee Jackson, Johnny Young and others from the Chicago Blues scene since the 1950's, as well as doing some recording on his own.

Carver, Warner

Country Fiddle, harmonica player
Warner Carver played the guitar and harmonica in *The Carver Boys,* a rural Country / Blues string band from Kentucky in the 1920's. Country Comedienne Cousin Emmy began her career by performing with *The Carver Boys.*

Cash, Johnny

Born: February 26, 1932 - Kingsland, AR

Country singer-songwriter, guitar, harmonica player

Though he is known primarily for his singing and guitar playing, Johnny Cash occasionally plays the harmonica as well as having top session musicians play it on his records.

1959 - **Greatest!**, *Sun* // 1965 - **The Original Sun Sound of Johnny Cash**, *Sun* // 1967 - **Johnny Cash's Greatest Hits, Vol. 1**, *Columbia* // 1985 - **The Sun Years**, *Charly* // 1986 - **Up Through the Years, 1955-1957**, *Bear Family* // 1987 - **Vintage Years: 1955-1963**, *Rhino* // 1987 - **Columbia Records 1958-1986**, *Columbia* // 1992 - **The Essential Johnny Cash 1955-1983**, *Columbia/Legacy*.

Cash, June Carter

Born: June 23, 1929 - Maces Spring, VA

Country singer-songwriter, multi-instrumentalist including harmonica

The daughter of Country music matriarch Mother Maybelle Carter, June Carter has been performing since 1937. She can play a large variety of instruments including the harmonica. She's been married to Country star Johnny Cash since 1968 and is the mother of Rosanne Cash and Carlene Carter, both of whom are country stars in their own right.

Discography:

1967 - **Carryin' On**, (AKA: Johnny Cash and his Woman), *Columbia* // 1976 - **Appalachian Pride**, *Columbia* // 1978 - **Gone Girl**, *Columbia* // 1999 - **Press On**, *Risk* // 1999 - **All in the Family**, *Bear Family* // **Johnny and June.**

Cash, Steve

Born: May 5, 1946 - Springfield, MO

Country / Rock vocals, harmonica

Steve Cash learned to play the harmonica from his mother and was the lead vocalist for the band, *The Ozark Mountain Daredevils*. He also played harmonica on albums by Emmylou Harris and

Brewer & Shipley.

Discography: (see - The Ozark Mountain Daredevils)

Cephas & Wiggins

Formed: 1977 - Washington, DC

Acoustic Blues duo

The acoustic Blues duo of guitarist John Cephas and harmonica player Phil Wiggins has been performing since 1976 and have become leading proponents of the Piedmont style of Blues.

See - Phil Wiggins

Discography:

1984 - **Sweet Bitter Blues**, *L&R Music* // 1985 - **Let It Roll: Bowling Green**, *Marimac* // 1986 - **Dog Days of August**, *Flying Fish* // 1987 - **Guitar Man**, *Flying Fish* // 1988 - **Walking Blues**, *Marimac* // 1992 - **Flip, Flop & Fly**, *Flying Fish* // 1993 - **Bluesmen**, *Chesky* // 1996 - **Cool Down**, *Alligator* // 1998 - **Goin' Down the Road Feelin' Bad**, *Evidence* // 1999 - **Homemade**, *Alligator* // 2000 - **From Richmond To Atlanta**, *Rounder*.

Chagrin, Francis

Born: 1905 - Hungary
Died: 1972

Classical composer

Francis Chagrin wrote "Roumanian Fantasy for Harmonica and Orchestra" for Larry Adler in 1956.

Recordings:

1997 - **Harmonica Virtuoso**, (soloist - Larry Adler), Legacy // **Classical Harmonicist**, (soloist - Larry Logan), *Logan*.

Chailly, Luciano

Born: 1920 - Italy

Classical composer

Luciano Chailly wrote "Improvvisazione No. 9 for Harmonica, Strings and Percussion" in 1962 for Classical harmonica player John Sebastian, Sr.

Chambers, Lester

Born: April 13, 1940 - Mississippi

Rock / Blues / Soul singer, harmonica player

Lester Chambers was a member of the Soul music group, *The Chambers Brothers*. He grew up in Mississippi, moved with his family to Los Angeles in the early 1950's and began performing with his brothers in the early 1960's. He played the harmonica on all of their albums as well as singing with the group.

Discography:

1964 - **Barbara Dane and The Chambers Brothers**, *Folkways* // 1965 - **People Get Ready**, *Vault* // 1965 -

Chambers Brothers Now, *Vault* // 1966 - **The Chambers Brothers Shout**, *Vault* // 1968 - **The Time Has Come**, *Columbia* // 1968 - **A New Time, a New Day**, *Columbia* // 1969 - **Love, Peace and Happiness**, *Columbia* // 1970 - **The Chambers Brothers Live at the Fillmore East**, *Columbia* // 1970 - **Feelin' the Blues**, *Vault* // 1971 - **A New Generation**, *Columbia* // 1971 - **The Chambers Brothers Greatest Hits**, *Columbia* // 1972 - **Oh My God!**, *Columbia* // 1973 - **The Best Of...**, *Fantasy* // 1974 - **Unbonded**, *Fantasy* // 1975 - **Right Move**, *Fantasy* // 1977 - **Live in Concert on Mars**, *Chelsea* // 1999 - **Lester Chambers**, *Complete* // 2001 - **Blues for Sale**.

Champion, Grady

Born: October 10, 1969 - Canton, MS

Blues singer, harmonica player

Grady Champion grew up in rural Mississippi and began his musical career singing in Gospel choirs and later picked up the harmonica as he began drifting into the Blues. He has been a regular on the Blues festival circuit since the mid-1990's.

Discography:
1998 - **Goin' Back Home**, *Grady Shady Music* // 1999 - **Payin' for My Sins**, *Shanachie*.

Chatmon, Sam

Born: January 10, 1897 - Bolton, MS
Died: February 2, 1983 - Hollandale, MS

Jug Band Blues multi-instrumentalist including harmonica

As part of the famous Chatmon family that included his brothers Bo and Lonnie and his half-brother, Charlie Patton, Sam Chatmon began playing music at age six and immediately joined his family's string band.

He played around Mississippi, Tennessee and Illinois from 1905 until the mid-1940's. He began recording in 1930 for the Okeh label with Texas Alexander and with his brothers as the group, *The Mississippi Sheiks* on the Bluebird label from 1934 to 1936.

Chatmon dropped out of music from 1942 until 1960, when he was re-discovered and then recorded by the Arhoolie label. He worked the Folk festival circuit through the 1960's and 70's as well as recording for the Blue Goose, Rounder and Albatross labels.

Discography:
1970 - **The Mississippi Sheik**, *Blue Goose* // 1972 - **The New Mississippi Sheiks** // 1977 - **Hollandale Blues** // 1979 - **Sam Chatmon's Advice**, *Rounder* // 1987 - **Sam Chatmon & his Barbecue Boys**, *Flying Fish* // 1989 - **Mississippi String Bands** // 1999 - **1970-1974**, *Flyright* // **The Mississippi Sheiks & Chatman Brothers, Complete Recorded Works, Vol 1-4**, *Document*.

Chenier, Clifton

Born: June 25, 1925 - Opelousas, LA
Died: December 12, 1987 - Lafayette, LA

Zydeco accordion, keyboards, harmonica player

Clifton Chenier learned how to play the accordion from his father and began playing professionally at age seventeen. He began recording in 1956 and became a leading proponent of Zydeco music. He would occasionally supplement his accordion by playing some harmonica.

Discography:
1955 - **Zydeco Blues and Boogie**, *Specialty* // 1960 - **Clifton Chenier and Rockin' Dopsie**, *Flyright* // 1965 - **Louisiana Blues and Zydeco**, *Arhoolie* // 1967 - **Black Snake Blues**, *Arhoolie* // 1969 - **Louisiana Blues**, *Arhoolie* // 1970 - **Clifton's Cajun Blues**, *Prophesy* // 1970 - **King of the Bayous**, *Arhoolie* // 1970 - **Bayou Blues**, *Specialty* // 1971 - **Live at a French Dance**, *Arhoolie* // 1974 - **Out West**, *Arhoolie* // 1975 - **Boogie 'n' Zydeco**, *Maison De Soul* // 1977 - **Red Hot Louisiana Band**, *Arhoolie* // 1978 - **Cajun Swamp Music Live**, *Tomato* // 1978 - **Clifton Chenier and his Red Hot Louisiana Band**, *Arhoolie* // 1979 - **The King of Zydeco**, *Arhoolie* // 1979 - **In New Orleans**, *GNP* // 1979 - **Bayou Soul**, *Maison De Soul* // 1979 - **Frenchin' the Boogie**, *Barclay* // 1980 - **Boogie 'n' Zydeco**, *Arhoolie* // 1980 - **Classic Clifton**, *Arhoolie* // 1981 - **Bon Ton Roulet**, *Arhoolie* // 1981 - **Blues & Zydeco**, *Arhoolie* // 1982 - **Live at the San Francisco Blues Festival**, *Arhoolie* // 1982 - **I'm Here!**, *Alligator* // 1984 - **Country Boy Now**, *Maison De Soul* // 1984 - **The King of Zydeco Live at Montreux**, *Arhoolie* // 1985 - **Live!**, *Arhoolie* // 1987 - **Sings the Blues**, *Arhoolie* // 1987 - **Bogalusa Boogie**, *Arhoolie* // 1988 - **My Baby Don't Wear No Shoes**, *Arhoolie* // 1988 - **Live at St. Mark's**, *Arhoolie* // 1988 - **60 Minutes with the King of Zydeco**, *Arhoolie* // 1993 - **Zydeco Dynamite: The Clifton Chenier Anthology**, *Rhino* // 1994 - **We're Gonna Party**, *Collectables* // 1996 - **I'm Coming Home**, *Magnum* // 1997 - **Zydeco Sont Pas Sale**, *Arhoolie* // 1999 - **Bayou Bayou**, *Import* // 1999 - **Squeezebox Boogie**, *Just a Memory* // 2000 - **Live at the 1966 Berkeley Blues Festival**, *Arhoolie* // **Boogie in Black and White**, *Jin*.

Movies:
1973 - **Dry Wood and Hot Peppers** // 1973 - **Getting' Back** // 1974 - **Within Southern Louisiana** // 1987 - **The King of Zydeco**.

The Chicago Blues Stars

Formed: 1969 - Chicago, IL

Blues band

The Chicago Blues Stars were a one-shot Blues supergroup put together by Charlie Musselwhite in order to get around contractual obligations to his record label. In addition to Musselwhite, the band featured Dave Myers, Fred Below and Louis Myers of *The Aces*.

See - Charlie Musselwhite, Louis Myers, The Aces

Discography:
1970 - **Coming Home,** *Blue Thumb.*

Chimes, Mike

Born: 1914
Died: 1984

Vaudeville / Pop harmonica player
Mike Chimes played the bass and chord harmonicas in *The Harmonica Rascals* from the mid-1920's through the mid-1930's. During that time he also worked with the M. Hohner Company to help develop the chord harmonica. He left *The Harmonica Rascals* to play in Carl Freed's *Harmonica Harlequins*, where he played chord and lead solo harmonicas as well as writing arrangements for the group.

When *The Harmonica Harlequins* disbanded in 1935, Freed and Chimes recruited Saul Webber and Sid Gould to put together a new band, The Harmonica Lads. Chime left that group in 1940. During the 1950's and 60's, Chimes teamed up with his wife and sons in a harmonica act called *The Chimes Family.*

He eventually returned to New York City where he worked steadily as a studio session player and recorded with Frank Sinatra, Neil Diamond, Johnny Mathis, Perry Como, Harry Belafonte, Pete Seeger, Gladys Knight and others.

Chmel, Franz

Born: St. Polten, Austria

Classical harmonica player
Franz Chmel began playing the harmonica at age six and was playing with his brothers in a harmonica band by the mid-1950's. Having won several competitions, Chmel started to work as a Classical soloist in the 1960's and has recorded several albums since that time.

Discography:
1997 - **Fantasia Baroque,** *PSB //* **Classic Harmonica, Vol 1.**

Chord Harmonica

The chord harmonica usually features two harmonicas hinged together and they feature clusters of notes enabling a player to play chords.

The first chord harmonica was developed to meet the growing musical needs of America's harmonica bands during the 1920's by the M. Hohner Company with the help of *Harmonica Rascal* Mike Chimes.

The first chord harmonica was the Hohner Model #267 which

was two feet long and featured 24 four-note chord positions (12 blow and 12 draw) with double reeds in every hole, for a total of 384 reeds in 96 double holes and a total of 48 possible chords. This harmonica supplies all of the major, minor, seventh chords as well as most of the augmented and diminished chords.

Chord playing can also be achieved on a limited basis by using regular harmonicas and playing chords through them. Many early Vaudeville players used this method, wedging several harmonicas between their fingers.

Some great chord harmonica players include: Al Fiore - *The Harmonicats //* Eddie Gordon - *The Harmonica Rascals, Johnny Puleo's Harmonica Gang //* Manny Smith - *The Stagg McMann Trio //* Michael Burton - *The Original Harmonica Band, The Dave McKelvey Trio //* Mike Chimes - *The Harmonica Rascals, The Harmonica Harlequins, The Harmonica Lads //* Bob Bauer - *The Harmonikings, The Harmonicats //* Fuzzy Feldman - *The Harmonica Rascals.*

Chowning, Randle

Born: 1950

Country / Rock singer, guitar and harmonica player
Randle Chowning played with *The Ozark Mountain Daredevils* from 1973 until 1976 and was featured playing the harmonica on their big hit, "If You Want To Go To Heaven."

Discography: (also see - Ozark Mountain Daredevils)
1978 - **Hearts On Fire,** *A&M.*

Chromatic Harmonica

Introduced in 1924 by the M. Hohner company, the chromatic harmonica typically has two sets of reed plates, tuned a half-step apart. The full chromatic scale is achieved by pushing a spring-action button which produces a half-step jump in notes. This enables the player to have the ability of playing the entire chromatic scale.

Clark, Gene

Born: November 17, 1941 - Tipton, MO
Died: May 24, 1991 - Sherman Oaks, CA

Folk / Country / Rock singer-songwriter, guitar, harmonica player
Gene Clark started his musical career playing 12-string guitar with *The New Christy Minstrels* during the early 1960's. He later moved to Los Angeles and became a co-founder of *The Byrds*. After leaving that group he worked in the Folk and Country music fields, playing guitar and harmonica, until his death at age 49.

Discography: (also see - The Byrds)
1967 - **Echoes,** (with The Gosdin Brothers), *Columbia //* 1967 - **Gene Clark with the Gosdin Brothers,** *Columbia //* 1968 - **Fantastic Expedition,** (as Dillard & Clark), *A&M //* 1969 -

Through the Morning, Through the Night, (as Dillard & Clark), *A&M* // 1969 - **Gene Clark,** *Together* // 1971 - **American Flyer, Media Arts** // 1972 - **Collector's Series: Early L.A. Sessions,** *Columbia* // 1972 - **White Light,** (AKA: Roadmaster), *A&M* // 1974 - **No Other,** *Asylum* // 1977 - **Two Sides To Every Story,** *RSP* // 1979 - **McGuinn,** *Hillman & Clark* // 1980 - **City,** (as McGuinn, Clark & Hillman) // 1984 - **Firebyrd,** *Allegiance* // 1987 - **So Rebellious a Lover,** *Razor & Tie* // 1992 - **Silhouetted in Light,** *Edsel* // 1995 - **This Byrd Has Flown,** *Edsel* // 1997 - **American Dreamer,** *Raven* // 1998 - **Flying High,** *A&M*.

Clarke, Michael

Real name: Michael Dick
Born: June 3, 1943 - New York City, NY
Died: December 19, 1993 - Treasure Island, FL

Country / Rock drummer, harmonica player

Michael Clarke played drums for the Folk / Rock band The Byrds from 1967 until 1976. He played some drums and harmonica for *The Flying Burrito Brothers* from 1970 to 1972 and for the group *Firefall* from 1976 until 1983.

Discography: (see - The Byrds, The Flying Burrito Brothers)

Clarke, William

Born: March 29, 1951 - Inglewood, CA
Died: November 3, 1996 - Fresno, CA

Blues harmonica player

William Clarke began playing the harmonica at age sixteen and was performing professionally two years later. He got some tutoring on the instrument from George "Harmonica" Smith.

Favoring the chromatic harmonica for playing the Blues, Clarke

performed and recorded steadily from the mid-1970's until his death in 1996. In addition to his solo albums, Clarke made appearances on recordings by Smokey Wilson, Steve Samuels, Cal Green and Shakey Jake Harris.

Discography:
1975 - **William Clarke** // 1978 - **Heavy Hittin',** *Good Times* // 1980 - **Blues From Los Angeles,** *Hittin' Heavy* // 1983 - **Can't You Hear Me Calling,** *Rivera* // 1987 - **Tip of the Top,** *Satch* // 1988 - **Rockin' the Boat,** *Rivera* // 1990 - **Blowin' Like Hell,** *Alligator* // 1992 - **Serious Intentions,** *Alligator* // 1994 - **Groove Time,** *Alligator* // 1996 - **The Hard Way,** *Alligator* // 1999 - **Deluxe Edition,** *Alligator* // **Blues Harmonica,** *Watch Dog.*

Classical Harmonica

Though the harmonica is usually shunned by traditionalists in the field of Classical music, there have been a small number of players who have made significant inroads in the genre. Some of the great Classical harmonica players include: Jerry Adler, Larry Adler, Robert Bonfiglio, George Fields, Stan Harper, Cham-Ber Huang, Larry Logan, Tommy Reilly, Alan "Blackie" Schackner, Corky Siegel, *The King's Harmonica Quintet* and others.

Composers who have written works specifically to include the harmonica include: Walter Anderson, Malcolm Arnold, Arthur Benjamin, Robert Russell Bennett, Jean Berger, Francis Chagrin, Luciano Chailly, Henry Cowell, Robert Farnon, Gordon Jacob, Norman Dello Joio, Alan Hovhaness, Aram Khachaturian, George Kleinsinger, Karl Heinz Koper, Joseph Kosma, Serge Lancen, Frank Lewin, Darius Milhaud, James Moody, Edward Robinson, William Russo, Cyril Scott, Henri Sauget, Matyas Seiber, Naresh Sohal, John Philip Sousa, Michael Spivakovsky, Alexander Tcherepnin, Vilem Tausky, Ralph Vaughan-Williams, Heitor Villa-Lobos, Fried Walter and Graham Whettam.

Cobb, Lee J.

Real name: Leo Jacobs
Born: December 8, 1911 - New York City, NY
Died: February 11,1976 - Woodland Hills, CA

Actor

Before embarking on his illustrious career as an actor, Lee J. Cobb was named the 1926 New York City Harmonica Champion in a competition held in Central Park.

Cobbs, Willie

Also known as: Willie C.
Born: July 15, 1932 - Monroe, AR

Blues guitar, harmonica

Willie Cobbs grew up singing in church choirs and was leading choirs by the age of eight. He moved to Chicago around 1951 and was soon working at the Maxwell Street Market with Little Walter Jacobs, from whom he took harmonica lessons. He sat in frequently with the *Muddy Waters Band* during the 1950's and served in the U.S. Marines from 1953 to 1957.

He opened his own Blues club in Chicago in 1957 and formed his own band in 1959, making his first recordings in 1961. His biggest hit, "You Don't Love Me," has been covered by *The Allman Brothers, Sonny and Cher* and *Albert Collins*. He moved back to Arkansas in 1969 and is still active in music.

Discography:
1991 - **Hey Little Girl,** *Wilco //* 1994 - **Down To Earth,** *Rooster Blues //* 1997 - **Pay or Do 11 Months and 29 Days,** *Wilco //* 2000 - **Jukin',** *Bullseye Blues.*

Movies:
1992 - **Mississippi Masala.**

Coffey, Bob
Vaudeville harmonica player
Bob Coffey was a harmonica soloist, working in Vaudeville, who specialized in popular music during the late 1920's and early 30's.

Coleman, Burl "Jaybird"
Born: May 20, 1896 - Gainesville, AL
Died: June 28, 1950 - Tuskegee, AL

Blues singer, guitar and harmonica player
Jaybird Coleman taught himself how to play the harmonica at age twelve. He served in the army during the First World War, where he spent his time entertaining troops with his music. It was during this time that he acquired his nickname for his singing.

After leaving the service, he teamed up with "Big" Joe Williams in *The Birmingham Jug Band* and toured with the Rabbit Foot Minstrel Show. His career was allegedly managed by a local chapter of the Ku Klux Klan.

He began recording in 1927 as a solo artist, with *The Birmingham Jug Band* and with *The Bessemer Blues Pickers.* He recorded eleven sides as a harmonica player and singer.

Largely inactive after 1930, he worked occasionally with various Jug bands and on the street for tips until his death from cancer in 1950.

Discography:
1988 - **Alabama Harmonica Kings,** (with George "Bullet" Williams) // 1993 - **Jaybird Coleman and The Birmingham Jug Band, Complete Recordings,** (1927-30), *Document.*

Comb
The comb of a harmonica is the body of wood or plastic in the center that the reed plates and covers are attached to. Air channels are cut into the comb to direct the players breath in or out of the appropriate reeds. The comb gets its name from its visual similarity to a hair comb.

Commander Cody and his Lost Planet Airmen
Formed: 1967 - Ann Arbor, MI
Disbanded: Late 1980's

Country Swing band
Originally formed as a college band, *Commander Cody and his Lost Planet Airmen* featured singer and guitarist Billy C. Farlow occasionally on the harmonica. Harmonica ace Norton Buffalo also played on several of their recordings.

See - Billy C. Farlow, Norton Buffalo

Discography:
1971 - **Lost in the Ozone,** *MCA //* 1972 - **Hot Licks, Cold Steel and Truckers' Favorites,** *MCA //* 1973 - **Country Casanova,** *MCA //* 1974 - **Live Deep in the Heart of Texas,** *Paramount //* 1975 - **Don't Let Go,** *Warner Brothers //* 1975 - **Commander Cody and his Lost Planet Airmen,** *Warner Brothers //* 1975 - **Tales from the Ozone,** *Warner Brothers //* 1976 - **We've Got a Live One Here,** *Warner Brothers //* 1977 - **Rock and Roll Again,** *Arista //* 1978 - **Flying Dreams,** *Arista //* 1980 - **Lose It Tonight,** *Line //* 1986 - **Let's Rock,** *Blind Pig //* 1986 - **The Very Best Of...,** *See for Miles //* 1986 - **Returns From Outer Space,** *Edsel //* 1988 - **Sleazy Roadside Stories,** *Relix //* 1990 - **Aces High,** *Relix //* 1990 - **Too Much Fun: The Best Of...,** *MCA //* 1993 - **Lost in Space,** *Relix //* 1994 - **Worst Case Scenario,** *Rounder //* 1995 - **The Best Of...,** *Relix.*

Cooksey, Robert

Also known as: Rabbit Foot

Blues singer, guitar and harmonica player

Robert Cooksey accompanied guitarists Bobby Leecan and Alfred Martin during the 1920's. He recorded 46 sides as a duet with Bobby Leecan from 1924 to 1928. He also recorded for the Victor label in 1926 as a member of The South Side Trio and for the Pathe label as a member of *The Dixie Jazzers Washboard Band* in 1927.

Discography: (see - Leecan and Cooksey)

Corley, Dewey

Born: June 18, 1898 - Halley, AR
Died: April 15, 1974 - Memphis, TN

Blues multi-instrumentalist including harmonica

Dewey Corley began playing the harmonica as a child growing up in Arkansas. He started hoboing around the U.S. at age eighteen. In the mid-1920's be worked with various Memphis-area Jug Bands, including *The South Memphis Jug Band*. He recorded with *The Memphis Jug Band* in 1934.

Corley worked in and out of music from the mid-1930's until he was rediscovered and recorded by the Arhoolie label in the 1960's. He also recorded for the Rounder, Albatross and Aldelphi labels in the mid-1960's and early 70's.

Discography:
1969 - **Mississippi Delta Blues, Vol. 1.**

Corritore, Bob

Born: September 27, 1956 - Chicago, IL

Blues harmonica player

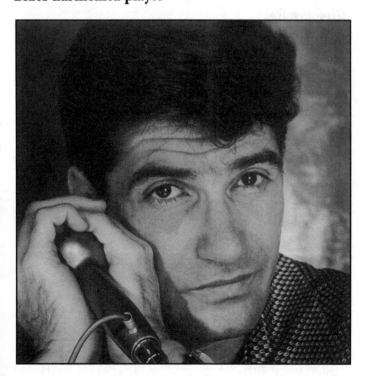

A highly influential player in the Arizona Blues scene, Bob Corritore began playing the harmonica at age twelve after hearing Muddy Waters on the radio. He played regularly with many of Chicago's Blues greats and started his own record label, recording Little Willie Anderson, Big Leon Brooks and many other Blues greats.

Moving to Arizona in 1981, Corritore established himself as a Blues disc jockey, record producer, talent booker for Phoenix's top Blues club as well a harmonica player.

Discography:
1999 - **The All-Star Blues Sessions,** *HMG.*

Cotton, James

Born: July 1, 1935 - Tunica, MS

Blues harmonica player

James Cotton learned how to play the harmonica from his mother as a child and was playing for tips by age nine. He started playing soon after, with Sonny Boy Williamson II (Rice Miller) and stayed with him for about six years.

After Williamson left for Chicago, Cotton returned to Memphis where he fronted *James Cotton and his Rhythm Playmates.* He also worked with Elmore James, Howlin' Wolf, Joe Willie Wilkins, Willie Nix and Junior Parker. Cotton began recording for the Sun label in 1953.

In 1954 he met Muddy Waters who brought him up to Chicago to play in his band and by 1957, Cotton had replaced Little Walter as Waters' full-time harmonica player, both live and in the studio. In 1966 Cotton left *The Muddy Waters Band* to perform solo, although he still performed occasionally with Waters until Waters died in 1983.

Since then Cotton has been a major force in Blues by recording his own albums on a regular basis as well as working with many of the Blues greatest names.

Discography:
1964 - **Chicago / The Blues / Today!, Vol. 2,** *Vanguard //* 1964 - **From Cotton with Verve,** *Verve //* 1966 - **Live and On the Move,** *One Way //* 1967 - **The James Cotton Blues Band,** *Verve //* 1967 - **Late Night Blues,** *Just a Memory //* 1967 - **Cut You Loose,** *Vanguard //* 1968 - **Cotton in Your Ears,** *Verve //* 1968 - **Pure Cotton,** *Verve //* 1971 - **Taking Care of Business,** *Vanguard //* 1974 - **100% Cotton,** *One Way //* 1975 - **Superharp Live and On The Move,** *Buddah //* 1975 - **High Energy,** *One Way //* 1980 - **Take Me Back,** *Blind Pig //* 1984 - **Two Sides of the Blues,** *Intermedia //* 1984 - **Dealing with The Devil,** *Intermedia //* 1984 - **High Compression,** *Alligator //* 1986 - **Live From Chicago Mr. Superharp Himself,** *Alligator //* 1986 - **James Cotton Live,** *Antone's //* 1990 - **Harp Attack!,** (with Billy Branch, Carey Bell & Junior Wells), *Alligator //* 1990 - **Mighty Long Time,** *Antone's //* 1994 - **3 Harp Boogie,** (with Billy Boy Arnold & Paul Butterfield), *Rhino //* 1994 - **Living the Blues,** *Verve //* 1995 - **Best of the Verve Years,** *Verve //* 1996 - **Deep in the Blues,** *Verve //* 1996 - **Feelin' Good,** *Eclipse //* 1998 - **Seems Like Yesterday: Collectors Classics,** *Just a Memory //* 1999 - **The Best of the Vanguard Years,** *Vanguard //* 1999 - **Superharps,** (with Charlie Musselwhite, Sugar Ray Norcia and Billy Branch), *Telarc //* 2000 - **Fire Down Under the Hill,** *Telarc //* **Live at Electric Lady,** *Sequel //* **Mystery Train,** (with Junior Parker), *Rounder.*

Country-Western Harmonica

The harmonica has served as a vital part of Country-Western music from its earliest roots and continues to thrive to this day. Country music's first million-selling record was harmonica player Vernon Dalhart's "Wreck of the Old 97." The first Country record cut in Nashville was an instrumental by the Grand Old Opry's harmonica star, Deford Bailey.

A large number of Country music's biggest stars can play the harmonica and Country music can boast some of the world's best players, including: Mickey Raphael, Don Brooks, Mike Stevens, George Thacker, Kirk "Jelly Roll" Johnson, Terry McMillan and, of course, harmonica legend Charlie McCoy.

Cousin Emmy

Real name: Cynthia May Carver
Born: 1903 - Lamb, KY
Died: April 11, 1980

Country singer-songwriter, comedienne, multi-instrumentalist including harmonica
Cousin Emmy, performed mostly as a comedienne, from the 1930's until well into the 1970's. Before working as a solo act, she worked with Warner Carver and *The Carver Boys.* She wrote the Country music standard "Ruby (Are You Mad At Your Man?)." Her act included her playing of over 15 different instruments, including the harmonica.

Discography:
1947 - **Kentucky Mountain Ballads,** *Decca //* 1968 - **The New Lost City Ramblers with Cousin Emmy,** *Folkways //* 1994 - **Old Time Music, (with The New Lost City Ramblers),** *Vanguard.*

Movies:
1955 - **The Second Greatest Sex.**

Cover Plates

Usually made of steel, tin, brass or some alloy, cover plates are attached to the comb over the reeds and help to direct the sound outwards from the harmonica.

Covington, Ben

Also known as: Bogus Ben, Blind Ben
Born: 1900 - Columbus, MS
Died: 1930's - Homer City, PA

Blues banjo, guitar, harmonica player
Ben Covington began playing music while he was in his teens. He frequently worked with Big Joe Williams doing street shows, medicine shows, carnivals and touring with the Rabbit Foot Minstrels. He often posed as a blind man to increase his tips and also worked as a sideshow attraction called "The Human Pretzel."

Covington recorded for the Paramount / Brunswick labels in 1928. He worked with Big Joe Williams, (as a fake blind man,) at the Century of Progress World's Fair of 1933 in Chicago as well as recording with Jaybird Coleman.

Discography:
1988 - **Alabama Jug and String Bands,** *Document.*

Cowell, Henry

Born: March 11, 1897 - Menlo Park, CA
Died: December 10, 1965 - Shady, NY

Classical composer
Henry Cowell wrote "Concerto for Harmonica and Orchestra" in 1961 for John Sebastian, Sr.

Cox, Billy

Real name: William Jennings Cox
Born: August 4, 1897 - Kanawha County, WV
Died: December 10, 1968

Country singer-songwriter, guitar, harmonica player
Billy Cox learned to play the harmonica from his mother as a child and later learned how to play the guitar. He performed at local functions in West Virginia throughout the 1920's. He start-

ed playing on the radio in 1927 and was recording by 1929. He played and recorded heavily through the 1930's.

In the 1940's he fell into obscurity due to his reckless behavior and heavy drinking. He was re-discovered and recorded shortly before his death in 1968.

Discography:
1967 - **The Dixie Songbird**, *Kanawha*.

Crane, Irvin

Vaudeville harmonica player

Irvin Crane was a member of *The Harmonica Rascals* during the 1930's.

Cranford, Bob

Country singer, harmonica player
Bob Cranford sang and played harmonica with *The Red Fox Chasers*, which formed in North Carolina in 1927. The group recorded a total of 48 sides for the Gennet label in 1928. They disbanded in the early 1930's.

Discography: (see - The Red Fox Chasers)

Crash Test Dummies

Formed: 1989 - Winnipeg, Manitoba, Canada

Alternative Rock Band
The Crash Test Dummies are an Alternative Rock band from Canada who have incorporated many traditional instruments like mandolin and harmonica into their sound. Benjamin Darvill plays both of those instruments for the group.

See - Benjamin Darvill

Discography:
1991 - **The Ghosts That Haunt Me**, *Arista* // 1993 - **God Shuffled his Feet**, *Arista* // 1996 - **A Worm's Life**, *Arista* // 1999 - **Give Yourself a Hand**, *Arista*.

Cream

Formed: 1966 - England
Disbanded 1968

British Hard-Rock band
Featuring former *Yardbirds* and *John Mayall's Bluesbreakers'* guitarist Eric Clapton and former *Blues Incorporated* veterans Ginger Baker and Jack Bruce, *Cream* was one of the pioneering Hard Rock bands of the late 1960's. Bass player Jack Bruce played harmonica on some of the band's songs.

See - Jack Bruce

Discography:
1966 - **Fresh Cream**, *Atco* // 1967 - **Disreali Gears**, *Atco* // 1968 - **Wheels of Fire**, *Atco* // 1968 - **The Savage Seven**, *Atco* // 1969 - **Goodbye Cream**, *Atco* // 1970 - **Live Cream**, *Atco* // 1972 - **Live Cream, Vol. Two**, *Atco* // 1975 - **The Best Of...**, *Polydor* // 1983 - **Strange Brew: The Very Best Of...**, *Polydor* // 1989 - **Live 1968**, *Koine*.

The Crook Brothers Band

Formed: 1920's
Disbanded: 1980's

Country string band
The Crook Brothers Band were regular performers at the Grand Old Opry from 1926 until the death of Herman Crook in 1988. The group included brothers Herman, Lewis and Matthew and featured a twin harmonica sound in its early days.

See - Herman Crook, Matthew Crook

Discography:
1962 - **Sam and Kirk McGee and The Crook Brothers Band**, *Starday*.

Crook, Herman

Born: December 2, 1898 - Scottsboro, TN
Died: June 10, 1988

Country harmonica player
Herman Crook played harmonica with the group, *The Crook Brothers Band* at the Grand Old Opry from 1926 until his death in 1988.

Discography: (see - The Crook Brothers Band)

Crook, Matthew

Born: 1896 - Scottsboro, TN

Country harmonica player
The brother of Herman Crook, Matthew Crook was a member of *The Crook Brothers Band* from its inception until he left in the late 1920's to become a full-time police officer.

Discography: (see - The Crook Brothers Band)

Cross Harp

A nickname for the second diatonic harmonica position, where the harmonica is played five steps above the music, thus placing the accent notes of the Blues scale into the draw position.

See - Positions

The Cumberland Ridge Runners

Formed: 1932
Disbanded: 1935

Country band
The Cumberland Ridge Runners were the house band for the WLS "National Barn Dance" radio show during the 1930's and featured John Lair on the harmonica. The group was also where future country music star Red Foley got his start on the radio.

See - John Lair, Red Foley

Cummings, "Blind Mississippi" Morris

Born: Clarksdale, MS

Blues harmonica player

Morris Cummings began playing harmonica at the age of four andwas playing in clubs in Memphis before he was ten. In the mid-1990's, after years of playing for tips, he began working in earnest with a band in the Memphis area. He has since released two albums of his music.

Discography:
1995 - **You Know What I Like,** *Priority* // 2000 - **Back Porch Blues,** (with Brad Webb), *Boogie Barbecue.*

Curtis, "Iron Man" Mike

Born: 1947, Los Angeles, CA

Pop / Rock singer, guitar, harmonica player

"Iron Man" Mike Curtis began playing the harmonica at the age of five and picked up drums and guitar as a teenager, working regularly in local Rock bands. He now works primarily as a one-man band out of Southern California, playing guitar, harmonica and foot-pedal bass.

Discography:
1997 - **Doin' It All Myself,** *USA Music Group.*

– D –

Daane, Art

Born: August 22, 1934 - Rotterdam, The Netherlands

Vaudeville harmonica player, historian
Art Daane began playing the harmonica at age ten and was playing with *The Hotcha Trio* by the late 1940's.

After moving to South Africa in 1954, he formed his first *Relda Trio,* a harmonica band that would have incarnations in The Netherlands and New Zealand as well.

In 1999 Daane opened the Harmonica Museum at the Muse in Malden, The Netherlands, which includes the "Harmonica Hall of Fame," a collection of over 100 harmonicas contributed by the greatest players in the world.

Dalhart, Vernon

Real name: Marion Try Slaughter II
Born: April 6, 1883 - Marion County, TX
Died: September 14, 1948 - Bridgeport, CT

Country singer, harmonica player

Vernon Dalhart was Country music's first major star. After starting out his career as an operatic singer in 1910, he switched over to Country music in 1924. He allegedly recorded over 1,000 sides under 100 aliases during the 1920's and 1930's. His recording of "Wreck of the Old 97" was the first Country record to sell over a million copies and his recording of "The Prisoner's Song" would eventually sell over 25 million copies.

His fortune and career collapsed after the stock market crash of 1929 and he never regained the success of his earlier years.

Discography:
1978 - **Vernon Dalhart, The First Singing Cowboy,** *Mark 56* // 1978 - **Vernon Dalhart, First Recorded Railroad Songs,** *Mark 56* // 1980 - **Ballads & Railroad Songs,** *Old Homestead* // 1985 - **Wreck of the Old 97,** *Old Homestead* // 1999 - 1981 - **Country Music Hall of Fame,** *King* // **On the Lighter Side** // **That Good Old Country Town, Vol. 4** // **Old Time Songs,** *Davis Unlimited.*

Daltry, Roger

Born: March 1, 1944 - London, England

Rock singer, harmonica player

Roger Daltry is the lead singer for the British Rock band, *The Who*. He occasionally plays the harmonica, most notably on live versions of "Magic Bus" and "Baba O'Riley."

Discography: (also see - The Who)

1973 - **Daltry,** *Repertoire* // 1975 - **Ride a Rock Horse,** *Repertoire* // 1977 - **One of the Boys,** *Repertoire* // 1981 - **The Best Of...,** *Polydor* // 1982 - **The Best Bits,** *MCA* // 1984 - **Parting Should Be Painless,** *Atlantic* // 1985 - **Under a Raging Moon,** *Atlantic* // 1987 - **Can't Wait to See the Movie,** *Atlantic* // 1992 - **Rocks in the Head,** *Atlantic* // 1992 - **The Best of Rockers & Ballads,** *Alex* // 1994 - **Celebration: The Music of the Who,** *Continuum* // 1996 - **McVicar,** *Polydor* // **Martyrs & Madmen: The Best Of...,** *Rhino.*

Dargie, Horrie

Born: July 7, 1917 - Australia
Died: August 30, 1999

Pop harmonica player

Horrie Dargie began his career playing in various harmonica bands in Australia during the 1930' and 40's. After serving in World War Two he continued to work with harmonica bands and as a soloist, recording several albums.

Movies:
1988 - **Crocodile Dundee II.**

Darling, Chuck

Blues harmonica player

Chuck Darling was a Blues harmonica player of the 1920's and 30's who specialized in playing Ragtime-styled harmonica.

Darvill, Benjamin

Born: January 4, 1967

Alternative Rock mandolin, harmonica player

Benjamin Darvill plays the mandolin and harmonica in the Alternative Rock band *The Crash Test Dummies.*

Discography: (see - Crash Test Dummies)

Davenport, Jed

Jug band leader, trumpet, harmonica player

Jed Davenport was the leader of *The Beale Street Jug Band,* performing on the streets and parks of Memphis beginning in the 1920's. He recorded for the Vocalion label in 1929 and 1930 with *The Beale Street Jug Band* and with Blues vocalist, Memphis Minnie. He continued playing on and off until his death in the 1960's.

Discography: (also see - The Beale Street Jug Band)
1983 - **Memphis Harmonica Kings** // 1992 - **Memphis Harp and Jug Blowers,** *Document.*

Davenport, Lester

Born: January 16, 1932

Blues drums, harmonica player

Lester Davenport began playing the harmonica at the age of five. After moving to Chicago in 1946, he took harmonica lessons from Snooky Pryor.

He is probably best remembered for having replaced Billy Boy Arnold in Bo Diddley's band. During the 1980's he did some playing with *The Kinsey Report* as well as playing and recording as a solo artist.

Discography:
1979 - **American Blues Legends 1979**, *Big Bear* // 1992 - **When The Blues Hit You**, *Earwig*.

Davies, Cyril

Born: 1932 - Denham, England
Died: January 7, 1964 - England

British Blues harmonica player
Cyril Davies began playing music professionally in the early 1950's, then taking up the harmonica after teaming up with Alexis Korner in the mid-1950's as an acoustic Blues duo. In the early 1960's they recruited drummer Charlie Watts and Bassist Jack Bruce, electrified their instruments and named themselves *Blues Incorporated*.

In 1962 they opened up the Ealing Club in London which attracted many Blues enthusiasts including: Mick Jagger, Keith Richards, Brian Jones, Eric Burdon and Rod Stewart, many of whom got their starts sitting in with the band. When Charlie Watts left *Blues Incorporated* he was replaced by Ginger Baker.

Blues Incorporated split up in 1963 and Davies put together *The Cyril Davies All-Stars*, which included Nicky Hopkins, Jimmy Page and Jeff Beck. They recorded 4 songs for Pye Records. While he was alive, Davies taught harmonica to Mick Jagger and Brian Jones. After Davies died of leukemia in 1964, his band was taken over by Long John Baldry.

See - Mick Jagger, Jack Bruce, Rod Stewart, Brian Jones, Long John Baldry

Discography: (also see - Blues Incorporated)
1957 - **The Legendary Cyril Davies**, *Folklore* // 1957-61 - **Alexis Korner and Cyril Davies**, *Krazy Kat* // 1962 - **Cyril Davies**, *Ace of Clubs* // 1971 - **R&B from the Marquee**, *Decca* // 1992 - **Dealing with the Devil: Immediate Blues, Vol. 2**, *CBS* // 1992 - **Stroll On**, *Sony*.

Davies, Rick

Born: July 22, 1944 - England

Rock keyboards, harmonica player
In addition to playing keyboards for the group *Supertramp*, Rick Davies occasionally played harmonica on the band's many hit records.

Discography: (see - Supertramp)

Davis, Reverend Gary

Also known as: Blind Gary
Born: April 30, 1896 - Laurens, SC
Died: May 5, 1972 - Hammonton, NJ

Blues singer, guitar, harmonica player
Gary Davis was blinded when he was two months old. He taught himself how to play the harmonica at age five and started playing in local string bands around 1910. He was ordained as a Baptist preacher in 1933 and began recording in 1935.

He worked with Blind Boy Fuller in the mid-1940's and was active recording and preaching all of his life. His music was a mixture of Gospel and religion-influenced Blues.

During the 1960's Davis was heavily active in the Folk music circuit, recording and making numerous appearances at many major music festivals. His biggest hits included "Candyman," "Samson and Delilah," "Death Don't Have No Mercy" and "Cocaine Blues."

Discography:
1935-40 - **Reverend Gary Davis**, *Yazoo* // 1950's - **The Singing Reverend**, *Stinson* // 1956 - **American Street Songs**, *Riverside* // 1959 - **At Newport**, *Vanguard* // 1960's - **When I Die I'll Live Again**, *Fantasy* // 1960 - **Harlem Street Singer**, *Bluesville* // 1961 - **Gospel, Blues and Street Songs**, *OBC* // 1961 - **Say No To the Devil**, *OBC* // 1962-63 - **I Am the True Vine**, *Heritage* // 1962-70 - **Ragtime Guitar**, *Heritage* // 1964 - **The Guitar and the Banjo of Rev. Gary Davis**, *Prestige* // 1966 - **At "Al Matthes"** // 1971 - **From Blues To Gospel**, *Biograph* // 1971 - **Lord I Wish I Could See**, *Biograph* // 1971 - **New Blues and Gospel** // 1973 - **At the Sign of the Sun**, *Gospel Heritage* // 1974 - **O Glory**, *Adelphi* // 1978 - **Guitar and Banjo of Rev.

Gary Davis, *Prestige //* 1991 - **Pure Religion and Bad Company,** *Smithsonian Folkways //* 1993 - **Blues and Ragtime,** *Shanachie //* 1994 - **Rev. Blind Gary Davis: Complete Recordings, (1935-1949),** *Document //* 1994 - **Complete Early Recordings,** *Yazoo //* 1997 - **Live & Kicking,** *Just a Memory //* 1999 - **Little More Faith,** *Original Blues Classics //* 2000 - **Live at Cambridge 1971,** *Catfish //* **Children of Zion,** *Heritage //* **Reverend Gary Davis,** *Heritage //* **Sun is Going Down,** *Folkways.*

Movies:
1967 - **Reverend Gary Davis //** 1972 - **Blind Gary Davis // Reverend Gary Davis and Sonny Terry: Masters of the Country Blues,** *Yazoo Video.*

Davis, Guy

Born: May 12, 1952 - New York, NY

Blues singer, guitar, harmonica player

The son of actors Ossie Davis and Ruby Dee, Guy Davis began playing Blues music at age thirteen after seeing Buddy Guy in concert. Primarily known as a singer and guitar player, Davis plays the harmonica on a neckbrace and specializes in acoustic Blues styles.

Discography:
1978 - **Dreams About Life,** *Folkways //* 1995 - **Stomp Down Rider,** *Red House //* 1996 - **Call Down the Thunder,** *Red House //* 1998 - **You Don't Know My Mind,** *Red House //* 2000 - **Butt Naked Free,** *Red House.*

Davis, Mac

Real name: Scott Davis
Born: January 21, 1942 - Lubbock, TX

Country singer-songwriter, guitar, harmonica player
Mac Davis has been working as a singer-songwriter since 1962. He wrote several hits for Elvis Presley, including: "Don't Cry Daddy" and "In the Ghetto." He's also had a number of top 40 hits as a solo artist and acted in several movies.

Discography:
1979 - **Greatest Hits of Mac Davis,** *Columbia //* 1984 - **20 Golden Greats,** *Astan //* 2000 - **Country Spotlight #1,** *Direct Source.*

Davis, "Little" Sammy

Born: November 28, 1928 - Mississippi

Blues singer, harmonica player

"Little" Sammy Davis began playing harmonica at age eight and began making records in 1952. After a few minor hits in the 1950's, his career was fairly quiet until he started to make a comeback in the mid-1990's.

Discography:
1995 - **I Ain't Lyin',** *Delmark.*

Davis, Spencer

Born: July 17, 1942 - Swansea, Wales

Rock singer, guitar, harmonica player
Spencer Davis founded *The Spencer Davis Group* in Birmingham, England in 1963. He was probably best known for having discovered Steve Winwood, who played keyboards and sang for the band. Their big hits included "Gimme Some Lovin'," "Keep On Running" and "I'm a Man."

Davis still plays occasionally, both with different line-ups of his group and guest-starring as a harmonica player and guitarist with other artists, as well as running his own artist management company.

Discography:
1965 - **First Album,** *Sonet UK* // 1966 - **Second Album,** *Sonet UK* // 1966 - **Autumn '66,** *Sonet UK* // 1967 - **Gimme Some Lovin',** *Sonet UK* // 1967 - **I'm a Man,** *Sonet UK* // 1968 - **The Very Best Of...,** *Sonet UK* // 1967 - **With Their New Face On,** *Repertoire* // 1968 - **Here We Go Round the Mulberry Bush,** *United Artists* // 1968 - **Funky,** *One Way* // 1969 - **Heavies,** *United Artists* // 1970 - **It's Been So Long,** *United Artists* // 1972 - **Mousetrap,** *United Artists* // 1973 - **Somebody Help Me,** *Island* // 1973 - **Gluggo,** *Repertoire* // 1974 - **Living in a Back Street,** *Repertoire* // 1978 - **Keep On Running,** *Island* // 1988 - **Live Together,** *Inakustik* // 1988 - **24 Hours, Live in Germany,** *Inakustik* // 2000 - **Catch You on the Rebop: Live 1973,** *RPM.*

Dawson, Julian

Born: July 4, 1954 - London, England

Rock singer-songwriter, guitar, harmonica player
Julian Dawson is an English singer-singer songwriter who has recorded several albums of solo material as well as playing harmonica with *Del Amitri, The Roches, Plainsong,* Gerry Rafferty, John Wesley Harding and many others. His music combines elements of Folk, Country, Bluegrass and Rock.

Discography:
1981 - **Cheap Pop for Poor People,** *Private* // 1982 - **Let Out the Pig,** *Plaene* // 1984 - **Cold Cold World,** *RT/Midnight* // 1987 - **As Real as Disneyland,** *Polygram* // 1988 - **Luckiest Man in the Western World,** *Polygram* // 1990 - **Live on the Radio,** *Nico Polo* // 1991 - **Fragile as China,** *BMG* // 1992 - **June Honeymoon,** *BMG* // 1993 - **Headlines,** *BMG* // 1993 - **Sunday Into Saturday Night,** *BMG* // 1994 - **How Human Hearts Behave,** *BMG* // 1995 - **Travel On,** *BMG* // 1996 - **Steal the Beat - The Lost Album,** *Hypertension* // 1996 - **Never Mind the Ballads,** *BMG* // 1997 - **Move Over Darling,** *Fledg'Ling Fled* // 1999 - **Spark USA,** *Gadfly* // 1999 - **Under the Sun,** *Blue Rose.*

Dean, Jimmy

Born: August 10, 1928 - Plainsview, TX

Country singer-songwriter, piano, guitar, harmonica
Jimmy Dean started playing the harmonica at age ten. He started recording as a singer-songwriter in 1952 and had a string of hits from the late 1950's through the mid-1960's. He now owns a very successful sausage company.

Discography:
1962 - **Portrait of Jimmy Dean,** *Columbia* // 1966 - **Jimmy Dean's Greatest Hits,** *Columbia* // 1988 - **American Originals,** *Columbia* // 1994 - **24 Greats,** *Deluxe* // 1995 - **Greatest Songs,** *Curb* // 1998 - **Greatest Hits,** *Sony* // 1999

- **20 Great Story Songs,** *Curb.*

DeFillipi, Bruno

Born: May 8, 1930 - Milan, Italy

Jazz guitar, harmonica player

Bruno DeFillipi began playing music at age seven and played Jazz professionally on the guitar for over forty years. In the 1970's he began playing the harmonica. He has since recorded several albums of Jazz harmonica as well as appearing in concert all over the world.

Discography:
1998 - **You My Love,** *Giants of Jazz* // 2000 - **I Love Paris,** *Giants of Jazz* // **Al S. Tecla,** *Bluebell* // **Sweet Jazz From Italy,** *Jump* // **Harmonica,** *Dire Music* // **In New York,** *Carosello* // **You and the Night and the Music,** *Carosello* // **Lilli Marlene,** *Giants of Jazz.*

deLay, Paul

Born: January 31, 1952 - Portland, OR

Blues harmonica player
From the Pacific Northwest, Paul deLay plays Blues on the chromatic harmonica. He began playing professionally in 1970 and by 1979, he had formed his own band.

The group's popularity as a performing and recording entity was put on hold in 1990 when deLay was arrested on drug charges and sentenced to three years in prison. They resumed their career upon his release and have been recording steadily ever since.

Discography:
1982 - **Teasin',** *Criminal* // 1984 - **American Voodoo,** *Criminal* // 1985 - **The Blue One,** *Criminal* // 1985 - **Live at**

the Jolly Roger // 1988 - **Burnin'**, *Criminal* // 1990 - **You're Fired, The Best Of...,** *Red Lightnin'* // 1990 - **The Other One,** *Criminal* // 1992 - **Paulzilla,** *Criminal* // 1996 - **Paul deLay Band,** *Criminal* // 1996 - **Ocean of Tears,** *Evidence* // 1996 - **Take It from the Turnaround,** *Evidence* // 1998 - **Nice & Strong,** *Evidence* // 1999 - **deLay Does Chicago,** *Evidence* // **Paul deLay,** *Criminal*.

Delin, Lou

Real name: Louis Delinsky
Born: June 20, 1910 - New York
Died: September 3, 1999 - New York

Vaudeville harmonica player

Lou Delin learned to play the harmonica in the Hebrew Orphan Asylum Harmonica Band. After taking fourth place in the 1926 Central Park harmonica competition, he was recruited by Borrah Minevitch to play in Minevitch's first band. In 1927 he joined his mentor, Charles Snow, in Charles Bennington's harmonica band. After Snow broke away from Bennington, Delin followed him into his *Broadway Pirates* harmonica group.

After leaving the music profession during the depression to work in carpentry, Delin kept forming harmonica bands and clubs in New York and Florida, many of which are still together to this day. Delin was honored by SPAH in 1998 with it's "Bernie Bray Player-of-the Year" award.

<u>Bibliography:</u>
1996 - **Backstage Harmonica,** *Oceanside Printing.*

Delisante, Pete
Vaudeville harmonica player
Pete Delisante played the chord harmonica in *The Three Harpers* with Stan Harper and Pro Robbins from the Mid-1930's through the late 1940's.

Del Junco, Carlos
Born: May 17, 1958 - Havana, Cuba

Blues harmonica player

Born in Cuba, Carlos Del Junco migrated to Canada with his family when he was a year old. He began playing the harmonica at the age of fourteen. He began playing professionally during the 1980's and studied harmonica under Howard Levy in the mid-1990's.

Since mastering the overblow technique, Carlos has won several major awards for his harmonica playing, including the 1993

Hohner World Harmonica Champion and 1996 Blues Musician of the Year.

Discography:
1993 - **Blues,** *Big Reed* // 1995 - **Just Your Fool,** *Big Reed* // 1995 - **Big Road Blues** // 1996 - **Old Way Blues,** *OWB* // 1998 - **Big Boy,** *Big Reed.*

Dello Joio, Norman

Born: January 24,1913 - New York, NY

Classical composer
Norman Dello Joio wrote "Concerto for Chamber Orchestra and Harmonica" in 1944 for John Sebastian Sr.

Dentz, Wally

Country bass guitar, harmonica player
Wally Dentz is a bass guitar and harmonica player who worked with *The Henry Paul Band* during the early 1980's and with *The Bellamy Brothers* from the late 1980's to the present.

Dexter, Al

Born: May 4, 1905 - Troup, TX
Died: January 28, 1984 - Lewisville, TX

Country singer, guitar, mandolin, harmonica player
Al Dexter learned harmonica as a youth, while growing up in Texas. He began playing professionally in the mid-1920's and made his first records in 1936. His biggest hit, "Pistol Packin' Mama' was covered by several artists, including Frank Sinatra and Bing Crosby. He left music in the late 1940's to run a night-club in Dallas, though he performed there until he retired.

Discography:
1954 - **Songs of the Southwest,** *CBS* // 1961 - **Pistol Packin' Mama,** *Harmony* // 1962 - **Al Dexter Sings and Plays,** *Capitol* // 1968 - **Al Dexter, The Original Pistol Packin' Mama,** *Pickwick* // 1990 - *Columbia* **Country Classics, Vol. 1: The Golden Era,** *Columbia* // 1995 - **Hillbilly Fever Vol. 2: Honky Tonk,** *Rhino* // 1999 - **Pistol Packin' Mama,** *ASV* // 2000 - **Sings and Plays his Greatest Hits,** *Longhorn.*

Diamond, Abe

Died: July 1996

Vaudeville harmonica player
The brother of Leo Diamond, Abe Diamond played in *The Harmonica Solidaires* with his brother, Richard Hayman and George Fields.

Diamond, Leo

Born: June 29, 1915 - New York City, NY
Died: September 15, 1966 - Los Angeles, CA

Vaudeville harmonica player

Leo Diamond played with and wrote arrangements for *The Harmonica Rascals* from the early 1930's until 1946. After leaving that group, he put together *The Harmonica Solidaires* with his brother Abe and Richard Hayman. When Hayman left the group, he was replaced by George Fields.

He worked as a studio harmonica player after he moved to California, including doing duel harmonica work with Tommy Morgan on the soundtrack of the movie "Rio Bravo." In 1956 he wrote and recorded "Skin Diver Suite" a twenty minute har-monica and orchestra epic.

He continued recording steadily from the 1950's until his death in 1966.

Discography:
1956 - **Skin Diver Suite,** *RCA* // 1961 - **Exciting Sounds from the South Seas,** *Reprise* // 1961 - **Themes From Great Foreign Films,** *Reprise* // **Ebb Tide,** *Harmony* // **Exciting Sounds From Romantic Places,** *ABC Paramount* // **The Harmonica Magic of Leo Diamond,** *RCA* // **Harmonica Sounds in Country Western Music,** *Reprise* // **Hi-Fi Harmonica,** *Roulette* // **Offshore,** *Reprise* // **Snuggled on Your Shoulder,** *RCA* // **Subliminal Sounds,** *ABC Paramount.*

Movies:
1942 - **Seven Days Leave** // 1943 - **As Thousands Cheer** // 1943 - **Girl Crazy** // 1943 - Sweet Rosie **O'Grady** // 1943 - **Coney Island** // 1953 - **Calamity Jane** // 1953 - **The Eddie Cantor Story** // 1953 - **Miss Sadie Thompson** // 1954 - **Living It Up** // 1954 - **Rear Window** // 1959 - **Rio Bravo** (with Tommy Morgan).

Diatonic Harmonica

The basic standard of harmonicas, the diatonic harmonica contains only the notes of the major, or diatonic scale. In the key of C, this would be the notes C, D, E, F, G, A and B or just the white keys on a piano. There have also been a limited number of diatonic harmonicas available in minor and other specialized tunings.

Diatonic players usually change keys by changing harmonicas, playing in different harmonica "positions," or by bending or overblowing and over drawing notes to accommodate the scale that they are playing in.

The diatonic is the harmonica most used by Folk, Country, Rock and Blues players; though it can be used for Classical, Jazz and most other styles.

Magic Dick

Real name: Dick Salwitz
Born: May 13, 1948 - New London, CT

Rock harmonica player

Magic Dick started playing the harmonica at age three. While attending college at Worchester Polytechnic Institute, he met guitarist Jay Geils and they immediately started playing together. After deciding to quit school to be in a band, they moved to Boston where they met up with vocalist Peter Wolf. The resulting group, *The J. Geils Band*, started recording in 1971. In 1983, after a long series of hits, the band broke up when Peter Wolf decided to pursue a solo career.

Magic Dick has since been working on new harmonica development with Pierre Beauregard and has worked with Jay Geils and the band, *Bluestime*. *The J. Geils Band* reunited briefly in 1999 for a concert tour.

Discography: (also see - The J. Geils Band)
1996 - **Little Car Blues,** *Rounder //* **Bluestime,** (with Jay Geils and Bluestime), *Rounder.*

Diddley, Bo

Real name: Ellas Otha Bates McDaniels
Born: December 30, 1928 - McComb, MS

Blues singer, guitar, violin, harmonica player
Known primarily for his trademark "Bo Diddley Beat," Bo Diddley can also play the harmonica, though he usually brings in great harmonica players to work with him, including Lester Davenport and Billy Boy Arnold.

Discography:
1960 - **Have Guitar, Will Travel,** *Chess //* 1962 - **Bo Diddley is a Twister,** *Chess //* 1962 - **Hey! Bo Diddley,** *Instant //* 1962 - **Bo Diddley & Company,** *Checker //* 1963 - **Bo Diddley is a Gunslinger,** *Chess //* 1963 - **Bo Diddley's Beach Party,** *Checker //* 1963 - **Surfin' with Bo,** *Checker //* 1963 - **Chuck & Bo,** *Pye //* 1964 - **Diddling,** *Pye //* 1964 - **Is a Lumberjack,** *Pye //* 1965 - **Hey, Good Lookin',** *Checker //* 1965 - **500% More Man,** *Checker //* 1966 - **The Originator,** *Checker //* 1967 - **Boss Man,** *Checker //* 1967 - **Road Runner,** *Checker //* **Super Blues,** (with Little Walter & Muddy Waters), *Chess //* 1970 - **The Black Gladiator,** *Checker //* 1971 - **Another Dimension,** *Chess //* 1972 - **Where It All Began,** *Chess //* 1972 - **Got My Own Bag of Tricks,** *Chess //* 1973 - **London Sessions,** *Chess //* 1974 - **Big Bad Bo,** *Chess //* 1983 - **It's Great to Be Rich,** *Red Lightnin' //* 1986 - **Bo Diddley / Go Bo Diddley,** *Chess //* 1987 - **In the Spotlight,** *Chess //* 1989 - **Live at the Ritz,** *JVC //* 1989 - **Pay Bo Diddley //** 1990 - **The Chess Box,** *Chess //* 1991 - **Rare and Well Done,** *Chess //* 1992 - **Two Great Guitars,** *Chess //* 1992 - **Who Do You Love,** *Sound Solution //* 1992 - **Bo's Guitar,** *Sound Solution //* 1993 - **Bo's Blues,** *Ace //* 1994 - **Bo Diddley is a Lover...Plus,** *See for Miles //* 1994 - **Let Me Pass...Plus,** *See for Miles //* 1994 - **Live,** *Triple X //* 1994 - **Promises,** *Triple X //* 1995 - **The Mighty Bo Diddley,** *Triple X //* 1995 - **Bo Knows Bo,** *MCA Special //* 1996 - **Mona,** *Drive //* 1996 - **A Man Amongst Men,** *Code Blue //* 1997 - **His Best,** *MCA Chess //* 1998 - **Road Runner Live,** *Mastertone //* **Diddley Daddy,** *Chess //* **His Greatest Hits, Vol. 1,** *Chess //* **The Super Blues Band,** (with Howlin' Wolf & Muddy Waters), *Chess.*

Movies:
1966 - **The Legend of Bo Diddley //** 1966 - **The Big TNT Show //** 1969 - **Sweet Toronto //** 1971 - **Fritz the Cat //** 1973 - **Let the Good Times Roll.**

Donovan

Real name: Donovan Leitch
Born: May 10, 1946 - Glasgow Scotland

British Folk singer-songwriter, guitar, harmonica

Donovan began performing in 1964 as a British equivalent to Bob Dylan, playing guitar and the harmonica on a neckbrace. After a series of acoustic Folk hits, Donovan went electric and had a string of chart successes. Though his career faded at the end of the 1960's, he has occasionally reappeared on the music scene.

Discography:
1965 - **What's Bin Did and What's Bin Hid,** *Pye* // 1965 - **Catch the Wind,** *Hickory* // 1965 - **Fairytale,** *Hickory* // 1966 - **The Real Donovan,** *Hickory* // 1966 - **Sunshine Superman,** *Epic* // 1967 - **Mellow Yellow,** *Epic* // 1967 - **For Little Ones,** *Epic* // 1967 - **Wear Your Love Like Heaven,** *Epic* // 1967 - **A Gift From a Flower To a Garden,** *Epic* // 1968 - **Donovan in Concert,** *Epic* // 1968 - **Like it Is, Was and Evermore Shall Be,** *Hickory* // 1968 - **The Hurdy Gurdy Man,** *Epic* // 1969 - **Donovan's Greatest Hits,** *Epic* // 1969 - **Barabajagal,** *Epic* // 1970 - **Open Road,** *Epic* // 1971 - **HMS Donovan,** *Dawn* // 1973 - **Live in Tokyo '73,** *Dirty 13* // **Cosmic Wheels,** *Epic* // 1973 - **Essence To Essence,** *Epic* // 1973 - **4 Shades,** *Pye* // 1974 - **7-Tease,** *Epic* // 1976 - **Slow Down World,** *Epic* // 1977 - **Donovan,** *Arista* // 1979 - **Troubadour,** *Mode* // 1981 - **Spotlight,** *PRT* // 1981 - **Love is Only Feeling,** *RCA* // 1981 - **Neurotic,** *RCA* // 1983 - **Lady of the Stars,** *Allegiance* // 1991 - **The Classics Live,** *Great Northern Arts* // 1992 - **Troubadour: The Definitive Collection,** 1964-76, *Epic/Legacy* // 1992 - **Live in Concert,** *QED* // 1995 - **Originals,** *EMI* // 1996 - **Sutras,** *American.*

Doucette, Dave

Died: 1983

Vaudeville harmonica player

Dave Doucette began his career playing lead harmonica and writing arrangements for Johnny O'Brien's *Harmonica Kings,* and eventually for *The Harmonica Hi-Hats.* He joined *The Harmonica Rascals* when the Diamond Brothers left the group. He played lead chromatic harmonica and wrote arrangements for *The Harmonica Rascals.*

Doucette was a part of the secret harmonica band that Johnny Puleo put together in 1942. Though that effort was short-lived, he rejoined Puleo in the mid-1950's as part of his *Harmonica Gang* after Borrah Minevitch died.

In 1968 he formed a harmonica band in Las Vegas called *The Stereomonics* and in 1975, a group called *The Big Harp* was brought together using Doucette's arrangements.

Doucette, Sherman "Tank"

Born: December 6, 1953 - North Battleford, Saskatchewan, Canada

Blues singer, harmonica player, historian

Sherman Doucette has been playing the harmonica since he was fifteen and has been the leader of the Vancouver-based Blues band, *Incognito* for over fifteen years. He has been collecting antique and rare harmonica since the 1960's and operates a harmonica web site on the internet.

Discography:
1996 - **Blues Alive,** *Incognito* // 1997 - **Bittersweet,** *Incognito.*

Douglass, Stephen "Tebes"

Died: January 12, 1984

Country singer keyboards, harmonica player
Stephen "Tebes" Douglass played keyboards and harmonica for the Country / Rock band *McGuffey Lane* from its inception until he was killed in a car accident in 1984.

Discography: (see - McGuffey Lane)

Mr. Downchild

Real name: Stephen Brazier
Born: May 15, 1950 - London, England

Blues singer, guitar, harmonica player

Mr. Downchild began playing the harmonica as a teenager after seeing Sonny Boy Williamson II (Rice Miller) perform in England. He also took his stage name from one of Williamson's songs. Since immigrating to America in 1985, he's been playing with his back-up band, *The Houserockers* and recorded several albums of Blues music.

Discography:
1994 - **They Call Me Mr. Downchild,** *Mascita* // 1997 - **Mr. Downchild Live at the Western Maryland Blues Festival,** *Mascita Music* // 1998 - **Steppin' on Time,** *Mascita Music* // 2000 - **Behind the Sun,** *Mascita Music.*

Dozzler, Christian

Born: September 22, 1958 - Vienna, Austria

Blues piano, guitar, harmonica player
Christian Dozzler began playing piano at the age of five and picked up the guitar and harmonica in his teens after getting hooked on Blues music. He's performed and recorded with *The Mojo Blues Band*, Magic Slim, Champion Jack Dupree and many others. In the spring of 2000 he joined up with Zydeco musician Larry Garner for a tour of the U.S.

Discography:
1984 - **Hot Bricks,** (with The Mojo Blues Band), *Bellaphon* // 1987 - **Midnight in Swampland,** (with The Mojo Blues Band), *EMI* // 1988 - **Champ's Housewarming,** (with Champion Jack Dupree and The Mojo Blues Band), *Vagabond* // 1989 - **The Wild Taste of Chicago,** *EMI* // 1992 - **Heat It Up,** (with Axel Zwingenberger and The Mojo Blues Band), *Vagabond* // 1994 - **Take It Easy,** *Wolf* // 1996 - **Perfect Day,** *Wolf* // 1998 - **Smile Awhile,** *Wolf* // 1999 - **Louisiana,** *Blueswave* // 2000 - **Christian Dozzler and the Blues Wave,** *Blueswave.*

Dr. Feelgood

Formed: 1971 - Canvey Island, England
Disbanded: 1994

British R&B band
Dr. Feelgood was one of the top groups in the British Pub Band movement of the mid-1970's. Vocalist and harmonica player Lee Brilleaux was one of the founding members and kept the group going until his death from cancer in 1994.

See - Lee Brilleaux

Discography:
1975 - **Down By the Jetty,** *United Artists* // 1975 - **Malpractice,** *Columbia* // 1976 - **Stupidity,** *United Artists* // 1977 - **Sneakin' Suspicion,** *Columbia* // 1977 - **Be Seeing You,** *United Artists* // 1978 - **Private Practice,** *United Artists* // 1979 - **As It Happens,** *United Artists* // 1979 - **Let It Roll,** *United Artists* // 1980 - **A Case of the Shakes,** *United Artists* // 1981 - **Casebook,** *Liberty* // 1981 - **On the Job,** *Liberty* // 1982 - **Fast Women & Slow Horses,** *Chiswick* // 1984 - **Doctor's Orders,** *Demon* // 1986 - **Mad Man Blues,** *ID* // 1986 - **Brilleaux,** *Grand* // 1990 - **Live in London,** *Grand* // 1995 - **Down at the Doctors,** *Grand* // 1998 - **Primo,** *Import* // 1998 - **On the Road Again,** *Import* // 1999 - **Feelgood Factor,** *Grand* // 1999 - **25 Years of Dr. Feelgood,** *Grand* // 1999 - **Live at the BBC,** *Grand* // 2000 - Chess Masters, *Grand.*

Dudgeon, Frank

Born: September 7, 1901 - Jackson County, WV
Died: March 16, 1987

Country singer-songwriter, guitar, harmonica player
Frank Dudgeon started his musical career in radio during the 1920's and made a limited number of recordings. He left music entirely in 1949.

Dufresne, Mark

Born: March 12, 1953 - Kansas City, MO

Blues singer, harmonica player

Mark Dufresne began playing the harmonica in the Kansas City area during the mid-1970's. Working out of Seattle since the early 1980's, Mark has worked with Lazy Lester, Chick Willis and other Blues greats as well as recording several albums of his own music.

Discography:
1996 - **Out of That Bed,** *Thumbs Up* // 1999 - **There's A Song in There,** *Thumbs Up* // 1999 - **Have Another Round,** *Thumbs Up.*

Duncan, "Little" Arthur

Born: 1934 - Indianola, MS

Blues singer, harmonica player
Blues harmonica player "Little" Arthur Duncan grew up on a plantation in Mississippi and moved to Chicago in the early 1950's. He became a part of the city's Blues scene, often working with guitarist Earl Hooker. Though not as famous as many of his peers, Duncan has maintained a steady club career for several decades.

Discography:
1989 - **Bad Reputation,** *Blues King* // 1999 - **Singin' with the Sun,** *Delmark* // 2000 - **Live in Chicago!,** *Random Chance.*

Duncan, Phil

Born: September 27, 1945 - Kansas City, KS

Harmonica educator

Phil Duncan was taught how to play the harmonica at age seven by his grandfather. He has written a variety of books and courses on how to play the harmonica that are available through Mel Bay Publications.

Bibliography:

Basic Blues Harp, *Mel Bay Publications //* **Basic Chromatic Harmonica,** *Mel Bay Publications //* **Blues Harmonica Starter Kit,** *Mel Bay Publications //* **Harmonica Classics,** *Mel Bay Publications //* **Holiday Collection for the Harmonica,** *Mel Bay Publications //* **Traditional Fiddle Tunes for the Harmonica,** *Mel Bay Publications //* **Easiest Blues Harp Book,** *Mel Bay Publications //* **Deluxe Harmonica Method,** *Mel Bay Publications //* **Blues Harp,** *Mel Bay Publications //* **Power Blues Harp,** (with Charlie Musselwhite), *Mel Bay Publications //* **Nashville Country Harmonica,** *Mel Bay Publications //* **Complete Chromatic Harmonica Method,** *Mel Bay Publications //* **Bluegrass & Country Music for Harmonica,** *Mel Bay Publications //* **Chromatic Harmonica Solos,** *Mel Bay Publications //* **Complete Harmonica Book,** *Mel Bay Publications //* **Gospel Harp,** *Mel Bay Publications //* **Harmonicare Chart,** *Mel Bay Publications //* **Hymns for Harmonica,** *Mel Bay Publications //* **Jazz Harp for Diatonic and Chromatic Harmonica,** *Mel Bay Publications //* **Harmonica Chord Chart,** *Mel Bay Publications //* **Great Hits for Harmonica,** *Mel Bay Publications //* **You Can Teach Yourself Harmonica,** *Mel Bay Publications //* **Christmas Songs for Harmonica,** *Mel Bay Publications //* **Irish Melodies for Harmonica,** *Mel Bay Publications //* **Chromatic Harmonica Pocketbook,** *Mel Bay Publications //* **Tremolo and Octave Tuned Harmonicas,** *Mel Bay Publications //* **Stephen Foster Tunes for Harmonica,** *Mel Bay Publications //* **Qwikguide: Basic Harmonica Book,** *Mel Bay Publications //* **Qwikguide: Basic Blues Harp,** *Mel Bay Publications //* **Qwikguide: Favorite Harmonica Songs,** *Mel Bay Publications.*

Videos:

You Can Teach Yourself Blues Harp, *Mel Bay Publications //* **Anyone Can Play Harmonica,** *Mel Bay Publications //* **Learn To Play Rock and Blues Harmonica,** *Mel Bay Publications //* **Blues Harp for Diatonic and Chromatic Harmonica,** *Mel Bay Publications //* **Complete Chromatic Harmonica Method,** *Mel Bay Publications //* **Deluxe Harmonica Method,** *Mel Bay Publications.*

Dunn, Roy Sidney

Born: April 13, 1922 - Eatonton, GA
Died: March 2, 1988 - Atlanta, GA

Blues guitar, harmonica player
Roy Sidney Dunn began playing music at age nine and worked in his family's Gospel group during the 1930's. During the 1940's he worked with Blind Willie McTell, Curley Weaver, Buddy Moss and others in the Atlanta area. After serving a sentence for manslaughter from 1956 to 1960, Dunn returned to music and recorded an album for the Trix label in 1972.

Discography:
1974 - **Know'd the All,** *Trix.*

Dyer, Johnny

Born: December 7, 1938 - Mississippi

Blues harmonica player

Johnny Dyer grew up on the Stovall plantation in Mississippi and began playing the harmonica at age seven. He began playing professionally at age sixteen. In 1958 he moved to California, where he hooked up with George "Harmonica" Smith and played with him and many other Blues greats.

He left music to work during the 1960's, but returned in the early 1980's. He played with Shakey Jake Harris, Harmonica Fats, Rod Piazza and many others. He cut his first record in 1983 and has continued playing and recording ever since.

Discography:
1994 - **Listen Up,** *Blacktop //* 1995 - Shake It!, *Blacktop //* 1995 - **Jukin',** *Blind Pig.*

Dykes, Omar Kent

Born: 1950 - McComb, MS

Blues singer, guitar, harmonica player
Omar Kent Dykes began playing music at age twelve. After relocating to Austin, Texas in 1976, he formed his own band, *Omar and the Howlers,* which became a steady presence on the national Blues scene. They've been touring and recording steadily ever since.

Discography: (see - Omar and the Howlers)

Dylan, Bob

Real name: Robert Alan Zimmerman
Born: May 24, 1941 - Duluth, MN

Folk singer-songwriter, guitar, harmonica player

Raised in Hibbing, Minnesota, Bob Dylan started playing music around the age of nine. He was a friend of and learned harmonica from Tony "Little Sun" Glover, and then learned how to play it on a neckbrace from Jesse "Lonecat" Fuller. By late 1960 he was concentrating on a straight harp style of playing with an emphasis on blow note clusters.

He moved to New York City in early 1961 and soon became the house harmonica player for Café Wha?. He did his first recording playing harmonica behind folksinger Carolyn Hester. He went on to do quite a lot of session work as a harmonica player with Harry Belafonte, Ramblin' Jack Elliott, "Big" Joe Williams and others.

In September of 1961 he met Columbia Records A&R man John Hammond, who signed Dylan to a recording contract. He proved to be an instant success as a singer-songwriter. He influenced nearly everyone who heard him, from *The Beatles* to Neil Young to today's Generation X songwriters.

Dylan has frequently risked the critics' wrath, experimenting in a large number of musical styles, often with mixed success. He continues to work both in electric and acoustic music and usually plays the harmonica with a neckbrace.

Discography:
1962 - **Bob Dylan,** *Columbia* // 1963 - **The Freewheelin' Bob Dylan,** *Columbia* // 1964 - **The Times They Are a Changin',** *Columbia* // 1964 - **Another Side of Bob Dylan,** *Columbia* // 1965 - **Bringing It All Back Home,** *Columbia* // 1961 - **Highway 61 Revisited,** *Columbia* // 1966 - **Blonde On Blonde,** *Columbia* // 1967 - **Bob Dylan's Greatest Hits,** *Columbia* // 1967 - **John Wesley Harding,** *Columbia* // 1969 - **Nashville Skyline,** *Columbia* // 1970 - **Self Portrait,** *Columbia* // 1970 - **New Morning,** *Columbia* // 1971 - **Bob Dylan's Greatest Hits, Vol. 2,** *Columbia* // 1973 - **Pat Garrett and Billy the Kid,** *Columbia* // 1973 - **Dylan,** *Columbia* // 1974 - **Planet Waves,** *Asylum* // 1974 - **Before the Flood,** *Asylum* // 1975 - **Blood on the Tracks,** *Columbia* // 1975 - **The Basement Tapes,** *Columbia* // 1976 - **Desire,** *Columbia* // 1976 - **Hard Rain,** *Columbia* // 1978 - **Bob Dylan at Budokan,** *Columbia* // 1978 - **Street Legal,** *Columbia* // 1979 - **Slow Train Coming,** *Columbia* // 1980 - **Saved,** *Columbia* // 1981 - **Shot of Love,** *Columbia* // 1983 - **Infidels,** *Columbia* // 1984 - **Real Live,** *Columbia* // 1985 - **Empire Burlesque,** *Columbia* // 1985 - **Biograph,** *Columbia* // 1986 - **Knocked Out Loaded,** *Columbia* // 1988 - **Down in the Groove,** *Columbia* // 1988 - **Oh Mercy,** *Columbia* // 1989 - **Dylan and the Dead,** *Columbia* // 1990 - **Under the Red Sky,** *Columbia* // 1991 - **The Bootleg Series, Vol. 1-3,** (1961-1991), *Columbia* // 1992 - **Good as I've Been To You,** *Columbia* // 1993 - **30th Anniversary Concert,** *Columbia* // 1993 - **World Gone Wrong,** *Columbia* // 1994 - **Greatest Hits, Vol. 3,** *Columbia* // 1995 - **MTV Unplugged,** *Columbia* // 1997 - **Time Out of Mind,** *Columbia* // 1998 - **Bootleg Series, Vol. 4: Live 1966 - Royal Albert Hall Concert,** *Columbia.*

Movies:
1965 - **Don't Look Back** // 1973 - **Pat Garrett and Billy the Kid** // 1977 - **Renaldo and Clara.**

– E –

Earle, Steve

Born: January 17, 1955 - Fort Monroe, VA

Country singer-songwriter, guitar, harmonica
Though he's best known as a guitar player, Country music singer-songwriter Steve Earle also plays the harmonica, usually on a neckbrace.

Discography:
1986 - **Guitar Town,** *MCA* // 1987 - **Exit 0,** *MCA* // 1988 - **Copperhead Road,** *MCA* // 1990 - **Shut Up and Die Like an Aviator,** *MCA* // 1991 - **The Hard Way,** *MCA* // 1993 - **Essential Steve Earle,** *MCA* // 1995 - **Train a Comin',** *Winter Harvest* // 1996 - **Ain't Never Satisfied,** *Hip-O* // 1996 - **I Feel Alright,** *WEA* // 1996 - **Fearless Heart,** *MCA* //

1996 - **Angry Young Man,** *Telstar* // 1997 - **El Corazon,** *WEA* // 1997 - **Steve Earle & the Supersuckers,** *Sub Pop* // 1999 - **Mountain,** *E Squared* // 2000 - **Transcendental Blues,** *E Squared.*

Earp, Wyatt

Born: March 19, 1848 -Monmouth, IL
Died: January 13, 1929 - Los Angeles, CA

Western lawman
As a gunfighter and sheriff, Wyatt Earp is probably one of the best known of the western lawmen. Legend has that he used to pass the time playing the harmonica.

Edwards, "Good Rockin'" Charles

Born: March 4, 1933 - Pratt City, AL
Died: May 18,1989 - Chicago, IL

Blues singer, harmonica player
"Good Rockin'" Charles Edwards moved to Chicago in 1949 and began working as a Blues singer shortly after. He started playing the harmonica in 1950 to help fill in the breaks in songs.

He worked with Willie "Long Time" Smith, Lee Jackson, James Richardson, Bo Diddley, Johnny Young, "Big Boy" Spires, "Smokey" Smothers and others at the Maxwell Street Market and at local clubs in the Chicago area from the late 1940's well into the 1980's. He made his first recordings in 1975 for the Mr. Blues label.

Discography:
1976 - **Good Rockin' Charles,** *Double Trouble.*

Edwards, David "Honeyboy"

Also known as: Honey Eddie, Mr. Honey
Born: June 28, 1915 - Shaw, MS

Blues singer, guitar, harmonica player
Honeyboy Edwards began playing music at age fourteen. He teamed up with Big Joe Williams in 1932 and toured briefly with Charlie Patton in 1934. He played with *The Memphis Jug Band* from 1935 to 1936 and worked with Walter Horton in 1936 and Robert Johnson in 1938.

He began recording for the Library of Congress in 1942, then traveled extensively around the U.S., stopping long enough to play with Little Walter in Chicago at the Maxwell Street Market. Dropping in and out of music, Honeyboy Edwards is still active in the Blues scene.

Discography:
1979 - **I've Been Around,** *Trix* // 1989 - **White Windows,** *Blue Suit* // 1991 - **Mississippi Blues: Library of Congress Recordings** // 1992 - **Delta Bluesman,** *Earwig* // 1997 - **Crawling Kingsnake,** *Testament* // 1997 - **The World Don't Owe Me Nothin',** *Earwig* // 1999 - **I Catch Trouble,** *Genes* // 1999 - **Don't Mistreat a Fool,** *Genes* // 2000 - **Shake 'Em On Down,** *Analogue* // **Back To the Roots,** *Wolf* // **Highway 61,** *Milestone* // **David "Honeyboy" Edwards, 1942-1991,** *Indigo.*

Bibliography:
1997 - **The World Don't Owe Me Nothin',** *Chicago Review Press.*

Edwards, Frank

Born: March 20, 1909 - Washington, GA
Died: 1990

Blues guitar, jug, harmonica player
Frank Edwards grew up in St. Petersburg, Florida and learned to play music as a child. He began playing music professionally at age fourteen and worked with Tampa Red in 1926.

He spent most of the 1920's through the 50's playing in juke joints, carnivals and minstrel shows, made an appearance on the "Major Bowes Amateur Hour" in 1940 and recorded for the Okeh label in 1941. Edwards stopped playing during the 1960's, but was re-discovered and resumed his career in the 1970's.

Discography:
1964 - **Living the Blues** // 1969 - **Sugar Mama Blues** // 1973 - **Done Some Travelin',** *Trix* // 1987 - **Chicago Blues** // 1990 - **Georgia Blues.**

Edwards, Jonathan

Born: July 28, 1946 - Aitkin, MN

Country singer-songwriter, guitar, piano, harmonica

Known mostly as a singer-songwriter, Jonathan Edwards took up playing the harmonica after hearing Bob Dylan and Donovan. In addition to recording several solo albums, Edwards has recorded with Emmylou Harris, Peter Kater, *The Seldom Scene* and *Orphan.*

Discography:
1971 - **Jonathan Edwards,** *Capricorn* // 1972 - **Honky Tonk Stardust Cowboy,** *Atco* // 1973 - **Have a Good Time for Me,** *Atco* // 1974 - **Lucky Day,** *Atco* // 1976 - **Rockin' Chair,** *Reprise* // 1977 - **Sailboat,** *Warner Brothers* // 1981 - **Jonathan Edwards Live,** *Chronic* // 1985 - **Blue Ridge,** *Sugarhill* // 1989 - **The Natural Thing,** *MCA* // 1994 - **One Day Closer,** *Rising* // 1997 - **Man in the Moon,** *Rising* // **Little Hands: Songs for and About Children,** *American Melody.*

Elliott, Ramblin' Jack

Real name: Elliott Charles Adnopoz
Born: August 1, 1931 - Brooklyn, NY

Folk singer-songwriter, guitar, harmonica player
Jack Elliott ran away from home at the age of fourteen and spent a great deal of time traveling around the U.S. He began performing publicly in the late 1940's and teamed up with Woody Guthrie in the early 1950's. He started to make records in 1955.

Elliott also worked with Cisco Houston, Jesse Fuller and Derroll Adams during the 1950's. He spent much of the 1960's and 70's touring in the U.S. and abroad. During the late 1970's he was a part of Bob Dylan's *Rolling Thunder Revue.*

Discography:
1957 - **The Ramblin' Boy,** *Topic UK* // 1957 - **Roll On Buddy** // 1960 - **Jack Elliott Sings the Songs of Woody Guthrie,** *Prestige* // 1961 - **Woody Guthrie's Songs To Grow On Sung By Ramblin' Jack Elliott,** *Folkways* // 1961 - **Ramblin' Jack Elliott,** *Prestige* // 1962 - **At the Second Fret,** *Prestige* // 1962 - **Jack Elliott Country Style,** *Prestige* // 1962 - **At the Main Point,** *Prestige* // 1964 - **Hootenanny with Jack Elliott,** *Prestige* // 1964 - **Jack Elliott,** *Vanguard* // 1965 - **Ramblin' Cowboy,** *Moniter* // 1968 - **Young Brigham,** *Reprise* // 1968 - **Talking Woody Guthrie,** *Delmark* // 1970 - **Bull Durham Sacks and Railroad Tracks,** *Reprise* // 1970 - **The Essential Ramblin' Jack Elliott,** *Vanguard* // 1976 - **Jack Elliott Sings Guthrie and Rogers,** *Moniter* // 1984 - **Kerouac's Last Dream,** *Appleseed* // 1989 - **Talking Dust Bowl - The Best Of...,** *Big Beat* // 1990 - **Hard Travelin',** *Fantasy* // 1995 - **Me & Bobby McGee,** *Rounder* // 1995 - **South Coast,** *Red House* // 1996 - **Ramblin' Jack,** *Topic* // 1997 - **America, a World of Music** // 1998 - **Friends of Mine,** *Hightone* // 1999 - **The Long Ride,** *Hightone* // 1999 - **Early Sessions,** *Tradition* // 2000 - **Ballad of Ramblin' Jack,** *Vanguard.*

Ely, "Brother" Claude

Born: July 21, 1922 - Lee County, VA
Died: May 7, 1978 - Newport, KY

Country/Gospel singer-songwriter, guitar, harmonica
Claude Ely developed tuberculosis at age twelve and learned how to play music while recovering. After attributing his recovery to a miracle, he spent his entire career working in the Country / Gospel field.

Discography:
1962 - **The Gospel Ranger,** *King* // 1968 - **At Home and At Church,** *King* // 1969 - **Child of the King,** *Gold Star* // 1979 - **Where Could I Go But Back To the Lord,** *Jordan* // 1993 - **Satan Get Back,** *King Masters.*

Epping, Rick

Born: August 22, 1949 - Santa Monica, CA

Country / Blues / Irish harmonica player
Rick Epping studied music in Ireland during the 1970's and 80's and was the 1975 All-Ireland harmonica champion. He also works as a product specialist for the M. Hohner Company in Virginia and has created several new harmonica and accordion designs.

Estrin, Rick

Born: October 5, 1949 - San Francisco, CA

Blues singer, harmonica player

Rick Estrin began playing the harmonica after his mother gave him one while he was in the hospital as a teenager, and he was playing professionally by the time he was eighteen.

Estrin is now the lead vocalist and harmonica player for *Little*

Charlie and The Nightcats as well as playing the harmonica on several albums by John Hammond. He favors the chromatic harmonica for playing Blues music.

Discography: (see - Little Charlie and The Nightcats)

Ezell, Buster "Buzz"

Blues singer, guitar, harmonica player

"Buzz Ezell" played Folk-styled acoustic Blues during the 1940's. He usually played the harmonica on a neckbrace. He made two records in 1941 and 1943.

Discography:
Field Recordings, Vol. 2, *Document.*

– F –

The Fabulous Thunderbirds

Formed: 1974 - Austin, TX

Blues / Rock band

Co-founded in 1974 by guitarist Jimmie Vaughan and Harmonica player Kim Wilson, *The Fabulous Thunderbirds* have been one of the leading Blues/Rock bands of the last twenty years. The band has had hits with songs like "Tough Enuff," "Wrap It Up" and others, many of which feature Wilson's dynamic harmonica playing.

See - Kim Wilson

Discography:
1979 - **The Fabulous Thunderbirds,** *Chrysalis //* 1980 - **What's the Word?,** *Chrysalis //* 1981 - **Butt Rockin',** *Chrysalis //* 1982 - **T-Bird Rhythm,** *Chrysalis //* 1986 - **Tuff Enuff,** *CBS //* 1987 - **Hot Number,** *Epic //* 1987 - **Portfolio,** *Chrysalis //* 1989 - **Powerful Stuff,** *Epic //* 1991 - **Walk That Walk, Talk That Talk,** *Epic //* 1991 - **The Essential,** *Chrysalis //* 1992 - **Hot Stuff: The Greatest Hits,** *Epic //* 1993 - **Wrap It Up,** *Sony //* 1995 - **Roll of the Dice,** *Private //* 1996 - **Different Tacos,** *Country Town //* 1997 - **High Water,** *Highstreet //* 1997 - **Best Of...,** *EMI //* 1997 - **Good Understanding,** *Bullseye //* 2000 - **Girls Go Wild,** *Benchmark //* **Will the Circle Be Unbroken?,** (with Snuff Johnson), *Black Magic.*

Fadden, Jimmie

Born: March 9, 1948 - Long Beach, CA

Country singer, drums, harmonica player

Jimmie Fadden has been playing drums and harmonica with *The Nitty Gritty Dirt Band* since 1967. He has also played the harmonica on records by Hoyt Axton, Jackson Browne, John Denver, Dan Fogelberg, Linda Ronstadt and others.

Discography: (see - The Nitty Gritty Dirt Band)

The Fall

Formed: 1977 - Manchester, England

British New-Wave band
The Fall has been one of England's leading New-Wave bands since it's inception in 1977. Leader Mark E. Smith plays harmonica in addition to keyboards and singing.

See - Mark E. Smith

Discography:
1979 - **Live at the Witch Trials,** *Step Forward //* 1979 - **Dragnet,** *Step Forward //* 1980 - **Grotesque,** *Rough Trade //* 1980 - **Totale's Turn,** (It's Now or Never), *Rough Trade //* 1981 - **Slates,** *Rough Trade //* 1981 - **The Early Years,** *Step Forward //* 1981 - **A Part of America Therein,** *Cottage //* 1982 - **Room To Live,** *Kamera //* 1982 - **Hex Enduction Hour,** *Kamera //* 1982 - **Live at Acklam Hall,** *Chaos //* 1983 - **Perverted By Language,** *Rough Trade //* 1983 - **Fall in a Hole,** *Flying Nun //* 1984 - **The Wonderful and Frightening World of the Fall,** *Beggar's Banquet //* 1984 - **Call for Escape Route,** *Beggar's Banquet //* 1985 - **This Nation's Saving Grace,** *Beggar's Banquet //* 1985 - **Hip Priests and Kamerads,** *Situation Two //* 1986 - **The Fall,** *Beggar's Banquet //* 1986 - **Bend Sinister,** *Beggar's Banquet //* 1987 - **The Fall In: Palace of Swords Revisited,** *Rough Trade //* 1988 - **The Frenz Experiment,** *Beggar's Banquet //* 1988 - **I Am Curious Orange,** *Beggar's Banquet //* 1989 - **Seminal Live,** *Beggar's Banquet //* 1990 - **Extricate,** *Cog Sinister //* 1990 - **458489 A-Sides / B-Sides,** *Beggar's Banquet //* 1991 - **Shift Work,** *Cog Sinister //* 1992 - **Code: Selfish,** *Cog Sinister //* 1993 - **The Infotainment Scan,** *Matador //* 1993 - **Kimble,** *Dutch East Indies //* 1993 - **BBC Radio 1 in Concert,** *Griffin //* 1994 - **Middle Class Revolt,** *Matador //* 1994 - **The League of Bald Headed Men,** *Matador //* 1995 - **Cerebral Caustic,** *Permanent //* 1995 - **27 Points,** *Permanent //* 1996 - **The Light User Syndrome,** *Jet //* 1996 - **Sinister Waltz,** *Receiver //* 1997 - **The Legendary Chaos Tape,** *Feel Good All //* 1997 -

Levitate, *Artful* // 1997 - **15 Ways To Leave Your Man,** *Receiver* // 1997 - **Oxymoron,** *Receiver* // 1997 - **Cheetham Hill,** *Receiver* // 1997 - **In the City,** *Artful* // 1998 - **Live To Air in Melbourne '82,** *Resurgent* // 1998 - **Room to Live,** *Resurgent* // 1998 - **Undilutable Slang Truth!,** *Cog Sinister* // 1999 - **Live in Nottingham,** *Resurgent* // 1999 - **The Marshall Suite,** *Artful.*

Falzarano, Michael

Folk / Blues guitar, mandolin, harmonica player

Michael Falzarano is a Folk/Blues multi-instrumentalist who has played harmonica with *Hot Tuna* on several of their albums.

Discography: (also see - Hot Tuna)
1996 - **Mecca,** *Relix.*

Farlow, Billy C.

Born: Decatur, AL

Country-Swing singer, harmonica player

Billy C. Farlow was the lead singer and harmonica player for the group *Commander Cody and his Lost Planet Airmen.* He also recorded with Homesick James, Sam Lay and Gene Vincent as well as recording some albums on his own.

Discography: (also see - Commander Cody and his Lost Planet Airmen)
1995 - **Blue Highway,** *Taxim* // 1996 - **Gulf Coast Blues,** *Appaloosa* // 1996 - **Ain't Never Had Too Much Fun,** *Appaloosa.*

Farnon, Robert

Born: 1917

Classical composer

Robert Farnon wrote "Prelude and Dance for Harmonica and Orchestra" and "Concerto for Harmonica and Orchestra" for Tommy Reilly.

Available recordings:
1968 - **Reilly Performs Villa-Lobos, Spivakovsky, Arnold and Others,** *Chandos* // 1993 - **Tommy Reilly Plays Harmonica Concertos,** *Chandos.*

Farr, Hugh

Vaudeville harmonica player

Hugh Farr was one of the players who took part in the secret harmonica band that Johnny Puleo assembled in the 1940's.

Farrar, Jay

Born: December 26, 1967 - Belleville, IL

Folk / Rock singer-songwriter, guitar, mandolin, harmonica player

As one of the founders of the band *Uncle Tupelo,* Jay Farrar is one of the leading proponents of the new wave of Alternative Country / Rock music. After *Uncle Tupelo* broke up in 1993, he founded the group, *Son Volt.* He plays the guitar, mandolin and harmonica as well as singing and writing much of material performed by the bands he has played in.

Discography: (see - Uncle Tupelo, Son Volt)

Feldman, Louis "Fuzzy"

Vaudeville harmonica player

Fuzzy Feldman played the chord harmonica for Borrah Minevitch's *Harmonica Rascals* in the 1920's and 30's, usually by playing with several Hohner Autovalve harmonicas wedged between his fingers. During the 1940's and 50's he worked in *The Don Henry Trio* with Pete Pedersen. Eventually he and Pete Pedersen worked as a duo.

Feltham, Mark

Rock harmonica player

Mark Feltham is a studio harmonica player who has been playing since the mid 1980's and has recorded with Paul Carrack, Joe Cocker, Roger Daltry, Rory Gallagher, Annie Lennox, *Godley & Creme, Nine Below Zero, Oasis, Talk Talk, The The,* Paul Young and many others.

Movies:
1998 - **The Mighty** // 1999 - **Notting Hill.**

Field, Kim

Born: May 23, 1951

Harmonica player, historian

Kim Field played the harmonica in the group *The Slamhound Hunters* as well as writing the book, "Harmonicas, Harps and Heavy Breathers," an overview of the history of the harmonica.

Discography: (with The Slamhound Hunters)
1984 - **Private Jungle,** *Satin* // **4/1 Mind,** *Satin.*

Bibliography:
1993 - **Harmonicas, Harps and Heavy Breathers,** *Fireside Press,* (2000 - 2ⁿᵈ edition, *Cooper Square Publishing*).

Fields, George

Born: April 22, 1921

Vaudeville, studio harmonica player

George Fields started playing the harmonica at about the age of ten. He formed the Brooklyn Harmonica Symphony Society while still in his early teens and at age fourteen he began taking lessons on the harmonica from Eddy Manson. In 1937 he won the New York City Park Department harmonica championship.

He began playing in Vaudeville during 1940 and 1941 with *The Cappy Barra Harmonica Ensemble* and spent part of 1942 playing with *The Harmonica Rascals.* He joined *The Harmonica Solidaires* when Richard Hayman left the group.

He settled in California and worked primarily in the movies and in the recording studio after World War Two. Two of his most memorable soundtracks include "Ruby Gentry" and "Breakfast At Tiffany's." He has been featured on recordings by Elvis Presley, Rosemary Clooney, Billy Vaughan and others.

Discography:
1950's - **Harmonica Favorites,** *Hi-Fi Tops* // 1978 - **The Pocket Bach,** *EMI Angel* // 1999 - **The Bach Stops Here,** *Aeolina.*

Movies:
1952 - **Ruby Gentry** // 1955 - **The Tall Men** // 1956 - **Goodbye My Lady** // 1957 - **Raintree County** // 1961 - **Breakfast At Tiffany's** // 1969 - **Paint Your Wagon** // **The Naked Sea.**

Filisko, Joe

Born: Germany

Blues harmonica player, custom builder
Perhaps the world's foremost builder of custom diatonic harmonicas, Joe Filisko began customizing harmonicas in the late 1980's and was soon making instruments for many of the world's best harmonica players, including Charlie Musselwhite, Corky Siegel, Howard Levy, Mickey Raphael, Peter "Madcat" Ruth, Mark Graham and many others.

Fiore, Al

Real name: Al Fiorentino
Born: December 30, 1922 - Chicago, IL
Died: October 25, 1996 - Chicago, IL

Vaudeville harmonica player
Al Fiore grew up on the West Side of Chicago. He first teamed

up with Jerry Murad, Pete Pedersen and Bob Hadamik in 1937 to form *The Harmonica Madcaps.* They stayed together until Murad and Pedersen left to join *The Harmonica Rascals.*

After Murad left the Rascals, they re-grouped with bass harmonica player Don Les, Ronny Salzman and a girl singer to form *The Quintones,* under the direction of Jimmy Mulcay. After Salzman left the group with the girl singer, the three remaining players decided to stay working as a trio and changed their name to *The Harmonicats.*

They recorded "Peg O' My Heart" in 1947, which would go on to become the number one record of that year and eventually one of the best selling singles of all time. During the next several years *The Harmonicats* recorded over 36 albums.

Al Fiore retired from the group in 1982. He remained active in the Windy City Harmonica Club until his death in 1996.

Discography: (see - The Harmonicats)

The Flamin' Groovies

Formed: 1965 - San Francisco, CA
Disbanded: 1979

Pop / Rock band
The Flamin' Groovies were a Pop band that specialized in playing short, three-minute songs. Bassist George Alexander and guitarist Chris Wilson both played harmonica.

See - George Alexander, Chris Wilson

Discography:
1968 - **Sneakers,** *Snazz* // 1969 - **Supersnazz,** *Epic* // 1970 - **Flamingo,** *Kama Sutra* // 1971 - **Teenage Head,** *Kama Sutra* // 1975 - **This is the Flamin' Groovies,** *Kama Sutra* // 1976 - **Slow Death,** *United Artists* // 1976 - **Shake Some Action,** *Sire* // 1976 - Still Shakin', *Buddah* // 1978 - **The Flamin' Groovies Now!,** *Sire* // 1979 - **Jumpin' the Night,** *Sire* // 1979 - **Absolutely Sweet Mary,** *Sire* // 1983 - **Flamin' Groovies '70,** *Eva* // 1983 - **Slow Death, Live!,** *Lolita* // 1983 - **Bucket Full of Brains,** *Voxx* // 1984 - **Flamin' Groovies Studio '68,** *Era* // 1984 - **The Gold Star Tapes,** *Sky Dog* // 1985 - **Live at the Whiskey A Go-Go '79,** *Lolita* // 1986 - **Roadhouse,** *Edsel* // 1989 - **The Groovies' Greatest Grooves,** *Sire* // 1989 - **The Rockfield Sessions,** *Aim* // 1991 - **Step Up,** *Aim* // 1993 - **Rock Juice,** *National* // 1994 - **Flamin' Groovies,** *Polydor* // 1994 - **Rockin' at the Roadhouse: Live,** *Mystery* // 1995 - **Live at the Festival of the Sun,** *Aim* // 1995 - **Live 68 / 70,** *New Rose* // 1995 - **16 Tunes,** *Sky Dog* // 1996 - **Groove In,** *New Rose* // 1997 - **In Person!,** *Norton* // 1998 - **Yesterday's Numbers,** *Camden* // 1999 - **Shake Some Action Live with The Flamin' Groovies,** *Dressed To Kill.*

Flanders, Tommy

Rock singer, harmonica player

Tommy Flanders played the harmonica and was the lead singer for the group *Blues Project*.

Discography: (also see - Blues Project)
1969 - **The Moonstone,** *Verve.*

Bela Fleck and the Flecktones

Formed: 1990 - Nashville, TN

Fusion Jazz band

Led by Fusion Jazz banjo virtuoso Bela Fleck, *The Flecktones* featured the Jazz harmonica stylings of Howard Levy on several of their earlier recordings.

See - Howard Levy

Discography: (with Howard Levy)
1990 - **Bela Fleck and the Flecktones,** *Warner Brothers //* 1991 - **Live Art,** *Warner Brothers //* 1992 - **Flight of the Cosmic Hippo,** *Warner Brothers //* 1993 - **UFO TOFU,** *Warner Brothers.*

The Fleshtones

Formed: 1976 - New York City, NY

Alternative Rock band

Deriving its sound from bands of the late 1950's and early 60's, *The Fleshtones* featured Peter Zaremba on vocals, keyboards and harmonica. The group has managed to maintain a presence on the charts for over twenty years.

See - Peter Zaremba

Discography:
1982 - **Roman Gods,** *A&M //* 1982 - **Blast Off!,** *ROIR //* 1983 - **Hexbreaker,** *A&M //* 1985 - **Speed Connection,** *IRS //* 1985 - **Speed Connection II: The Final Chapter,** *IRS //* 1987 - **Fleshtones vs. Reality,** *Emergo //* 1989 - **Soul Madrid,** *Impossible //* 1992 - **Powerstance,** *Naked Language //* 1994 - **Beautiful Light,** *Naked Language //* 1995 - **Laboratory of Sound,** *Ichiban //* 1996 - **Fleshtones,** *Restless //* 1997 - **Hitsburg, USA,** *Telstar //* 1998 - **More Than Skin Deep,** *Ichiban //* 1999 - **Angry Years,** *Amsterdamned //* 2000 - **Return To Hitsburg,** *Telstar.*

Flowers, Danny

Country guitar, harmonica player

Raised in North Carolina, Danny Flowers came to Nashville to work as a studio musician in 1971. He plays lead guitar and harmonica in *The Scratch Band,* Don Williams' back-up group. Flowers co-wrote "Tulsa Time" which was a big hit for Williams and Eric Clapton. Flowers has also worked with Emmylou Harris, Nanci Griffith, *The Spencer Davis Group* and others.

Discography:
1982 - **The Scratch Band with Danny Flowers,** *MCA //* 2000 - **Forbidden Fruits and Vegetables.**

Floyd, "Harmonica" Frank

Also known as: The Silly Kid
Born: October 11, 1908 - Toccopola, MS
Died: August 7, 1984 - Blanchester, OH

Blues guitar, harmonica player

Born and raised without being given a proper name, Frank Floyd named himself as a teenager. He taught himself how to play the harmonica at age ten and ran away from home at age twelve, working as a comedian and harmonica player at carnivals and medicine shows.

Harmonica Frank developed a technique of playing the harmonica without a neckbrace, simply slipping it into his mouth and playing, leaving his hands free to play the guitar. He could also play two harmonicas at once, one with his mouth and one with his nose. He spent over thirty years hoboing around the U.S.

He started working in radio in 1932 and began recording for the Chess label in 1951. His recordings for the Sun label are considered to be some of the earliest examples of Rockabilly music. He continued recording and performing until his death in 1984.

Discography:
1974 - **The Great Original Recordings of Harmonica Frank,** *Puritan //* 1975 - **Harmonica Frank Floyd,** *Barrelhouse //* 1997 - **The Great Medical Menagarist,** *Genes //* **Swamproot,** *Genes.*

The Flying Burrito Brothers

Formed: 1968 - Los Angeles, CA
Disbanded: 1973

Country / Rock band

Made up primarily of ex-members of *The Byrds, The Flying Burrito Brothers* were leading proponents of the Country / Rock movement of the early 1970's. The group included Michael Clarke on the drums and harmonica from 1968 until the late 1970's.

See - Michael Clarke

Discography:
1969 - **The Gilded Palace of Sin,** *A&M //* 1970 - **Burrito Deluxe,** *A&M //* 1971 - **The Flying Burrito Brothers,** *A&M //* 1971 - **Last of the Red Hot Burritos,** *A&M //* 1974 - **Close Up the Honky Tonks,** *A&M //* 1974 - **Honky Tonk Heaven,** *Ariola //* 1976 - **Sleepless Nights,** *A&M //* 1987 - **Dim Lights, Thick Smoke and Loud Music,** *Edsel //* 1988 - **Farther Along: The Best Of...,** *A&M //* 1999 - **Sin City,** *Relix.*

Foley, Red

Real name: Claude Julian Foley
Born: June 17, 1910 - Blue Lick, KY
Died: September 19, 1968 - Fort Wayne, IN

Country singer-songwriter, guitar, harmonica player
Red Foley began playing guitar and harmonica while growing up in Indiana. He played on the "National Barn Dance" radio show with *The Cumberland Ridge Runners* from 1930 through 1937. He started recording in 1933 and had a string of Country hits from the late 1930's through the 1960's.

Discography:
1959 - **Red Foley's Golden Favorites,** *Decca* // 1964 - **The Red Foley Story,** *Decca* // 1965 - **Red Foley's Greatest Hits,** *Decca* // **Red Foley, 1937-39,** *Document.*

Folk Harmonica

The harmonica has played a major part in Folk music throughout its history. Usually played by guitarists using the harmonica on a neckbrace, some of Folk music's greatest practitioners, including Woody Guthrie, Neil Young and Bob Dylan, have used the harmonica for fills and lead breaks in their songs.

Harmonica also plays a part in the traditional Folk musics of Ireland, Appalachia, the South, the West and other parts of the world.

Ford, Carl

Vaudeville harmonica player
Carl Ford played harmonica with *The Harmonica Rascals* during the 1940's.

Ford, Mark

Born: October 21, 1953 - Ukiah, CA

Blues harmonica player

Mark Ford plays harmonica in *The Charles Ford Blues Band* with his brothers Robben and Patrick. The group has also featured Gary Smith and also backed Charlie Musselwhite on several of his albums. Mark has also played with Garth Webber, Brownie McGhee and Jimmy Witherspoon as well as on solo albums by his brother Robben.

Discography:
1972 - **The Charles Ford Blues Band,** *Arhoolie* // 1982 - **A Reunion,** *Blue Rock-It* // 1990 - **Here We Go,** *Crosscut* // 1991 - **Mark and Robben Ford,** *Blue Rock-It* // 1991 - **The Ford Blues Band,** *Blue Rock-It* // 1994 - **Reunion Live,** *Blue Rock-It* // 1994 - **On the Edge,** *Blue Rock-It* // 1996 - **As Real as it Gets,** *Blue Rock-It* // 1997 - **Fords and Friends,** *Blue Rock-It* // 1998 - **Mark Ford and the Blue Line,** *Blue Rock-It* // **As Real as it Gets,** *Blue Rock-It* // **Garth Webber and the Ford Blues Band,** *Blue Rock-It* // **Up from the Streets,** *Blue Rock-It.*

Forest City Joe: (see - Joe Pugh)

Fortier, Lee

Blues singer, harmonica player

Lee Fortier began playing the harmonica at the age of twelve. During the 1970's he worked closely with Sonny Terry, as well as playing in several bands on the East Coast. Semi-retired from the music scene to pursue a career as a lawyer during the 1980's, he made a return to music in the late 1990's with a debut album on his own Fine as Wine label.

Discography:
1997 - **Turn It Up,** *Fine as Wine.*

Foster, Garley

Born: January 10, 1905 - Wilkes County, NC
Died: October 1968

Country singer, harmonica player
Garley Foster played the harmonica with *The Carolina Tarheels* from the late 1920's until the mid-1930's. He also performed and recorded with Doc Watson during the late 1950's and early 60's.

Discography: (see - The Carolina Tarheels)

Foster, Gwen

Born: Gaston County, NC

Country singer, harmonica player
Gwen Foster played the harmonica with *The Carolina Tarheels* from the late 1920's until the mid-1930's. Over the years he developed a very distinctive growling tone to his harmonica playing. He also played harmonica in a duet with guitarist Tom Ashley during the 1930's.

Discography: (also see - The Carolina Tarheels)
Ashley & Foster, *Yazoo* // **Ashley & Foster,** *Rounder.*

Foster, "Little" Willy

Born: April 5, 1922 - Clarksdale, MS

Blues piano, harmonica player
Willie Foster was raised as a sharecropper in Mississippi and moved to Chicago when he was nineteen years old. He learned how to play the harmonica from Big Walter Horton and frequently worked the Maxwell Street Market for tips.

During the 1950's he played with *The Floyd Jones Band*, Baby Face Leroy, Snooky Pryor and other in Chicago's southside Blues clubs. Foster began recording in 1954 and was fairly active through the mid-1950's.

Foster was shot and paralyzed in 1956 and made a slow recovery, performing sporadically starting in the late 1960's. He reportedly served time for a fatal shooting in 1974, but has been recording and performing again since the 1990's.

Discography:
1965 - **Chicago Blues, The Early 1950's** // 1980 - **King Cobras** // 1999 - **Live at the Airport Grocery,** Memphis // **I Found Joy,** *Palindrome.*

Fox, George

Born: March 23, 1950 - Cochrane, Alberta, Canada

Country singer-songwriter, guitar, harmonica player
George Fox is one of Canada's top Country-Western artists. He began playing music at age 21 and has been recording since 1988. Like many Country artists, he also plays the harmonica and guitar as well as singing.

Discography:
1988 - **George Fox,** *Warner Brothers* // 1989 - **With All My Might,** *Warner Brothers* // 1991 - **Spice of Life,** *Warner Brothers* // 1993 - **Mustang Heart,** *Warner Brothers.*

Freddie and the Dreamers

Formed: 1960 - Manchester, England
Disbanded: 1968

British Invasion Pop band
Freddie and the Dreamers were one of the groups that emerged during the British Invasion of the early 1960's. They featured Derek Quinn on guitar and harmonica.

See - Derek Quinn

Discography:
1963 - **Freddie and the Dreamers,** *Columbia* // 1963 - **If You Make a Fool,** *Columbia* // 1964 - **You Were Made for Me,** *Columbia* // 1964 - **Crazy World,** *Columbia* // 1964 - **Just for You,** *Columbia* // 1965 - **Sing Along,** *Columbia* // 1965 - **Ready Freddie Go,** *Columbia* // 1965 - **Freddie and the Dreamers,** *Mercury* // 1965 - **Do the Freddie,** *Mercury* // 1966 - **Freddie and the Dreamers in Disneyland,** *Columbia* // 1967 - **King Freddie & Dreaming Knights,** *Columbia* // 1970 - **Oliver in Overworld,** *Starline* // 1974 - **Freddy Garrity,** *Bus Stop* // 1977 - **The Best Of...,** *Capitol* // 2000 - **Best of the 60's,** *Disky.*

Movies:
1965 - **Every Day's a Holiday (AKA: Seaside Swingers).**

Free-reed

The harmonica is classified as a free-reeded instrument. A free-reeded instrument is one that can produce a tone without the help of any other surface to determine its pitch when air is blown over it. The pitch is determined by the length and thickness of the reed.

Other free-reeded instruments include: accordion, concertina and the melodica. Most free-reeded instruments are descended from an Asian instrument called the Yu. Other Asian free-reeded instruments include the Sheng, the Khaen and the Sho.

Freed, Carl

Born: 1896 - Turkey
Died: 1984

Vaudeville harmonica band leader
Carl Freed assembled a harmonica band called *The Harmonica Harlequins* in 1934. Their trademark was that they all wore clown suits while performing. The group lasted about a year.

After *The Harmonica Harlequins* broke up in 1935, Freed regrouped with *The Harmonica Lads* featuring Mike Chimes, Saul Webber and Sid Gould. In 1940 Chime and Gould left the group and were replaced by Byron Bouchard and Pete Blasberg. The group dissolved after the outbreak of World War Two.

Freeman, Milton
Vaudeville harmonica player
Milton Freeman played the bass harmonica in *The Harmonica Harlequins* during the mid-1930's.

French Harp
A southern colloquial name for the harmonica.

Friedman, Carl
Vaudeville harmonica player
Carl Friedman played the bass harmonica in Johnny O'Brien's *Harmonica Hi-Hats* during the late 1930's.

Friedman, Leo
Died: July 13, 2000

Vaudeville harmonica player
Leo Friedman was a member of *The Harmonica Rascals* from 1942 until 1945 and also *The Cappy Barra Harmonica Gentleman* during the 1940's. During the late 1940's he worked in Hollywood doing movie soundtracks.

Frost, Frank Otis
Born: April 15, 1936 - Augusta, AR
Died: October 12, 1999 - Helena, AR

Blues singer, guitar, piano, harmonica player
Frank Otis Frost grew up in the St. Louis area and learned to play the harmonica from Little Willie Foster and Sonny Boy Williamson II (Rice Miller). He began working professionally with Williamson during the mid-1950's.

He began recording as a solo artist in the early 1960's and worked with B.B. King, Albert King, Little Milton, Sam Carr and others. He worked with the group, *The Jelly Roll Kings* well into the 1990's.

Discography:
1960's - **Ride with Your Daddy Tonight**, *Charly* // 1962 - **Hey Boss Man**, *P-Vine* // 1966 - **Frank Frost**, *Jewel* // 1966 - **Harp and Soul**, *P-Vine* // 1973 - **Frank Frost**, *Paula* // 1989 - **Midnight Prowler**, *Earwig* // 1990 - **Jelly Roll King**, *Charly* // 1990 - **The Jelly `Roll Kings Rockin' the Juke Joint Down**, *Earwig* // 1991 - **Jelly Roll Blues**, *Paula* // 1992 - **Deep Blues**, *Appaloosa* // 1994 - **Screamers**, *Appalossa* // 1996 - **Keep Yourself Together**, *Evidence* // 1998 - **The Jelly Roll Kings**, *Earwig* // 1999 - **Big Boss Man: The Very Best Of...**, *Collectables* // **Frost Music**, *Vanguard*.

Movies:
1986 - **Crossroads** // **Deep Blues**.

Fuller, Jesse "Lone Cat"
Born: March 12, 1896 - Jonesboro, GA
Died January 29, 1976 - Oakland, CA

Blues singer, guitar, harmonica player
Jesse Fuller began playing music at age five. He ran away from home at age ten and traveled extensively around the United States until the mid-1920's, when he settled for a time in the Los Angeles area and worked as an extra in the movies.

Fuller moved to Oakland in 1929, where he worked for shipyards and railroads. He returned to music in the 1940's and did shows with Folk music legend, Leadbelly. He worked steadily as a one-man band throughout the 40's, 50's and 60's and reportedly taught a young Bob Dylan how to play the harmonica on a neckbrace.

He recorded steadily from the 1950's until the early 1970's, when he became inactive due to ill health. His big hits included; "San Francisco Bay Blues," "Beat It On Down the Line" and "Monkey and the Engineer."

Discography:
1950's - **Frisco Bound**, *Arhoolie* // 1959 - **Brother Lowdown**, *Fantasy* // 1961 - **The Lone Cat Sings and Plays Jazz, Folksongs, Spirituals and Blues**, *Good Time Jazz* // 1963 - **San Francisco Bay Blues**, *Prestige* // 1965 - **Favorites**, *Prestige* // 1993 - **Jazz, Folk Songs, Spirituals and Blues**, *Fantasy* // **Folk, Blues and Spirituals**, *Good Time Jazz* // **Move On Down the Line**, *Topic*.

Movies:
1924 - **The Thief of Bagdad** // 1924 - **East of Suez** // 1929 - **Hearts in Dixie** // 1929 - **End of the World** // 1970 - **The Great White Hope**, (Soundtrack).

Anson Funderburgh and the Rockets
Formed: 1978 - Texas

Blues band
The Rockets are the back-up group for Blues guitarist Anson Funderburgh. Darrell Nulisch played harmonica for the group starting in 1978. He was replaced by veteran Blues man Sam Myers in 1986, and Myers has continued fronting the band ever since.

See - Darrell Nulisch, Sam Myers

Discography:
1981 - **Talk To You By Hand**, *Black Top* // 1985 - **She Knocks Me Out!**, *Black Top* // 1985 - **Knock You Out**, *Spindrift* // 1986 - **My Love is Here To Stay**, *Black Top* // 1987 - **Sins**, *Black Top* // 1988 - **Black Top Blues-A-Rama Live**, *Black Top* // 1989 - **Rack 'Em Up**, *Black Top* // 1991 - **Tell Me What I Want To Hear**, *Black Top* // 1992 - **Thru the Years: A Retrospective, (1981-1992)**, *Black Top* // 1995

- Live at the Grand Emporium, *Black Top* // 1997 - **That's What They Want,** *Black Top* // 1999 - **Change in My Pocket,** *Bullseye Blues.*

Furbish, Al
Vaudeville harmonica player

Al Furbish played harmonica in *The Harmonica Rascals* during the 1930's.

– G –

Galison, William

Born: February 19, 1958

Jazz harmonica player

William Galison began playing harmonica at age two. In his late teens he studied music at the Berklee School of Music in Boston and has specialized in playing Jazz on the chromatic harmonica.

He has worked with Sting, Chaka Khan, *The O'Jays*, Ruth Brown, Marla BB, Dion Farris, Peggy Lee, Ivan Neville, Christy Brown, Maureen McGovern and many others as well as recording three albums as a solo artist.

Discography:
1988 - **Overjoyed,** *Polygram* // 1997 - **Midnight Sun,** *Eclipse Collage* // 2000 - **Waking Up with You,** *JVC* // **Calling You,** *Polygram.*

Movies
1988 - **Bagdad Café** // 1992 - **Prelude To a Kiss** // 1994 - **Crooklyn** // 1995 - **Way West** // TV - **Sesame Street.**

Gapping

Gapping refers to the distance between the reed plate and the free end of the reed. Adjusting the gapping changes how the reed will respond to the air pressure that runs across the reed's surface. The farther the free end of the reed is from the reed plate, the greater the amount of air pressure a player will need to create to make the reed respond.

Garden, Claude
Pop/Classical harmonica soloist

French harmonica player Claude Garden has been performing in the Classical music field since the 1960's. He has also composed several pieces for the instrument including "Concerto for Harmonica and Orchestra" in 1970.

Discography:
1993 - **Listener's Choice: Gentle Harmonica,** *Metacom* // **Melodies,** *Victor* // **Alexandra's Secret Garden,** *Intermede* // **Tender Harmonica Stories,** *Intermede* // **Mes Rappels Preferes Harmonica,** *Production CG* // **Claude Garden Plays Bach, Chopin, Ibert, Garden,** *Production CG* // **That's What Friends are For,** *Amplitude.*

Gardner, Dick

Born: October 24, 1934

Vaudeville bass harmonica player

Dick Gardner joined *The Harmonicats* in 1971 to replace Don Les on the bass harmonica. After *The Harmonicats* disbanded permanently, Gardner became a full-time harmonica repairman.

Discography: (see - The Harmonicats)

Garrett, Peter

Rock singer, harmonica player

Peter Garrett has been the lead singer for the Australian Rock band, *Midnight Oil* since 1975. In addition to singing and fronting the group, Garrett also plays the harmonica occasionally.

Discography: (see - Midnight Oil)

Gary, Tommy

Born: January 9, 1919 - Brownsville, TN
Died: July 31, 1975

Blues harmonica player

During the 1920's Tommy Gary played with Son Borum. He started playing with Sleepy John Estes at age twelve and continued with him until Hammie Nixon became Estes' full-time harmonica player. Gary played with Robert Wilkins during the 1930's and re-united with Sleepy John Estes in the 1960's.

Discography:

1969 - **Memphis Swamp Jam,** *Blue Thumb* // **The Memphis Blues Again, Vol. 2,** *Adelphi.*

The J. Geils Band

Formed: 1967 - Boston, MA
Disbanded: 1983

Blues / Rock band

An enormously popular Blues / Rock band of the 1970's and 80's, *The J. Geils Band* enjoyed a tremendous following for their high energy shows that were centered around the harmonica pyrotechnics of Magic Dick. Their big hits included: "I Must Have Got Lost," "Lookin' for a Love," "Give It To Me" and the harmonica showcase, "Whammer Jammer."

See - Magic Dick

Discography:

1971 - **The J. Geils Band,** *Atlantic* // 1972 - **The Morning After,** *Atlantic* // 1972 - **Full House,** *Atlantic* // 1973 - **Bloodshot,** *Atlantic* // 1973 - **Ladies Invited,** *Atlantic* // 1974 - **Nightmares (and Other Tales from the Vinyl Jungle),** *Atlantic* // 1975 - **Hot Line,** *Atlantic* // 1976 - **Blow Your Face Out,** *Atlantic* // 1977 - **Monkey Island,** *Atlantic* // 1978 - **Sanctuary,** *EMI* // 1979 - **The Best Of...,** *Atlantic* // 1980 - **Love Stinks,** *EMI* // 1981 - **Freeze-Frame,** *EMI* // 1982 - **Showtime!,** *EMI* // 1984 - **You're Gettin' Even While I'm Gettin' Odd,** *EMI* // 1985 - **Flashback: The Best Of...,** *EMI* // 1993 - **House Party: The J. Geils Band Anthology,** *Rhino.*

Geldray, Max

Real name: Max Van Gelder
Born: 1916 - Amsterdam

Pop / Jazz harmonica player

Max Geldray began playing the harmonica when he was sixteen years old. In the mid-1930's he put together a harmonica band in the Netherlands and did a tour and some radio appearances with them. After the group broke up, Max began working as a Jazz harmonica soloist.

He moved to England to escape persecution during World War Two. In 1951 he began working on "The Goon Show' on the BBC with Spike Milligan and Peter Sellers, playing a regular part of the show's comedy antics and playing Jazz harmonica pieces as well. During the 1960's he began working on cruise ships as an entertainer. He has remained active playing Pop and Jazz harmonica since then.

Geneva Red

Born: April 23, 1969 - McHenry, IL

Blues singer, harmonica player

From a musical family, Geneva Red began playing the harmonica after attending a Chicago Blues Festival in the late 1980's. After recording several demo songs in the mid-1990's, she was signed to Full Cyrkle Records and has recorded several albums for the label.

Discography:

1997 - **Alley Ways,** *Full Cyrkle* // 1997 - **Geneva Red and the Roadsters,** *Full Cyrkle* // 2000 - **In the Red,** *Full Cyrkle.*

George, Lowell

Born: April 13, 1945 - Hollywood, CA
Died: June 29, 1979 - Arlington, VA

Rock singer, slide guitar, harmonica player

Lowell George made his first national public appearance on the

"Ted Mack's Amateur Hour" Television show playing a harmonica duet with his brother, Hampton. He got into the Rock scene in the late 1960's and worked with *Frank Zappa and the Mothers of Invention.*

He went on to become more famous as a slide guitarist and founder of the Rock band *Little Feat,* occasionally playing the harmonica whenever it was needed

Discography: (also see - Little Feat)
1979 - **Thanks, I'll Eat It Here,** *Warner Brothers* // 1993 - **Lightning Rod Man,** *Bizarre.*

Geremia, Paul

Born: April 21, 1944 - Providence, RI

Blues singer, guitar, harmonica player
Playing since the 1960's, Paul Geremia has specialized in playing acoustic Blues music and has worked with Eric Von Schmidt, Dave Von Ronk and many other Folk and Blues artists.

Discography:
1968 - **Just Enough,** *Verve* // 1968 - **Paul Geremia,** *Sire* // 1982 - **I Really Don't Mind Livin',** *Flying Fish* // 1986 - **My Kinda Place,** *Flying Fish* // 1993 - **Gamblin' Woman Blues,** *Red House* // 1995 - **Self Portrait in Blues,** *Vanguard* // 1997 - **Live From Uncle Sam's Backyard,** *Red House* // 1999 - **Devil's Music,** *Red House* // 2000 - **Hard Life Rockin' Chair,** *Genes.*

German, Sandy

Born: 1932 - Cleveland, OH

Jazz harmonica player
Sandy German began playing trumpet at age eight and picked up the harmonica a few years later after seeing Larry Adler perform in a movie. After spending most of his adult life away from music, Sandy got back into playing the harmonica after attending a SPAH convention in 1982.

Discography:
1998 - **Tenderley,** *German.*

Gerritsen, Rinus

Born: August 9, 1946 - The Hague, Netherlands

Rock bass, keyboards, harmonica player
Rinus Gerritsen co-founded the Dutch Rock group *Golden Earring* with George Kooymans in 1961. Though primarily a European act, during the 1970's and 80's they were able to score some American hits with "Radar Love" and "Twilight Zone."

Discography: (also see - Golden Earring)
1979 - **De G.V.D. Band** // 1985 - **Labyrinth.**

Gillum, Jazz

Real name: William McKinley Gillum
Born: September 11, 1904 - Indianola, MS
Died: March 29, 1966 - Chicago, IL

Blues harmonica player
Orphaned at an early age, Jazz Gillum was raised by an uncle, a church deacon, who taught him how to play the organ and the harmonica. By age fourteen he had run away from home and was playing the harmonica on the streets for tips. He came to Chicago in 1923 and was soon working with Blues guitarist Big Bill Broonzy. Gillum worked primarily as a sideman throughout the 1920's and 30's and began recording in 1934.

Largely inactive during the 1950's, Gillum was just starting to make a comeback in the early 1960's, recording with Memphis Slim, when he died from gunshot wounds he received during an argument.

Discography:
1970 - **You Got To Reap What You Sow** // 1985 - **Jazz Gillum,** *Travelin' Man* // 1993 - **Best of Blues, 1935-46,** *Best of Blues* // 1997 - **The Bluebird Recordings, 1934-1938,** *RCA* // 1998 - **Harmonica Chicago Blues 1934-1947,** *Formeaux* // **Roll Dem Bones 1938-1949,** *Wolf* // **Key To the Highway, 1935-1942,** *Blues Collection* // **Complete Recorded Works, Volumes 1-4,** *Document.*

Gindick, Jon
Folk guitar, harmonica player, writer

Jon Gindick has been playing the harmonica since around 1964. He is a well-respected performer and author of instructional books on how to play the harmonica.

Discography:
1993 - **Westward Vision,** *Cross Harp* // 2000 - **Banished Moon,** *Cross Harp.*

Bibliography:
The Natural Blues and Country Western Harmonica, *Cross Harp Press* // **Country and Blues Harmonica for the Musically Hopeless,** *Cross Harp Press* // **Four Positions of Blues, Jazz and Country Harmonica,** *Cross Harp Press* // **Harmonica Americana,** *Cross Harp Press* // **The Robert Johnson Lesson,** *Cross Harp Press* // **Gospel Plow,** *Cross Harp Press* // **Rock and Blues Accompaniment Lesson,** *Cross Harp Press* // **Rock N' Blues Harmonica,** *Cross Harp Press.*

Video:
Beginners Video, (with B.B. King), *Cross Harp Press.*

Glosson, Lonnie

Born: February 14, 1908 - Judsonia, AR

Country harmonica player

Lonnie Glosson learned to play the harmonica from his mother when he was ten years old. During the 1920's he played on the WLS "National Barn Dance" radio show. He moved to California in 1934, where he played on various radio shows, but soon moved back to the Midwest to work in radio and to do some recording.

In 1936 he started playing with fellow Country harmonica player Wayne Raney, a partnership that would last on and off until 1960. In 1949 he began working on television, broadcasting on WSB in Atlanta. He has been active recording and performing ever since.

Discography:
1981 - **Lonnie Glosson with Wayne Raney,** *Collectors Item* // 1982 - **The Living Legend,** *Old Homestead* // 1989 - **Live at Tres Rios** // **All Harmonica,** *Rimrock* // **The Blues Harp Man,** *Rimrock* // **Smell the Roses** // **Gospel Snakes.**

Glover, Tony "Little Sun"

Folk / Blues harmonica player

As a boyhood friend of Bob Dylan, Tony Glover is credited with teaching him how to play the harmonica. Glover was a part of the Folk / Blues trio *Koerner, Ray and Glover* during the early 1960's. He has also written several books of harmonica instruction and continues to perform on a regular basis in the Minneapolis area.

Discography: (also see - Koerner, Ray and Glover, John Koerner)
1965 - **Snaker's Here,** (with David Ray), *Elektra* // 1968 - **Sleep Faster, We Need the Pillow,** (with Michael Lessac), *Columbia* // 1985 - **From the West Bank,** (with David Ray), *Treehouse* // 1987 - **Legends in Their Spare Time,** (with David Ray), *Treehouse* // 1990 - **Ashes in my Whiskey,** (with David Ray), *Rough Trade* // 1993 - **The Picture has Faded,** (with David Ray), *Tim Kerr Records* // 2000 - **By the Water,** (with The Back Porch Rockers), *Back Porch Rockers.*

Bibliography:
Blues Harp, *Oak Publications* // **Blues Harp Songbook,** *Oak Publications* // **Rock Harp,** *Oak Publications.*

Gob Iron
A Scottish nickname for the harmonica.

Golbey, Brian

Born: February 5, 1939 - Pycombe, England

Country singer-songwriter, fiddle, harmonica player
Brian Golbey was taught to play the harmonica at age eleven by his father. He has been performing since the mid-1950's and is one of England's top Country-Western stars.

Discography:
1970 - **The Old and the New,** *Lucky* // 1972 - **Virginia Waters,** *Phoenix* // 1973 - **Silver Haired Daddy of Mine,** *Avenue* // 1974 - **Moments,** *Emerald Gem* // 1976 - **Cajun Moon,** *Chrysalis* // 1977 - **The London Tapes,** *Waterfall* // 1979 - **When the Dealing is Done,** *Waterfront* // 1983 - **Last Train South,** *Waterfront* // **Line Up Later,** (with Cajun Moon).

Golden Earring

Formed: 1961 - The Hague, Netherlands

Dutch Rock band
Golden Earring was a Dutch Rock band that had hits in America during the 1970's and 80's with the songs "Radar Love" and

"Twilight Zone." Their bass guitar player, Rinus Gerritsen, also played the harmonica.

See - Rinus Gerritsen

<u>Discography:</u>
1964 - **Just Earring,** *Polydor* // 1967 - **Winter Harvest,** *Capitol* // 1968 - **Miracle Mirror,** *Capitol* // 1969 - **On the Double,** *Polydor* // 1970 - **Eight Miles High,** *Polydor* // 1970 - **Golden Earring,** *Polydor* // 1970 - **Sing My Song,** *Karusell* // 1971 - **Seven Years,** *Polydor* // 1972 - **Together,** *Polydor* // 1973 - **Hearing Earring,** *Track* // 1974 - **Moontan,** *MCA* // 1975 - **Switch,** *MCA* // 1976 - **To the Hilt,** *MCA* // 1976 - **Contraband,** *Polydor* // 1977 - **Mad Love,** *MCA* // 1977 - **Live,** *Polydor* // 1977 - **Golden Earring Live,** *MCA* // 1979 - **Grab It for a Second,** *MCA* // 1979 - **No Promises, No Debts,** *Polydor* // 1980 - **Long Blond Animal,** *Polydor* // 1980 - **Prisoner of the Night,** *Polydor* // 1981 - **2nd Live,** *Polydor* // 1982 - **Cut,** *21 Records* // 1984 - **N.E.W.S.,** *21 Records* // 1984 - **Something Heavy Going Down Live from the Twilight Zone,** *21 Records* // 1986 - **The Hole,** *21 Records* // 1989 - **Keeper of the Flame,** *Baktabak* // 1991 - **Bloody Buccaneers,** *Capitol* // 1995 - **Face It,** *Columbia* // 1997 - **Naked II,** *CNR* // 1999 - **Paradise in Distress,** *Import* // **Naked Truth,** *First Quake.*

Gordon, Eddie

Born: October 7, 1941

Vaudeville / Pop harmonica player

Eddie Gordon began his musical career playing with *The Harmonica Rascals* at age nine. He played the chord harmonica in *Johnny Puleo's Harmonica Gang* during the mid-1950's and in Dave Doucette's *Stereomonics* in the late 1960's. He has been playing in duos since 1972 with guitarists Jimmy Thomas and Steve Ono.

<u>Discography:</u> (also see - Johnny Puleo's Harmonica Gang)
1980 - **Harmonitalk,** *Sloan/Gordon* // 1982 - **Love's Way - Alive in Alaska,** *Gordon/Thomas* // 1983 - **Eddie Gordon & Friends,** *Michael F. Scott* // 1985 - **Eddie Gordon,** *Gordon* // 1995 - **Harmonicas and Guitars,** *Gordon/Ono* // 1996 - **Steve Ono - Voice of a Friend,** *Onomuse.*

Gordon, Jimmy

Born: 1960 - Massachusetts

Jimmy Gordon began playing the harmonica at age four and was playing professionally by the time he was 13. By the time he was twenty he had played with Jerry Lee Lewis, Bonnie Raitt, J.J. Cale and many others

<u>Discography:</u>
1998 - **Come On Over,** *Uncle Dummy's World Records.*

Gould, Sid

Vaudeville harmonica player

Sid Gould played harmonica with *The Harmonica Harlequins* during the 1930's. He also made a cameo appearance, playing the harmonica with his nose, in the movie "Police Academy 4."

<u>Movies:</u>
1987 - **Police Academy 4.**

Graham, Mark

Born: 1953 - Renton, WA

Folk harmonica player

Mark Graham began playing the harmonica in 1971, played with *The Hurricane Ridgerunners* from 1979 until 1982 and with *The Chicken Chokers* from 1984 until 1986. He specializes in playing Folk, Celtic and Traditional old-time music.

Discography:
1981 - **Hurricane Ridgerunners,** *Topaz* // 1985 - **Chokers & Flies,** (with The Chicken Chokers), *Rounder* // 1987 - **Natural Selections,** *Fronthall* // 1995 - **Second Story,** *Green Linnet* // 1997 - **The Kings of Mongrel Folk,** *Graham* // 1998 - **Inner Life,** *Graham* // 1998 - **Hoof and Mouth,** *Green Linnet* // 2000 - **Southern Old-Time Harmonica,** *Graham* // 2000 - **The Funniest Songs in the World** // **Open House,** (with Kevin Burke), *Green Linnet.*

The Grateful Dead

Formed: 1965 - San Francisco, CA
Disbanded: 1995

Rock Band
The Grateful Dead was one of the leading groups to come from the San Francisco area in the late 1960's. During the first few years, the band was co-led by Ron "Pigpen" McKernan, who played organ and harmonica.

After Pigpen died in 1972, another harmonica player did not replace him. However, Matt Kelly, the harmonica player from the band Kingfish, did a guest appearance on the song "I Need a Miracle" on The Grateful Dead album, "Shakedown Street" in 1978.

See - Pigpen, Matt Kelly

Discography: (with Pigpen & Matt Kelly)
1967 - **The Grateful Dead,** *Warner Brothers* // 1968 - **Anthem of the Sun,** *Warner Brothers* // 1969 - **Aoxomoxoa,** *Warner Brothers* // 1969 - **Live Dead,** *Warner Brothers* // 1970 - **Workingman's Dead,** *Warner Brothers* // 1970 - **American Beauty,** *Warner Brothers* // 1971 - **Grateful Dead (AKA: Skull and Roses),** *Warner Brothers* // 1972 - **Europe 72,** *Warner Brothers* // 1973 - **History of The Grateful Dead, Vol. 1: Bear's Choice,** *Warner Brothers* // 1974 - **Skeletons from the Closet,** *Warner Brothers* // 1978 - **Shakedown Street,** *Arista* // 1992 - **Two from the Vault,** *Grateful Dead* // 1995 - **Hundred Year Hall,** *Grateful Dead* // 1996 - **Dick's Pick's Volume 4,** *Grateful Dead.*

Green, Karl

Born: July 31, 1947 - Salford, England

Rock bass guitar, harmonica player
Karl Green played the bass guitar and harmonica in the 1960's British Invasion Pop band Herman's Hermits.

Discography: (see - Herman's Hermits)

Greene, Alan

Vaudeville harmonica player
Alan Greene played in *The Cappy Barra Harmonica Ensemble* during the 1930's and 40's.

Greene, Buddy

Born: October 30, 1953

Country / Gospel harmonica player

Buddy Greene began playing the harmonica when he was 21 and played for Country music star Jerry Reed until 1987. Since then he has established himself as a pre-eminent harmonica player in the field of Country Gospel, recording several albums of his own.

Discography:
1987 - **Praise Harmonica** // 1990 - **Sojourner's Song,** *Fortress* // 1994 - **Grace for the Moment,** *Fortress* // 1995 - **Minstrel of the Lord,** *Fortress* // 1996 - **Quiet Harmonica Praise,** *Fortress* // 1996 - **Simple Praise,** *Fortress* // 2000 - **Sinners and Saints,** *Fortress* // **Buddy Greene,** *Fortress* // **So Far,** *Fortress* // **Slice of Life,** *Fortress* // **Buddy Greene and Friends Live,** *Fortress* // **Praise You, Lord,** *Fortress* // **Christmas: Not Just Any Night,** *Fortress* // **Pro-Trax,** *Fortress.*

Greenwell, Smoky

Blues harmonica player

New Orleans harmonica player Smoky Greenwell has been playing the harmonica since his childhood. He has played with *War*, Coco Robicheaux, Rockie Charles and others as well as recording three albums of his own.

Discography:
1996 - **Smoke Alarm,** *Greenwell* // 1996 - **Smokin',** *Greenwell* // 1998 - **Blowout,** *Greenwell.*

Grimaldi, "Studebaker" John

Born: November 5, 1952 - Chicago, IL

Blues singer, guitar, harmonica player

"Studebaker" John Grimaldi started playing the harmonica at age seven and has been playing professionally in the Chicago area since the late 1960's. He formed his back-up band, *The Hawks*, in 1971 and has been a presence on the Chicago Blues scene ever since.

Discography:
1985 - **Rocking the Blues,** *Double Trouble* // 1994 - **Too Tough,** *Blind Pig* // 1994 - **Born To Win,** *Double Trouble* // 1995 - **Outside Looking In,** *Blind Pig* // 1996 - **Tremoluxe,** *Blind Pig* // 1996 - **Studebaker John & the Hawks,** *Blind Pig* // 1997 - **Time Will Tell,** *Blind Pig.*

Griswald, Roman

Born: 1936 - Arkansas

Blues singer, organ, harmonica player
Originally from Helena, Arkansas, Roman Griswald joined his brother Art in Toledo, Ohio in 1959 to form the Blues group, *The Griswalds.* They recorded a few singles during the 1960's and have been performing and recording steadily ever since.

Discography:
1979 - **All the Way Down,** *JSP* // 1987 - **Two Aces and a Jack,** *Blues Suit* // 1990 - **Full Time Blues,** *Highball* // **The Reel Deal,** *Buckeye.*

The Ground Hogs

Formed: 1963 - England
Disbanded: 1975

Blues / Heavy Metal Rock band
Originally formed in 1963 as a Blues band, *The Groundhogs* failed to achieve any reasonable success until regrouping in 1968, at which time they added harmonica player Steve Rye, who stayed with the band until at least the 1970's.

See - Steve Rye

Discography:
1968 - **Scratching the Surface,** *Liberty* // 1968 - **The Groundhogs with John Lee Hooker and John Mayall,** *Cleve* // 1969 - **Blues Obituary,** *Liberty* // 1970 - **Thank Christ for the Bomb,** *Liberty* // 1971 - **Split,** *Liberty* // 1972 - **Who Will Save the World?,** *United Artists* // 1972 - **Got To Get Enough,** *Turbo* // 1972 - **Hogwash,** *United Artists* // 1974 - **Solid,** *WWA* // 1974 - **Groundhogs Best 1969-1972,** *United Artists* // 1976 - **Crosscut Saw,** *United Artists* // 1976 - **Black Diamond,** *United Artists* // 1984 - **Hoggin' the Stage,** *Psycho* // 1985 - **Razor's Edge,** *Conquest* // 1986 - **Moving Fast, Standing Still,** *Raw Power* // 1987 - **Back Against the Wall,** *Demi-Monde* // 1988 - **Hogs On the Road,** *Demi-Monde* // 1990 - **No Surrender,** *Total* // 1994 - **Groundhog Night,** *Gopaco* // 1996 - **Who Said Cherry Red,** *Indigo* // 1999 - **Hogs in Wolf's Clothing,** *Tranatlantic* // 2000 - **11 Classic Tracks,** *Cleopatra.*

Groven, Sigmund

Born: Heddal, Telemark, Norway

Pop / Classical harmonica player

Sigmund Groven began playing the harmonica at about the age of nine after hearing Tommy Reilly. Groven spent several years working with Reilly and specialized in Classical music. He has performed at Carnegie Hall as well as writing symphonic pieces for a variety of events in his native Norway.

Discography:
1975 - **Sa Spiller Vi Harmonica**, *Polydor* // 1976 - **Music for Two Harmonicas**, (with Tommy Reilly), *Polydor* // 1977 - **Musikk for En Lang Natt**, *Polydor* // 1979 - **Motlys**, *Polydor* // 1981 - **Musikken Inni Oss**, *Polydor* // 1981 - **Kom Sol Pa Alle Mine Berg**, *Sonet* // 1981 - **Laevandes Dikt**, *Viton* // 1983 - **Songar Utan Ord**, *Polydor* // 1985 - **Colour Slides**, *NOPA* // 1986 - **Trollestenen**, *NOPA* // 1988 - **Sigmund Groven**, *Polydor* // 1988 - **Aria**, *Sonet* // 1990 - **Nordisk Natt**, *Sonet* // 1991 - **Nattonsker**, *Sonet* // 1993 - **Siesta**, *NOPA* // 1995 - **Til Telemark**, *Sonet* // 1996 - **I Godt Lag**, *Sonet* // 1999 - **Harmonica Album**, *Grappa* // 2000 - **Innunder Jul**, *Grappa*.

Gruenling, Dennis

Blues harmonica player

A leading proponent of Jump Blues music, Dennis Gruenling is also an expert on Chicago Blues harmonica styles, especially the playing of George "Harmonica" Smith. He tours and performs extensively and has recorded albums of both Jump and Chicago style Blues.

Discography:
1999 - **Jump Time!**, *Backbender* // 2000 - **Up All Night**, *Backbender*.

Gussow, Adam

Born: April 3, 1958 - Congers, NY

Blues harmonica player

After graduating from Princeton in 1979, Adam Gussow worked as a street musician in Paris and Amsterdam. After returning to America, a chance meeting with Blues guitarist Sterling "Mr. Satan" Magee led to their teaming up as the Blues duo, *Satan and Adam*.

Gussow got some early training on the harmonica from Nat Riddles and played harmonica in the road version of the Broadway musical "Big River."

Discography: (see - Satan and Adam)
Bibliography:
1998 - **Mr. Satan's Apprentice**, *Pantheon Books.*

Guthrie, Arlo

Born: July 10, 1947 - Coney Island, NY

Folk singer-songwriter, guitar, harmonica player

Arlo Guthrie is the son of Folk music legend Woody Guthrie and has been a performer in his own right since the mid-1960's. He usually plays the harmonica on a neckbrace. His big hits include; "Alice's Restaurant," "Coming into Los Angeles" and "City of New Orleans."

Discography:
1967 - **Alice's Restaurant**, *Reprise* // 1968 - **Arlo**, *Reprise* // 1969 - **Running Down the Road**, *Reprise* // 1969 - **Alice's Restaurant Soundtrack**, *United Artists* // 1970 - **Washington County**, *United Artists* // 1972 - **Hobo's Lullaby**, *Reprise* // 1973 - **Last of the Brooklyn Cowboys**, *Reprise* // 1974 - **Arlo Guthrie**, *Reprise* // 1975 - **Pete Seeger / Arlo Guthrie: Together in Concert**, *Reprise* // 1976 - **Amigos**, *Reprise* // 1977 - **The Best Of...**, *Warner Brothers* // 1978 - **One Night**, *Warner Brothers* // 1979 - **Outlasting the Blues**, *Warner Brothers* // 1981 - **The Power of Love**, *Warner Brothers* // 1982 - **Precious Friend**, *Reprise* // 1986 - **Some Day**, *Rising Son* // 1991 - **All Over the World**, *Rising Son* // 1992 - **Son of the Wind**, *Rising Son* // 1992 - **Baby's Storytime**, *Lightyear* // 1994 - **More Together Again, Vol. 1 & 2**, *Rising Son* // 1995 - **Alice's Restaurant, Vol. 2: The Massacre**, *Rising Son* // 1996 - **Mystic Journey**, *Rising Son.*

Movies:
1969 - **Alice's Restaurant.**

Guthrie, Woodie

Born: July 14, 1912 - Okemah, OK
Died: October 3, 1967 - Queens, NY

Folk singer-songwriter, guitar, harmonica player

Woody Guthrie is considered by many to be one of the most influential of America's folksingers. Using music as a format for social commentary, he influenced generations of Folk artists, including Bob Dylan.

Woody probably learned to play music from his father, who was also a musician. His first instrument was the harmonica. After years of traveling and performing, he was able to eke out a living as a musician. Over the years he worked with Cisco Houston, Will Geer, Burl Ives, Leadbelly, Sonny Terry, Brownie McGhee, *The Almanac Singers* and others.

His big hits included such standards as; "Deportee," "I Ain't Got No Home," "Rueben James," "This Land is Your Land" and many others.

Discography:
1933 - **The Science of Sound,** *Smithsonian* // 1950's - **Talking Dust Bowl,** *Smithsonian* // 1958 - **Nursery Days,** *Smithsonian* // 1960 - **Sacco and Vanzetti,** *Folkways* // 1961 - **Bound for Glory,** *Folkways* // 1961 - **Dust Bowl Ballads,** *Folkways* // 1962-64 - **Woody Guthrie Sings Folk Songs, Vol. 1 & 2,** *Folkways* // 1964 - **Woody Guthrie,** *Everest* // 1964 - **One of a Kind,** *Pair* // 1965 - **Woody Guthrie,** *Extra* // 1967 - **This Land is Your Land,** *Folkways* // 1969 - **Blind Sonny Terry and Woodie Guthrie,** *Archive of Folk* // 1976 - **Struggle,** *Smithsonian* // 1977 - **Songs From Bound for Glory,** *Warner Brothers* // 1977 - **A Legendary Performer,** *RCA* // 1981 - **Poor Boy,** *Xtra* // 1988 - **The Greatest Songs of Woody Guthrie,** *Vanguard* // 1988 - **The Columbia River Collection,** *Rounder* // 1988 - **Sings Folksongs of Leadbelly,** *Smithsonian* // 1989 - *Folkways: The Original Vision,* *Folkways* // 1989 - **The Library of Congress Recordings,** *Rounder* // 1992 - **Grow Big Songs, Vol. 1-3,** *Warner Brothers* // 1993 - **Songs To Grow On, Vol. 1-3,** *Smithsonian Folkways* // 1994 - **Long Ways To Travel, 1944-1949,** *Smithsonian Folkways* // 1996 - **Folk Hero, Collector's Edition** // **Why Oh Why,** *Smithsonian* // **A Tribute To Woody Guthrie, Part 2,** *Warner Brothers* // **Chain Gangs,** *Stinson* // **Folk Songs,** *Stinson* // **Cowboy Songs,** *Stinson* // **Songs To Grow On for Mother and Child,** *Smithsonian* // **We Ain't Down Yet!,** *Cream.*

Guyger, Steve
Blues harmonica player

Philadelphian Steve Guyger has been playing Blues harmonica since he was seventeen and has been performing regularly with the group, *The Excellos,* since the mid-1970's. Guyger has toured with Jimmy Rogers and has guest-starred on two albums by former Muddy Waters harmonica player Paul Oscher.

Discography:
1997 - **Last Train To Dover,** *Hot Records* // 1998 - **Live at the Dinosaur BBQ,** *Horseplay* // 1999 - **Past Life Blues,** *Severn* // 2000 - **Paul Oscher & Steve Guyger: Living Legends Deep in the Blues,** *Bluesleaf* // **Blues at the 5 Burro Café,** (with Paul Oscher), *Mo-Jo Productions.*

– H –

Hadamick, Bob
Vaudeville harmonica player
Bob Hadamik played the bass harmonica in *The Harmonica Madcaps* during the mid-1930's. The Madcaps also featured Jerry Murad and Al Fiore who would go on to form *The Harmonicats* with Don Les on bass harmonica.

Hager, Jon
Born: August 30, 1946 - Chicago, IL

Country singer, guitar, harmonica player
Jon Hager was half of the Country music singing act, *The Hagers,* with his twin brother Jim. After a stint in the Army they started performing professionally, first in Chicago, then in California.

They were discovered by Buck Owens, who got them signed to Capitol Records. They were regulars on the "Hee-Haw" television show for eighteen years, from 1969 until 1987.

Discography:
1970 - **The Hagers,** *Capitol* // 1970 - **Two Hagers Are Better Than One,** *Capitol* // 1971 - **Motherhood, Apple Pie and the Flag,** *Capitol* // 1972 - **Countryside,** *Barnaby* // 1974 - **The Hagers,** *Elektra.*

Halicki, Harry
Vaudeville harmonica player
During the mid-1930's, Harry Halicki was a member of *The Philharmonicas,* a band formed from students of Borrah Minevitch's Harmonica Institute of America. He also played in *The Philharmonica Trio* during World War Two with Charles and Joe Pitello.

Hall, Jimmy
Rock singer, saxophone, harmonica player

Jimmy Hall was the lead singer, saxophonist and harmonica player for the group, *Wet Willie* from 1970 until 1980. The group had one major hit with the song "Keep On Smiling" on which Hall played the harmonica.

Hall also worked with *The Allman Brothers Band* from 1980 to 1981, *The Nighthawks* from 1985 until 1990 and various other artists throughout his career. He has also recorded some solo albums.

Discography: (also see - Wet Willie, The Nighthawks)
1980 - **Touch You**, *Epic* // 1982 - **Cadillac Tracks**, *Epic* // 1996 - **Rendezvous with The Blues**, *Capricorn*.

Hall, Kenny
Folk / Country mandolin, fiddle, harmonica player

Kenny Hall is considered to be a virtuoso of the mandolin though he also plays several other instruments, including the harmonica. He is the leader of *The Sweets Mill String Band*.

Discography:
Kenny Hall and the Sweets Mill String Band, *Bay* // **Kenny Hall**, *Philo*.

Hall, "Flattop" Tom
Jump Blues singer, harmonica player

"Flattop" Tom Hall got his start in Jump Blues as a dancer during the 1980's. After seeing Paul Butterfield and William Clarke at a Blues festival in 1987, he took up the harmonica, eventually getting some tutelage on the instrument from Clarke. He formed his own band in 1992, *Flattop Tom and his Jump Cats* and they have released three albums to date as well as performing regularly at clubs and festivals.

Discography:
Jumping Blues for Your Dancing Shoes // **Rockin' and Jumpin' the Blues** // 2000 - **Swing Dance Party**, *Palamar*.

Hammond, John Paul
Born: November 13, 1942 - New York City, NY

Folk / Blues singer, guitar, harmonica player

The son of the legendary Columbia Records talent scout, John Hammond, John Paul Hammond learned Delta Blues-styled guitar from records. He concentrated on the works of Robert Johnson and other artists of the 1920's and 30's. He began performing in the early 1960's and signed with the Vanguard label in 1962.

He has been recording and performing steadily ever since with an emphasis on acoustic Blues. He usually plays the harmonica on a neckbrace.

Discography:
1962 - **John Hammond**, *Vanguard* // 1964 - **Big City Blues**, *Vanguard* // 1964 - **Country Blues**, *Vanguard* // 1965 - **So Many Roads**, *Vanguard* // 1967 - **Mirrors**, *Vanguard* // 1967 - **I Can Tell**, *Atlantic* // 1968 - **Sooner or Later**, *Atlantic* // 1969 - **Southern Fried**, *Atlantic* // 1970 - **Source Point**, *Columbia* // 1970 - **The Best Of...**, *Vanguard* // 1971 - **Little Big Man**, (soundtrack), *Columbia* // 1972 - **I'm Satisfied**, *Columbia* // 1973 - **When I Need**, *Columbia* // 1973 - **Triumvirate**, (with Mike Bloomfield and Dr. John), *Columbia* // 1973 - **Spirituals To Swing**, *Vanguard* // 1975 - **Can't Beat the Kid**, *Capricorn* // 1975 - **My Spanish Album**, *Coytronics* // 1976 - **John Hammond Solo**, *Vanguard* // 1978 - **Footwork**, *Vanguard* // 1979 - **Hot Tracks**, *Vanguard* // 1980 - **Milage**, *Sonet* // 1982 - **Frogs for Snakes**, *Rounder* // 1983 - **Hits for the Highway**, *Aim* // 1984 - **Spoonful**, *Edsel* //

1984 - **John Hammond Live in Greece**, *Lyra* // 1988 - **Nobody But You**, *Flying Fish* // 1992 - **Got Love if You Want it**, *Pointblank* // 1992 - **Live**, *Rounder* // 1992 - **Gears / Forever Taurus**, *BGP* // 1993 - **You Can't Judge a Book By It's Cover**, *Vanguard* // 1994 - **Trouble No More**, *Pointblank* // 1996 - **Found True Love**, *Pointblank* // 1998 - **Long as I Have You**, *Virgin* // 2000 - **The Best of the Vanguard Years**, *Vanguard* // **The Search for Robert Johnson**, *Sony* // **John Hammond**, *Rounder*.

Movies:
1971 - **Little Big Man**.

The Harlemonicats

Formed: 1930's - New Orleans, LA

Jazz harmonica trio
The Harlemonicats was a Jazz harmonica trio led by drummer Wilbert Kirk. Kirk used a variety of harmonicas, including diatonics, chromatics and polyphonias.

See - Wilbert Kirk

Harman, James

Born: June 8, 1946 - Anniston, AL

Blues harmonica player

The nephew of Fate Norris, James Harman learned to play the harmonica from his father while growing up in Alabama and was leading Blues bands through the late 1960's. He moved to Los Angeles in 1970, but soon left music due to poor health. He returned to music in the early 1980's and has been playing the harmonica and leading his own band ever since.

Discography:
1981 - **This Band Won't Behave**, *Icepick* // 1983 - **Thank**

You Baby, *Enigma* // 1987 - **Those Dangerous Gentlemens**, *Rhino* // 1988 - **Extra Napkins**, *Rivera* // 1990 - **Strictly Live in 85, Vol. One**, *Rivera* // 1991 - **Do Not Disturb**, *Blacktop* // 1993 - **Two Sides To Every Story**, *Blacktop* // 1994 - **Cards on the Table**, *Blacktop* // 1995 - **Black and White**, *Blacktop* // 1999 - **Takin' Chances**, *Cannonball* // 2000 - **Mo' Na'Kins Please!**, *Cannonball* // **The James Harman Band**, *Blacktop*.

Harmonica Bands

The first big harmonica band was the brainchild of philanthropist Albert Hoxie. Following the first harmonica competition that he sponsored in 1924, Hoxie organized his boys harmonica band in Philadelphia, Pennsylvania. The band was patterned after the marching bands of the day, wore full uniforms and they were featured in parades and concerts.

In 1927, harmonica salesman Borrah Minevitch organized is own harmonica band, *The Harmonica Rascals*, around the comedy antics of Johnny Puleo, a harmonica playing midget. *The Harmonica Rascals* were an instant success in Vaudeville and soon spawned hundreds of imitators, many of which featured harmonica playing midgets.

In order to meet the musical needs of these bands, the M. Hohner Company developed several new harmonicas, including the polyphonia, the chromatic, bass and chord harmonicas.

With the outbreak of World War II, harmonica bands, like their Big Band counterparts, pared down to smaller units, usually trios. The most famous of these was a trio from Chicago, *The Harmonicats*. In 1947, they recorded "Peg O' My Heart" which eventually sold over 25 million copies.

With the growth in popularity of Rock and other modern forms of music, the interest in harmonica bands declined during the 1950's and 60's. There are still a small number of harmonica trios still in existence and many harmonica clubs have been established since the 1960's that provide an opportunity for players to perform in a band setting.

Harmonica Fats

Real name: Harvey Blackston
Born: September 8, 1927 - McDade, LA
Died: January 3, 2000 - Los Angeles, CA

Blues harmonica player
Harmonica Fats got his first harmonica at age three and learned to play from his father while growing up in Louisiana. After moving to California in 1946 he began playing professionally in 1956 and had a minor hit in the early 1960's with "Tore Up." He played as a duet with guitarist Bernie Pearl from 1986 until his death in 2000.

Discography:
1990 - **Live at the Café Lido**, *Pearl Til-Black* // 1991 - **I Had**

To Get Nasty, *Bee Bump* // 1995 - **Two Heads Are Better Than One,** *Bee Bump* // 1996 - **Blow, Fat Daddy, Blow,** *Bee Bump*.

Johnny Puleo's Harmonica Gang

Formed: 1955
Disbanded: 1973

Vaudeville harmonica band

Organized by Johnny Puleo shortly after the death of *Harmonica Rascals* leader Borrah Minevitch in the mid-1950's, *Johnny Puleo's Harmonica Gang* featured the talents of Eddie Gordon, Dom Sgro, Tony Sgro, Al Smith, Dave Doucette, Dave McKelvey, Michael Burton and several others. They made numerous TV appearances, recorded several albums for the Audio Fidelity label and played together until Puleo retired in 1973.

Discography:

1958 - **Johnny Puleo and his Harmonica Gang,** *Audio Fidelity* // 1958 - **Volume Two,** *Audio Fidelity* // 1958 - **Molto Italiano!,** *Audio Fidelity* // 1959 - **Western Songs,** *Audio Fidelity* // 1959 - **Encore Italiano!,** *Audio Fidelity* // 1961 - **Jewish & Israeli Favorites,** *Audio Fidelity* // 1962 - **Great Movie Themes,** *Audio Fidelity* // 1964 - **Volume 7,** *Audio Fidelity*.

The Harmonica Harlequins

Formed: 1934

Vaudeville harmonica band

Carl Freed organized *The Harmonica Harlequins* in 1934 as a competitor to Borrah Minevitch's *Harmonica Rascals*. The group's trademark was that they all wore garish clown outfits. Players in the band included Carl Freed, Sam Scheckter, Mike Chimes, Phil Solomon, Nat Bergman, Milton Freeman, Sid Gould, Joe Mullendore and Leon Lafell.

They worked in Vaudeville, radio and even cut one record. In 1935 all of the players except for Chimes and Gould left to form *The Cappy Barra Harmonica Ensemble*. Freed changed the name to *The Harmonica Lads* and then eventually to *Senor Carlos and his Caballeros*.

The Harmonica Hi-Hats

Formed: 1937 - San Francisco, CA
Disbanded: 1940

Vaudeville harmonica band

The Harmonica Hi-Hats were put together by Vaudevillian Johnny O'Brien from remnants of the group *The Harmonica Kings*. O'Brien was said to be an accomplished performer on the diatonic harmonica and is said to be one of the first to master playing chromatic scales on the instrument.

Players in the group included Dave Doucette, Lenny Schwartz, Alan Pogson, Sam Blanco, Carl Friedman, Eddy Manson and Sid Goodman.

The Harmonica Hotshots
Pop harmonica duo

Made up of the husband-wife team of Al Smith and Judy Simpson-Smith, *The Harmonica Hotshots* have been playing together since the mid-1980's on cruise ships and at harmonica gatherings.

See - Al Smith, Judy Simpson Smith

The Harmonica Kings

Formed: 1937 - New York City, NY

Vaudeville harmonica band

The Harmonica Kings were an attempt by Dave Doucette to put together a harmonica band during the 1930's. Its members included Lenny Schwartz, Alan Pogson, Sam Blanco and Carl Friedman. The group moved to San Francisco, where all of the members were incorporated into Johnny O'Brien's *Harmonica Hi-Hats*.

The Harmonica Lads

Formed: 1935

Vaudeville harmonica band

The Harmonica Lads was formed from the remnants of Carl Freed's *Harmonica Harlequins*. Players in the group included Carl Freed, Mike Chimes, Sid Gould and Saul Webber.

Chimes and Gould left the band in 1940 and they were replaced by Byron Bouchard and Pete Blasberg. In 1941 the group went to Mexico to perform. Upon returning they billed themselves as *Senor Carlos and his Caballeros*. The group dissolved shortly after the outbreak of World War Two.

The Harmonica Madcaps

Formed: 1937 - Chicago, IL

Vaudeville harmonica band

The Harmonica Madcaps was a small harmonica band put together from members of the Walla Walla Harmonica Club from Crane Tech High School in Chicago. Its members included Jerry Murad, Pete Pedersen, Harry Halicki and Al Fiore.

The nucleus of the group, Fiore and Murad, would eventually become *The Harmonicats,* with Pedersen writing most of the arrangements. The group disbanded when Jerry Murad and Pete Pedersen joined Borrah Minevitch's *Harmonica Rascals.*

The Harmonica Rascals

Formed: 1927 - New York City, NY
Disbanded: 1955

Vaudeville harmonica band

The Harmonica Rascals was the first and most popular of the Vaudeville harmonica bands. Formed in 1927 after harmonica salesman Borrah Minevitch met fourteen year old Johnny Puleo, *The Harmonica Rascals* blended slapstick comedy with a large harmonica band sound. Minevitch built his band's image around a newsboy/ragmuffin motif with Puleo, a harmonica player midget, as the core of the act. Minevitch had him play the polyphonia, the largest harmonica available at the time, simply because it looked funny.

The group went on to become one of Vaudeville's biggest attractions, grossing over $3,000 per week, although the players, most of them teenagers, were paid only a pittance for their work. The group became so popular that Minevitch was able to operate three different *Harmonica Rascals* groups: west coast, midwest and east coast, each with their own harmonica playing midget. They also appeared in several movies during the 1930's and 40's.

During the many decades that the group was together it featured hundreds of players, including: Borrah Minevitch, Johnny Puleo, Leo Diamond, Mike Chimes, Pete Pedersen, Ray Tankersley, Jerry Murad, Ernie Morris, Don Les, Carl Ford, Sammy Ross, Abe Diamond, Irvin Crane, Hal Leighton, Hugh McCaskey, Fuzzy Feldman, Alex Novelle, Eddy Manson, Leo Friedman, Richard Bain, Bill Walden, Dave Doucette, Richard Hayman, George Fields, Lou Delin, George Ross, Don Henry, Al Furbish and many others, most of whom went on to successful careers in music.

The Harmonica Rascals remained under the control of Borrah Minevitch until his death in 1955. The name was taken over by Paul Baron, who started his own *Harmonica Rascals* band and by Borrah's daughter, Lydia Minevitch, whose version of the band lasted only a short time.

Discography:
1997 - **Peg O' My Heart,** *Simitar.*

Movies:
1928 - **The Patriot** // 1934 - **Lazy Bones** // 1935 - **Dreamland** // 1936 - **One in a Million** // 1937 - **Love Under Fire** // 1938 - **Rascals** // 1941 - **Always in My Heart** // 1941 - **Rhythm and Romance** // 1942 - **Tramp, Tramp, Tramp** // 1942 - **Borrah Minevitch Harmonica School** // 1943 - **Top Man.**

The Harmonica Scamps

Formed: Early 1930's

Vaudeville harmonica band

The Harmonica Scamps was a Vaudeville harmonica band patterned after *The Harmonica Rascals* except that it featured a black midget. Players included Murray Lane, Alan "Blackie" Schackner, Nat Bergman and Stan Harper.

Harmonica Slim

Real name: Travis L. Blaylock
Born: December 21, 1934 - Douglassville, TX

Blues harmonica player

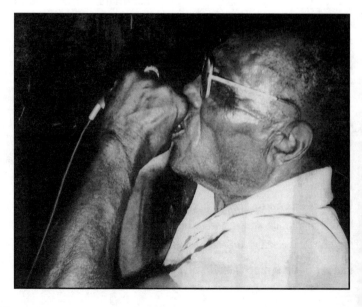

Harmonica Slim started playing the harmonica at age twelve and was performing professionally by the late 1940's. While he worked mostly in Texas, he managed to play with Lowell Fulson, Percy Mayfield, T-Bone Walker and others. He began recording in the mid-1950's for the Aladdin label and remained fairly active after that.

Discography:
1995 - **Black Bottom Blues**, *Trix* // 1997 - **Give Me My Shotgun**, *Fedora* // 2000 - **Cold Tacos and Warm Beer**, *Fedora*.

The Harmonica Solidaires

Formed: Early 1940's

Vaudeville harmonica band
The Harmonica Solidaires were organized by the Diamond brothers, Leo and Abe, during the early 1940's and also included the talents of Richard Hayman and George Fields.

The Harmonicats

Formed: mid-1940's - Chicago, IL

Pop / Vaudeville harmonica band

The Harmonicats were formed around 1944 from the remnants of *The Quintones* and featured Jerry Murad on lead chromatic, Al Fiore on chord and Don Les on bass harmonica.

After a couple of years of playing in lounges and nightclubs, the group recorded "Peg O' My Heart" as a demo. The song went on to become the number one record of 1947 and ultimately sold over 25 million copies. Though they were never able to recapture the enormous success of their first hit, *The Harmonicats* did enjoy enormous popularity and went on to record over 30 albums.

Don Les left the group to form his own *Harmonicats* band in 1972 and was replaced by Dick Gardner on bass harmonica. Al Fiore retired from music in 1982 and was replaced by Bob Bauer on the chord harmonica. Over the years, several outstanding players also sat in with *The Harmonicats*, including Pete Pedersen, Bud

Boblink, Leon Lafell, George Miklas, Danny Wilson, Al Data and several others.

The Harmonicats career came to an end when Jerry Murad passed away in 1996.

Discography:
1987 - **Fascinatin'**, *Sony* // 1990 - **The Harmonicats Greatest Hits**, *Columbia* // 1997 - **The Original RKO & Unique Masters**, *Varese* // **Cherry Pink and Apple Blossom White**, *Columbia* // **Peg O' My Heart**, *Columbia* // **Senimental Serenade**, *Columbia* // **Fiesta**, *Columbia* // **Forgotten Dreams**, *Columbia* // **Try a Little Tenderness**, *Columbia* // **The Love Songs of Tom Jones**, *Columbia* // **Harmonica Rhapsody**, *Columbia* // **Harmonicats' Selected Favorites**, *Mercury* // **South American Nights**, *Mercury* // **Command Performance**, *Mercury* // **The Cat's Meow**, *Mercury* // **In the Land of Hi-fi**, *Mercury* // **Hamonicha-cha-cha**, *Mercury* // **Selected Favorites**, *Mercury* // **Cats Around the Horn**, *Mercury* // **Dolls, Dolls, Dolls**, *Mercury* // **El Cid, Moon River & Other Movie Music**, *Columbia* // **That New Gang of Mine**, *Columbia* // **What's New Harmonicats?**, *Columbia*.

The Harmonicuties

Formed: 1930's

Vaudeville harmonica band
An all-girl version of *The Harmonica Rascals*, *The Harmonicuties* was a Vaudeville harmonica band of the 1930's that even featured its own harmonica playing female midget.

Harp
A nickname for the harmonica, "Harp" is usually used to describe a Blues-styled harmonica.

Harper, Stan

Born: September 2, 1921

Vaudeville / Classical harmonica soloist
Stan Harper started playing the harmonica as a ten year old and quickly graduated up to the chromatic. He played briefly in the 1930's with Murray Lane's *Harmonica Scamps*.

During World War Two he performed with fellow harmonica player Eddie Shu, entertaining the troops. After the war he returned to Vaudeville, where he put together a group called *The Three Harpers* with Pro Robbins and Pete Delisante.

During the 1950's he became a solo performer and studio musician and concentrated on a Classical / Baroque repertoire. He continues to do concerts and cruise ships to this day.

Discography:
Stan Harper Plays the Great Novellettes // **Stan Harper Plays Fritz Kreisler** // **Stan Harper Live On**

Harpo, Slim

Real name: James Moore
Born: January 11, 1924 - Baton Rouge, LA
Died: January 31, 1970

Blues harmonica player

Slim Harpo learned to play guitar and harmonica while working on the docks in New Orleans. By the early 1940's he was playing in local clubs. He started recording in the mid-1950's and had a string of hits with "I'm a King Bee," "Rainin' in My Heart," "Scratch My Back" and many others, many of which have been covered by white Blues rockers.

His success led him to play as a favorite of the psychedelic concert circuit during the late 1960's. He remained popular until his death from a heart attack in 1970.

Discography:
1961 - **I'm a King Bee,** *Flyright* // 1961 - **Rainin' in My Heart,** *Excello* // 1965 - **A Long Drink of the Blues,** *Stateside* // 1966 - **Baby, Scratch My Back,** *Excello* // 1968 - **Tip On In,** *Ace* // 1969 - **The Best Of...,** *Excello* // 1970 - **He Knew the Blues,** *Excello* // 1971 - **Trigger Finger,** *Blue Horizon* // 1976 - **Blues Hangover,** *Flyright* // 1980 - **Got Love If You Want It,** *Flyright* // 1986 - **Shake Your Hips,** *Flyright* // 1989 - **The Best Of...,** *Rhino* // 1989 - **I'm a King Bee,** *Flyright* // 1994 - **Hip Shakin',** *Excello* // 1996 - **The Scratch: Rare and Unissued,** *Excello* // 1997 - **The Best of Slim Harpo,** *Hip-O* // 1997 - **Sting It Then!, Live,** *Excello/Ace*.

Harris, Don "Sugarcane"

Born: June 18, 1938 - Pasadena, CA
Died: December 1, 1999 - Los Angeles, CA

R&B violin, guitar, piano, harmonica player

Best known as a multi-instrumentalist who worked in a number of different musical styles, Don "Sugarcane" Harris often cited harmonica players Jimmy Reed and Little Walter as being very influential to his musical development.

After teaming up with vocalist Dewey Terry in the 1950's, Harris worked with a number of popular artists including Johnny Otis, Little Richard, Frank Zappa, Jean-Luc Ponty and John Mayall, as well as working with the group *Pure Food and Drug Act.*

Discography:
1960 - **Don and Dewey,** *Specialty* // 1970 - **Fiddler on the Rock,** *Polydor* // 1970 - **Sugarcane,** *Epic* // 1970 - **Don "Sugarcane" Harris,** *Epic* // 1970 - **USA Union,** (with John Mayall) // 1971 - **Fiddler on the Rock,** *Musicdisc* // 1971 - **New Violin Summit,** *Metronome* // 1972 - **Choice Cuts,** (with Pure Food and Drug Act), *Epic* // 1973 - **Cup Full of Dreams,** *Epic* // 1973 - **Sugarcane's Got the Blues,** *BASF* // 1973 - **Key Stop,** *BASF* // 1974 - **Cupful of Dreams,** *BASF* // // 1974 - **They're Rockin' Till Midnight,** *Specialty* // 1985 - **Midnight DJ** // **Keep On Driving,** *Musicdisc* // **Got the Blues,** *Polydor.*

Harris, "Shakey" Jake

Born: April 12, 1921 - Earle, AR
Died: March 2, 1990 - Pine Bluff, AR

Blues harmonica player

After learning how to play the harmonica from John Lee "Sonny Boy" Williamson, "Shakey" Jake Harris began playing professionally in the late 1940's in Chicago. During his career he worked with Little Walter, Magic Sam, Muddy Waters, John Mayall, Sunnyland Slim and others. He got his nickname from his favorite pastime of playing dice.

Discography:
1960 - **Good Times,** *Bluesville* // 1961 - **Mouth Harp Blues,** *Bluesville* // 1969 - **Further Up the Road,** *Sequel* // 1972 - **The Devil's Harmonica,** *Polydor* // 1980 - **Magic Rocker** // 1983 - **Magic Touch** // 1985 - **The Key Won't Fit,** *Murray Brothers.*

Hastings, Peter
Folk guitar, harmonica player

Peter Hastings plays guitar and harmonica with *No Strings Attached,* a Folk string band that incorporated Jazz and World music into it's sound. Hastings plays both diatonic and chromatic harmonicas and has studied with Howard Levy.

Discography: (see - No Strings Attached)

Hatch, Provine

Also known as: Little Hatch
Born: October 21, 1921 - Sledge, MS

Blues singer, harmonica player

Blues harmonica player and singer Provine Hatch began playing the instrument when he was a child and was working professionally by his early teens. He moved to Kansas City in 1946 and formed his own band in 1962. Hatch recorded on his own Little Hatchet label in 1970. He is still active, recording an album in 1998.

Discography:
1974 - **The Little Hatchet Band,** *M&M* // 1993 - **Well, All Right!,** *Modern Blues* // 1998 - **Goin' Back,** *Analogue Productions.*

Hatcher, Sam "Dynamite"

Country singer, guitar, harmonica player

Sam Hatcher played harmonica in Roy Acuff's band during the 1930's.

Hayman, Richard

Born: March 27, 1920 - Cambridge, MA

Pop / Vaudeville harmonica player

Richard Hayman taught himself how to play the harmonica and joined *The Harmonica Rascals* after he finished high school in 1938. Two years later, when the Diamond brothers left the group, he took over as the main arranger for the band. Hayman left *The Harmonica Rascals* in 1940 to join the Diamond brothers in forming *The Harmonica Solidaires.*

During the 1940's he worked as a composer and arranger in Hollywood where he worked on such musicals as "Girl Crazy," "As Thousands Cheer," "Meet Me in St. Louis" and others. In 1952 he scored a huge hit with the record of the theme from the movie "Ruby Gentry."

Hayman served as the musical director for Mercury Records from 1953 to 1965 and also worked as an arranger for *The Boston Pops Orchestra* from the 1950's through the 1980's.

During the 1950's he also worked on various harmonica projects including *Richard Hayman's Harmonica Orchestra* (with Charles Leighton, Blackie Schackner, Eddy Manson and others), *The Harmonica Sparklers* and several projects with Jerry Murad of *The Harmonicats.* In 1978 he composed the "Concerto for Harmonica and Orchestra."

Hayman has worked as the musical director for numerous musical superstars, including Tom Jones, Engelbert Humperdinck, Cannonball Adderley, *The Carpenters, The Osmonds,* Roy Clark, Pat Boone, Bobby Vinton and others.

Discography:
1950's - **Reminiscing,** *Mercury* // 1950's - **My Fair Lady,** *Mercury* // 1950's - **Two Tickets To Paris** // 1950's - **Around the Campfire,** *Mercury* // 1950's - **Harmonica Holiday** // 1950's - **Love is a Many Splendored Thing,** *Mercury* // 1950's - **Only Memories,** *Mercury* // 1950's - **Let's Get Together,** *Mercury* // 1957 - **Two Tickets To Rome** // 1957 - **Havana in Hi-Fi,** *Mercury* // 1958 - **Great Motion Picture Themes of Victor Young,** *Mercury* // 1959 - **Caramba!** // 1960 - **Come with Me To Faraway Places,** *Mercury* // 1960 - **The Sound of Music** // 1960 - **Serenade for Love** // 1960 - **Pop Concert in Sound,** *Mercury* // 1961 - **Tender Moments,** *Bainbridge* // 1963 - **Era of Cleopatra** // 1964 - **Gypsy** // 1964 - **Hits of the 40's** // 1964 - **Songs of Wonderful Girls** // 1964 - **Richard Hayman** // 1996 - **Stepping Out Classics II,** *Victor Red Seal* // **Harlem Nocturne and Other Hits,** *Kem-disc* // **Voodoo!,** *Mercury* // **Cinematic,** *Command* // **Genuine Electric Latin Love Machine,** *Command* // **Italy - The Pride and the Passion,** *Bainbridge* // **Harlem Nocturne and Other Hits,** *KEM.*

Movies:
1943 - **Girl Crazy** // 1944 - **Meet Me in St. Louis** // 1945 - **State Fair.**

Hazell, Patrick

Born: September 23, 1945 - Burlington, IA

Blues singer, piano, drums, harmonica player

Based out of Washington, Iowa, Patrick Hazell has been playing the harmonica since he was nineteen years old. He began playing music professionally in 1960 and was playing in full Blues bands by 1969. He started working as a one-man band in 1983, where he played the harmonica on a neckbrace and has released several albums since then.

Discography:
1978 - **Harvest Dance,** *Blue Rhythm* // 1979 - **Back Country Shuffle,** *Blue Rhythm* // 1980 - **Patrick Hazell,** *Blue Rhythm* // 1980 - **After Hours,** *Blue Rhythm* // 1982 - **Christmas Visions,** *Blue Rhythm* // 1985 - **Studio Solos,** *Blue Rhythm* // 1986 - **The New Cool,** *Blue Rhythm* // 1986 - **Solo Improvisations,** *Blue Rhythm* // 1987 - **Patrick Hazell - Live!,** *Blue Rhythm* // 1988 - **East of Midnight,** *Blue Rhythm* // 1988 - **Nemos' Island,** *Blue Rhythm* // 1989 - **Mystery Winds,** *Blue Rhythm* // 1990 - **Tuba-Piano Jam Session,** *Blue Rhythm* // 1996 - **Blues on the Run,** *Blue Rhythm* // 1996 - **Patrick Hazell and the Mother Blues Band,** *Blue Rhythm* // 1996 - **In the Prairieland,** *Blue Rhythm* // 1996 - **Dream Catcher,** *Blue Rhythm* // 1997 - **Sound Tracks,** *Blue Rhythm* // 1997 - **Blue Blood,** *Blue Rhythm.*

He, Jia-Yi

Born: 1953 - Beijing, China

Classical harmonica soloist
Jia-Yi He began playing the harmonica in 1964 and studied with Cham-Ber Huang starting in 1981. He took top prizes in several harmonica competitions during the 1980's and 90's and has since served as a juror for several of these events. He appears regularly with orchestras in Asia as well as developing new harmonica designs and teaching.

Discography:
2000 - **Rhapsody in Blue,** *Harmonica.*

Heart's Horn
A nickname for the harmonica.

Helm, Levon

Born: May 26, 1942 - Arkansas

Folk/Rock singer, drums, mandolin, harmonica player
Levon Helm plays the harmonica as well as drums, mandolin and singing for the Folk / Rock group, *The Band.*

Discography: (also see - The Band)
1977 - **Levon Helm and the RCO All-Stars,** *Mobile Fidelity* // 1978 - **Levon Helm,** *Mobile Fidelity* // 1980 - **American Son,** *MCA* // 1982 - **Levon Helm,** *Capitol* // 1999 - **Ties That Bind: The Best Of...,** *Raven* // 2000 - **Souvenir, Vol. 1,** *Breeze Hill.*

Henderson, Mike

Born: January 16, 1954

Country multi-instrumentalist, including harmonica
Mike Henderson began playing the harmonica at age five and later added the guitar, fiddle and mandolin to the instruments that he could play. When he moved to Nashville in the mid-1980's, he became a session musician and has recorded with Randy Travis, John Hiatt, Delbert McClinton, Emmylou Harris and many more.

Discography:
1994 - **Country Music Made Me Do It,** *RCA* // 1996 - **Edge of Night,** *Dead Reckoning* // 1996 - **First Blood,** *Dead Reckoning* // 1998 - **Oakland Blues,** *Dead Reckoning* // 1999 - **Thicker Than Water,** *Dead Reckoning.*

Henley, John Lee

Also known as: John Lee
Born: February 13, 1919 -Canton, MS

Blues harmonica player
John Lee Henley taught himself how to play the harmonica as a child in Mississippi and as a teenager he worked at local parties and dances. He moved to Chicago in 1943.

Soon after arriving in Chicago he started spending time with John Lee "Sonny Boy" Williamson, who taught him about harmonica technique. He began sitting in with *The Muddy Waters Band* in 1945 as well as working with Big Boy Spires, Carl Martin, Buddy Cobbs, Big Joe Williams, Honeyboy Edwards and others.

Discography:
1982 - **World of Trouble.**

Henry, Don

Real name: Dominic Quagenti
Died: February 5, 1995 - New York City, NY

Vaudeville harmonica player
Don Henry started his career as the bass harmonica player in the secret harmonica band that Johnny Puleo formed during his 1942 departure from *The Harmonica Rascals*. During the 1950's he put together *The Don Henry Trio* with Pete Pedersen on chromatic and Fuzzy Feldman on the chord harmonica. They worked together for about three years and had a minor hit with their recording of "The Saber Dance."

Herman's Hermits

Formed: 1963 - Manchester, England
Disbanded: 1971

British Pop band
As one of the top groups in the British Invasion of the early 1960's, Herman's Hermits had eleven top ten hits, including: "I'm Henry the Eighth," "I'm Into Something Good," "Mrs. Brown You've Got a Lovely Daughter" and others. Bass guitarist Karl Green also played the harmonica.

See - Karl Green

Discography:
1965 - **The Best Of...**, *MGM* // 1966 - **The Best Of..., Vol. 2**, *MGM* // 1968 - **The Best Of..., Vol. 3**, *MGM* // 1973 - **Their Greatest Hits**, *ABKCO.*

Hicks, Dan

Born: December 9, 1941 - Little Rock, AR

Jazz singer, guitar, harmonica player
Dan Hicks emerged from the San Francisco music scene of the late 1960's as an acoustic guitar-driven bandleader of great repute. His bands, *Dan Hicks and his Hot Licks* from 1968 to 1974 and *Dan Hicks and his Acoustic Warriors,* formed in the mid-1980's, have always been on the cutting edge of acoustic music. In addition to guitar and vocals, Hicks occasionally plays the harmonica.

Discography:
1969 - **Original Recordings,** *Epic* // 1971 - **Where's the Money?,** *Blue Thumb* // 1972 - **Strikin' It Rich,** *Blue Thumb* // 1973 - **Last Train To Hicksville,** *Blue Thumb* // 1975 - **Hey Good Lookin',** *Warner Brothers* // 1978 - **It Happened One Bite,** *Warner Brothers* // 1986 - **Rich & Happy in Hicksville,** *See for Miles* // 1988 - **Mistletoe Jam,** *Relix* // 1991 - **The Very Best Of...,** *Blue Thumb* // 1991 - **Dan Hicks and his Hot Licks,** *Columbia* // 1994 - **Shootin' Straight,** *On the Spot* // 1994 - **Lost in the Eighties,** *Blue Thumb* // 1994 - **At the Boardinghouse - 1971,** *Blue Thumb* // 1994 - **Paramount Theatre 1990,** *Blue Thumb* // 1997 - **Return To Hicksville: The Best Of...,** *Hip-O* // 1998 - **Early Years,** *Big Beat* // 2000 - **Beatin' the Heat,** *Hollywood* // **Moody Richard,** *MCA.*

Hill, Blind Joe

Born:1941 - Pennsylvania
Died: November 17, 1999 - Los Angeles, CA

Blues singer, drums, guitar, harmonica player
"Blind" Joe Hill was a one-man Blues band who played in the style of Joe Hill Louis, playing drums guitar and harmonica simultaneously.

Discography:
1978 - **Boogie in the Dark,** *Barrelhouse.*

Hill, King Solomon - (see Joe Holmes)

The Hillsiders

Formed: 1964 - England

English Country-Western band
Originally formed as *The Country Three* in 1959, *The Hillsiders* were one of England's top Country music bands well into the 1980's. Brian Hilton joined the band in 1964 as the lead guitar and harmonica player. In addition to their own material, they recorded albums with Bobby Bare, George Hamilton IV and Kenny Johnson.

See - Brian Hilton

Discography:
1960's - **The Hillsiders Play the Country Hits** // 1965 - **It Takes a Lot of Money,** *Lucky UK* // 1965 - **The English Countryside,** *RCA* // 1968 - **The Leaving of Liverpool,** *RCA* // 1970 - **Heritage,** *RCA* // 1972 - **By Request,** *Polydor* // 1973 - **Our Country,** *Polydor* // 1975 - **To Please You,** *Stile UK* // 1978 - **On the Road,** *LP UK* // 1984 - **Only One**

You, *Suitcase* // 1986 - **If That's the Way You Feel**, *Suitcase* // 1988 - **15-25**, *Suitcase*.

Hilton, Brian

Country singer, guitar, harmonica player

Brian Hilton played lead guitar and harmonica for the British Country music group, *The Hillsiders*, from 1964 until the mid-1980's.

Discography: (see - The Hillsiders)

Hinds, Mervyn "Harmonica"

Born: Trinidad

Blues guitar, harmonica player

Mervyn "Harmonica" Hinds has been a regular fixture on the Chicago Blues scene for since the mid-1970's, working with Koko Taylor, John Primer and others.

Hinton, Sam

Born: March 21, 1917 - Tulsa, OK

Folk singer, harmonica player

Sam Hinton specializes in playing traditional music on the harmonica and has been performing as a folklorist since 1936. He began playing the harmonica at age five while growing up in Texas. He made his first recordings in the late 1940's.

One of his specialties was to play the harmonica without a neckbrace while playing the guitar, simply placing the harmonica into his mouth and using his tongue to block out the notes he wanted.

Discography:

1947 - **Buffalo Boy and the Barnyard Song**, *Library of Congress* // 1950 - **Old Man Atom**, *Columbia* // 1952 - **Folk Songs of California** // 1955 - **Singing Across the Land**, *Decca* // 1956 - **A Family Tree of Folk Songs**, *Decca* // 1957 - **The Real McCoy**, *Decca* // 1961 - **Whoever Shall Have Some Peanuts**, *Folkways* // 1967 - **The Wandering Folk Song**, *Folkways* // 1972 - **I'll Sing You a Story**, *Folkways* // 1999 - **Library of Congress Recordings**, *Bear Family* // **I'll Sing a Song**, *Folkways* // **Sam Hinton Sings the Songs of Man**, *Folkways*.

Hite, Bob "The Bear"

Born: February 26, 1943 - Torrance, CA
Died: April 5, 1981 - Venice, CA

Blues singer, guitar, harmonica player

A collector and historian of pre-war Blues, Bob Hite co-founded the band *Canned Heat* in 1966 with fellow Blues enthusiast Al Wilson. He was nicknamed "The Bear" because of his height and weight, (over 6 feet tall and 300 pounds). He died of an apparent heart attack in 1981.

Discography: (see - Canned Heat)

Hogan, Silas

Born: September 15, 1911 - Westover, LA
Died: January 9, 1994 - Scotlandville, LA

Blues guitar, harmonica player

Silas Hogan learned to play Blues guitar and harmonica in his teens from his uncles and was playing at local parties during the 1930's. Though he played with bands in and around the Baton Rouge area starting in the mid-1930's, he didn't make his first recordings until the late 1950's. His career was sporadic, but he managed to make a few records before his death in 1994.

Discography:

1961-65 - **I'm a Free Hearted Man**, *Flyright* // 1972 - **Trouble At Home**, *Blue Horizon* // 1972 - **Trouble**, *Excello* // 1989 - **The Godfather**, *Blues Southwest* // 1995 - **So Long Blues**, *Ace* // 1995 - **Trouble, The Best of The Excello Masters**, *AVI-Excello* // 1999 - **Silas Hogan, The Godfather: Louisiana Swamp Blues, Vol. 6**, *Wolf* // **Louisiana Blues**, *Arhoolie*.

Hohner, Matthias

Born: December 13, 1833 - Germany
Died: December 11, 1902 - Germany

Harmonica manufacturer

Like many of the early harmonica makers, Matthias Hohner began his career as a clockmaker. While visiting the harmonica factory of Messner and Weiss, he learned how to make harmonicas. He was soon producing the instruments in his kitchen with the help of his family and 1 or 2 workmen. During his first year, 1857, he was able to produce about 650 harmonicas.

In 1862, at the request of some relatives who had previously immigrated to America, Hohner started exporting harmonicas to the U.S. The market seemed almost limitless and Hohner became the first of the German harmonica makers to incorporate mass production techniques to building harmonicas. By 1887, the M. Hohner Company was producing over a million harmonicas a year.

Matthias Hohner retired from business in 1900, passing control of his company to his five sons. He passed away two years later.

M. Hohner, Inc.

Founded: 1857

Harmonica manufacturer

M. Hohner, Inc. was founded in 1857 by Matthias Hohner, a clockmaker from Trossingen, Germany. M. Hohner managed to outsell its competitors by introducing mass production to the making of harmonicas. In 1878 they perfected machinery that could stamp out the metal reeds of the instrument. Previously, each reed had to be hand-fabricated.

In 1896 they introduced the Marine Band model harmonica, which would become the biggest selling musical instrument in the world and the standard by which all future diatonic harmonica designs would be judged.

During the 1920's Hohner introduced chromatic harmonicas, the polyphonia, chord and bass models to its line in order to meet the musical needs of harmonica bands. By 1930 Hohner was producing over 28 million harmonicas a year.

World War Two and the decline in popularity of harmonica bands caused lean times for the company in the 1940's and early 50's, but the resurgence of Blues, the Folk music revival of the 1960's and the growth in interest in the instrument by Rock players has helped M. Hohner, Inc. to maintain an annual sales level of around two million instruments a year.

Holmes, Joe

Also known as: King Solomon Hill
Born: 1897 - McComb, MS
Died: 1949 - Sibley, MS

Blues guitar, harmonica player

Joe Holmes learned to play Blues guitar and harmonica as a child. He worked with Ramblin' Thomas and Blind Lemon Jefferson during the late 1920's. He made some recordings for the Paramount label in 1932 and spent the rest of his life traveling around the south as a hobo.

Discography:

Blues from the Western States, 1929-49, *Yazoo* // **Giants of Country Blues, 1927-32,** *Wolf,* // **Greatest Country Blues** // **Mississippi Masters, 1927-35** // **Backwoods Blues,** *Document.*

Holmes, Floyd "Salty"

Born: March 6, 1909 - Glasgow, KY
Died: January 1, 1970

Country jug, guitar, harmonica player

Salty Holmes specialized in "talking" harmonica pieces where he would use vocal tones while playing the harmonica. He played with *The Prairie Ramblers* during the 1930's and also worked with his wife as *Salty and Maddie* with the Grand Old Opry.

Discography: (also see - The Prairie Ramblers)
Harmonica Masters, *Yazoo.*

Movies:
1936 - **Banjo On My Knee** // 1937 - **Arizona Days.**

Holt, David

Born: October 15, 1946 - Gatesville, TX

Country singer-songwriter, banjo, harmonica player

Best known for his banjo playing and storytelling, David Holt learned how to play the harmonica when he was a teenager from old-time cowboy singer Carl T. Sprague. Holt has been the host of the "Fire on the Mountain" and "The American Music Shop" television shows as well as touring and recording on a regular basis.

Discography:

1986 - **Reel & Rock,** *Flying Fish* // 1994 - **I Got a Bullfrog: Folksongs for the Fun of It,** *High Windy* // **Tailybone & Other Strange Stories,** *High Windy* // **Doodle Daddle Day: Old Time Sing-Alongs,** *High Windy* // **Hairyman - Southern Folktales,** *High Windy* // **Grandfather's Greatest Hits,** *High Windy.*

Homesick James

Real name: John Williamson
Born: April 30, 1910 - Somerville, TN

Blues singer, guitar, bass, harmonica player

A cousin of Blues guitarist Elmore James, Homesick James taught himself how to play guitar when he was ten years old. He promptly ran away from home and during the 1920's he worked with Blind Boy Fuller, Sleepy John Estes and Frank Stokes. He settled in Chicago around 1930.

He began making recordings in 1937 and over the next sixty years he played and recorded with Big Joe Williams, John Lee "Sonny Boy" Williamson, Baby Face Leroy, Big Bill Broonzy, Roosevelt Sykes, Snooky Pryor and of course his cousin, Elmore James, who died in Homesick's apartment in 1963. He is still active in the Blues scene.

Discography:

1964 - **Blues from the Southside,** *Prestige* // 1970's -

Chicago Blues Festival, *Black & Blue* // 1972 - **The Country Blues,** *Blues On Blues* // 1973 - **Homesick James and Snooky Pryor,** *Wolf* // 1973 - **Ain't Sick No More** // 1973 - **Shake Your Money Maker,** *Krazy Kat* // 1976 - **Home Sweet Homesick James,** *Big Bear* // 1977 - **Goin' Back Home,** *Trix* // 1992 - **Sweet Home Tennessee,** *Appaloosa* // 1994 - **Goin' Back To the Times,** *Earwig* // 1995 - **Got To Move,** *Trix* // 1997 - **Words of Wisdom,** *Icehouse* // 1997 - **Juanita,** *Evidence* // 1998 - **Last of the Broomdusters,** *Fedora* // 1998 - **Chicago Slide Guitar Legend,** *Official.*

Hooker, Earl

Born: January 15, 1930 - Clarksdale, MS
Died: April 21, 1970 - Chicago, IL

Blues guitar, piano, harmonica player

A cousin of Blues legend John Lee Hooker, Earl Hooker taught himself how to play guitar at age ten and began attending Chicago's Lyon and Healy School of Music in 1941. He occasionally worked the streets of Chicago for tips with Bo Diddley.

During the mid-1940's he took guitar lessons from Robert Nighthawk, toured with Ike Turner and appeared on the "King Biscuit Time" radio program with Sonny Boy Williamson II. He began making records in 1952. Over the next two decades he would perform and record prolifically and even appeared with *The Beatles* on the "Ready, Steady, Go" television program. He died of tuberculosis in 1970.

Discography:

1966 - **Two Bugs and a Roach,** *Arhoolie* // 1969 - **The Genius of Earl Hooker,** *Cucu* // 1969 - **Don't Have To Worry,** *Bluesway* // 1970 - **Sweet Black Angel,** *One Way* // 1972 - **Funk Last of the Great Earl Hooker,** *Blues On Blues* // 1972 - **There's a Fungus Amung Us,** *Red Lightnin'* // 1973 - **Do You Remember the Great Earl Hooker,** *Bluesway* // 1975 - **Hooker N' Steve,** *Arhoolie* // 1978 - **Leading Brand,** *Red Lightnin'* // 1981 - **Blue Guitar,** *P-Vine* // 1985 - **Play Your Guitar Mr. Hooker!,** *Blacktop* // 1986 - **His First and Last Recordings,** *Arhoolie* // 1986 - **Calling All Blues,** *Charly* // 1998 - **Smooth Slidin,** *CLP* // 1998 - **Moon is Rising,** *Arhoolie* // 1999 - **Simply the Best: Earl Hooker Collection,** *MCA.*

Hoover, Clint

Jazz harmonica player

Clint Hoover began playing the harmonica at the age of seventeen, switching to the chromatic after joining his first band. He's studied with Robert Bonfiglio and has recorded with Peter Mayer, *The Rim Rock Ramblers,* Pat Shelby and others.

Discography:

1999 - **Dream of the Serpent Dog,** *Hoover* // 2000 - **Take Your Time Mr. Brown,** (with The Sugar Kings), *Hoover.*

Horton, Walter

Also known as: Mumbles, Big Walter, Shakey
Born: April 6, 1917 - Horn Lake, MS
Died: December 8, 1981 - Chicago, IL

Blues harmonica player

Walter Horton got his first harmonica from his father when he was five years old. By the time he was nine he was taking lessons from Will Shade and allegedly recording with *The Memphis Jug Band.* By the end of the 1930's he had worked with Buddy Doyle, Big Joe Williams and Floyd Jones.

He gave up music due to poor health in 1940 and worked at odd jobs for the next few years. He reappeared in Chicago in 1948, playing at the local Blues clubs and by 1950 was back in Memphis where he started to make records for the Sun label in 1952.

In 1952 he took over as the harmonica player for *The Muddy Waters Band*, replacing Junior Wells and in 1953 he had his first big hit with "Easy." He spent the rest of the 50's, 60's and 70's recording solo and working as a sideman for Muddy Waters, Willie Dixon, Otis Rush, JB Hutto and others. He had a cameo appearance in the movie "The Blues Brothers" just before he died in 1981.

Discography:
1951 - **Mouth Harp Maestro,** *Virgin* // 1964 - **The Soul of Blues Harmonica,** *Chess* // 1969 - **Southern Comfort,** *Sire* // 1972 - **Back,** *Crosscut* // 1972 - **Big Walter Horton with Carey Bell,** *Alligator* // 1972 - **An Offer You Can't Refuse,** (with Paul Butterfield), *Red Lightnin'* // 1973 - **Live at El Mocambo,** *Red Lightnin'* // 1978 - **Fine Cuts,** *Blind Pig* // 1980 - **Little Boy Blue,** (with Sugar Blue), *JSP* // 1984 - **The Deep Blues Harmonica,** *JSP* // 1986 - **Walter Horton,** *Black Magic* // 1987 - **Harmonica Blues Kings,** (with Alfred Harris), *Pearl* // 1989 - **Can't Keep Lovin' You,** *Blind Pig* // 1991 - **Memphis Recordings 1951,** *Kent* // 1993 - **The Be-Bop Boy,** (with Joe Hill Louis) // 1996 - **Ann Arbor Blues and Jazz Festival 1973, Vol. 4,** *Schoolkids* // 1996 - **Walter Shakey Horton with Hot Cottage,** *Stony Plain* // 1996 - **They Call Me Big Walter Horton,** *Blues Alliance* // 1998 - **Toronto '73,** *M.I.L. Multine* // **With Johnny Shines,** *TCD* // **King of Blues Harmonica,** *Chess* // **Memphis Harp and Jug Blowers,** *Document* // **Chicago Blues,** *Arhoolie* // **Harmonica Genius,** (with Carey Bell), *Black Magic.*

Movies:
1980 - **The Blues Brothers.**

Hot Tuna

Formed: 1970

Acoustic / Electric Blues band
Formed as a side project from *The Jefferson Airplane* by guitarist Jorma Kaukonen and bassist Jack Cassidy, Hot Tuna specialized in old-time Blues music. The band featured the harmonica playing of Will Scarlett from 1970 to 1971. The group also featured guitar, mandolin and harmonica player Michael Falzarano beginning in 1990.

See - Will Scarlett, Michael Falzarano

Discography: (with Will Scarlett, Michael Falzarano)
1970 - **Hot Tuna,** *RCA* // 1971 - **First Pull Up, Then Pull Down,** *RCA* // 1971 - **Electric,** *RCA* // 1992 - **Live at Sweetwater,** *Relix* // 1993 - **Live at Sweetwater 2,** *Relix.*

Hotz, Friedrick
Harmonica manufacturer
Friedrick Hotz was a 19ᵗʰ century harmonica builder from Wuerttemburg, Germany.

Hovhaness, Alan
Born: March 8, 1911 - USA
Died: 2000

Classical Composer
Alan Hovhaness wrote "Concerto for Harmonica and Orchestra" in 1953 and "Seven Greek Folk Dances, Opus 150" in 1956 for John Sebastian, Sr.

Howard and The White Boys
Formed: 1988 - Dekalb, IL

Blues band
Originally put together as a weekend college band at Northern Illinois University, *Howard and the White Boys* features the guitar and harmonica playing of Dan Bellini. They have been regulars on the Chicago Blues scene for many years and have recorded several albums.

See - Dan Bellini

Discography:
1994 - **Strung Out on the Blues,** *Mighty Tiger* // 1997 - **Guess Who's Coming To Dinner?,** *Mighty Tiger* // 1999 - **The Big Score,** *Evidence* // 2000 - **Live at Chord on Blues,** *Evidence.*

Howlin' Wolf
Real name: Chester Burnett
Born: June 10, 1910 - West Point, MS
Died: January 10, 1976 - Hines, IL

Blues singer, guitar, harmonica player
Raised on a cotton plantation in Ruleville, Mississippi, Chester Burnett started playing music as a teenager. He learned how to play the guitar from Charlie Patton and the harmonica from his brother-in-law, Sonny Boy Williamson II (Rice Miller).

He put together his first band, *The House Rockers,* during the late 1940's, which included Ike Turner, Little Junior Parker and James Cotton. He made his first recordings for the Sun label in 1951. Moving to Chicago in 1952, he soon became a major player in the local Blues scene. The competition between him and Muddy Waters was fierce and their rivalry drove them to greater heights, vying for the best Blues players and the best songs, especially those by Willie Dixon.

He became a legend in Blues circles, touring and recording often during the 1960's. Among his hits were "Evil," "Spoonful," "Back Door Man," "Sitting On Top of the World," "Smokestack Lightning" "I Ain't Superstitious" and many more, most of which have been covered by major Rock and Blues bands.

He remained active until 1975 when he was forced to retire to ill health. He died the next year.

Discography:
1950 - **Ridin' in the Moonlight,** *Ace* // 1951-52 - **Memphis Days, The Definitive Collection, Vol. I&II,** *Bear Family* // 1951-64 - **Moanin' and Howlin',** *Chess* // 1954-63 - **His Greatest Hits,** *Chess* // 1958 - **Howlin' Wolf,** *Chess* // 1962 - **Rocking Chair,** *Chess* // 1962 - **Howlin' Wolf,** *Chess* // 1962 - **Howlin' Wolf Sings the Blues,** *Crown* // 1964 - **Tell Me,** *Pye* // 1964 - **Moanin' in the Moonlight,** *Chess* // 1964 - **Live in Europe 1964,** *Sundown* // 1965 - **Poor Boy,** *Chess* // 1966 - **Big City Blues,** *Custom* // 1966 - **The Real Folk Blues,** *Chess* // 1967 - **Live and Cookin' At Alice's Revisited,** *Chess* // 1967 - **Evil,** *Chess* // 1967 - **More Real Folk Blues,** *Chess* // 1967 - **The Original Folk Blues,** *United* // 1967 - **Super Super Blues Band,** (with Bo Diddley and Muddy Waters), *Chess* // 1969 - **This is Howlin' Wolf's New Album,** *Cadet* // 1970 - **Goin' Back Home,** *Syndicate* // 1971 - **Message To the Young,** *Chess* // 1971 - **The London Sessions,** *Chess* // 1973 - **I'm the Wolf,** *Vogue* // 1974 - **London Revisited,** *Chess* // 1974 - **Muddy and the Wolf,** *Chess* // 1974 - **Howlin' Wolf AKA Chester Burnett,** *Chess* // 1975 - **Live 1975,** *Wolf* // 1970's - **Change My Way,** *Chess* // 1979 - **Heart Like Railroad Steel,** *Blues Ball* // 1979 - **Can't Put Me Out,** *Blues Ball* // 1984 - **The Wolf,** *Blue Moon* // 1984 - **All Night Boogie,** *Blue Moon* // 1987 - **Cadillac Daddy, Memphis Recordings,** *Rounder* // 1988 - **Smokestack Lightning,** *Vogue* // 1988 - **Red Rooster,** *Joker* // 1991 - **The Chess Box,** *Chess* // 1992 - **Back Door Man,** *Sound Solution* // 1993 - **Howlin' Wolf Rides Again,** *Flair/Virgin* // 1994 - **Ain't Gonna Be Your Dog,** *Chess* // 1995 - **Chicago Blue,** *Rhino* // 1996 - **The Back Door Wolf,** *MCA/Chess* // 1996 - **Killing Floor,** *Charly* // 1996 - **Rockin' the Blues,** *Collectables* // 1997 - **Cause of It All,** *Dove* // 1997 - **His Best,** *MCA/Chess* // 1997 - **Howlin' at the Sun,** *Charly* // 1999 - **His Best, Vol. 2,** *MCA / Chess* // **Demon Drivin' Blues,** *Black Label* // **Wolf is At Your Door,** *New Rose* // **Live at Joe's 1973,** *Wolf* // **Tail Dragger,** *Onyx Classic* // **Live in Cambridge, 1966,** *New Rose.*

Hoxie, Albert

Harmonica band organizer
Philanthropist Albert Hoxie began organizing harmonica contests during the Boy Council of Philadelphia's 1923 "Boy Week" celebration. It became an annual event and winners included Leon Lafell in 1924 and John Sebastian, Sr. in 1930.

Soon he began organizing harmonica bands, complete with military-style marching band uniforms. Throughout the 1920's and 30's he took his bands on tours, played for presidents, royalty and visiting dignitaries.

His desire to spread the gospel of the harmonica was ceaseless. He sent assistants across the country to organize and train harmonica bands. By the end of the 1930's there were over 150 harmonica bands in Chicago alone. 1200 children received weekly instruction in the Dayton, Ohio public schools. In Los Angeles, over 100,000 youngsters enrolled in harmonica courses. By the end of the Great Depression over 2,000 harmonica bands were formed, thanks to his efforts.

Hoy, Johnnie

Born: January 10, 1957 - Middletown, CT

Blues harmonica player

Johnny Hoy began playing the harmonica when he was eighteen years old. After spending several years traveling and working at various jobs he settled down in Martha's Vineyard, Massachusetts. In the 1980's he began playing professionally, eventually recording several albums for the Tone-Cool label.

Discography:
1995 - **Trolling the Hootchy,** *Tone-Cool* // 1998 - **You Gonna Lose Your Head,** *Tone-Cool* // 1998 - **Walk the Plank,** *Tone-Cool.*

Huang, Cham-Ber

Born: October 17, 1925 - Shanghai, China

Classical harmonica soloist, harmonica manufacturer
Cham-Ber Huang got his first harmonica from his grandfather. Because the reeds were reversed on it, he learned to play the instrument upside-down. He began taking harmonica lessons and learned to read music in school at age seven. By high school he was teaching harmonica as well as conducting a harmonica

orchestra of 150 pieces in his native Shanghai. He began appearing with The Shanghai Symphony in 1946 and toured Europe in 1949 as a classical harmonica soloist.

While on tour in America, Mao's revolution took place. Huang became a U.S. citizen and settled in New York, where he worked as a harmonica soloist. He began teaching at the Turtle Bay School of Music in 1957. He regularly holds seminars on the harmonica and even gave lessons to Robert Bonfiglio. In the 1970's Huang was the first American artist to be asked to perform by the Chinese Ministry of Culture.

He started working as a product specialist for the Hohner Harmonica Company and started introducing new models in the late 1960's. In 1982 Huang began exporting harmonicas from China with his brother Frank, who had also worked for Hohner as a harmonica technician. Huang Harmonicas has been making inroads into the American harmonica market ever since.

Discography:
Music That Touches the Heart, *Huang.*

Bibliography:
Blues and All That Jazz, (Book and CD), *Huang.*

Huang Harmonica Co.

Harmonica manufacturing company

Established in 1982, the Huang Harmonica Company was founded by harmonica virtuoso Cham-Ber Huang and his brother Frank. By importing their harmonicas from China, Huang has managed to make great inroads into the American harmonica market.

Hummel, Mark

Born: December 15, 1955 - New Haven, CT

Blues harmonica player

Mark Hummel grew up in Los Angeles and has been playing the harmonica since his teens. After moving to the Oakland area in 1972, he began playing with many of the local Blues greats in the area. He plays with his own back-up group, *The Blues Survivors,* in the San Francisco Bay area.

Discography:
1980's - **Harmonica Party,** *Double Trouble //* 1985 - **Playin' in Your Town,** *Rockinitus//* 1988 - **Up and Jumpin',** *Rockinitus //* 1992 - **Hard Lovin' 90's,** *Double Trouble //* 1994 - **Feel Like Rockin',** *Flying Fish //* 1995 - **Married to the Blues,** *Flying Fish //* 1997 - **Heart of Chicago,** *Tone-Cool //* 1998 - **Lowdown To Uptown,** *Tone-Cool //* **High Steppin',** *Double Trouble.*

On Video:
Harmonica Party, *Mountain Top Video.*

Hunt, "Sleepy" Otis

Born: April 29, 1923 - Pine Bluff, AR
Died: July 4, 1998 - Chicago, IL

Blues, singer, drums, organ, harmonica player
"Sleepy" Otis Hunt Began playing Blues harmonica in Chicago in the 1950's when his wife took up with Howlin' Wolf and he wanted to win her back by playing the instrument. He was given his first instrument by Little Walter and was mentored on the harmonica by Eddie Taylor.

He managed to make a name for himself on the instrument with Muddy Waters, Howlin' Wolf, (they eventually became friends),

Freddie King, Elmore James and many others. He left music to pursue regular employment in the early 1960's, but started to make a comeback shortly before his death in 1998.

Discography:
1998 - **Lost American Bluesmen,** *Midnight Creeper.*

Hunter, Richard

Born: April 1, 1952

Jazz piano, harmonica player

Richard Hunter began by playing piano and started playing the harmonica around 1967 and worked in Rock and Blues music. After attending college he started experimenting in Jazz and eventually wrote the book "Jazz Harp." He has been recording and performing steadily ever since.

Discography:
1994 - **The Act of Being Free in One Act,** *Turtle Hill* // 1998 - **The Second Act of Being Free,** *Turtle Hill.*

Bibliography:
1980 - **Jazz Harp,** *Oak Publications.*

Movies:
1991 - **City of Hope** // 1997 - **Prefontaine.**

Hurt, "Mississippi" John

Born: July 3, 1893 - Teoc, MS
Died: November 2, 1966 - Grenada, MS

Blues singer, guitar, harmonica player
"Mississippi" John Hurt dropped out of school to work on his family's farm and to take up music at age ten. By the time he was twelve he was playing at local parties and dances. He recorded several sides for the Okeh label in 1928, but then returned to farming until he was rediscovered in 1963. He was an instant success on the Folk / Blues circuit and worked steadily until his death in 1966.

Discography:
1963 - **Monday Morning Blues,** *Flyright* // 1963 - **Mississippi John Hurt - Folk Songs and Blues** // 1964 - **Worried Blues,** *Rounder* // 1964 - **Memorial Anthology,** *Adelphi* // 1965 - **Avalon Blues,** *Rounder* // 1965 - **Blues At Newport,** *Vanguard* // 1965 - **The Best Of...,** *Vanguard* // 1966 - **The Last Sessions,** *Vanguard* // 1967 - **Mississippi John Hurt - Today!,** *Vanguard* // 1968 - **The Immortal,** *Vanguard* // 1968 - **The Mississippi John Hurt,** *Vanguard* // 1980 - **Candy Man,** *Intermedia* // 1980's - **Satisfied,** *Intermedia* // 1986 - **Shake That Thing,** *Blue Moon* // 1988 - **Sacred and Secular, Vol. 3,** *Heritage* // 1988 - **1928 Sessions,** *Yazoo* // 1989 - **The Best Of...,** *Start* // 1990 - **The Greatest Songsters: Complete Works,** (1927-29), *Document* // 1995 - **Satisfying Blues,** *Collectables* // 1995 - **In Concert,** *Magnum* // 1996 - **Coffee Blues,** *Iris* // 1996 - **Avalon Blues: The Complete 1928 Okeh Sessions,** *Sony* // 1997 - **Legend,** *Rounder* // 1997 - **Satisfied: Live,** *Beacon* // 1997 - **Memorial Anthology, Vol. 2,** *Edsel* // 1998 - **Live!,** *Columbia River* // 1998 - **Rediscovered,** *Vanguard* // 1998 - **The Best Of...,** *Aim* // 2000 - **Songster,** *King Bee* // **The Piedmont Sessions, Vol. 1, Origin.**

Hutchison, Frank

Born: March 20, 1897 - Raleigh County, WV
Died: November 9, 1945 - Columbus, OH

Country guitar, harmonica player
Frank Hutchison started playing the harmonica at age eight and was playing professionally in the mid-1920's. He recorded 32 sides for the Okeh label from 1926 until 1929. His style was heavily influenced by black rural Blues and he is considered by many to be one of the first white musicians to record Blues music. He stopped performing during the Great Depression and never returned to music.

Discography:
1973 - **The Train That Carried My Girl From Town,** *Rounder* // 1997 - **Frank Hutchison, Complete Recorded Works, Vol. 1 (1926-29),** *Document* // 1997 - **Old-Time Music From West Virginia,** *Document* // **Frank Hutchison,** *Rounder.*

Hynde, Chrissie

Born: September 7, 1951 - Akron, Ohio

Rock singer-songwriter, guitar, harmonica player
Chrissie Hynde is the leader of the Rock band, *The Pretenders.* She occasionally plays the harmonica on some of the groups songs.

Discography: (all with The Pretenders)
1980 - **The Pretenders**, *Sire* // 1981 - **The Pretenders II**, *Sire* // 1984 - **Learning To Crawl**, *Sire* // 1986 - **Get Close**, *Sire* // 1987 - **The Singles**, *Sire* // 1990 - **Packed!**, *Sire* // 1994 - **Last of the Independents**, *Sire* // 1995 - **Isle of View**, *Warner Brothers* // 1999 - **Viva El Amor**, *Warner Brothers*.

I

Ingham, Tom
Country / Rock harmonica player
Tom Ingham played the harmonica for the Country / Rock group, *McGuffey Lane* for a short time during 1990 and appeared on their "Live On High Street" album. The group dissolved shortly thereafter.

Discography: (see - McGuffey Lane)

-J-

Jackson, Joe
Born: August 11, 1955 - Burton-Upon-Trent, England

Rock singer, keyboards, harmonica player
Generally regarded as one of Rock music's premiere singer-songwriters, Joe Jackson usually plays the harmonica once or twice on each of his albums.

Discography:
1979 - **Look Sharp!**, *A&M* // 1979 - **I'm the Man**, *A&M* // 1980 - **Beat Crazy**, *A&M* // 1981 - **Jumpin' Jive**, *A&M* // 1982 - **Night & Day**, *A&M* // 1983 - **Mike's Murder Soundtrack**, *A&M* // 1984 - **Body & Soul**, *A&M* // 1986 - **Big World**, *A&M* // 1987 - **Will Power**, *A&M* // 1988 - **Tucker**, *A&M* // 1988 - **Live...1980-1986**, *A&M* // 1989 - **Blaze of Glory**, *A&M* // 1990 - **Steppin' Out: The Very Best Of...**, *A&M* // 1991 - **Laughter & Lust**, *Virgin* // 1994 - **Night Music**, *Virgin* // 1995 - **I'm the Man: The Classic Tracks, 1979-1989**, *A&M* // 1996 - **Greatest Hits**, *A&M* // 1997 - **This is It! The A&M Years**, *A&M* // 1997 - **Heaven & Hell**, *Sony* // 1999 - **Symphony 1**, *Sony* // 2000 - **Summer in the City: Live in New York**, *Sony*.

Jackson, Julian
Jazz harmonica player
Raised in Liverpool, England, Julian Jackson studied harmonica under James Hughes and Toots Thielemans. He has spent much of his musical career working in movies and television.

Movies:
1998 - **The Full Monty**.

Jackson, Ray
Born: December 12, 1948

Folk / Rock guitar, mandolin, harmonica player
Ray Jackson is an English multi-instrumentalist who has played harmonica on records by Chris DeBurgh, Alan Hull, *Lindisfarne*, Peter Hamill and others.

Discography:
1980 - **Into the Night**, *Mercury*.

Jackson, Arthur "Peg Leg Sam"
Born: December 18, 1911 - Jonesville, SC
Died: October 27, 1977 - Jonesville, SC

Blues harmonica player
"Peg Leg Sam" Jackson taught himself to play harmonica at age nine. He may have taken some lessons from a local Blues player named Elmon Bell. Jackson began playing professionally at about age ten. Jackson hoboed around the country for the next several years until 1930, when he lost his right leg in a railroad accident. He carved his own wooden leg.

Jackson began working on the radio in 1936, broadcasting from Rocky Mount, North Carolina during tobacco marketing season and spending the rest of the year working with carnivals and medicine shows. He would amuse audiences with his humorous stories and harmonica playing, sometimes playing two harmonicas at once, one with his mouth and one with his nose.

In 1960, during a domestic dispute, he was shot in the face and lost most of his right ear and part of his jaw. He started making a comeback in 1972 and spent the rest of his life playing at Folk Festivals.

Discography:
1973 - **Medicine Show Man**, *Trix* // 1975 - **Joshua**, *Tomato* // 1996 - **Early in the Morning**, *The Blues Alliance* // **Peg Leg Sam**, *Tomato*.

Jacob, Gordon
Born: September 5, 1895 - England
Died: June 1, 1984

Classical composer
Gordon Jacob wrote "Pieces (5) for Harmonica and Orchestra" and "Divertimento for Harmonica and String Quartet" in 1957 for Tommy Reilly and Larry Adler respectively.

Recording Availability:
1977 - **Vaughan-Williams, Tausky, Moody, Jacob,** (Tommy Reilly - soloist), *Chandos* // **Divertimento for Harmonica and String Quartet,** (Tommy Reilly - soloist), *Chandos.*

Jacobs, Marion "Little" Walter

Born: May 1, 1930 - Marksville, LA
Died: February 15, 1968 - Chicago, IL

Blues singer, harmonica player

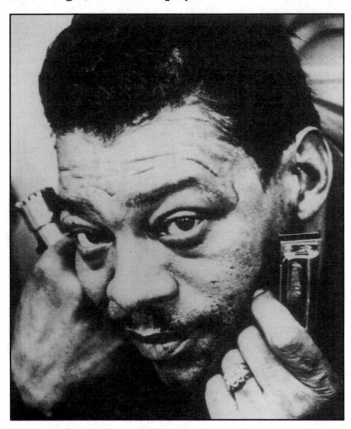

"Little" Walter Jacobs taught himself to play the harmonica at age eight. He ran away from home and was playing for tips in New Orleans by age twelve. By the time he was fifteen he was in Helena, Arkansas studying harmonica with Sonny Boy Williamson II (Rice Miller).

He moved to Chicago in 1947 and was soon playing on Maxwell Street for tips, as well as playing in the clubs and recording. He first teamed up with Muddy Waters in 1948. During a recording session with Waters on July 11, 1951, Little Walter plugged the microphone from his harmonica into a guitar amplifier and became one of the first to play what has become known as Chicago-style electric harmonica.

Also recording solo, Walter scored his first big hit in 1952 with the song "Juke." He quit *The Muddy Waters Band* and started playing with *The Aces,* which had been Junior Wells' group. He continued to perform and record heavily during the 1950's and early 60's. His big hits included "Mellow Down Easy," "Blues with a Feeling," "Last Night," "Easy," "My Babe" and many others, as well as an immense body of work backing various artists for Chess Records. During the Mid-1960's he toured Europe and even used *The Rolling Stones* as a back-up group in 1964.

By the late 1960's he was quickly deteriorating from alcohol abuse and eventually died of injuries that he received in a street brawl. He has been cited by many Blues harmonica players as being the major influence on their playing.

Discography:
1958 - **The Best of Little Walter,** *Chess* // 1964 - **Little Walter,** *Pye* // 1967 - **Super Blues,** *Chess* // 1969 - **Hate To See You Go,** *Chess* // 1971 - **Thunderbird,** *Syndicate* // 1972 - **Boss Blues Harmonica,** *Chess* // 1974 - **Confessin' the Blues,** *Chess* // 1979 - **Chess Masters,** (with Otis Rush), *Rhino* // 1982 - **Quarter To Twelve,** *Red Lightnin'* // 1983 - **We Three Kings,** *Syndicate* // 1986 - **Blues World of Little Walter,** *Delmark* // 1986 - **Windy City Blues,** *Blue Moon* // 1987 - **Collection: Little Walter 20 Blues Greats** // 1990 - **Best Of..., Vol. 2,** *Chess* // 1992 - **Juke,** *Sound Solution* // 1993 - **Essential Little Walter,** *Chess* // 1993 - **The Chess Years, 1952-63,** *Chess* // 1995 - **Chess Collectibles, Vol. 3 - Blues with a Feeling,** *Chess* // 2000 - **Live in the Windy City,** *Columbia River* // **Little Walter and his Jukes,** *Python* // **Blue Midnight,** *Le Roi de Blues* // **Blue and Lonesome,** *Le Roi de Blues* // **Southern Feeling,** *Le Roi de Blues.*

Jagger, Mick

Born: July 26, 1943 - Dartford, England

Rock singer, harmonica player
Mick Jagger learned to play the harmonica from Cyril Davies of *Blues Incorporated.* During the early 1960's Jagger would sing with the group, which also featured drummer Charlie Watts. After *Blues Incorporated* disbanded Watts and Jagger would go on to form *The Rolling Stones.*

The Rolling Stones went on to become one of the biggest Rock bands in history. They toured with Blues greats Little Walter and Junior Wells, both of whom gave some harmonica instruction to Jagger. He occasionally plays the harmonica on records and in concert.

Discography: (also see - The Rolling Stones)
1985 - **She's the Boss,** *Columbia* // 1987 - **Primitive Cool,** *Rolling Stones* // 1993 - **Wandering Spirit,** *Atlantic.*

James, Frank

Born: January 10, 1843 - Clay County, MO
Died: February 18, 1915

Bank robber
According to legend, Frank James of the James Gang played the harmonica when he wasn't busy robbing banks. There is a story that his life was spared when a bullet that was headed for his heart was stopped by a harmonica that he kept in his breast pocket.

Jason and The Scorchers

Formed: 1981 - Nashville, TN
Disbanded: 1989
Re-united: 1993

Country / Punk band

Jason and The Scorchers were originally brought together as a Hard-Country or "Cow-Punk" band. Although they garnered much critical acclaim, they never achieved the commercial success they wanted and they disbanded in 1989. They were led by singer/guitarist Jason Ringenberg, who also played the harmonica.

The group re-united in 1993 and has since recorded several albums with Ringenberg.

See - Jason Ringenberg

Discography:

1985 - **Lost & Found**, *EMI* // 1986 - **Still Standing**, *EMI* // 1989 - **Thunder & Fire**, *A&M* // 1992 - **Essential Jason and The Scorchers** // 1995 - **A Blazing Grace**, *Mammoth* // 1996 - **Both Sides of the Line**, *EMI* // 1996 - **Clear Impetuous Morning**, *Mammoth* // 1998 - **Midnight Roads & Stages Seen**, *Mammoth*.

Jass, Joe

Vaudeville harmonica player

Joe Jass played the lead chromatic harmonica in *The Philharmonicas* during the 1930's.

The Jayhawks

Formed: 1985 - Minneapolis, MN

Country / Rock band

The Jayhawks were one of the leading bands in the Country / Rock revival of the 1990's. They scored several hit albums and toured extensively during the decade. The band was co-founded by guitar and harmonica player Mark Olson.

See - Mark Olson

Discography:

1986 - **The Jayhawks**, *Bunkhouse* // 1989 - **Blue Earth**, *Twin/Tone* // 1992 - **Hollywood Town Hall**, *Def American* // 1995 - **Tomorrow the Green Grass**, *American* // 1997 - **Sound of Lies**, *Warner Brothers* // 2000 - **Smile**, *Sony*.

Jazz Harmonica

The harmonica, while not being overly popular with many Jazz fans, has never the less played an important role in the history of Jazz. During the 1930's, several of the harmonica bands based their sound on big band arrangements and as soloists like Larry Adler emerged, they showed very definite tendencies towards Jazz-styled music.

During the 1950's, 60's and 70's, Jean "Toots" Thielemans dominated Jazz harmonica playing with his work in The George Shearing Quintet, with Quincy Jones and also by recording dozens of great solo albums as well. In the 1980's, Howard Levy's use of overblows on the diatonic harmonica revolutionized the way that instrument was played.

Presently there are several outstanding Jazz harmonica players including: William Galison, Richard Hunter, Mike Turk, Sandy Weltman, Ron Kalina, Hendrik Meurkens, Howard Levy and a host of others.

Jenkins, John Pickens "Bobo"

Born: January 7, 1916 - Forkland, AL
Died: August 14, 1984 - Detroit, MI

Blues guitar, harmonica player

"Bobo" Jenkins began in music at age five by singing in his family's Gospel choir. He ran away from home at age twelve and hoboed extensively for the next few years.

He came to the public's attention when he appeared on the King Biscuit Time radio program in 1941. After serving in the Army from 1942 to 1944 he settled in the Detroit area. While working mostly in the Midwest, he began recording in the mid-1950's and continued to pursue music as well as working as a photographer and running his own record label, Big Star.

Discography:

1966 - **Detroit Blues - The Early 1960's** // 1972 - **The Life of Bobo Jenkins** // 1975 - **Here I Am a Fool in Love Again** // 1978 - **Detroit All Purpose Blues** // 1989 - **Blues for Big Town**.

Johansen, David

Also known as: Buster Poindexter
Born: January 9, 1950 - Staten Island, NY

Rock / Blues singer, harmonica player

Singer David Johansen has been a presence has been a steady presence in the Rock and Blues fields, playing with *The New York Dolls* as well as recording as a solo artist. He also plays the harmonica to augment his singing.

Discography: (also see - The New York Dolls)

1978 - **David Johansen**, *Razor & Tie* // 1978 - **Live**, *Columbia* // 1979 - **In Style**, *Razor & Tie* // 1982 - **Live It Up**, *Razor & Tie* // 1982 - **Here Comes the Night**, *Razor & Tie* // 1984 - **Sweet Revenge**, *M.I.L.* // 1987 - **Buster Poindexter**, *RCA* // 1989 - **Buster Goes Berserk**, *RCA* // 1990 - **International Playboy**, *RCA* // 1990 - **Crucial Music: Collection**, *Combat* // 1993 - **Live at the Bottom Line**, *CBS* // 1994 - **Buster's Happy Hour**, *Rhino* // 1995 - **Hot Hot Hot**, *RCA* // 1995 - **From Pumps To Pompadour**, *Rhino* // 1996 - **Looking Good**, *Sony* // 1997 - **Buster's Spanish Rocketship**, *Polygram* // 2000 - **David Johansen & The Harry Smiths**, *Chesky*.

Johnson, Henry "Rufe"

Born: December 8, 1908 - Union, SC
Died: February 1974 - Union, SC

Blues piano, guitar, harmonica player
"Rufe" Johnson began playing music after learning guitar from his brother at the age of fifteen. While popular in his immediate area, he didn't start to catch on until the 1970's, when he was discovered by Blues enthusiasts. He started working the club and festival circuit and even did some appearances with "Peg Leg" Sam Jackson. He was able to make a couple of recordings before he died of kidney failure in 1974.

Discography:
1973 - **Union County Flash,** *Trix* // 1993 - **New Beginnings.**

Johnson, Jimmy

Real name: Jim Thompson
Born: November 25, 1928 - Holly Springs, MS

Blues singer, guitar, keyboards, harmonica player
The brother of Blues great Syl Johnson, Jimmy Johnson came from a musical family that moved to Chicago in 1950. While playing music as a hobby for most of his early years, he began performing professionally in 1959.

Working mostly as a journeyman Blues artist over the next few years, he recorded his first album in 1975. Since then he has recorded for several labels including Delmark and Alligator.

Discography:
1975 - **Ma Bea's Rock,** *MCM* // 1977 - **Jimmy Johnson & Luther Johnson,** *MCM* // 1978 - **Tobacco Road,** *MCM* // 1979 - **Johnson's Whacks,** *Delmark* // 1982 - **North / South,** *Delmark* // 1983 - **Barroom Preacher,** *Alligator* // 1995 - **I'm a Jockey,** *Verve* // 1999 - **Every Road Ends,** *Ruf.*

Johnson, Joe

Born: January 19, 1942 - Independence, LA

Blues singer, guitar, harmonica player
Joe Johnson taught himself to play the harmonica as a youth and also sang in local Gospel groups in his teens. He began performing professionally in 1959 and began recording in 1966.

Johnson, Kirk "Jelly Roll"

Born: July 4, 1953

Country studio harmonica player
Kirk "Jelly Roll" Johnson began playing harmonica at age nineteen. He has since worked with *The Judds*, Randy Travis, Trisha Yearwood, Reba McEntire and many others as well as recording some albums of his own.

Discography:
1996 - **Red Hot Christmas Blues,** (with Mark Baldwin), *Unison* // 1999 - **Jelly Roll Johnson and a Few Close Friends,** *JMJ Records* // Kirk "Jelly Roll" Johnson.

Johnson, Larry

Born: May 15, 1938 - Atlanta, GA

Blues guitar, banjo, harmonica player
Larry Johnson learned how to play the harmonica from his father, a Gospel preacher who often had his son tour with him. As a teen he frequently played at local parties in the Atlanta area. He served in the Navy from 1954 to 1959.

After his hitch in the Navy he settled in New York City and studied guitar with Reverend Gary Davis. Johnson began recording in 1962. Since then he's been active in the Folk / Blues music scene and has worked and recorded with Big Joe Williams, Reverend Gary Davis, John Hammond, Bobby Robinson and others. In 1970 a short documentary, "Larry Johnson" was made about him. He often worked with harmonica player Nat Riddles.

Discography:
1970 - **Fast and Funky,** *Blue Goose* // 1970 - **Presenting the Country Blues,** *Blue Horizon* // 1974 - **Country Blues,** *Blue Horizon* // 1980's - **Larry Johnson and Nat Riddles,** *Spivey* // 1990 - **Railroad Man,** *JSP* // 1995 - **Saturday Night Blues,** *Biograph* // 1995 - **Midnight Hour Blues,** *Biograph* // 1999 - **Blues for Harlem,** *Armadillo* // **Johnson! Where Did You Get That Sound?,** (with Nat Riddles), *L&R.*

Movies:
1970 - **Larry Johnson** // 1970 - **Black Roots.**

Johnson, "Lazy" Lester

Real name: Leslie Johnson
Born: June 20, 1933 - Torras, LA

Blues harmonica player
Nicknamed "Lazy Lester" for his laid-back approach to Blues music, Lester Johnson taught himself to play the harmonica and started working in bands in the early 1950's.

He frequently worked with Lightnin' Slim from the mid to late 1950's and began recording on his own in 1958. He quit music and moved to Detroit to work in the auto plants in the 1960's, but started making a comeback in the early 1970's.

Discography:
1960's - **True Blues**, *Excello* // 1987 - **Lester's Stomp**, *Flyright* // 1988 - **Harp and Soul**, *Alligator* // 1988 - **Lazy Lester Rides Again**, *Sunjay* // 1989 - **Lazy Lester**, *Flyright* // 1989 - **Lazy Lester**, *Excello* // 1995 - **I Hear You Knockin'!!!**, *Excello* // **Poor Boy Blues**, *Flyright* // **They Call Me Lazy**, *Flyright* // **I'm a Lover Not a Fighter**, *Excello/Ace* // **All Over You**, *Antone's*.

Johnson, Robert

Born: May 8, 1912(?) - Hazelhurst, MS
Died: August 16, 1938 - Greenwood, MS

Blues singer-songwriter, guitar, harmonica player
The great patriarch of Mississippi Delta Blues, Robert Johnson has influenced several generations of Blues musicians. Though his small recorded output, (40 sides), featured only his singing and guitar playing, friends recall that Johnson began his musical career playing the harmonica and was talented enough to make a living from it for a while. The 1990 release of his complete recordings became the biggest-selling Blues re-issue recording of all time.

Discography:
1990 - **The Complete Recordings**, *Columbia*.

Johnson, Syl

Real name: Syl Thompson
Born: July 1, 1936 - Holly Springs, MS

Blues guitar, harmonica player
Syl Johnson learned how to play the harmonica as a child from his father. From a musical family, one of his brothers played bass guitar for Magic Sam and another, Jimmy Johnson, is a Blues artist in his own right. After his family moved to Chicago in the late 1940's, Syl started sitting in with Howlin' Wolf, Muddy Waters, Junior Wells and others. He made his first recordings in 1956 with Billy Boy Arnold and was soon recording and playing with Jimmy Reed, Shakey Jake, Elmore James and many more.

He remained busy in music until the mid-1980's, when he semi-retired to open a string of fast food fish restaurants. During the 1990's he made a number of appearances at major Blues clubs and festivals.

Discography:
1968 - **Dresses Too Short**, *Twinight* // 1970 - **Is It Because I'm Black?**, *Charly* // 1973 - **Back for a Taste of Your Love**, *Hi* // 1974 - **Diamond in the Rough**, *Hi* // 1976 - **Total Explosion**, *Hi* // 1979 - **Uptown Shakedown**, *Hi* // 1980 - **Brings Out the Blues in Me**, *Shama* // 1983 - **Ms. Fine Brown Frame** // 1984 - **Suicide Blues** // 1986 - **The Love Chimes** // 1988 - **Foxy Brown** // 1989 - **Stuck in Chicago** // 1994 - **A-Sides**, *Hi* // 1995 - **Back in the Game**, *Delmark* // 1995 - **This Time Together By Father and Daughter**, *Twinight* // 1996 - **The Best of Syl Johnson: The Hi Years**, *Capitol* // 1998 - **Bridge To a Legacy**, *Antone's* // 1998 - **Hi Masters**, *Hi* // 1998 - **Back for a Taste**, *Hi* // 1999 - **Talkin' About Chicago**, *Delmark* // 2000 - **Hands of Time**, *Hep' Me* // **Music To My Ears**, *Hi*.

Jones, Birmingham

Born: January 9, 1937 - Saginaw, MI

Blues guitar, saxophone, harmonica player
Birmingham Jones began playing music on the saxophone and worked as a sideman for J.B. Lenoir during the early 1950's. While working with Elmore James, he also learned how to play the guitar. Finally he learned to play the harmonica and formed his own band, *Birmingham Jones and his Lover Boys*.

He began recording in 1956 and remained active until retiring from music in the mid-1970's.

Discography:
1985 - **Chills and Fever**.

Jones, Brian

Real name: Lewis Brian Hopkins-Jones
Born: February 28, 1942 - Cheltenham, England
Died: July 3, 1969 - London, England

Rock guitar, harmonica player

A talented multi-instrumentalist, Brian Jones was one of the founders of *The Rolling Stones* with fellow Blues fans Mick Jagger, Charlie Watts, Keith Richards and Bill Wyman. He shared harmonica duties with Mick Jagger on most of *The Rolling Stones* albums until his death from drowning in 1969.

Discography: (see - The Rolling Stones)

Jones, "Little" Johnny

Born: November 1, 1924 - Jackson, MS
Died: November 19, 1964 - Chicago, IL

Blues singer, piano, harmonica player
Though he was primarily known as a piano player, "Little" Johnny Jones learned to play the harmonica while growing up in Mississippi. His family moved to Chicago in 1945. He began working with Tampa Red two years later.

He began recording with Tampa Red in 1949 and with Muddy Waters in 1950. Over the years he played with Elmore James, Joe Turner, Howlin' Wolf, JB Hutto, Magic Sam, Albert King, Billy Boy Arnold and others until his death from pneumonia in 1964.

Discography:
1963 - **Johnny Jones with Billy Boy Arnold,** *Alligator* // 1972 - **Chicago Piano Plus** // 1982 - **Tampa Red** // 1983 - **King of the Slide Guitar** // 1987 - **Midnight Blues** // 1988 - **Knights of the Keyboard** // 1998 - **Raised On Blues,** *Black Magic.*

Jones, Johnny "Yarddog"

Born: June 21, 1941 - Crawfordsville, AR

Blues singer, guitar, harmonica player

Johnny "Yarddog" Jones started playing the harmonica at age

ten and got his first real harmonica from Little Walter Jacobs. He moved to Detroit in 1971, worked with Bobo Jenkins and has been a steady presence on the Detroit Blues scene ever since.

Discography:
1996 - **Ain't Gonna Worry,** *Earwig.*

Jones, Paul

Real name: Paul Pond
Born: February 24, 1942 - Portsmouth, England

Blues/Rock singer, harmonica player
Paul Jones sang the lead vocals and played the harmonica for *Manfred Mann* from 1963 to 1966. They had a string of hits including "Pretty Flamingo" and "Do Wah Diddy." Although the band would resurface periodically, Paul Jones wasn't a part of any of its later incarnations.

He embarked on a solo career and scored a few minor hits with "High Time" and "I've Been a Bad, Bad Boy" and even landed a part in the movie "Privilege." He put together a group called *The Blues Band* in the 1970's and has been working steadily in music since then. Jones has played the harmonica and recorded with Eric Clapton, Dave Edmunds, Memphis Slim, Gerry Rafferty, Steve Winwood and others.

Discography: (also see - The Blues band, Manfred Mann)
1966 - **My Way,** *HMV* // 1967 - **Privilege,** *HMV* // 1968 - **Love Me Love My Friends,** *HMV* // 1969 - **Come Into My Music Box,** *Columbia* // 1971 - **Crucix on a Horse,** *London* // 1980 - **Hits and Blues, One Up** // 1996 - **The Paul Jones Collection, Vol. 1-3,** *RPM* // 1999 - **Pucker Up Butter Cup,** *Fat Possum.*

Movies:
1967 - **Privilege.**

Jostyn, Mindy

Born: June 5, 1956

Folk / Blues / World violin, guitar, harmonica player

Mindy Jostyn began playing music at age two and was playing in bands by the time she was eleven. In addition to the harmonica, she plays violin, guitar, piano and accordion.

Mindy worked primarily as a "sideman" during the early stages of her career, playing with Dolly Parton, Billy Joel, John Cougar Mellencamp, Joe Jackson, *The Hooters*, Andreas Vollenweider and Cyndi Lauper. She recorded her first solo album in 1994.

Discography:
1994 - **Five Miles From Hope,** *Prime* // 1997 - **Cedar Lane,** *Palmetto* // 1998 - **In His Eyes,** *Moonboy.*

Movies:
1999 - **Anywhere But Here.**

Jug Bands

Jug bands emerged as a musical style in the American south during the early 1920's. They usually consisted of several inexpensive instruments, including washboards, kazoos, spoons, guitars, banjos, mandolins, harmonicas and sometimes fiddles.

Some of the great harmonica players to emerge from this style included Will Shade, Walter Horton, Noah Lewis, Jed Davenport, Jaybird Coleman, Robert Lee McCoy, Walter "Furry" Lewis and a host of others.

Personnel in these bands changed frequently and they were popular for local dances. Many Jug bands were recorded in the 1920's and early 30's until the popularity of these bands died out.

The sound was revived by the Folk movement of the 1960's and several bands, including *The Lovin' Spoonful* and *The Grateful Dead,* actually started out as Jug bands.

Just, Andy

Born: December 5, 1954

Blues / Rock harmonica player

Andy Just is a Blues harmonica player from the San Francisco Bay area who has recorded on several occasions with *The Ford Blues Band* in addition to releasing several solo albums of his own.

Discography:
1981 - **Rockinitis,** *Blue Rock'it* // 1983 - **Andy Just and The Defenders,** *S&M* // 1994 - **Don't Cry,** *Blue Rock'it.*

– K –

Kalina, Ron

Born; August 4, 1928

Jazz piano, harmonica player
Ron Kalina works mostly as a studio musician out of Los Angeles. He started playing the harmonica at the age of four and moved up to the chromatic at the age of six. He performed with *The New Word Harmonica Trio* with Danny Wilson and Michael Burton. As a pianist he has played with Anita O'Day, Dakota Station, Gloria Lynne and others.

Discography:
Solid Gold Harmonica, *Malvern* // **Children At Play,** *Discovery.*

Movies:
1998 - **Bird** // 1991 - **One for the Boys** // 1992 - **Mississippi Masala** // 1999 - **Magnolia.**

Television:
Moonlighting // **Wild Wild West.**

Katz, Steve

Born: May 9, 1945 - Brooklyn, NY

Rock Singer, guitar, harmonica player

Steve Katz has led a multi-faceted career in music. During the mid-1960's he was a part of the Jug Band movement, working with Dave Von Ronk's *Ragtime Jug Stompers* and Jim Kweskin's *Even Dozen Jug Band.*

In 1965 he played the guitar, harmonica and sang in the group Blues Project. In 1967 he was one of the co-founders of *Blood, Sweat and Tears* with Al Kooper. He left *Blood, Sweat and Tears* in 1972 and joined the group, *American Flyer* for a brief time before taking a job at Mercury Records.

As a studio harmonica player, Steve has recorded with Duke Jupiter, Mark James, Lou Reed, *Lynyrd Skynyrd* and others.

Discography: (see - Blues Project, Blood, Sweat & Tears)

Keaton, Buster

Real name: Joseph Francis Keaton
Born: October 4, 1895 - Piqua, KS
Died: February 1, 1966

Actor, comedian

Silent film comedy star Buster Keaton played and endorsed Hohner harmonicas during the 1920's.

Kelly, Matt

Rock guitar, congas, harmonica player

Matt Kelly played the harmonica, guitar and congas for Bob Weir's groups Kingfish and *Bobby and The Midnites*. He also appeared on *The Grateful Dead* song, "I Need a Miracle" from the album "Shakedown Street."

Discography: (also see - Bobby and The Midnites, Kingfish)
1994 - **Wing and a Prayer,** (with John Lee Hooker and Mike Bloomfield), *Relix.*

Khachaturian, Aram

Born: June 6, 1903 - Russia
Died: May 1, 1978

Classical composer

Aram Khachaturian wrote "Armenian Rhapsody for Mouth Organ and Orchestra" in the 1970's for Larry Adler.

King Biscuit Boy

Real name: Richard Newell
Born: March 9, 1944 - Hamilton, Ontario, Canada

Blues harmonica player

King Biscuit Boy is a Blues singer and harmonica player from Canada who has been performing and recording since the early 1960's. After several years of working in various bands he pur-

sued a solo career and has released about half a dozen albums of Blues music.

Discography:
1970 - **Official Music,** *Stony Plain* // 1971 - **Good 'Uns,** *Stony Plain* // 1974 - **King Biscuit Boy,** *Epic* // 1982 - **Mouth of Steel,** *Red Lightnin'* //1995 - **Urban Blues: Re Newell,** *Blue Wave* // 1996 - **Badly Bent: The Best Of...,** *Stony Plain* // 1997 - **Down the Line,** *Sequel.*

King, Phil

Vaudeville harmonica player

During the 1920's Phil King was a member of *The Cappy Barra Harmonica Ensemble* and became the leader of the New York-based unit when the band split into two groups. He led the entire ensemble when it reconsolidated after the outbreak of World War Two. The group permanently disbanded in 1944.

Kingfish

Formed: 1975 - California

Rock band

A group formed as a solo project for *Grateful Dead* guitarist Bob Weir, *Kingfish* features Matt Kelly on guitar and harmonica. The band has managed to release several albums, mostly live recordings, over the past twenty years.

See - Matt Kelly

Discography:
1976 - **Kingfish,** *Round* // 1977 - **Kingfish Live and Kickin',** *Jet* // 1978 - **Trident,** *Jet* // 1985 - **Alive in 85,** *Relix* // 1996 - **King Biscuit Flower Hour,** *King Biscuit* // 1997 - **Night in New York,** *Relix* // 1997 - **The Relix's Best of Kingfish,** *Relix* // 1999 - **Sundown on the Forest,** *Phoenix*

Rising // 2000 - **Live**, *EMI*.

The King's Harmonica Quintet

Formed: 1987 - Hong Kong

Classical harmonica ensemble

The King's Harmonica Quintet is made up of former members of the *King's College Harmonica Band* of Hong Kong. The players include Lau Chun-bong and Lok Ying-kei on tenor harmonicas, Chan Shu-keung and Ho Pak-cheong on treble harmonicas and Kuan Man-hou on bass harmonica. Their repertoire consists mostly of Classical pieces adapted for the harmonica as well as some traditional Chinese music.

Discography:
A Sampler // In Concert // Blowing Up a Real Harmonica Storm.

Kinsella, Mick

Celtic harmonica player

Mick Kinsella began playing the harmonica during the mid-1980's. Specializing in the Celtic music of his native Ireland, Kinsella has appeared on numerous albums by Irish artists as well as performing with "Riverdance."

Discography:
2000 - **Harmonica**, *OBM*.

Bibliography:
1998 - **Blues Harp From Scratch**, *Music Sales Corp.*

Kinsey, "Big Daddy" Lester

Born: March 18, 1927 - Pleasant Grove, MS

Blues singer, guitar, harmonica player
The patriarch of the Gary, Indiana-based Blues band *Big Daddy Kinsey and The Kinsey Report*, Lester Kinsey had been playing slide guitar and harmonica long before founding the group in 1984. The band is made up primarily of his sons, all accomplished Blues musicians in their own right.

Discography: (with The Kinsey Report)
1985 - **Bad Situation**, *Rooster Blues* // 1989 - **Midnight Drive**, *Alligator* // 1990 - **Can't Let Go**, *Blind Pig* // 1991 - **Powerhouse**, *Point Blank* // 1993 - **I Am the Blues**, *Verve* // 1993 - **Crossing Bridges**, *Virgin* // 1995 - **Ramblin' Man**, *Polygram*.

Kirk, Wilbert

Jazz drum, harmonica player
Though primarily a Jazz drummer, Wilbert Kirk was also proficient on the harmonica and could play diatonics, chromatics and polyphonias. He led *The Harlemonicats*, a harmonica trio that specialized in Jazz arrangements as well as playing drums and harmonica with Sidney Bechet, Wilbur DeParis, Lena Horne and Rex Stewart on a regular basis.

Kirkland, "Little" Eddie

Also known as: Eddie Kirk
Born: August 16, 1928 - Jamaica

Blues guitar, organ, harmonica player
Eddie Kirkland, who taught himself how to play the harmonica as a child, was working the streets for tips in Dothan, Alabama by age eight. He moved to Detroit in 1943 to work at Ford Motors and soon was playing with fellow Detroit Bluesman John Lee Hooker, with whom he worked on and off through the 1960's.

Kirkland made his first solo recordings in 1953 and has maintained a fairly regular career as a Bluesman ever since.

Discography:
1950's - **Detroit Blues: The Early 1950's**, *Blues Classics* // 1961 - **That's the Blues**, *Tru-Sound* // 1962 - **It's the Blues Man!**, *OBC* // 1972 - **The Devil and Other Blues Demons**, *Trix* // 1980's - **Three Shades of Blue**, *Relic* // 1983 - **The Way it Was** // 1985 - **Pickin' Up the Pieces** // 1993 - **Have Mercy**, *Pulsar* // 1993 - **All Around the World**, *Deluge* // 1994 - **Some Like It Raw**, *Deluge* // 1995 - **Front and Center**, *Trix* // 1995 - **Where Do You Get Your**

Sugar?, *Deluge* // 1997 - **Lonely Street,** *Telarc* // 1999 - **Movin' On,** *JSP* // 1999 - **The Complete Trix Recordings,** *32 Blues.*

Kleinsinger, George
Classical composer
George Kleinsinger wrote "Street Corner Concerto" in 1943 for John Sebastian, Sr.

Kline, Phil
Avant-Garde composer, harmonica player
Phil Kline wrote "Bachman's Warbler" in 1993.

Recording Availability:
1993 - **Emergency Music - Bang on a Can Volume 2,** (Phil Kline - soloist), *Composers Recordings.*

Koda, Michael "Cub"
Born: October 1, 1948 - Detroit, MI
Died: July 1, 2000

Rock singer-songwriter, guitar, harmonica player, writer
Cub Koda began playing music at age five, starting with the drums and later picking up the guitar and harmonica.

As a teenager he played in a local band before founding *Brownsville Station* in 1969. The band produced one major hit, "Smoking in the Boys' Room," in 1973 and disbanded in 1979. After that Koda pursued a solo musical career, including playing a harmonica solo on *Blackfoot's* hit "Train, Train," in addition to working steadily as a Rock and Blues writer for several publications. In 2000 he died from complications from kidney dialysis.

Discography: (also see - Brownsville Station)
1980 - **Cub Koda & The Points,** *Fan Club* // 1981 - **It's the Blues,** *Fan Club* // 1989 - **Cub Digs Chuck,** *Garageland* // 1991 - **Cub Digs Bo,** *Garageland* // 1991 - **Live at B.L.U.E.S. 1982,** *Wolf* // 1993 - **Welcome To My Job: The Cub Koda Collection,** *Blue Wave* // 1994 - **Abba Dabba Dabba: A Bonanza of Hits,** *Schoolkids* // 1996 - **The Joint Was Rockin',** *Deluxe* // 1997 - **Box Lunch,** *J-Bird* // 2000 - **Noise Monkeys,** *J-Bird.*

Koerner, Ray and Glover
Formed: Early 1960's
Disbanded: Mid-1960's

Folk / Blues trio
Consisting of "Spider" John Koerner, Tony "Little Sun" Glover and Dave "Snaker" Ray, *Koerner, Ray and Glover* was an acoustic Folk / Blues trio of the early 1960's. The trio got together as students at the University of Minnesota, where they were pioneers of the white Blues revival of that era. While their original grouping only lasted a short time, they have occasionally reunited from time to time.

See -John Koerner, Tony Glover

Discography:
1963 - **Blues, Rags and Hollers,** *Red House* // 1964 - **More Blues, Rags and Hollers,** *Elektra* // 1964 - **The Blues Project,** *Elektra* // 1964 - **The Folk Box,** *Elektra* // 1965 - **Folk Song 65,** *Elektra* // 1965 - **The Return of Koerner, Ray and Glover,** *Elektra* // 1966 - **Festival - Newport Folk Festival 1965,** *Elektra* // 1970 - **Live at St. Olaf Festival** // 1972 - **Good Old Koerner, Ray and Glover,** *Mill City* // 1974 - **Some American Folk Songs like they Used to Be,** *Sweet Jane* // 1996 - **One Foot in the Groove,** *Tim Kerr.*

Koerner, "Spider" John
Born: August 31, 1938 - Rochester, NY

John Koerner grew up in Rochester, New York and attended the University of Minnesota about the same time as Bob Dylan. He was a part of the Folk / Blues trio *Koerner, Ray and Glover* during the 1960's. After a couple of albums he left the group to record solo in 1965, but has returned occasionally for reunion concerts and recordings.

Discography: (also see - Koerner, Ray and Glover)
1965 - **Spider's Blues,** *Elektra* // 1968 - **Running, Jumping, Standing Still,** (with Willie Murphy), *Red House* // 1972 - **Music is Just a Bunch of Notes,** *Sweet Jane* // 1986 - **Nobody Knows the Trouble I've Been,** *Red House* // 1990 - **Legends of Folk,** (with Ramblin' Jack Elliott), *Red House* // 1992 - **Raised By Humans,** *Red House* // 1996 - **Stargeezer,** *Red House.*

Koper, Karl Heinz
Classical Composer

Karl Heinz Koper wrote "Concerto for Harmonica and Orchestra" in 1961 for Tommy Reilly.

William Kratt Harmonica Co.

Harmonica manufacturer

The William Kratt Harmonica Company was established on the east coast around the turn of the century. Kratt Harmonicas reached their peak in sales during the harmonica boom of the 1920's and 30's and they were one of Hohner's chief U.S. competitors.

Although they are now largely out of the manufacturing, Kratt still maintains an office in New Jersey and does some `custom harmonica work.

Jim Kweskin Jug Band

Formed: 1963 - Cambridge, MA
Disbanded: Late 1960's

Jug band

Cofounded by Jim Kweskin and harmonica player Mel Lyman, *The Jim Kweskin Jug Band* emerged from the Cambridge, Massachusetts Folk music scene of the early 1960's. The band also featured Bruno Wolfe on the harmonica, as well as Geoff and Maria Muldaur, who would both later work with *The Paul Butterfield Blues Band*.

See - Mel Lyman

<u>Discography:</u>
1963 - **Jim Kweskin and The Jug Band I**, *Vanguard* // 1965 - **Jug Band Music**, *Vanguard* // 1966 - **Relax Your Mind**, *Vanguard* // 1966 - **Jim Kweskin and The Jug Band II** // 1967 - **See Reverse Side for Title**, *Fontana* // 1967 - **Garden of Joy**, *Reprise* // 1967 - **Jump for Joy**, *Vanguard* // 1968 - **Whatever Happened To Those Good Old Days**, *Vanguard* // 1968 - **The Best Of...**, *Vanguard* // 1969 - **American Aviator**, *Reprise* // 1970 - **Greatest Hits**, *Vanguard* // 1971 - **Jim Kweskin's America**, *Reprise* // 1977 - **Lives Again**, *Mountain Railroad* // 1978 - **Jim Kweskin**, *Mountain Railroad* // 1979 - **Side By Side**, *Mountain Railroad* // 1998 - **Acoustic Swing and Jug**, *Vanguard* // **Jug Band Blues**, *Mountain Railroad* // **With Jim Kweskin and The Jug Band: Jug Band**, (with Sippie Wallace and Otis Spann), *Mountain Railroad*.

– L –

LaCocque, Pierre

Born: October 13, 1952 - Belgium

Blues harmonica player

Pierre LaCocque came to Chicago originally from Belgium in 1969. He began playing harmonica after seeing Walter Horton perform in concert and was performing professionally by 1991.

He is the harmonica player and leader of *Mississippi Heat*, a Chicago area Blues band.

<u>Discography:</u> (see - Mississippi Heat)

Lafell, Leon "Cappy"

Real name: Leon Lehrfeld
Born: February 5, 1913

Vaudeville harmonica player

Leon Lafell first started playing the harmonica at age five and by the time he was fifteen he competed and came in second in an Albert Hoxie harmonica competition in Philadelphia. He immediately joined Hoxie's harmonica orchestra and played in it for several years.

In 1934 he joined Carl Freed's *Harmonica Harlequins* and when that broke up in 1935 he joined *The Cappy Barra Harmonica Ensemble*. Specializing on the polyphonia, Lafell played with the *Cappy Barra* group until the outbreak of World War Two. After the war he played polyphonia with *The Harmonicats* for a couple of years during the late 1940's.

A capable vocalist, Leon Lafell also recorded with Johnny Hodges, Frankie Newton and Duke Ellington during the 1930's.

Lair, John

Born: July 1, 1894 - Livingston, KY
Died: November 13, 1985 - Lexington, KY

Country jug, harmonica player

As program director for WLS radio in Chicago, John Lair put together the group *The Cumberland Ridge Runners* in 1932. John himself played jug and harmonica and the group was the house band for the station's "National Barn Dance" program.

Moving to Cincinnati in 1937, he started the "Renfro Valley Barn Dance" radio show for WLW radio, which became an enormous success and ran for more than 25 years.

Lamb, Paul

Born: Newcastle, England

Blues harmonica player

Paul Lamb began playing the harmonica at the age of fifteen and was playing professionally within four years. He competed in the World Harmonica Championships in Trossingen, Germany. He has been working with his back-up band, *The King Snakes* since the late 1980's.

Discography:
1990 - **Paul Lamb and The King Snakes**, *Blue Horizon* // 1995 - **Fine Condition**, *Indigo* // 1996 - **She's a Killer**, *Indigo* // 1997 - **Shifting Into Gear**, *Indigo* // 1998 - **John Henry Jumps In**, *Indigo* // 1999 - **The Blue Album**, *Indigo* // 1999 - **Blues Burglars - Whoopin'**, *Indigo* // 2000 - **Take Your Time and Get It Right**, *Indigo*.

Lancen, Serge

Classical Composer

Serge Lancen wrote "Concerto for Harmonica and Orchestra" in 1958 for Larry Adler.

Lane, Murray

Vaudeville harmonica band leader

Murray Lane was the leader of *The Harmonica Scamps* during the 1930's. He also put together the all-female harmonica band, *The Harmonicuties*.

Leadbelly

Real name: Huddie Ledbetter
Born: January 29, 1889 - Mooringsport, LA
Died: December 6, 1949 - New York, NY

Folk singer-songwriter, guitar, accordion, harmonica player

Along with Woody Guthrie, Leadbelly is regarded as one of America's founding fathers of modern Folk music. Although known mostly for his singing and mastery of the 12-string guitar, he was also well-versed in accordion and harmonica.

His musical career was sporadic, punctuated by prison sentences for various violent crimes, but he had the good fortune to work with Blind Lemon Jefferson, Woody Guthrie, Sonny Terry, Brownie McGhee and others.

Leadbelly's output as a songwriter was legendary. Amongst the songs he penned included "Rock Island Line," "Good Morning Blues," "Black Betty," "Cotton Fields," "Boll Weevil Blues," "Goodnight Irene" and "Midnight Special," all of which became hits for him and other singers who performed them.

His long and turbulent life came to an end in 1949, when he died of lateral sclerosis at New York's Bellevue Hospital.

Discography:
1935 - **Convict Blues**, *Aldabra* // 1935 - **Leadbelly**, *Columbia* // 1940's - **Congress Blues**, *Aldabra* // 1951 - **Leadbelly Memorial, Vol. 1-4**, *Stinson* // 1951 - **Leadbelly Plays Party Songs**, *Stinson* // 1951 - **Huddie Ledbetter**, *Smithsonian/Folkways* // 1951 - **Rock Island Line**, *Smithsonian/Folkways* // 1951 - **More Party Songs**, *Stinson* // 1952 - **Includes Legendary Performances Never Before Released**, *Columbia* // 1965 - **Take This Hammer**, *Smithsonian/Folkways* // 1965 - **Keep Your Hands Off Her**, *Smithsonian/Folkways* // 1966 - **Library of Congress Recordings**, *Elektra* // 1969 - **Good Mornin' Blues**, *Biograph* // 1989 - **Negro Folk Songs for Young People**, *Smithsonian/Folkways* // 1990 - **Alabama Bound**, *RCA* // 1990 - **Leadbelly Sings Folksongs**, (with Woody Guthrie, Cisco Houston, Sonny Terry and Brownie McGhee), *Smithsonian/Folkways* // 1990 - **Golden Classics**, *Collectables* // 1991 - **Gwine Dig a Hole to Put the Devil In**, *Rounder* // 1991 - **Let it Shine on Me**, *Rounder* // 1991 - **Midnight Special**, *Rounder* // 1992 - **Leadbelly**, *Blues Encores* // 1994 - **Kisses Sweeter Than Wine**, *Omega* // 1994 - **Nobody Knows the Trouble I've Seen**, *Rounder* // 1994 - **Pick Up on This**, *Rounder* // 1994 - **The Titanic, Vol. 4**, *Rounder* // 1994 - **Storyteller Blues**, *Drive Archive* // 1995 - **Leadbelly's Last Sessions**, *Smithsonian/Folkways* // 1995 - **Go Down Old Hannah**, *Rounder* // // 1995 - **The Complete Recordings, 1934-46**, *Document* 1996 - **Goodnight Irene**, *Tradition* // 1996 - **Leadbelly in Concert**, *Magnum* // 1996 - **Where Did You Sleep Last Night**, *Smithsonian/Folkways* // 1996 - **Masters of the Country Blues**, (with Blind Willie McTell), *Biograph* // 1996 - **In the Shadow of the Gallows Pole**, *Tradition* // 1996 - **Good Morning Blues**, *Topaz Jazz* // 1996 - **Leadbelly in Concert**, *Collector's Edition* // 1997 - **Bourgeois Blues**, *Smithsonian/Folkways* // 1999 - **Bridging Leadbelly**, *Rounder* // 2000 - **Private Party, Minneapolis, Minnesota, 1948**, *Document* // **Defense Blues**, *Collectables* // **Huddie Ledbetter's Best**, *Capitol* // **King of the 12-String Guitar**, *Columbia*.

Led Zepplin

Formed: 1968 - England
Disbanded: 1980

English Hard-Rock band

One of the groundbreaking Hard-Rock groups that dominated

the 1970's, *Led Zepplin* featured lead vocalist Robert Plant, who sometimes played the harmonica.

See - Robert Plant

<u>Discography:</u>
1969 - **Led Zepplin,** *Atlantic* // 1969 - **Led Zepplin II,** *Atlantic* // 1970 - **Led Zepplin III,** *Atlantic* // 1971 - **Led Zepplin IV,** *Atlantic* // 1973 - **Houses of the Holy,** *Atlantic* // 1975 - **Physical Graffiti,** *Atlantic* // 1976 - **Presence,** *Swan Song* // 1976 - **The Song Remains the Same,** *Swan Song* // 1979 - **In Through the Out Door,** *Swan Song* // 1982 - **Coda,** *Swan Song* // 1993 - **Complete Studio Recordings,** *Swan Song* // 1997 - **BBC Sessions,** *Atlantic.*

<u>Movies:</u>
1986 - **The Song Remains the Same.**

LeDoux, Chris

Born: October 2, 1948 - Biloxi, MS

Country singer, guitar, harmonica player
Having learned to play the guitar and harmonica while he was a teenager, Chris LeDoux has been performing and recording cowboy songs since the early 1970's, as well as having a highly successful career as a champion rodeo star.

<u>Discography:</u>
1971 - **Songs of Rodeo Life,** *Liberty* // 1972 - **Chris LeDoux Sings his Rodeo Songs,** *Liberty* // 1973 - **Rodeo Songs - Old and New,** *Liberty* // 1974 - **Songs of Rodeo and Country,** *Liberty* // 1974 - **Songs of Rodeo and Living Free,** *Liberty* // 1975 - **Life as a Rodeo Man,** *Liberty* // 1976 - **Songbook of the American West,** *Liberty* // 1977 - **Sing Me a Song, Mr. Rodeo Man,** *Liberty* // 1978 - **Western-Country** (Cowboys Ain't Easy to Love), *Liberty* // 1979 - **Paint Me Back Home in Wyoming,** *Liberty* // 1979 - **Rodeo's Singing Bronc Rider,** *Liberty* // 1980 - **Western Tunesmith,** *Liberty* // 1980 - **Sounds of the Western Country,** *Liberty* // 1980 - **Old Cowboy Heroes,** *Liberty* // 1981 - **He Rides the Wild Horses,** *Liberty* // 1982 - **Used To Want to Be a Cowboy,** *Liberty* // 1983 - **Thirty Dollar Cowboy,** *Liberty* // 1983 - **Old Cowboy Classics,** *Liberty* // 1984 - **Melodies and Memories,** *Liberty* // 1986 - **Wild and Wooly,** *Liberty* // 1990 - **Radio & Rodeo Hits,** *Liberty* // 1990 - **Powder River,** *Liberty* // 1991 - **Chris LeDoux & the Saddle Boogie Band,** *Liberty* // 1991 - **Gold Buckle Dreams,** *Liberty* // 1991 - **Western Underground,** *Capitol* // 1992 - **What Ya Gonna Do with a Cowboy,** *Capitol* // 1993 - **Under This Old Hat,** *Liberty* // 1994 - **Haywire,** *Liberty* // 1994 - **The Best Of..,** *Liberty* // 1994 - **American Cowboy,** *Liberty* // 1995 - **Rodeo Rock and Roll Collection,** *Liberty* // 1996 - **Stampede,** *Capitol* // 1997 - **Live,** *Capitol* // 1998 - **One Road Man,** *Capitol* // 1999 - **20 Greatest Hits,** *Capitol* // 2000 - **Cowboy,** *Capitol.*

Leecan and Cooksey
Acoustic Blues duo
Leecan and Cooksey were an acoustic Blues duo of the 1920's and 30's that featured guitarist Bobby Leecan and harmonica player Robert Cooksey.

See - Robert Cooksey

<u>Discography:</u>
1975 - **The Blues of Bobby Leecan and Robert Cooksey** // 1986 - **The Remaining Titles,** *Matchbox* // 1996 - **Complete Recorded Works, Vol. 1&2,** *Document.*

The Legendary Blues Band
Formed: 1980 - Chicago, IL

Blues band
Formed by former members of *The Muddy Waters Band, The Legendary Blues Band* featured Jerry Portnoy on the harmonica from 1980 until 1986, when he was replaced by Walter "Madison Slim" Koenig.

See - Jerry Portnoy, Madison Slim

<u>Discography:</u>
1980 - **Life of Ease,** *Rounder* // 1985 - **Red, Hot and Blue,** *Rounder* // 1989 - **Woke Up with the Blues,** *Ichiban* // 1990 - **Keepin' the Blues Alive,** *Ichiban* // 1991 - **U B Da Judge,** *Wild Dog* // 1992 - **Primetime Blues,** *Wild Dog* // 1993 - **Money Talks,** *Wild Dog.*

Leigh, Keri

Born: April 21, 1969 - Birmingham, AL

Blues singer, guitar, bass, harmonica player
Originally from Oklahoma, Keri Leigh settled in Austin, Texas in 1990 and has been performing and recording steadily ever since. She also works as a writer and publishes books and articles on a variety of Blues-related topics.

<u>Discography:</u>
1991 - **Blue Devil Blues,** *Amazing* // 1993 - **No Beginner,** *Amazing* // 1995 - **Arrival,** *Malaco.*

Leighton, Charles

Born: June 24, 1921 - NY

Jazz / Classical harmonica player
Charles Leighton started playing the harmonica at age twelve and took lessons at Borrah Minevitch's Harmonica Institute of America. During the late 1930's he played with *The Philharmonicas* and *The Cappy Barra Harmonica Ensemble.*

He began playing solo after World War Two, doing a lot of session work in the recording studio as well as appearing in movies. Artists he worked with include *The Andrews Sisters,* Dean Martin, Harry Belafonte, Dinah Shore, Harry Belafonte and Mitch

Miller. He also started working as a recording engineer and produced albums for Alan "Blackie" Schackner and Stan Harper as well as taking part in Richard Hayman's *Harmonica Sparklers*.

From the mid-1950's on, he spent most of his time concentrating on running his recording studio. In the 1990's he began working with harmonica players like William Galison and Susan Rosenberg as well as recording an album of Classical music and making limited personal appearances.

Discography:
2000 - **Charles Leighton - Classical,** *Mega Mouth* // **Old Standard Songs** // **Classical Album #1** // **Classical Album #2** // **Yesterdays.**

Leighton, Hal
Vaudeville harmonica player
Hal Leighton was a harmonica player and arranger for *The Harmonica Rascals* as well as authoring a book of harmonica instruction.

Bibliography:
1978 - **How To Play the Harmonica for Fun and Profit,** *Borden.*

Lennon, John
Born: October 9, 1940 - Liverpool, England
Died: December 8, 1980 - New York City, NY

Rock singer-songwriter, guitar, harmonica player
A co-founder of *The Beatles,* John Lennon played the harmonica on several of their early hits. He learned how to play cross-harp style from Delbert McClinton. Lennon stopped featuring his harmonica playing after the first few albums.

Discography: (see - The Beatles)

Lenoir, J.B.
Born: March 5, 1929 - Monticello, MS
Died: April 29, 1967 - Urbana, IL

Blues guitar, harmonica player
Known primarily as a guitar player, J.B. Lenoir learned to play Blues music from his father in the late 1930's. Traveling around the south, he worked with Elmore James and Sonny Boy Williamson II (Rice Miller) before settling in Chicago in 1949.

During the 1950's he worked with Memphis Minnie, Big Maceo, Muddy Waters, Big Bill Broonzy and others. He started his own band, *JB and The Bayou Boys* in 1950 and recorded for the JOB label starting in 1951. He worked steadily through the 1950's and 60's. Lenoir died as a result of injuries he received in a car crash in 1967.

Discography:
1965 - **Alabama Blues,** *L&R* // 1968 - **Natural Man,** *Chess* // 1970 - **Crusade,** *Polydor* // 1976 - *Chess* **Blues Masters,** *Chess* // 1980 - **Mojo Boogie,** *Flyright* // 1980 - **Down in Mississippi,** *L&R* // 1989 - **The Parrot Sessions, 1954-55,** *Relic* // 1991 - **J.B. Lenoir,** *Chess* // 1991 - **J.B. Lenoir, 1951-54: His JOB Recordings,** *Paula* // 1992 - **1951/1958,** *New Rose* // 1993 - **Mama Watch Your Daughter** // 1995 - **Viet Nam Blues,** *Evidence* // **I Don't Know,** *Vogue.*

Les, Don
Real name: Dominick Leshinski
Born: November 15, 1914 - Lorain, OH
Died: August 25, 1994 - Chicago, IL

Vaudeville harmonica player
Don Les grew up in Lorain, Ohio and started playing the Harmonica at age fifteen. He joined Borrah Minevitch's

Harmonica Rascals in 1942. It was there that he met Jerry Murad. When Murad left the group to return to Chicago, Les followed and was brought in to play the bass harmonica in *The Quintones*, which became *The Harmonicats* when it became a trio.

The Harmonicats recorded "Peg O' My Heart" in 1947 and it became the best-selling song of that year. Les stayed with the group until 1972. Following an argument with Jerry Murad, Les formed his own *Harmonicats* group with Mildred Mulcay playing the lead harmonica.

Les mastered playing chromatic Jazz on the diatonic harmonica and took over playing lead when Mildred Mulcay left. He was joined by Mo Vint, who played the chord harmonica and foot pedal bass. Les continued playing until his death in 1995.

Discography: (also see - The Harmonicats)
Don Les' Harmonicats - Vol. 1&2.

Levy, Howard

Born: July 31, 1951 - Brooklyn, NY

Jazz piano, harmonica player

Howard Levy is the modern master of playing chromatic jazz on the diatonic harmonica. Originally from New York, he started out as a piano player and didn't pick up the harmonica until he was eighteen.

As Levy tells it, he was experimenting on the high-end blow bends one day when he started to figure out how to play them in the lower registers of the instrument. Since mastering this technique, he can play a full chromatic scale in any key on any diatonic harmonica.

Heavily in demand for studio work, Levy has done over 1,000 sessions and has appeared on countless albums as a guest artist, including work with Holly Cole, Ralph Covert, Dennis

Deyoung, Steve Goodman, Bonnie Koloc, Kenny Loggins, Ken Nordine, Tom Paxton, John Prine, Pete Seeger, Ben Sidran, Dolly Parton, *The Freddy Jones Band* and many others.

In 1989 he joined *Bela Fleck and The Flecktones* for three outstanding Jazz albums. He currently works with *Trio Globo*, a World music group, as well as doing solo and group projects. In addition to playing harmonica and piano, Levy also has mastered several other intruments, including the ocarina, flute, saxophones, percussion instruments and others.

Discography: (also see - Bela Fleck and The Flecktones)
1986 - **Harmonica Jazz,** *Tall Thin* // 1994 - **Trio Globo,** *Silverwave* // 1995 - **Carnival of Souls,** (with Trio Globo), *Silverwave* // 1996 - **The Old Country,** *M.A.*

Movies:
1992 - **Straight Talk** // 1996 - **Time to Kill** // 1997 - **Family Thing** // 1998 - **Striptease.**

Lewin, Frank
Classical composer
Frank Lewin wrote "Concerto for Harmonica and Orchestra" in 1960 for John Sebastian, Sr.

Lewis, Huey

Real name: Hugh Cregg III
Born: July 5, 1951 - New York City, NY

Rock singer, harmonica player
Huey Lewis is the lead vocalist and harmonica player with *Huey Lewis and The News.* Founded in 1980, The News had a string of hits in the mid-1980's, many of which featured Huey Lewis on the harmonica.

Discography:
1980 - **Huey Lewis and The News,** *Chrysalis* // 1982 - **Picture This,** *Chrysalis* // 1983 - **Sports,** *Chrysalis* // 1986 - **Fore!,** *Chrysalis* // 1988 - **Small World,** *Chrysalis* // 1991 - **Hard At Play,** *EMI* // 1992 - **The Heart of Rock and Roll: The Best Of...,** *Chrysalis* // 1994 - **Four Chords and Several Years Ago,** *Elektra* // 2000 - **Greatest,** *EMI.*

Lewis, Noah

Born: September 3, 1895 - Henning, TN
Died: February 7, 1961 - Ripley, TN

Blues harmonica player
Noah Lewis taught himself how to play the harmonica as a child in Tennessee. He began playing for tips in Memphis around 1912. He had the ability to play two harmonicas at once, one with his mouth and one with his nose.

He started working with Gus Cannon around 1916 and together they formed *Cannon's Jug Stompers,* a top Memphis-styled Jug band. They recorded for the Victor label during the late 1920's.

After leaving the Jug band in the early 1930's, Lewis played around at juke joints and dances and even did some recordings with Yank Rachell and Sleepy John Estes, though he eventually dropped out of music. He died as a consequence of frostbite in 1961.

Discography: (also see - Cannon's Jug Stompers)
Gus Cannon & Noah Lewis, Complete Recorded Works, Vol. 2, *Document.*

Lewis, Walter "Furry"

Born: March 6, 1893 - Greenwood, MS
Died: September 14, 1981 - Memphis, TN

Blues singer, guitar, harmonica player
"Furry" Lewis began his musical career early, playing on the streets of Memphis at age seven. During his early career he played guitar with W.C. Handy's orchestra. Hoboing around the country, he lost a leg in a railroad accident in 1916.

After settling in Memphis, Tennessee, he played music for tips and swept the streets. During the late 1920's he recorded approximately 20 sides for various record labels. He was largely unheard of for the next thirty years.

Folklorists rediscovered him in 1959 and he had a highly successful career playing the Folk club and festival circuits, as well as recording prolifically until his death in 1981.

Discography:
1959 - **Furry Lewis Blues,** *Smithsonian/Folkways* // 1960's - **Shake Em On Down,** *Fantasy* // 1961 - **Back On My Feet Again,** *Bluesway* // 1962 - **Done Changed My Mind,** *Ace* // 1969 - **Presenting the Country Blues,** *Blue Horizon* // 1970's - **Beale Street Blues,** *Barclay* // 1970 - **Mississippi Fred McDowell & Furry Lewis,** *Biograph* // 1975 - **Fourth and Beale,** *Lucky Seven* // 1970 - **In Memphis** // 1970 - **On the Road Again,** *Adelphi* // 1970 - **When I Lay My Burden Down** // 1971 - **Live at the Gaslight,** *Ampex* // 1972 - **Blues Masters, Vol. 5,** *Blue Horizon* // 1976 - **The Fabulous Furry Lewis,** *Southland* // 1988 - **Furry Lewis in his Prime, 1927-29,** *Yazoo* // 1990 - **Complete Recorded Works, (1927-29),** *Document* // 1992 - **Canned Heat Blues: Masters of Memphis Blues,** *BMG* // 1998 - **Furry Lewis,** *Xtra* // 1999 - **Take Your Time,** *Genes* // 1999 - **Blues Magician,** *Lucky Seven* // 1999 - **On the Road Again,** (with Bukka White), *Genes* // **American Blues Heritage, Vol. 3,** *Southland* // **House of Blues, Vol. 2,** *Blue Star* // **The Remaining Titles,** *Wolf* // **Furry Lewis, 1927-29,** *Wolf.*

Movies
1975 - **W.W. and The Dixie Dance Kings.**

Lightfoot, "Papa" Alexander

Also known as: Papa George, Little Papa Walter
Born: March 2, 1924 - Natchez, MS
Died: November 28, 1971 - Natchez, MS

Blues singer, washboard, harmonica player
"Papa" Alexander Lightfoot was known primarily as a vocalist and made his first recordings in 1949 with *The Gondoliers,* a vocal group from New Orleans. Self-taught on the harmonica as a child, he drifted into the Blues and recorded for several labels during the 1950's.

During the course of his career he worked with "Champion" Jack Dupree, "Fats" Domino, Dinah Washington, Sonny Boy Williamson II (Rice Miller) and others. Largely unheard of during the 1960's, he was re-discovered by Bob Hite of the group *Canned Heat* who managed to get several of his records re-released. Lightfoot was just starting his comeback when he died of a heart attack in 1971.

Discography:
1969 - **Natchez Trace,** *Crosscut* // 1969 - **Rural Blues, Vol. 2,** *Liberty* // 1995 - **Goin' Back To Natchez Trace,** *Ace.*

Linz, Phil

Born: June 4, 1939 - Baltimore, MD

Baseball player
A utility infielder for the New York Yankees, Phil Linz was fined $250 by manager Yogi Berra on August 20, 1964 for playing his harmonica on the team bus. The public outcry was so tremendous that Berra refunded the fine in the form of music lessons and the Hohner company gave Linz $5,000 to endorse it's products.

Lip Blocking

Lip blocking is a technique where the harmonica player puckers in order to determine the size of the hole and consequently the number of holes to be played.

Also see - Blocking

Little Charlie and The Nightcats

Formed: 1976 - California

Blues band
Little Charlie and The Nightcats came into existence after a chance meeting in 1973 by harmonica players Rick Estrin and Charlie Baty. Estrin had been playing around northern California since 1968, including playing with Lowell Fulson. The group came in 1976 with Baty switching over to guitar and Estrin handling the harmonica and vocals. They cut their first single in 1982 and signed with Alligator Records in 1987.

See - Rick Estrin

Discography:
1987 - **All the Way Crazy,** *Alligator* // 1988 - **Disturbing the Peace,** *Alligator* // 1989 - **The Big Break!,** *Alligator* // 1991 - **Captured Live,** *Alligator* // 1993 - **Night Vision,** *Alligator* // 1995 - **Straight Up!,** *Alligator* // 1997 - **Deluxe Edition,** *Alligator* // 1998 - **Shadow of the Blues,** *Alligator.*

Little Feat

Formed: 1969 - Los Angeles, CA
Disbanded 1979 Reformed: 1988

Southern Rock band

Founded by ex-*Mothers of Invention* members Roy Estrada and Lowell George, *Little Feat's* sound was an eclectic blend of Country, Rock, New Orleans R&B and Funk. George led the group through the 1970's with his songwriting, vocals and slide guitar as well as taking an occasional turn on the harmonica.

After Lowell died in 1979, the band's career stalled. They reunited in the mid-1990's with limited commercial success.

See - Lowell George

Discography: (with Lowell George)
1971 - **Little Feat,** *Warner Brothers* // 1972 - **Sailin' Shoes,** *Warner Brothers* // 1973 - **Dixie Chicken,** *Warner Brothers* // 1974 - **Feats Don't Fail Me Now,** *Warner Brothers* // 1975 - **The Last Record Album,** *Warner Brothers* // 1975 - **Two Originals,** *Warner Brothers* // 1977 - **Time Loves a Hero,** *Warner Brothers* // 1978 - **Waiting for Columbus,** *Warner Brothers* // 1979 - **Down on the Farm,** *Warner Brothers* // 1994 - **The Best Of...,** *Warner Brothers* // 2000 - **Hotcakes and Outtakes: 30 Years of Little Feat,** *Rhino.*

Little Mike and The Tornadoes

Formed: 1978 - New York City, NY

Blues band

Originally based out of New York City, *Little Mike and The Tornadoes* is led by vocalist Mike Markowitz, who also plays piano and harmonica. Before recording on their own, *The Tornadoes* did albums backing Pinetop Perkins and ex-Howlin' Wolf guitarist Hubert Sumlin. They continue to tour and record in the U.S. and Europe.

See - Mike Markowitz

Discography:
1988 - **After Hours,** (with Pinetop Perkins), *Blind Pig* // 1989 - **Heart and Soul,** *Blind Pig* // 1990 - **Heart Attack,** *Blind Pig* // 1992 - **Pay Day,** *Blind Pig* // 1995 - **Flynn's Place,** *Flying Fish* // 1998 - **Hot Shot,** *Wild Dog.*

Lockwood, Robert Jr.

Born: March 27, 1915 - Marvell, AR
Blues guitar, harmonica player

Robert Lockwood is the stepson of Delta Blues legend Robert Johnson, who taught him how to play guitar. Lockwood played at local parties and dances around the Helena, Arkansas, area until 1938, when he started working with Sonny Boy Williamson II (Rice Miller), from whom he probably picked up some of his harmonica playing.

Over the next few years he would work with various Blues musicians in the Mississippi Delta area, including Williamson, Howlin' Wolf and Baby Boy Warren. He moved to Chicago in 1950 and worked with Muddy Waters, Little Walter, Otis Spann, Roosevelt Sykes and Sunnyland Slim, as well as recording and performing on his own.

He has continued to work in the Blues and is a leading proponent of the Delta Blues style that his father taught him in addition to being a terrific guitar player in his own right.

Discography:
1967 - **Steady Rollin' Man,** *Delmark* // 1974 - **Contrasts,** *Trix* // 1975 - **Blues Live in Japan,** *Advent* // 1976 - **Windy City Blues** // 1977 - **Does 12,** *Trix* // 1979 - **Hangin' On,** *Rounder* // 1980 - **Johnny Shines and Robert Lockwood - Dust My Broom,** *Flyright* // 1981 - **Johnny Shines and Robert Lockwood: Mr. Blues is Here to Stay,** *Rounder* // 1982 - **Plays Robert and Robert,** *Black & Blue* // 1990 - **What's the Score** // 1991 - **Robert Lockwood,** *Paula* // 1998 - **I Got To Find Me a Woman,** *Verve* // 1999 - **Complete Trix Recordings,** *32 Jazz* // 1999 - **Just the Blues,** *Bullseye Blues* // 2000 - **Delta Crossroads,** *Telarc* // **Robert Lockwood Jr.,** *Black & Blue.*

Logan, John "Juke"
Blues harmonica player, DJ

Working mostly as a studio harmonica player, John "Juke" Logan has played and recorded with Ry Cooder, Albert Collins,

Dobie Gray, Leon Russell, John Lee Hooker and others as well as doing several movies and TV Shows.

Discography:
1995 - **The Chill,** *Razor & Tie* // 1999 - **Juke Rhythm,** *Mocombo* // 1999 - **Live as it Gets,** *Mocombo.*

Movies:
1984 - **Streets of Fire** // 1986 - **Crossroads** // 1987 - **La Bamba** // 1996 - **Two Days in the Valley** // TV - **Rosanne** // TV - **Home Improvement.**

Logan, Larry

Born: October 23, Lafayette, LA

Classical harmonica soloist

Larry Logan began playing the harmonica in the 1930's with his brother's *Harmonica Rascal*-like band. He took up the chromatic harmonica in earnest and decided to pursue a career as a Pop/Classical harmonica soloist after hearing Larry Adler.

From the 1950's on he has worked with orchestras and piano accompanists worldwide, playing a mixture of Classical and Popular music.

Discography:
1988 - **Concert Encores,** *Logan* // 1989 - **Classical Harmonicist,** *Logan* // 1993 - **Live in Concert,** *Logan* // 1996 - **Souvenirs,** *Logan* // 2000 - **Logan Plays Gershwin,** *Logan.*

Video:
2000 - **An Evening with Larry Logan.**

Bibliography:
2001 - **Logan's Run,** *First Books.*

Loudermilk, John D.

Also known as: Johnny Dee
Born: March 31, 1934 - Durham NC

Folk / Country / Rock singer-songwriter, guitar, harmonica player

Known primarily as a songwriter, John D. Loudermilk is probably best remembered as having written the Blues/Rock classics "Tobacco Road" and "Indian Reservation." He began performing professionally as Johnny Dee when he was thirteen, including singing, playing guitar and harmonica.

Although he had a few minor hits, his greatest success came as a songwriter when he penned hits for Eddie Cochran, *The Everly Brothers,* Bobby Vee, Johnny Cash and others. Although his concentration is on songwriting, he continues to perform occasionally.

Discography:
1962 - **Language of Love,** *RCA* // 1962 - **12 Sides Of,** *RCA* // 1965 - **Sings a Bizarre Collection,** *RCA* // 1967 - **Suburban Attitudes,** *RCA* // 1968 - **Country Love Songs,** *RCA* // 1969 - **The Open Mind of J D Loudermilk,** *RCA* // 1971 - **Elloree, Vol. 1,** *Warner Brothers* // 1973 - **The Best Of...,** *RCA* // 1975 - **Encores,** *RCA* // 1977 - **Just Passing Through,** *Mim* // 1989 - **Blue Train,** *Bear Family* // 1989 - **It's My Time,** *Bear Family* // 1995 - **Sittin' in the Balcony,** *Bear Family.*

Louis, Joe Hill

Real name: Lester Hill
Also known as: The Bee-Bop Boy
Born: September 23, 1921 - Raines, TN
Died: August 5, 1957 - Memphis, TN

Blues drum, guitar, harmonica player

Joe Hill Louis learned how to play the harmonica and guitar from Will Shade, leader of *The Memphis Jug Band.* Louis hoboed extensively during the 1930's and 40's and did not settle down until after he recorded for the Columbia label in 1949.

Louis made his home in Memphis, Tennessee, where he took over B.B. King's radio show. By adding a drum set to his guitar and harmonica, Louis billed himself as "Joe Hill Louis, The Be-Bop Boy and his One Man Band." He made several recordings over the next few years, including some for the Sun label with harmonica ace, Big Walter Horton. Louis died of a tetanus infection in 1957.

Discography:
1972 - **Blues in the Morning** // 1979 - **The One Man Band 1949-56,** *Muskadine* // 1992 - **The Be-Bop Boy,** (with Walter Horton and Mose Vinson), *Bear Family.*

Louisiana Red (see - Iverson Minter)

Louisiana Saxophone

A southern colloquial term for the harmonica.

The Lovin' Spoonful

Formed: 1965 - New York City, NY
Disbanded: 1968

Folk / Rock band

Originally started as a Jug band, *The Lovin' Spoonful* featured lead vocalist and guitarist John Sebastian on the harmonica. Sebastian was the son of Classical soloist John Sebastian, Sr. and wrote most of the band's original material. He went on to a steady solo career after *The Lovin' Spoonful* disbanded in 1968.

See - John Sebastian, Jr.

Discography:
1965 - **Do You Believe in Magic?**, *Kama Sutra* // 1966 - **Day Dream**, *Kama Sutra* // 1966 - **Did You Ever**, *Kama Sutra* // 1966 - **What's Up Tiger Lily?**, *Kama Sutra* // 1966 - **Hums of The Lovin' Spoonful**, *Kama Sutra* // 1967 - **Day Blues**, *Kama Sutra* // 1967 - **Nashville Cats**, *Kama Sutra* // 1967 - **Loving You**, *Kama Sutra* // 1967 - **Something in the Night**, *Kama Sutra* // 1967 - **You're a Big Boy Now**, *Kama Sutra* // 1967 - **The Best Of...**, *Kama Sutra* // 1968 - **Revelation Revolution 69**, *Kama Sutra* // 1968 - **Everything Playing**, *Kama Sutra* // 1990 - **Anthology**, *Rhino*.

Movies:
1966 - **What's Up Tiger Lily?** // 1967 - **You're a Big Boy Now.**

Lowe, Jez

Born: 1956 - Easington, Durham, England

Folk singer-songwriter, guitar, harmonica player

Jez Lowe first began playing music professionally in the early 1970's where he specialized in traditional English Folk music. Now working with his back-up band, *The Bad Pennies*, Lowe plays guitar and harmonica to augment his singing and songwriting.

Discography:
1983 - **The Old Durham Road**, *Felside* // 1987 - **Jez Lowe**, *Felside* // 1988 - **Bad Penny**, *Felside* // 1990 - **Briefly on the Street**, *Felside* // 1992 - **Back Shift**, *Felside* // 1993 - **Bede Weeps**, *Felside* // 1994 - **Banners**, *Easington District Council* // 1995 - **Tenterhooks**, *Green Linnet* // 1996 - **Galloways**, *Musica Pangea* // 1998 - **The Parish Notices**, *Green Linnet*.

Lucas, Robert

Born: July 25, 1962 - Long Beach, CA

Blues singer guitar, harmonica player

Robert Lucas began playing harmonica as a teenager and later picked up the slide guitar. He played for several years with his guitar teacher, Bernie Pearl, before going solo in 1990. He has recorded several solo albums as well as doing a brief stint playing guitar and harmonica with *Canned Heat*.

Discography: (also see - Canned Heat)
1990 - **Across the River** // 1990 - **Usin' Man Blues**, *Audioquest* // 1991 - **Luke and The Locomotives**, *Audioquest* // 1992 - **Built for Comfort**, *Audioquest* // 1994 - **Layaway**, *Audioquest* // 1997 - **Completely Blue**, *Audioquest*.

Lyman, Mel

Folk harmonica player

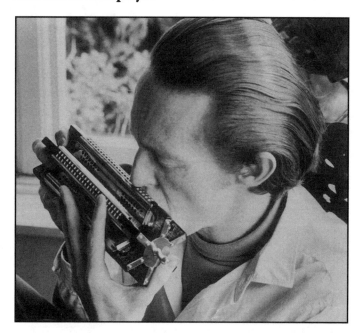

An almost mythical musician, Mel Lyman was part of the Cambridge, Massachusetts Folk music scene in the mid-1960's. While playing banjo and harmonica in *The Jim Kweskin Jug Band*, he appeared at several Newport Folk Festivals before departing music to start his own commune.

Discography: (see - The Jim Kweskin Jug band)

Lynwood Slim

Real name: Richard Duran
Born: August 19, 1953

Blues singer, harmonica player

Lynwood Slim began playing the harmonica at age fifteen while growing up in California. After moving to Minnesota in the mid-1980's, he took over the Blues band that Kim Wilson left to join *The Fabulous Thunderbirds*. Eventually forming *The Lynwood Slim Band*, he has formed bands in Los Angeles and Chicago and recorded several albums.

Discography:
1996 - **Soul Feet**, *Atomic Theory* // 1997 - **Lost in America**, *Black Magic* // 1998 - **Back To Back**, *Crosscut* // 2000 - **World Wide Wood**, *Pacific Blues*.

Lyon, "Southside" Johnny

Born: December 4, 1948 - Neptune, NJ

Rock singer, harmonica player

"Southside" Johnny Lyon played in several bands with Bruce Springsteen and "Miami" Steve Van Zandt during the late 1960's before forming his own band, *Southside Johnny and The Asbury Jukes,* in 1974. He has been recording and performing steadily ever since.

Discography: (also see - Southside Johnny and The Asbury Jukes)
1988 - *Slow Dance, Cypress //* 1991 - **Better Days,** *Impact.*

– M –

Mabon, "Big" Willie

Born: October 24, 1925 - Hollywood TN
Died: April 19, 1985 - Paris France

Blues piano, vocals, harmonica

Willie Mabon taught himself to play the piano at age sixteen. His family moved to Chicago in 1942 and he started playing the harmonica shortly thereafter. After serving in the Marines for two years he returned to Chicago and immediately started working in music by playing with Bill Lucas and Earl Dranes. He formed his own band, *The House Rockers,* in 1947 and began recording in 1949.

He signed with Chess Records in 1950 and over the next few years he had hits with "I'm Mad," "I Don't Know," "Poison Ivy" and "Seventh Son" as well as playing behind several artists on the Chess label. After a falling out with Leonard Chess in 1956, Mabon spent the rest of his life moving from label to label and performing, both in the U.S. and in Europe. He did some harmonica playing on recordings by Mickey Baker and Sunnyland Slim.

Discography:
1972 - **Funky //** 1973 - **Cold Chilly Woman,** *Black & Blue //* 1973 - **Come Back,** *America //* 1974 - **Live and Well //** 1974 - **Chicago 1963,** *America //* 1975 - **Shake That Thing,** *Black & Blue //* 1976 - **Sings 'I Don't Know' and Other Chicago Blues Hits,** *Antilles //* 1979 - **Chicago Blues Sessions,** *L&R //* 1980 - **I'm the Fixer (Original USA Recordings 1963-64),** *Flyright //* 1982 - **The Seventh Son,** *Crown Prince //* 1982 - **Blues Roots Vol. 16,** *Chess //* 1993 - **Seventh Son,** *Charly //* 1995 - **I Don't Know: The Best Of...,** *Wolf //* **Willie Mabon,** *Chess.*

Macklin, Dave

Vaudeville harmonica player, instructor, band leader

Dave Macklin was an instructor at the Borrah Minevitch Harmonica Institute in New York City during the 1930's. He organized his best pupils into *The Philharmonicas,* a Vaudeville harmonica band that lasted until World War Two.

Maddox, Cal

Born: November 3, 1915 - Boaz, AL
Died: 1968

Country singer, guitar, harmonica player

Cal Maddox was known primarily as a singer, guitarist and harmonica player for his family's group, *The Maddox Brothers and Rose.* They were popular from the mid-1940's until the mid-1950's.

Discography:
1956 - **A Collection of Standard Sacred Songs,** *King //* 1961 - **America's Most Colorful Hillbilly, Vol. 1&2,** *Arhoolie //* 1961 - **I'll Write Your Name in the Sand,** *King //* 1962 - **The Maddox Brothers and Rose,** *Wrangler //* 1965 - **Go Honky Tonkin',** *Hilltop //* 1976 - **The Maddox Brothers and Rose, 1945-51, Vol. 1&2,** *Arhoolie //* 1983 - **On the Air: The 1940's, Vol. 1&2,** *Arhoolie //* 1997 - **The Maddox Brothers and Rose,** *King //* **Family Folks,** *Bear Family //* **Rockin' and Rollin',** *Bear Family //* *Columbia* **Historic Collection,** *Columbia //* **The Hillbilly Boogie Years,** *Rockateer //* **Talk About 50 Years in Country Music,** *Arhoolie.*

Madison Slim

Real name: Walter Koenig

Blues harmonica player

Madison Slim is the harmonica player who replaced Jerry Portnoy in *The Legendary Blues Band* in the late 1980's. He has also toured with Jimmy Rogers and most recently has been playing with *Reverend Raven and The Chain Smokin' Choir Boys*.

Discography: (see - The Legendary Blues Band)

Magann, Les

Died: August 7, 1999

Vaudeville harmonica player

Les Magann played the bass and chord harmonicas with The Harmaniacs, *The Harmonica Rascals* and with *Johnny Puleo's Harmonica Gang* during the 1950's.

Taj Mahal

Real name: Henry St. Clair Fredericks
Born: May 17, 1940 - New York City, NY

Folk / Blues singer, multi-instrumentalist including harmonica

The son of musical parents, Taj Mahal learned to play the guitar at age fifteen and has picked up several other instruments, including the harmonica, since that time. While studying at the University of Massachusetts he joined a local folklore society and began studying rural Blues styles. After graduating from college, he played in the local Folk and Blues clubs around Boston before moving to California in 1965.

After arriving in California, he teamed up with drummer Ed Cassidy and guitarist Ry Cooder to form *The Rising Suns*. They were signed to a recording contract with the Columbia label in 1965, but broke up before the album could be released. Columbia kept Taj Mahal on as a solo artist. He has been releasing quality albums on a regular basis ever since.

During the 1970's he became involved in movies, where he made several guest appearances as an actor as well as doing several soundtracks. He has managed to maintain a fairly consistent, if not eclectic performing and recording career, by exploring the many styles of African-American music.

Discography:
1967 - **Taj Mahal,** *Columbia* // 1969 - **The Natch'l Blues,** *Columbia* // 1969 - **Giant Step / De Ole Folks at Home,** *Columbia* // 1971 - **The Real Thing,** *Columbia* // 1971 - **Happy Just to Be Like I Am,** *Columbia* // 1972 - **Recycling the Blues and Other Stuff,** *Columbia* // 1973 - **OOOH So Good 'n' Blues,** *Columbia* // 1973 - **Sounder,** *Columbia* // 1974 - **Mo' Roots,** *Columbia* // 1975 - **Music Keeps Me Together,** *Columbia* // 1976 - **Anthology, Vol. 1,** *Columbia* // 1976 - **Satisfied 'n' Tickled Too,** *Columbia* // 1977 - **Brothers,** *Warner Brothers* // 1977 - **Music Fuh Ya,** *Warner Brothers* // 1978 - **Evolution,** *Warner Brothers* // 1979 - **Taj Mahal and The International Rhythm Band Live,** *Crystal Clear* // 1980 - **Taj Mahal and The International Rhythm Band,** *Magnet* // 1981 - **The Best Of...,** *Magnet* // 1981 - **The Best Of, Vol. 1,** *Columbia* // 1981 - Live, *Magnet* // 1986 - **Taj,** *Gramavision* // 1987 - **Live and Direct,** *Laserlight* // 1988 - **Shake Sugaree,** *Music for Little People* // 1989 - **Peace is the World Smiling** // 1990 - **Brer Rabbit and The Wonderful Tar Baby** // 1991 - **Don't Call Us,** *Atlantic* // 1991 - **Mule Bone,** *Gramavision* // 1991 - **Like Never Before,** *Private Music* // 1992 - **Taj's Blues,** *Columbia* // 1993 - **Dancin' the Blues,** *Private Music* // 1993 - **World Music,** *Legacy* // 1994 - **Taj Mahal 1980,** *Just a Memory* // 1994 - **The Rising Sun Collection,** *Just a Memory* // 1995 - **Mumatz, Mahal,** *Waterlily Acoustic* // 1996 - **Live at Ronnie Scott's,** *DRG* // 1996 - **Phantom Blues,** *Private Music* // 1997 - **An Evening of Acoustic Music,** *RUF* // 1997 - **Senor Blues,** *Private Music* // 1997 - **Shakin' a Tail Feather,** *Rhino* // 1998 - **Real Blues,** *Sony* // 1998 - **In Progress & in Motion (1965-1998),** *Columbia* // 1998 - **Sacred Island,** *Private Music* // 1998 - **Taj Mahal & The Hula Blues,** *Tradition* // 1999 - **Kulanjan,** *Hannibal* // 1999 - **Blue Light Boogie,** *Private Music* // 2000 - **Shoutin in Key,** *Hannibal* // 2000 - **The Best Of...,** *Private Music* // **Taj Mahal,** *Yazoo* // **Big Blues,** *Essential* // **Shake It To the One,** *Music for Little People* // **The Collection,** *Castle*.

Movies:
1971 - **Clay Pigeon** // 1972 - **Sounder** // 1974 - **Fighting for Our Lives** // 1975 - **Play it Again Sam** // 1976 - **Scott Joplin** // 1976 - **Sounder, Part Two** // 1977 - **Brothers.**

Maiden, Sidney

Born: 1923 - Mansfield, LA

Blues harmonica player

Sidney Maiden learned how to play the harmonica as a child growing up in rural Louisiana. He left home in his late teens, traveled around the U.S. and eventually settled in the San Francisco Bay area in the late 1940's.

He started working with KC Douglas in 1947 and by 1948 they were recording together. Since staying mostly in California, Maiden has worked in music sporadically ever since.

Discography:
1961 - **Trouble An' Blues**, *Original Blues Classics* // 1988 - **Jericho Alley Blues Flash**.

Manfred Mann

Formed: 1964 - England
Original line-up disbanded: 1968

British Pop band

One of the bands to hit it big during the British invasion of the early 1960's, *Manfred Mann* was fronted by vocalist and harmonica player Paul Jones, who stayed with the group until 1966. They had big hits with "Pretty Flamingo" and "Do Wah Diddy."

See - Paul Jones

Discography: (with Paul Jones)
1964 - **Five Faces of Manfred Mann**, *EMI* // 1964 - **The Manfred Mann Album**, *Ascot* // 1965 - **My Little Red Book of Winners**, *Ascot* // 1965 - **Mann Made**, *Ascot* // 1966 - **Mann Made Hits**, *HMV* // 1966 - **Pretty Flamingo**, *United Artists* // 1966 - **As Is**, *Fontana*.

Mansfield, Darrell

Born: April 10, 1950 - Sioux City, IA

Christian Rock guitar, harmonica player

One of the top harmonica players in the field of Christian Rock music, Darrell Mansfield began playing music after meeting Paul McCartney in the Late 1960's. After a series of personal misfortunes, he turned his music over to the Contemporary Christian genre. He's performed on nearly every continent and leads a busy schedule of touring and recording.

Discography:
1976 - **Gentle Faith**, *Marantha* // 1979 - **Higher Power**, *Marantha* // 1980 - **Get Ready**, *Polydor* // 1983 - **Darrell Mansfield Band Live**, *Marantha* // 1983 - **The Vision**, *Marantha* // 1988 - **Darrell Mansfield Live at Calvary Chapel**, *Asaph* // 1990 - **Trimmed and Burnin'**, *Grrr Records* // 1991 - **Blues with a Feelin'**, *Ocean* // 1991 - **Live at Flevo**, *Asaph* // 1992 - **Give Me Your Blues**, *Asaph* // 1993 - **Slow Burn**, *Grrr Records* // 1993 - **Shack of Peasants**,

Vol. 1 & 2, *Metro One* // 1995 - **Mansfield & Company**, *Ocean* // 1995 - **Into the Night**, *Grrr Records* // 1996 - **The Lord's House** // 1997 - **Delta Blues** // 1997 - *Crossroads* // 1997 - **Revelation**, *Word* // 1998 - **Last Chance Boogie**, *Full Moon* // 1999 - **The Darrell Mansfield Blues Band Live in Europe**, *Sparks* // 2000 - **Soul'D Out**, *Son* // 2000 - **Darrell Mansfield Band Live On Tour**, *Micah* // **Collection**.

Manson, Eddy

Born: 1919
Died: July 17, 1996 - Los Angeles

Vaudeville / Studio harmonica player

Eddy Manson began playing the harmonica as a child and was playing in Vaudeville at age fifteen with *The Harmonica Rascals*. He joined Johnny O'Brien's *Harmonica Hi-Hats* in 1938 and later studied the clarinet at Julliard.

During the 1950's he worked with Richard Hayman on several projects and was the featured harmonica player on Mitch Miller's "Sing Along" television series. Manson also wrote several orchestral pieces for the harmonica, including "Little Fugitive Suite for Harmonica and Orchestra" in 1953, "Bachiana Americana" in 1972, "Kol Nidrei for Harmonica and String Quartet" in 1977 and "Analogues for Harmonica and String Quartet" in 1978.

His main work was in Hollywood, where he worked as an arranger and a studio harmonica player. He won five Venice Film Awards, two Emmy nominations, sixteen Clios and co-scored the movie "Day of the Painter," which was nominated for an Oscar for best score. In addition to that, he guest-starred with several recording artists, including an appearance on Michael Jackson's "One Day In Your Life."

Discography:
1956 - **Little Fugitive Suite and Other Harmonica Solos,** *Smithsonian/Folkways.*

Movies:
1953 - **The Little Fugitive** // 1960 - **Day of the Painter** // 1962 - **The Longest Day** // 1973 - **Oklahoma Crude** // 1975 - **Hard Times** // 1979 - **Coal Miner's Daughter** // 1983 - **Sting II** // 1984 - **Maria's Lovers** // 1989 - **Born on the Fourth of July** // TV - **The Virginian** // TV - **Ben Casey.**

Markowitz, "Little" Mike

Born: November 23, 1955 - Queens, NY

Blues singer, piano, harmonica player

Mike Markowitz began playing the harmonica at age fourteen and took up the piano two years later. He founded the band *Little Mike and The Tornadoes* in 1978. Based out of New York City, Markowitz plays piano and harmonica as well as being the lead singer for the group. He has also produced albums for Hubert Sumlin and Pinetop Perkins.

Discography: (see - Little Mike and The Tornadoes)

Marr, Johnny

Real name: John Maher
Born: October 31, 1963 - Manchester, England

Rock singer, guitar, harmonica player
Best known as the lead singer and guitar player for The Smiths, Johnny Marr also plays the harmonica. He has also worked with *The The, The Talking Heads,* Billy Bragg, *Electronic, The Pet Shop Boys* and Tom Jones, with whom he has played harmonica.

Discography: (see - The Smiths)

Mars, Johnny

Born: December 7, 1942 - Laurens, SC

Blues guitar, harmonica player

Johnny Mars taught himself how to play the harmonica when he was thirteen years old. After moving to New York State in 1957, he formed his own band, *Johnny Mars and The Cotton Brothers.* They played local dances, parties and clubs until 1967, when they recorded for the Mercury label.

Shortly after, Mars moved to San Francisco where he formed *The Johnny Mars Blues Band.* They worked extensively, playing clubs until Mars moved to England in 1972, where he's been working steadily ever since.

Discography:
1972 - **Blues On Mars,** *Polydor* // 1975 - **Life On Mars,** *Beat Goes On* // 1976 - **Oakland Boogie,** *Big Bear* // 1980 - **King of the Blues Harp,** *JSP* // 1980 - **Mighty Mars,** *JSP* // 1994 - **Stateside,** *MM&K.*

Masterson, Damien

Born: 1970 - Berkeley, CA

Latin harmonica player

Damien Masterson began playing the harmonica at age of fourteen. At age eighteen he studied in Brazil, where he acquired an affinity towards Latin music in it's many forms. He has since made himself a presence in the San Francisco Bay area Jazz scene, specializing in Cuban and Brazilian music.

Discography:
1997 - **Intercambio**, *Good Omen* // 1999 - **Cubacambio**, *Good Omen* // **Masterson Jazz Quartet**, *Good Omen*.

Mayall, John

Born: November 29, 1933 - Macclesfield, England

Blues singer, guitar, harmonica player

The son of a Jazz guitarist, John Mayall started playing guitar at age twelve and piano at age fourteen. He formed his first band while in college. After serving in the British Army he put together a Blues band that would become his *Bluesbreakers*.

His groups would shift personnel on a regular basis and it's alumnus reads like a Who's Who of British Blues/Rock: John McVie, Mick Fleetwood, Peter Green, Eric Clapton, Ainsley Dunbar, Mick Taylor, Sugarcane Harris, Coco Montoya and a host of others.

Mayall has had a very steady career since 1965 and often features his stellar harmonica playing on his records. His biggest hit, "Room To Move," has a spectacular harmonica solo running through it.

Discography:
1964 - **Live at Klooks Kleek**, *Polydor* // 1965 - **John Mayall Plays John Mayall**, *Decca* // 1966 - **Blues Breakers**, (with Eric Clapton), *Deram* // 1967 - **Raw Blues**, *Polydor* // 1967 - **A Hard Road**, *Deram* // 1967 - **Crusade**, *London* // 1967 - **The Blues Alone**, *London* // 1968 - **Diary of a Band, Vol. 1&2**, *London* // 1968 - **Bare Wires**, *Rebound* // 1968 - **Blues Giant**, *Decca* // 1969 - **So Many Roads**, *Decca* // 1969 - **Live**, *Decca* // 1969 - **Blues From Laurel Canyon**, *London* // 1969 - **Looking Back**, *London* // 1969 - **The Turning Point**, *Polydor* // 1970 - **Empty Rooms**, *Polydor* // 1970 - **USA Union**, *Polydor* // 1971 - **Back To the Roots**, *Polydor* // 1971 - **Through the Years**, *London* // 1971 - **Memories**, *Polydor* // 1971 - **Beyond the Turning Point**, *Polydor* // 1971 - **The World of John Mayall, Vol. 1&2**, *Decca* // 1972 - **Jazz - Blues Fusion**, *Polydor* // 1972 - **Moving On**, *Polydor* // 1973 - **The Best Of...**, *Polydor* // 1973 - **Ten Years Are Gone**, *Polydor* // 1973 - **Down the Line**, *London* // 1975 - **The Latest Edition**, *Polydor* // 1975 - **New Year, New Band, New Company**, *Blue Thumb* // 1975 - **Notice To Appear**, *Blue Thumb* // 1976 - **A Banquet of Roses**, *ABC* // 1976 - **John Mayall**, *Polydor* // 1977 - **Lots of People**, *ABC* // 1977 - **A Hard Core Package**, *ABC* // 1977 - **The Last of the British Blues Bands**, *ABC* // 1977 - **Primal Solos**, *Deram* // 1978 - **Blues Roots**, *Decca* // 1979 - **Bottom Line**, *ABC* // 1979 - **No More Interviews**, *ABC* // 1980 - **Roadshow Blues**, *ABC* // 1982 - **Return of The Bluesbreakers**, *AIM* // 1983 - **Last Edition**, *Polydor* // 1983 - **The John Mayall Story**, *Decca* // 1986 - **The Collection**, *Castle* // 1986 - **Some of My Best Friends are Blues**, *Charly* // 1986 - **Behind the Iron Curtain**, *GRP Crescendo* // 1987 - **The Power of the Blues**, *Entente* // 1987 - **Road Show**, *Magnum* // 1988 - **Chicago Line**, *Island* // 1988 - **Archives To Eighties**, *Polydor* // 1988 - **Primal Solos**, *Polygram* // 1990 - **Crocidile Walk**, *Lost Rose* // 1990 - **A Sense of Place**, *Island* // 1992 - **London Blues, 1964-1969**, *Polygram* // 1992 - **Room To Move, 1969-74**, *Polygram* // 1993 - **Wake Up Call**, *Jive/Novus* // 1994 - **The 1982 Reunion Concert**, *One-Way* // 1994 - **Cross Country Blues**, *One-Way* // 1995 - **Spinning Coin**, *Silvertone* // 1997 - **Blues for the Lost Days**, *Silvertone* // 1998 - **As It All Began 1964-69: The Best Of...**, *Polygram* // 1998 - **Drivin' On: The ABC Years (1975-1982)**, *MCA* // 1998 - **Silver Tones: The Best Of...**, *Jive* // 1999 - **Rock the Blues Tonight**, *Indigo* // 1999 - **Padlock on the Blues**, *Cleopatra* // 2000 - **The Masters**, *Spitfire* // 2000 - **Live at the Marquee 1969**, *Spitfire* // 2000 - **Reaching for the Blues**, *Pyramid* // **Crusade**, *London* // **Live in Europe**, *London*.

Mayberry, Lynn
Vaudeville comedienne, harmonica player
Lynn Mayberry was a Vaudeville comedienne who used the harmonica as a part of her act in the 1930's.

Maynard, Ken

Born: July 21, 1895 - Vevay, IN
Died: March 1973

Cowboy actor, guitar, harmonica player
Although he was best known as a singing cowboy in the movies

from the 1920's and 30's, Ken Maynard also played the fiddle, harmonica and guitar. As one of the first singing cowboys he served as a role model for others that followed and he even gave Gene Autry his first job.

Movies:

1923 - **The Man Who Won** // 1929 - The Wagon Master // 1929 - **In Old Arizona** // 1929 - **Mountain Justice** // 1929 - **Song of the Caballero** // 1929 - **Sons of the Saddle** // 1930 - **Roarin' Ranch** // 1930 - **Trigger Tricks** // 1931 - **Range Law** // 1932 - **Dynamite Ranch** // 1932 - **Between Fighting Men** // 1932 - **Arizona Terror** // 1932 - **Branded Men** // 1932 - **Alias - The Bad Men** // 1932 - **Hell-Fire Austin** // 1932 - **Come On, Tarzan** // 1932 - **Fargo Express** // 1932 - **Tombstone Canyon** // 1933 - **Drum Taps** // 1933 - **King of the Arena** // 1933 - **Fiddlin' Buckaroo** // 1933 - **Strawberry Roan** // 1933 - **Trail Drive** // 1934 - **Gun Justice** // 1934 - **Wheels of Destiny** // 1934 - **Smoking Guns** // 1934 - **In Old Santa Fe** // 1934 - **Mystery Mountain** // 1935 - **Western Frontier** // 1935 - **Western Courage** // 1937 - **Boots of Destiny** // 1937 - **Trailin' Trouble** // 1938 - **Whirlwind Horseman** // 1938 - **Six Shootin' Sheriff** // 1939 - **Flaming Lead** // 1939 - **Phantom Rancher** // 1940 - **Death Rides the Range** // 1940 - **Lightning Strikes West** // 1941 - **Death Valley Outlaws** // 1943 - **Blazing Guns** // 1943 - **The Law Rides Again** // 1943 - **Death Valley Riders** // 1943 - **Wild Horse Stampede** // 1944 - **Arizona Whirlwind** // 1944 - **Harmony Trail** // 1944 - **Blazing Frontier** // 1944 - **Westward Bound** // 1947 - **White Stallion** // 1972 - **Big Foot** // 1972 - **Buck and the Preacher.**

McAbee, Palmer
Rural Blues harmonica player
Palmer McAbee was a rural Blues harmonica player who recorded during the late 1920's.

McBee, Lee
Born: March 23, 1951 - Kansas City, MO

Blues harmonica player
Lee McBee is probably best known as having been the lead singer and harmonica player for *Mike Morgan and The Crawl* since it's inception in the late 1980's.

Discography: (also see - Mike Morgan & The Crawl)
1995 - **44**, *Red Hot.*

McCain, Jerry "Boogie"
Born: June 19, 1930 - Gadsden, AL

Blues guitar, drums, harmonica player
Jerry McCain began playing the harmonica at age five. He fre-

quently worked in juke joints, street corners and on the radio during the late 1940's through the early 1950's. He formed the group, *The Upstarts* in the early 1950's and they recorded for the Trumpet label in 1953.

Usually fronting his own bands, Jerry McCain has recorded and performed steadily into the 1990's, as well as working as a private detective.

Discography:
1950's - **Choo Choo Rock**, *White Label* // 1954 - **Strange Kind of Feeling**, *Alligator* // 1973 - **Sings Slim Harpo** // 1989 - **Blues 'n' Stuff**, *Ichiban* // 1991 - **Love Desperado**, *Wild Dog Blues* // 1992 - **Struttin' My Stuff**, *Wild Dog Blues* // 1993 - **I've Got the Blues All Over Me**, *Wild Dog Blues* // 1995 - **That's What They Want: The Best Of...**, *Excello* // 1998 - **Retrospectives**, *Ichiban* // 1999 - **Good Stuff!**, *Varese* // 2000 - **This Stuff Just Kills Me**, *Music Maker* // **Midnight Beat**, *Charly.*

McCarn, Dave
Born: 1905 - Gaston, NC
Died: November 7, 1964 - Stanley, NC

Country singer-songwriter, guitar, harmonica player
Dave McCarn grew up in the Piedmont area of North Carolina. He developed a guitar style similar to that of Blues guitarists Blind Boy Fuller and Rev. Gary Davis while playing Country-style music.

Best known for his protest songs against the cotton industry, McCarn also worked with fellow harmonica player Gwen Foster. He recorded in the late 1920's and early 30's and by the end of the depression had drifted away from music entirely.

Discography:
Dave McCarn and Gwen Foster - Singers of the Piedmont, *Bear Family.*

McCaskey, Hugh "Pud"
Also known as: Stagg McMann
Born: December 25, 1922
Died: 1989

Vaudeville harmonica player
Hugh McCaskey started playing the harmonica as a child while growing up in Lancaster, Pennsylvania. He was playing in a WPA harmonica band when he met Manny Smith and Paul Steigerwald. After they graduated from high school in 1936, they formed a harmonica trio, went to New York City and got a job backing former *Harmonica Rascal* star Alex Novelle.

After Novelle got drafted in World War Two, the three went on as *The Stagg McMann Trio*, deriving the name from the first few letters of each of their names. When Steigerwald and Smith were drafted, McCaskey joined up with the secret harmonica band that Johnny Puleo was trying to form. When that group didn't work out, McCaskey joined up with *The Harmonica Rascals*.

After the war ended, *Stagg McMann* regrouped and worked in nightclubs and Vaudeville. They recorded an album in 1950 and broke up the following year. McCaskey began doing a solo act.

Around 1964 Hugh McCaskey ended up in Chicago. He would substitute for various members of *The Harmonicats* when he was needed and even recorded with Jerry Murad on a "Happy Harmonica" series of recordings. He continued to play until his death in 1989.

Discography: (see - Stagg McMann)

McClinton, Delbert

Born: November 4, 1940 - Lubbock, TX

Blues singer, harmonica player

While growing up in Fort Worth, Texas, Delbert McClinton took an early interest in music, especially Blues. By his late teens he was backing up artists like Howlin' Wolf, Jimmy Reed, Sonny Boy Williamson II and Lightnin' Hopkins. He made his first recordings as a member of *The Ron-Dels*.

In 1962 McClinton played the harmonica on Bruce Chanel's "Hey Baby." The song was a huge hit and McClinton toured England backing Chanel. During the tour he met John Lennon and taught him how to play cross harp style. After returning to the U.S. McClinton worked in nightclubs.

In the early 1970's he relocated to Los Angeles and formed a partnership with Country/Soul artist Glen Clark. After recording two albums together, McClinton embarked on a solo career as a singer-songwriter as well as concentrating on his harmonica playing.

Successful as a songwriter, his songs have been covered by *The*

Blues Brothers, Emmylou Harris and a host of others. He won a Grammy award in 1991 for a duet he recorded with Bonnie Raitt. He remains active by maintaining a heavy schedule of recording and performing.

Discography:
1972 - **Delbert and Glen**, *Clean* // 1973 - **Subject To Change**, *Clean* // 1975 - **Victim of Life's Circumstances**, *ABC* // 1976 - **Genuine Cowhide**, *ABC* // 1977 - **Love Rustler**, *ABC* // 1978 - **Second Wind**, *Capricorn* // 1978 - **Very Early Delbert McClinton with The Ron-Dels**, *Le Cam* // 1979 - **Keeper of the Flame**, *Capricorn* // 1980 - **The Jealous Kind**, *Capitol* // 1981 - **Plain from the Heart**, *Capitol* // 1987 - **Honky Tonkin'**, *MCA* // 1989 - **Live From Austin**, *Alligator* // 1990 - **I'm With You**, *Curb* // 1991 - **The Best Of...**, *Curb* // 1992 - **Never Been Rocked Enough**, *Curb* // 1993 - **Delbert McClinton**, *Curb* // 1994 - **Honky Tonkin' Blues**, *MCA* // 1994 - **Classics, Vol. 1 & 2**, *Curb* // 1995 - **Great Songs: Come Together**, *Curb* // 1995 - **Shot from the Saddle**, *Curb* // 1995 - **Let the Good Times Roll**, *MCA* // 1997 - **One of the Fortunate Few**, *Rising Tide* // 1999 - **Crazy Cajun Recordings**, *Edsel* // 1999 - **The Ultimate Collection**, *Hip-O* // 2000 - **Don't Let Go: The Collection**, *Music Club* // 2000 - **Genuine Rhythm and Blues**, *Polygram* // **Feelin' Allright**, *Intermedia*.

McCluskey, Kenneth

Born: February 8, 1962 - Scotland

Soul / Folk singer, harmonica player

Kenneth McCluskey was the lead singer and harmonica player for *The Bluebells*, a Soul music group from Scotland that was active during the early 1980's. After they disbanded, McCluskey teamed up with his brother David as a Folk music duo.

Discography: (see - The Bluebells)

McCoy, Charlie

Born: March 28, 1941 - Oak Hill, WV

Country studio harmonica player

Charlie McCoy is considered by many to be the greatest Country music session harmonica player in existence. He has played on over 6,000 session recordings since 1960, as well as recording a large number of albums under his own name.

Charlie got his first harmonica for fifty cents and a box top when he was eight years old. While spending most of his childhood living in Florida and West Virginia, he picked up on both Blues and Country styles. While playing guitar in Rock and Roll bands, Country star Mel Tillis heard him and suggested he come to Nashville to work. After a brief attempt at a career as a Rock singer, Charlie began working as a studio session musician.

During his first week in the studio, McCoy played on sessions with Ann-Margret and Roy Orbison that yielded best selling records. This led him to become one of the most sought after harmonica players in the Country music field, doing up to 400 sessions a year. In 1965 he started working with Bob Dylan and ended up playing on three of his albums: "Blonde On Blonde," "John Wesley Harding" and "Nashville Skyline." He also played the bass harmonica on *Simon and Garfunkle's* "The Boxer."

During the 1970's he banded together with other Nashville studio musicians to form *Area Code 615*. The group was short-lived, but made a terrific impact on the field of Country/Rock music. The remnants of the group went on to form *Barefoot Jerry* and Charlie played on all of their albums.

In 1977 Charlie McCoy was named musical director for the television series "Hee-Haw" and served through its entire run. He began recording solo albums to showcase his harmonica talents in 1969 and has released new albums on a regular basis ever since. He remains active to this day, both performing and recording.

Discography: (also see - Area Code 615, Barefoot Jerry)
1968 - **The World of Charlie McCoy,** *Monument* // 1969 - **The Real McCoy,** *Columbia* // 1969 - **Charlie McCoy,** *Monument* // 1973 - **Good Time Charlie,** *Monument* // 1973 - **The Fastest Harp in the South,** *CBS* // 1974 - **The Nashville Hitman,** *Monument* // 1974 - **Christmas Album,** *Monument* // 1975 - **Harpin' the Blues,** *Monument* // 1975 - **Charlie My Boy,** *Monument* // 1976 - **Play It Again Charlie,** *Monument* // 1977 - **Country Cookin',** *Monument* // 1979 - **Appalachian Fever,** *Monument* // 1982 - **Greatest Hits,** *Monument* // 1986 - **One for the Road** // 1987 - **Harmonica Jones,** *Worldwide* // 1988 - **Another Side of Charlie McCoy,** *Worldwide* // 1988 - **Charlie McCoy's 13th,** *Step One* // 1989 - **Beam Me Up Charlie,** *Step One* // 1989 - **Candle Light, Wine & Charlie,** *Worldwide* // 1990 -

International Incident // 1991 - **Out on a Limb,** *Monument* // 1992 - **Live in Paris,** *PSB Disques France* // 1993 - **Live in Paris** // 1993 - **International Airport** // 1994 - **Choo Choo Ch'Boogie** // 1996 - **American Roots** // 1998 - **Precious Memories,** *Revival* // 1998 - **Christmas,** *Sony* // **Country Western & Swing,** *Adventures in Sound.*

Video:
1994 - **Beginning Country Harp** // 1994 - **Complete Country Harp Techniques with Charlie McCoy.**

Book and CD:
Beginning Country Harp with Charlie McCoy // **All-American Harp Solos** // **Learn To Play All-American Harp.**

McCoy, Robert Lee

Also known as: Robert Nighthawk, Ramblin' Bob
Real name: Robert McCollum
Born: November 30, 1909 - Helena, AR
Died: November 5, 1967 - Helena, AR

Blues guitar, harmonica player
Robert Lee McCoy came from a large musical family. His cousins included Houston Stackhouse, Charlie McCoy, (the Blues guitarist, not the harmonica player), and Kansas Joe McCoy. He began working with Will Shade and *The Memphis Jug Band* during the mid-1920's, as well as working with his cousins periodically.

During the 1930's he performed and recorded with several Jug bands as a harmonica player in addition to working with John Lee Hooker, Sleepy John Estes, Henry Townsend, Joe Williams and others before coming to Chicago around 1937.

After moving to Chicago, McCoy changed his name to Robert Nighthawk and switched his focus over to guitar. He was well respected in the Blues field and worked with many of its greats, including Little Walter and others.

Discography as Robert Lee McCoy:
1963 - **Barrelhouse Blues and Jook Piano,** *Vulcan* // 1985 - **Complete Recorded Works, 1937-1940,** *Wolf* // 1997 - **The Bluebird Recordings 1937-38,** *RCA* // 2000 - **Prowline Nighthawk,** *Catfish.*

As Robert Nighthawk:
1977 - **Bricks in My Pillow,** *Pearl Flapper* // 1985 - **Complete Recorded Works,** *Wolf* // 1991 - **Live On Maxwell Street, 1964,** *Rounder* // 1991 - **Black Angel Blues,** *Charly* // 1994 - **Masters of Modern Blues,** *Testament* // 1995 - **Toasting the Blues,** *Inside Sounds.*

McCracken, Hugh
Studio guitar, harmonica player
Hugh McCracken is a studio guitar and harmonica player who has been playing since the 1970's and has recorded with Mose

Allison, Laurie Anderson, Jimmy Buffett, Neil Diamond, Dr. John, Donald Fagen, Garland Jeffreys, Chaka Khan, Freddie King, Graham Parker, Tom Scott, Phoebe Snow, James Taylor and many others.

McCracklin, Jimmy

Born: August 13, 1921 - St. Louis, MO

Blues singer, piano, harmonica player
Jimmy McCracklin started playing piano in the mid-1940's and began recording with *The JD Nicholson Band* in 1945. Although he played the harmonica, Jimmy has been known primarily as a Blues vocalist and has been working steadily since the 1940's.

Discography:
1961 - **Twist with**, *Crown* // 1961 - **I Just Gotta Know**, *Imperial* // 1961 - **Jimmy McCracklin Sings**, *Chess* // 1963 - **My Rockin' Soul**, *United* // 1965 - **Everynight Everyday**, *Imperial* // 1965 - **Think**, *Imperial* // 1966 - **My Answer**, *Imperial* // 1966 - **New Soul of Jimmy McCracklin**, *Imperial* // 1968 - **Let's Get Together**, *Minit* // 1969 - **Stinger Man**, *Minit* // 1971 - **High on the Blues**, *Stax* // 1972 - **Yesterday is Gone**, *Stax* // 1981 - **Jimmy McCracklin and his Bluesblasters**, *Ace* // 1983 - **Blasting the Blues**, *JSP* // 1989 - **Same Lovin'**, *Ichiban* // 1991 - **Jimmy Mccracklin & Paul Gayten**, *Huub* // 1991 - **My Story**, *Rounder* // 1992 - **The Mercury Recordings**, *Bear Family* // 1994 - **A Taste of the Blues: West Coast**, *Bullseye* // 1995 - **Swing Time Shouters, Vol. 2**, *Night Train* // 1999 - **Tell It To the Judge**, *Gunsmoke* // 1999 - **Modern Recordings 1948-1950**, *Ace* // **Roots of Rhythm & Blues**, *Roots* // **Blast 'Em Dead**, *Ace*.

McDonald, Barbara K.

Born: October 4, 1957 - Wausau, WI

New-wave singer, guitar, harmonica player
Best known as half of the New-Wave, husband and wife duo *Timbuk 3*, Barbara K. plays the harmonica as well as the guitar, fiddle and singing. She left music for a while during the early 1990's but has recently returned with a solo album.

Discography: (also see - Timbuk 3)
1998 - **Madmen and Lovers**, *White Eagle*.

McDonald, Pat

Born: August 6, 1952 - Green Bay, WI

New-wave singer, guitar, harmonica player
Pat McDonald was the other half of *Timbuk 3*. Along with his wife, Barbara K., Pat plays harmonica, guitar and sings. Since *Timbuk 3* was disbanded, Pat has gone on to record two solo albums as well as appearing on several other recordings.

Discography: (also see - Timbuk 3)
1997 - **Pat McDonald Sleeps with his Guitar**, *Ark 21* //

Lowdown, *Mountain Railroad*.

McFalls, Willie

Also known as: Blues Boy Willie
Born: November 28, 1946 - Memphis, TX

Blues singer, harmonica player
Willie McFalls has been working as a Blues musician for several years. He scored his first hit in 1990 with "Be-Who?."

Discography:
1989 - **Strange Things Happening**, *Ichiban* // 1990 - **Be Who? 2**, *Ichiban* // 1992 - **I Got the Blues**, *Ichiban* // 1993 - **Don't Look Down**, *Ichiban* // 1995 - **Juke Joint Blues**, *Ichiban*.

McGhee, John

Born: April 9, 1882 - Griffithville, WV
Died: May 9, 1945

Country guitar, harmonica player
Harmonica player John McGhee teamed up with guitarist Frank Welling from 1917 through the mid-1930's. Starting in 1927 they recorded over 250 sides for the Gennett, Paramount, Brunswick and the American Record Company labels.

Discography:
1987 - **Sacred, Sentimental and Silly Songs**, *Old Homestead*.

McGuffey Lane

Formed: 1972 - Ohio
Disbanded: 1990

Country / Rock band
McGuffey Lane was a contender to be one of the top Country/Rock bands of the 1980's, unfortunately bad luck plagued them throughout their career, culminating in 1984 when harmonica player Tebes Douglass was killed in a car accident while returning from a gig.

He would not be replaced on the harmonica by Tom Ingham until just before the band broke up in 1990.

See - Tebes Douglass, Tom Ingham

Discography:
1980 - **McGuffey Lane**, *Atco* // 1981 - **Aqua Dream**, *Atco* // 1983 - **Let the Hard Times Roll**, *Atco* // 1984 - **Day By Day**, *Atlantic America* // 1995 - **A McGuffey Lane Christmas**, *High Chief* // 1995 - **Live and More**, *High Chief* // **Call Me Lucky**, *Lick* // **Greatest Hits: Live and More**, *High Chief*.

McGuire, Barry

Born: October 15, 1935 - Oklahoma City, OK

Folk singer-songwriter, guitar, harmonica player

Originally with *The New Christy Minstrels*, (which also featured Kenny Rogers, Kim Carnes and Roger McGuinn), Barry McGuire was the featured vocalist on their hit, "Green, Green."

McGuire left the group to pursue a solo career and in 1965 had a #1 hit with "Eve of Destruction." He became a born-again Christian in the 1970's and moved to New Zealand.

Discography:
1962 - **Barry Here and Now**, *Horizon* // 1965 - **Eve of Destruction**, *Dunhill* // 1966 - **This Precious Time**, *Dunhill* // 1967 - **The World's Last Private Citizen**, *Dunhill* // 1971 - **Barry McGuire and The Doctor**, *Ode* // 1973 - **Seeds**, *Myrrh* // 1974 - **Narnia**, *Myrrh* // 1975 - **Lighten Up**, *Myrrh* // 1976 - **C'Mon Along**, *Sparrow* // 1976 - **Have You Heard**, *Sparrow* // 1976 - **Jubilation**, *Myrrh* // 1976 - **Jubilation Too**, *Myrrh* // 1978 - **Happy Roads**, *DJM* // 1979 - **Cosmic Cowboy**, *Sparrow* // 1981 - **Finer Than Gold** // 1982 - **Inside Out** // 1982 - **To the Bride**, *Myrrh* // 1982 - **Best of Barry**, *Sparrow* // 1993 - **Anthology**, *One-Way* // **Let's Tend God's Earth**, *Marantha* // **Pilgrim**, *Word* // **The Eve of Destruction Man**, *Spalax* // **The Best Of...**, *Sparrow*.

McKelvey, Dave
Pop harmonica player

Dave McKelvey has been a member of harmonica bands since the 1970's. He has worked with *Johnny Puleo's Harmonica Gang*, *The Original Harmonica Band* and *The Dave McKelvey Trio*, which includes Danny Wilson and Michael Burton. As a studio musician, McKelvey has worked with Brian Wilson, Nelson Riddle, Judy Collins, Leon Redbone, Terrence Blanchard and others

Discography:
1988 - **Hymns & Carols**, *Major Label* // 1999 - **Live From Boulevard Music**, (with The Dave McKelvey Trio), *Major*.

Bibliography:
Blues Harmonica // **Instant Harmonica Christmas Favorites** // **Instant Harmonica Christmas Treasures**.

McMillan, Terry
Born: October 12, 1953 - Lexington, NC

Country studio drum, harmonica player

Terry McMillan is a Country harmonica player who began playing professionally in 1973 and switched to full-time studio work in 1976. He has played with Chet Atkins, Jeanie C. Riley, Jerry Reed, Ray Charles, Elvis Presley, J.J. Cale, Amy Grant, *Brooks & Dunn*, Dolly Parton, *Alabama*, Garth Brooks, Suzy Bogguss, Johnny Cash, Randy Travis, George Jones, Tanya Tucker, Lacy J. Dalton and others.

Discography:
1993 - **I've Got a Feeling**, *Step One* // 1996 - **Somebody's Comin'**, *Warner Brothers*.

McNeely, Larry
Born: January 3, 1948 - Lafayette, LA

Country singer-songwriter, multi-instrumentalist, including harmonica

Larry McNeely began playing music at age thirteen and plays a number of instruments, including the harmonica. He moved to Nashville in 1965 and was soon working with Roy Acuff, a relationship that would last until McNeely joined Glen Campbell's band in 1970.

McNeely began record his own material in 1970 and has since worked as a session musician, playing with dozens of musicians from Tom Jones to Roger Miller.

Discography:
1971 - **Glen Campbell Presents Larry McNeely**, *Capitol* // 1979 - **Rhapsody for Banjo**, *Flying Fish* // 1990 - **After Midnight**, *Sheffield Lab* // **Confederation**, *Sheffield Lab* // **Live**

at McCabes, *Takoma* // **Power Play**, *Flying Fish* // **Larry McNeely**, *Capitol*.

McTell, "Blind" Willie Samuel

Born: May 5, 1901 - Thomson, GA
Died: August 19, 1959 - Milledgeville, GA

Blues guitar, harmonica player
Blinded from birth, Willie McTell began playing music on the accordion and harmonica and took up the guitar at age thirteen. By 1927 he was recording and specialized in 12-string guitar pieces. Occasionally playing the harmonica himself, McTell also worked with harmonica player Buddy Moss from time to time.

His biggest hit was "Statesboro Blues," which was later covered by The Allman Brothers Band.

Discography:
1949 - **Atlanta Twelve String**, *Atco* // 1950 - **Pig 'n' Whistle Red**, *Biograph* // 1956 - **Last Session**, *Original Blues Classics* // 1967 - **Legendary Library of Congress Session**, *Elektra* // 1972 - **Blues Originals, Vol. 1**, *Atlantic* // 1989 - **Blind Willie McTell**, *Yazoo* // 1990 - **The Early Years, 1927-1935**, *Yazoo* // 1990 - **Complete Library of Congress Recordings**, *Document* // 1990 - **Complete Recorded Works, Vol. 1, 2 & 3**, *Document* // 1994 - **The Complete Blind Willie McTell**, *Columbia* // 1994 - **The Definitive Blind Willie McTell**, *Columbia/Legacy* // 1995 - **Statesboro Blues**, *Indigo* // 1995 - **Stompdown Rider**, **(1927-31)**, *Collectables* // 1997 - **The Victor Recordings, 1927-34**, *RCA* // 1999 - **Traveling Blues**, *Catfish* // **Jazz Heritage: Blues in the Dark**, *MCA* // **Love Changin' Blues**, *Biograph* // **Trying To Get Home**, *Biograph* // **Blind Willie McTell**, *Wolf* // **Blues in the Dark**, *MCA* // **Doing That Atlanta, (1927-1935)**, *Yazoo* // **The Postwar Recordings of Blind Willie McTell and Curly Weaver**, *Document*.

Melton, Mel

Real Name: Roy Melton, Jr.
Born: August 19, 1949 -Gastonia, NC

Blues, Zydeco singer, harmonica player
The son of a musical father, Mel Melton began playing the harmonica after receiving one for his eleventh birthday. He began playing blues after hearing Paul Butterfield and Little Walter records in college. After moving to Louisiana in the late 1960's, Melton started to play with the local bands, including Clifton Chenier and Sonny Landreth. He continues to perform with his band, *The Wicked Mojos* as well as being an award-winning chef.

Discography:
1997 - **Swamp Slinger**, *New Moon* // 2000 - **Mojo Dream**.

The Memphis Jug Band

Formed: 1920's - Memphis, TN
Disbanded: 1960's

Jug band
The Memphis Jug Band was the most popular group to emerge from Memphis during the Jug band craze that lasted from the early 1920's until the mid-1930's. Harmonica player Will Shade led the group, while Furry Lewis and a young Walter Horton occasionally sat in.

Though the group never recorded after the mid-1930's, Will Shade kept the group going with various line-ups until his death in the mid-1960's.

See - Will Shade, Walter Horton, Furry Lewis

Discography:
1990 - **Complete Recorded Works, Vol. 1-3**, *Document* // 1990 - **American Skiffle Bands**, *Smithsonian/Folkways* // 1995 - **State of Tennessee Blues**, *Memphis Archives* // 2000 - **The Memphis Jug Band Story: 1927-1934**, *EPM Musique* // **Associates and Outtakes**, *Wolf* // **Memphis Jug Band**, *Yazoo* // **Memphis Jug Band, Volume 1-3**, *JSP* // **The Remaining Titles**, *Matchbox*.

Mersènne, Marin

17th century French writer
In 1636, Marin Mersènne wrote about the Sheng, an Asian wind instrument, thus bringing the concept of the free-reeded instrument to Europe.

Messner, Christian

19th century German harmonica maker
Christian Messner reportedly started building harmonicas around 1827 in Trossingen, Germany with his cousin Christian Weiss. According to legend, clockmaker Matthias Hohner learned how to build harmonicas while visiting the harmonica factory of Messner and Weiss.

Meurkins, Hendrik

Born: 1957 - Hamburg, Germany

Jazz harmonica player
A pioneer in recording Brazilian Jazz on the harmonica, Hendrik Meurkins began by playing the vibes as a teenager. At nineteen he began playing the harmonica after hearing Toots Thieleman. After studying at the Berklee School of Music he lived in Brazil for several years, where he picked up an affinity towards the Jazz music of that country. He's recorded several albums since the early 1990's featuring his harmonica playing.

Discography:
1989 - **Samba Importado**, *Bellaphon* // 1990 - **Sambahia**, *Concord Jazz* // 1992 - **Clear of Clouds**, *Concord Jazz* // 1993

- **A View of Manhattan**, *Concord Jazz* // 1994 - **Slidin'**, *Concord Jazz* // 1994 - **October Colors**, *Concord Picant* // 1996 - **Poema Brasileiro**, *Concord Picant* // 1998 - **Quiet Moments**, *Evidence* // 1998 - **Dig This Samba!**, *Candid* // 1999 - **In a Sentimental Mood**, *Challenge*.

Mickle, Elmon

Also known as: Driftin' Slim, Harmonica Harry, Model T. Slim
Born: February 24, 1919 - Keo, AR
Died: September 15, 1977 - Los Angeles, CA

Blues drums, guitar, harmonica player
While working under a variety of stage names, Elmon Mickle learned how to play the harmonica from John Lee "Sonny Boy" Williamson and worked with "Sonny Boy" Williamson II (Rice Miller) during the 1940's. Mickle began recording during the early 1950's and remained active in the Blues music scene until his death from lung cancer in 1977.

Discography:
1967 - **Model T. Slim**, *Flyright* // 1969 - **Drifting Slim and his Blues Band**, *Milestone* // 1999 - **Somebody Hoo-Doo'd the Hoo-Doo Man**, *Original Blues*.

Midnight Oil

Formed: 1975 - Sydney, Australia

Alternative Rock band
Midnight Oil has been one of Australia's top Rock bands since the 1980's. Lead singer Peter Garrett sometimes plays the harmonica.

See - Peter Garrett

Discography:
1978 - **Midnight Oil**, *Columbia* // 1979 - **Head Injuries**, *Columbia* // 1981 - **Place without a Postcard**, *Columbia* // 1983 - **10, 9, 8, 7, 6, 5, 4, 3, 2, 1**, *Columbia* // 1984 - **Red Sails in the Sunset**, *Columbia* // 1987 - **Diesel and Dust**, *Columbia* // 1990 - **Blue Sky Morning**, *Columbia* // 1992 - **Scream in Blue Live**, *Columbia* // 1993 - **Earth and Sun and Moon**, *Columbia* // 1996 - **Breathe**, *Sony* // 1997 - **20,000 Watt R.S.L.: Greatest Hits**, *Columbia* // 1998 - **Redneck Wonderland**, *Sony*.

Mike Morgan and The Crawl

Formed: late 1980's

Blues band
Texas-based Blues band, *Mike Morgan and The Crawl*, has featured singer and harmonica player Lee McBee since it's founding in the late 1980's.

See - Lee McBee

Discography:
1990 - **Raw and Ready**, *Black Top* // 1991 - **Mighty Fine**

Dancin', *Black Top* // 1992 - *Full Moon* **Over Dallas**, *Black Top* // 1994 - **Ain't Worried No More**, *Black Top* // 1994 - **Let the Dogs Run**, *Black Top* // 1996 - **Looky Here!**, *Black Top* // 1998 - **The Road**, *Black Top* // 1999 - **I Like the Way You Work It!**, *Black Top* // **Lowdown Evil** // *Texas Man*.

Milhaud, Darius

Born: September 4, 1892 - France
Died: June 22, 1974 - Switzerland

Classical composer
Darius Milhaud wrote "Suite for Harmonica and Orchestra" in 1943 for Larry Adler.

Miller, "Big" Clarence

Born: December 18, 1922 - Sioux City, IA

Blues / Jazz singer, bass, drums, harmonica player
Though best known as a Jazz vocalist and saxophone player, "Big" Clarence Miller can also play several other instruments, including the harmonica.

Discography:
1959 - **Did You Ever Hear the Blues?**, *United Artists* // 1961 - **Revelation and the Blues**, *Columbia* // 1962 - **Big Miller Sings, Twists, Shouts and Preaches**, *Columbia*.

Miller, Rice (see - Sonny Boy Williamson II)

Miller, Steve

Born: October 5, 1943 - Milwaukee, WI

Rock singer, guitar, harmonica player
As a guitarist, Steve Miller took lessons from guitar legend Les Paul while growing up in the Milwaukee area. By 1955 he was playing in his own band that also included guitarist Boz Scaggs. While attending the University of Wisconsin, he put together a Blues band that included Scaggs and Ben Sidran. The group moved to Chicago and played at southside Blues clubs for awhile.

After moving to San Francisco in 1966 he started The *Steve Miller Band*. They were signed to Capitol Records after their performance at the Monterey Pop Festival. Their second album featured the hit, "Living in The USA," which featured a Steve Miller harmonica solo in it's opening.

Throughout his lengthy career, Miller has played the harmonica as well as featuring harmonica ace Norton Buffalo on several recordings.

Discography:
1968 - **Children of the Future**, *Capitol* // 1968 - **Sailor**, *Capitol* // 1969 - **Brave New World**, *Capitol* // 1969 - **Your Saving Grace**, *Capitol* // 1970 - **Number 5**, *Capitol* // 1971 - **Rock Love**, *Capitol* // 1972 - **Recall the Beginning**, *Capitol*

// 1972 - **Anthology,** *Capitol* // 1973 - **The Joker,** *Capitol* // 1973 - **Living in the USA,** *Capitol* // 1976 - **Fly Like an Eagle,** *Capitol* // 1977 - **Book of Dreams,** *Capitol* // 1978 - **Greatest Hits, 1974-1978,** *Capitol* // 1981 - **Circle of Love,** *Capitol* // 1982 - **Abracadabra,** *Capitol* // 1983 - **Live,** *Capitol* // 1984 - **Italian X-Rays,** *Capitol* // 1986 - **Living in the 20th Century,** *Capitol* // 1988 - **Born 2B Blue,** *Capitol* // 1990 - **The Best of Steve Miller (1968-1973),** *Capitol* // 1993 - **Wide River,** *Polydor* // 1994 - **Boxed Set,** *Capitol.*

Milteau, Jean-Jacques "J.J."

Born: April 17, 1950

Blues harmonica player

J.J. Milteau began playing Blues harmonica in the late 1960's. While touring extensively, he has performed with Yves Montand, Charles Aznavours and others, as well as recording several albums of his own music.

Discography:
1989 - **Blues Harp,** *Le Chant du Monde* // 1992 - **Explorer,** *Saphir* // 1993 - Live, *Saphir* // 1995 - **Routes,** *EMI* // 1996 - **Merci d'etre Venus,** *Odeon* // 1998 - **Blues Live,** *Mister Music* // 1999 - **Bastille Blues,** *Mister Music* // 2000 - **Honky Tonk Blues,** *Mister Music.*

Minevitch, Borrah

Born: November 5, 1902 - Kiev, Russia
Died: June 26, 1955 - Paris, France

Vaudeville harmonica band leader

Borrah Minevitch was a Russian immigrant who came to Boston in 1912. He got his first harmonica from his mother after asking her for a violin. After mastering the instrument, he gave lessons in the New York City area.

In 1925 Minevitch recruited forty boys from a junior high school in the Bronx for his first harmonica band. In 1927 he met Johnny Puleo, a diminutive harmonica contest winner. After deciding to go into Vaudeville, Minevitch combined slapstick comedy and harmonica playing into *The Harmonica Rascals.*

They were an instant success and soon were one of the highest paid acts on the Vaudeville circuit, though Minevitch's stinginess led him to recruit youngsters and severely underpay them. By the early 1930's Minevitch was bringing in over $3,000 a week, but only paying his player a maximum $100 a week as well as making them pay for all of the own travel and living expenses.

In spite of his cheapness, Minevitch's group was the pinnacle of the harmonica world and some of the world's greatest players were veterans of the band, including: Pete Pedersen, Jerry Murad, Don Les, Hugh McCaskey, Eddie Gordon, Ernie Morris, Hal Leighton, Eddy Manson, Al Smith, Sammy Ross, Mike Chimes, Abe and Leo Diamond, Richard Hayman, Alex Novelle, Dom and Tony Sgro, Ray Tankersley, Dave Doucette and dozens of others.

By the mid-1930's the group was split into three units to cover the country's Vaudeville circuits, each group featuring it's own harmonica playing midget. Minevitch also branched into acting and made several appearances in the movies and on Broadway.

After World War Two Minevitch moved to Paris. He married a young model and was reportedly killed by her lover, who threw Minevitch down a flight of stairs, breaking his neck.

Discography: (see - The Harmonica Rascals)

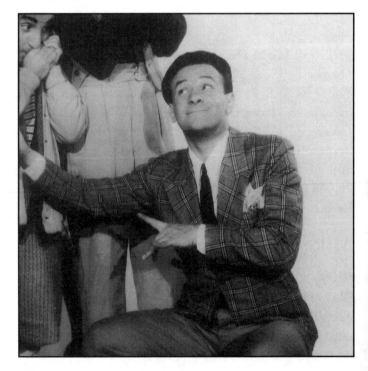

Minter, Iverson "Red"

Also known as: Louisiana Red, Rocky Fuller
Born: March 23, 1936 - Vicksburg, MS

Blues singer, guitar, harmonica player

After having lost both of his parents at an early age, (his mother died shortly after childbirth, his father was lynched by the Ku Klux Klan when Minter was five years old), Iverson Minter grew up with relatives and in orphanages. He started playing the harmonica before he was in his teens and took up the guitar a few years later.

After sitting in with *The Muddy Waters Band* while it was in Pittsburgh in 1949, Minter moved to Chicago and immediately got into the local Blues scene by working under the names "Rocky Fuller" and "Louisiana Red." He recorded for the Checker label that year.

After serving a hitch in the U.S. Army from 1951 until 1958, Minter returned to music. He's managed to tour extensively and has performed with Brownie McGhee, Albert King, Peg Leg Sam Jackson, Roosevelt Sykes, John Lee Hooker, Jimmy Reed and others.

Discography:
1963 - **Seventh Son,** *Carnival* // 1965 - **Lowdown Back Porch Blues,** *Collectables* // 1972 - **Louisiana Red Sings the Blues,** *Atlantic* // 1975 - **Sweet Blood Call,** *Blue Labor* // 1975 - **Midnight Rambler,** *Tomato* // 1976 - **Dead Stray Dog,** *Blue Labor* // 1978 - **Red Funk & Blue,** *Black Panther* // 1983 - **Blues from the Heart,** *JSP* // 1984 - **Blues Man,** *JSP* // 1992 - **Live at 55,** (with Carey Bell), *Blues Beacon* // 1994 - **Always Played the Blues,** *JSP* // 1994 - **Blues for Ida B,** *JSP* // 1995 - **Sittin' Here Wonderin',** *Earwig* // 1995 - **The Best Of...,** *Evidence* // 1995 - **Sugar Hips,** *CMA* // 1996 - **Nobody Knows,** *Uptown Video* // 1996 - **The Rising Sun**

Collection, *Just A Memory* // 1997 - **Walked All Night Long,** *Blues Alliance* // 1997 - **Louisiana Guitar Red,** *Uptown Video* // 1998 - **Blues Spectrum of Louisiana Red,** *JSP* // 1999 - **Millenium Blues,** *Earwig* // 2000 - **Live in Montreux,** *Labor* // 2000 - **Driftin',** *Earwig* // **Louisiana Red,** *Forum* // **Boy From Black Bayou,** *L&R*.

Mischo, R.J.

Born: March 18, 1960 - Chilton, WI

Blues harmonica player

R.J. Mischo began playing Blues harmonica at age sixteen after hearing Muddy Waters perform in Minneapolis. After more than a decade of playing and touring he released the first of several Blues albums. He has been touring and recording albums on a steady basis ever since.

Discography:
1992 - **Ready To Go,** *Atomic Theory* // 1994 - **Gonna Rock Tonight,** *Blue Loon* // 1996 - **Rough 'n' Tough,** *CrossCut* // 1997 - **Cool Disposition,** *Crosscut* // 1999 - **West Wind Blowin',** *Cross Cut*.

Mississippi Heat

Formed: 1991 - Chicago, IL

Blues band
Mississippi Heat is a Blues band out of Chicago that features Pierre LaCocque on the harmonica. They have been regulars on the local club and festival scene for over a decade.

See - Pierre LaCocque

Discography:
1992 - **Straight from the Heart,** *Van Der Linden Recordings* // 1994 - **Learned the Hard Way,** *Van Der Linden Recordings* //

1995 - **Thunder in My Heart,** *Van Der Linden Recordings* // 1999 - **Handyman,** *Van Der Linden Recordings.*

Mississippi Saxophone
A southern colloquial term for the harmonica.

Mitkowski, Frank
Vaudeville harmonica player
Frank Mitowski was a member of *The Philharmonicas* band that played in Vaudeville during the 1930's.

Keb' Mo'
Real name: Kevin Moore
Born: October 3, 1952 - Compton, CA

Blues singer, guitar, harmonica player
Blues star Keb' Mo' sometimes plays the harmonica on a neck-brace to accompany his guitar playing and singing. As a sideman he has played with Santana, Papa John Creach, Joe Cocker and Buddy Guy.

Discography:
1980 - **Rainmaker,** *Casablanca* // 1994 - **Keb' Mo',** *Okeh/Epic* // 1996 - **Just Like You,** *Okeh/Epic* // 1998 - **Slow Down,** *Sony* // 2000 - **The Door,** *Sony.*

Monque'd, J.
Born: April 10, 1946 - Pointe a la Hache, LA

Blues harmonica player

J. Monque'd is a New Orleans Blues harmonica player who learned how to play the instrument from his grandmother at age four and made his first television appearance at age seven. He has been performing in the Blues clubs of new Orleans since his teens, made several tours of Europe and was inducted into the Louisiana Music Hall of Fame in 1999.

Discography:
1994 - **Butter Churnin' Man,** *Real To Reel* // 1998 - **After the Beep,** *Real To Reel* // 1999 - **Chitlin' Eatin' Music,** *Real To Reel.*

The Moody Blues
Formed: 1964 - England

Rock Band
Though generally thought of as an Art-Rock band, *The Moody Blues* started out as a Blues band in the mid-1960's and featured Ray Thomas on the harmonica.

See - Ray Thomas

Discography:
1965 - **Go Now!,** *Decca* // 1965 - **Moody Blues,** *Decca* // 1967 - **Days of Future Passed,** *London* // 1968 - **In Search of the Lost Chord,** *Polydor* // 1969 - **On the Threshold of a Dream,** *Polydor* // 1969 - **To Our Children's Children's Children,** *Polydor* // 1970 - **A Question of Balance,** *Polydor* // 1971 - **Every Good Boy Deserves Favour,** *Polydor* // 1972 - **Seventh Sojourn,** *Polydor* // 1977 - **Caught Live + 5,** *Polygram* // 1978 - **Octave,** *Polydor* // 1981 - **Long Distance Voyager,** *Polydor* // 1983 - **The Present,** *Polydor* // 1986 - **The Other Side of Life,** *Polydor* // 1988 - **Sur La Mer,** *Polydor* // 1991 - **Keys of the Kingdom,** *Polydor* // 1993 - **A Night At Red Rocks,** *Polygram* // 1994 - **Time Traveler,** *Polygram* // 1997 - **The Best Of...,** *Polygram* // 1998 - **Anthology,** *Polygram* // 1999 - **Strange Times,** *Universal* // 2000 - **Live at Royal Albert Hall 2000,** *Ark 21.*

The Moody Brothers
Formed: 1968 - North Carolina

Country / Gospel / Bluegrass band
Though failing to chart in the U.S., *The Moody Brothers* have continued to sell heavily in England and Czechoslovakia and feature David Moody on the harmonica.

See - David Moody

Discography:
1988 - **Friends,** *Lamon* // 1993 - **Home for the Holidays,** *Pro Arte* // **No Hard Feelings,** *Lamon* // **Gimme a Smile,** *Lamon* // **We've Got It in North Carolina,** *Lamon* // **Cotton Eyed Joe,** *Lamon* // **Do the Sugar-Foot Rag,** *Lamon* // **Start with the Talking,** *Lamon* // **Carlton Moody and The Moody Brothers,** *Lamon* // **Christmas with The Moody Brothers,** *Lamon.*

Moody, David
Born: May 24, 1952 - Fayetteville, NC

Bluegrass multi-instrumentalist, including harmonica
David Moody is a Bluegrass multi-instrumentalist who counts the harmonica amongst the many instruments that he plays. He's been playing with his family's group, *The Moody Brothers,* since it's inception in 1968.

Discography: (see - The Moody Brothers)

Moody, James

Born: 1907
Died: 2000

Classical Composer
Composing chiefly for harmonica soloist Tommy Reilly, James Moody wrote "Quintet for Harmonica and Orchestra' in 1970, "Spanish Fantasy," "Irish Fallen Suite," "Dance Suite Francais," "Bulgarian Wedding Dance for Harmonica and Strings," and "Little Suite for Harmonica and Orchestra."

Available Discography:
1976 - **Reilly Performs Vaughan-Williams, Tausky, Moody and Others,** (Tommy Reilly - Soloist), *Chandos //* 1978 - **Reilly Performs Villa-Lobos, Spivakovsky, Arnold and Others,** (Tommy Reilly - Soloist), *Chandos //* 1986 - **Moody, Faure, Grieg and Others,** *Chandos //* 1994 - **Tommy Reilly Plays Harmonica Concertos,** *Chandos //* 1994 - **Orff, Diedrich, Wuytack and Others,** *Sound . 'on //* **Beethoven, Porter, Lara and Others,** *Norway Mus.*

Moore, "Whistling" Alex

Born: November 22, 1899 - Dallas, TX
Died: January 20, 1989 - Dallas, Texas

Blues piano, harmonica player
Alexander Moore began playing the harmonica at age sixteen and piano the next year. After serving in the Army during World War One, he returned to the Dallas area and began working professionally in music.

He began recording for the *Columbia* label in 1929 and continued performing and recording on and off well into the 1970's. His career was severely limited by his reluctance to tour.

Discography:
1960 - **From North Dallas To the East Side,** *Arhoolie //* 1988 - **Wiggle Tail,** *Rounder //* 1994 - **Whistlin' Alex Moore, (1929-51),** *Document //* 1995 - **Ice Pick Blues //** In Europe, *Arhoolie //* **Piano Blues,** *Arhoolie*

Morgan, Tommy

Born: December 4, 1932

Studio harmonica player
One of the most sought after Hollywood studio harmonica players, Tommy Morgan started playing the harmonica at age four. After getting some lessons from Jerry Adler and Leo Diamond,

he embarked on a career that has placed him in the studio for hundreds of film and television scores as well as playing with *The Beach Boys,* Henry Mancini, Neil Diamond, Barbra Streisand, Linda Ronstadt, *The Carpenters,* Randy Newman, Gary Puckett and a lot of others.

Discography:
Faith Songs // *Christmas.*

Movies:
1954 - **Seven Brides for Seven Brothers //** 1959 - **Rio Bravo** (with Leo Diamond) // 1963 - **Lilies of the Field //** 1967 - **Cool Hand Luke //** 1968 - **Hang Em High //** 1972 - **The Getaway** (with Toots Thielemans) // 1972 - **Buck and the Preacher** (with Sonny Terry) // 1979 - **All That Jazz //** 1978 - **Heart To Heart //** 1982 - **Annie //** 1984 - **The Soldier's Story //** 1985 - **The Color Purple** (with Sonny Terry) // 1989 - **Next of Kin //** 1990 - **Dances with Wolves //** 1990 - **Arachnophobia //** 1991 - **City Slickers //** 1993 - **Dennis the Menace //** 1993 - **The Muppet Movie //** 1996 - **The Mirror Has Two Faces //** 1996 - **Escape From L.A. //** 1997 - **For Richer or Poorer //** 1997 - **Rosewood //** 1998 - **The Odd Couple II //** 1998 - **Paulie //** 1999 - **Stuart Little //** 1999 - **Crazy In Alabama.**

Television:
Green Acres // Rockford Files // The Waltons // Dukes of Hazzard // Newhart // The Twilight Zone // Sanford and Son // Bonanza // China Beach.

Bibliography:
Chromatic Harmonica, *Alfred Publishing.*

Morisette, Alanis

Born: June 1, 1974 - Ottawa, Canada

Rock singer, harmonica player

Alanis Morisette began playing the piano at age six and was writing songs by age nine. Her debut album on Maverick Records featured Morisette's singing and harmonica playing as well as her songwriting skills.

Discography:
1995 - **Jagged Little Pill**, *Maverick* // 1996 - **Ironic**, *Maverick* 1998 - **Supposed Former Infatuation Junkie**, *Warner Brothers* // 1999 - **Alanis Unplugged**, *Maverick* // 2000 - **Still**, *WEA International*.

Morris, Ernie

Died: 1950's

Vaudeville harmonica player

The lone black member of *The Harmonica Rascals*, Ernie Morris handled the low harmony parts for the group. He developed a throat vibrato that became the trademark sound of the band.

Frequently mistreated by Borrah Minevitch, Morris left the group in 1944 to pursue a solo career. His career never caught on so he took to drinking and died sometime in the 1950's.

Morris, Willie, Jr.

Born: January 3, 1925 - Camden, AL

Blues singer, guitar, harmonica player

Willie Morris Jr. began playing the harmonica and guitar when he was ten years old. During the 1950's he did some recordings for the Decca label, but gave up music after injuring his hand in 1968.

Morrison, Van

Real name: George Ivan
Born: August 31, 1945 - Belfast, Ireland

Rock singer-songwriter, sax, guitar, harmonica player

The son of a Jazz and Blues enthusiast, Van Morrison began his career as the lead singer for the group *Them*. They had a hit with Morrison's songs "Here Comes the Night" and "Gloria." Since leaving the group in 1966, Morrison has had a stellar career as a singer-songwriter. He occasionally plays the harmonica.

Discography: (also see - Them)
1967 - **Blowin Your Mind!**, *Bang* // 1968 - **Astral Weeks**, *Warner Brothers* // 1970 - **Moondance**, *Warner Brothers* // 1970 - **His Band and Street Choir**, *Warner Brothers* // 1971 - **Tupelo Honey**, *Warner Brothers* // 1972 - **St. Domenic's Preview**, *Warner Brothers* // 1973 - **Hard Nose to the Highway**, *Warner Brothers* // 1974 - **It's Too Late to Stop Now**, *Warner Brothers* // 1974 - **Veedon Fleece**, *Warner Brothers* // 1974 - **T. B. Sheets**, *Bang* // 1977 - **This is Where I Came In**, *Warner Brothers* // 1977 - **A Period of Transition**, *Warner Brothers* // 1978 - **Wavelength**, *Warner Brothers* // 1979 - **Into the Mystic**, *Warner Brothers* // 1980 - **Common One**, *Warner Brothers* // 1982 - **Beautiful Vision**, *Warner Brothers* // 1983 - **Inarticulate Speech of the Heart**, *Warner Brothers* // 1985 - **A Sense of Wonder**, *Mercury* // 1985 - **Live at the Grand Opera House, Belfast**, *Mercury* // 1986 - **No Guru, No Method, No Teacher**, *Mercury* // 1987 - **Poetic Champions Compose**, *Mercury* // 1988 - **Irish Heartbeat**, *Mercury* // 1989 - **Avalon Sunset**, *Mercury* // 1990 - **Enlightenment**, *Mercury* // 1990 - **The Best Of...**, *Polydor* // 1991 - **Bang Masters**, *Epic* // 1991 - **Hymns To the Silence**, *Polydor* // 1993 - **The Best Of..., Vol. 2**, *Polydor* // 1993 - **Too Long in Exile**, *Polydor* // 1994 - **A Night in San Francisco**, (with Junior Wells), *Polydor* // 1995 - **Days Like This**, *Polydor* // 1996 - **How Long Has This Been Going On**, *Verve* // 1996 - **Tell Me Something: Songs of Mose Allison**, *Verve* // 1997 - **The Healing Game**, *Polydor* // 1997 - **The Philosopher's Stone**, *Polydor* // 1999 - **Back On Top**, *Point Blank* // 1999 - **Super Hits**, *Sony* // 2000 - **The Skiffle Sessions: Live in Belfast 1998**, *Pointblank* // 2000 - **You Win Again**, *Virgin* // 2000 - **The Early Years: 1967-1968**, *Metro*.

Morton, Tex

Real name: Robert William Lane
Born: August 30, 1916 - Nelson, New Zealand
Died: July 23, 1983

Country singer, guitar, harmonica player

Known as the "Yodeling Boundary Rider," Tex Morton was one of the biggest Country/Western stars in the Australian music scene. Beginning his musical career in 1934, he was recording within two years and was a major draw, remaining active until his death in 1983. Only leaving Australia once in the early 1950's to tour the U.S. and Canada, he spent most of his career in New Zealand and Australia.

Discography:
1970 - **Tex Morton Today**, *Columbia* // 1977 - **Tex Morton's Gooniwindi Grey**, *Festival* // 1981 - **You and My Old Guitar**, *Festival* // 1982 - **The Man From Snowy River and Other Poems**, *Festival* // 1987 - **The Tex Morton Collection**, *Regal Zonophone*.

Moss, Eugene "Buddy"

Born: January 26, 1906 - Jewell, GA
Died: October 19, 1984 - Atlanta, GA

Jug band guitar, harmonica player

Buddy Moss began playing the harmonica professionally at parties and juke joints when he was twelve years old. During the late 1920's and early 30's he worked with a variety of Jug bands and in duets with people like Barbecue Bob, Curley Weaver and Blind Willie McTell. In the mid-1930's he served a term in prison for killing his wife and his career never fully recovered, although he continued playing until the 1970's.

Discography:
1983 - **Georgia Blues,** *Travelin' Man* // 1992 - **The Complete Recorded Works, Vol. 1-3,** *Document* // 1995 - **Atlanta Blues Legend,** *Biograph* // **Buddy Moss with Sonny Terry,** *Travelin' Man* // **Country Blues from the Eastern States,** (with Tallahassee Tight), *Document* // **Red River Blues, 1933-1941,** *Travelin' Man* // **Rediscovery,** *Biograph* // **Buddy Moss 1933-1941,** *Travelin' Man.*

Mouth Harp
A colloquial name for the harmonica.

Mouth Organ
A colloquial name for the harmonica.

The Mulcays
Formed: 1940's

Pop / Vaudeville harmonica duo

The Mulcays were a husband and wife Pop/Vaudeville harmonica duo that performed primarily in the 1940's and 50's.

Mulcay, Jimmy
Died: 1968

Vaudeville harmonica player

Jimmy Mulcay was a Vaudeville harmonica soloist when he teamed up with his wife Mildred to form *The Mulcays.* Jimmy played the chord harmonica and he was also instrumental in putting together *The Quintones,* the group that would later become *The Harmonicats.*

Mulcay, Mildred
Vaudeville Harmonica player

Originally a Vaudeville performer herself, Mildred Mulcay took up the chromatic harmonica after meeting Jimmy Mulcay. They worked together as *The Mulcays* until Jimmy's death in 1968. In later years Mildred played in Don Les' *Harmonicats* until the mid-1970's, when she permanently retired in Las Vegas.

Mullendore, Joe
Vaudeville harmonica player

Joe Mullendore began his career playing in Albert Hoxie's harmonica band. During the mid-1930's he joined *The Harmonica Harlequins,* where he played fourth chromatic harmonica, in addition to writing many of the band's arrangements.

When that band broke up, Mullendore joined *The Cappy Barra Harmonica Ensemble* and stayed with them until the outbreak of World War Two. After the war he moved to California and did studio work, mostly as a composer.

Movies: (as score composer)
1953 - **Wicked Woman** // 1955 - **New York Confidential** // 1956 - **While the City Sleeps** // 1966 - **I Deal in Danger.**

Mundaeoline
A 19th century German name for the harmonica.

Mundharmonika
A German name for the harmonica that Americas would later shorten to harmonica.

Murad, Jerry
Real name: Jerry Muradian
Born: December 1, 1918 - Constantinople, Turkey
Died: May 11, 1996 - Liberty Township, Ohio

Vaudeville harmonica player

Jerry Murad was born in Turkey, but grew up on the west side of Chicago. His mother bought him his first harmonica, a Hohner Marine Band, when he was six years old. While playing in Chicago's Walla Walla Harmonica Club, he met Al Fiore and Bob Hadamik. Along with Pete Pedersen they would form *The Harmonica Madcaps* in 1937.

Murad took the opportunity to join *The Harmonica Rascals* in 1942, but quickly found that it wasn't to his liking and soon was back in Chicago. Reteaming with Fiore and adding Harmonica Rascals bass harmonica player Don Les, they were recruited by Jimmy Mulcay to become *The Quintones* with harmonica player Ronny Salzman and singer Barbara Engels. When Salzman ran away with Engels, the remaining three players became *The Harmonicats.*

After recording "Peg 'O' My Heart" in 1947, the group was an instant success. Over the next few decades they recorded over thirty albums. Murad remained active as a harmonica player until his death in 1996.

Discography: (see - The Harmonicats)

Murphey, Michael Martin
Country singer-songwriter, guitar, harmonica player
Michael Martin Murphey is a long time veteran of the Folk and Country music scenes where he scored his biggest hit with the song, "Wildfire." Among his other accomplishments, he taught Waylon Jennings' harmonica player, Don Brooks, how to play in the cross harp position.

Discography:
1967 - **Lewis & Clark Expedition,** *Colgems* // 1972 - **Geronimo's Cadillac,** *A&M* // 1973 - **Cosmic Cowboy Souvenir,** *A&M* // 1973 - **Michael Murphey,** *Epic* // 1975 - **Blue Sky - Night Thunder,** *Epic* // 1976 - **Flowing Free Forever,** *Epic* // 1976 - **Swans Against the Sun,** *Epic* // 1978 - **Lone Wolf,** *Epic* // 1979 - **Peaks, Valleys, Honky Tonks & Alleys,** *Epic* // 1981 - **Hard Country,** *Epic* // 1982 - **Michael Martin Murphey,** *Liberty* // 1982 - **The Best Of...,** *EMI* // 1986 - **Tonight We Ride,** *Warner Brothers* // 1987 - **Americana,** *Warner Brothers* // 1988 - **River of Time,** *Warner Brothers* // 1989 - **Land of Enchantment,** *Warner Brothers* // 1990 - **Cowboy Songs,** *Warner Brothers* // 1990 - **The Best of Country,** *Curb* // 1991 - **Cowboy Christmas,** *Warner Brothers* // 1992 - **What's Forever For,** *CEMA* // 1993 - **Cowboy Songs 3,** *Warner Brothers* // 1993 - **Wide Open Country,** *Warner Brothers* // 1995 - **Sagebrush Symphony,** *Warner Brothers* // 1995 - **America's Heroes,** *Warner Brothers* // 1997 - **Horse Legends,** *Warner Brothers* // 1998 - **Wildfire (1972-1984),** *Raven* // 1998 - **Cowboy Songs 4,** *Valley* // 1999 - **Acoustic Christmas Carols,** *Valley* // **Roses and Thorns,** *Warner Brothers.*

Musial, Stan
Also known as: Stan the Man
Born: November 21, 1920 - Donora, PA

Baseball player
A star player for the St. Louis Cardinals, Stan Musial is also a harmonica player and once wrote an instruction book for the instrument.

Bibliography:
1994 - **Stan Musial Plays the Harmonica,** *Mel Bay Publications.*

Musselwhite, Charlie
Born: January 31, 1944 - Kosciuko, MS

Blues harmonica player

One of the greatest of the white Blues harmonica players, Charlie Musselwhite was raised in Memphis, Tennessee, where he made the acquaintance of Will Shade, who taught him the basics of Blues harmonica playing.

Upon moving to Chicago in the mid-1960's, Musselwhite was soon playing in the city's black Blues clubs with JB Hutto, Muddy Waters, Mike Bloomfield, Big Joe Williams and others. An appearance on a Chicago Blues sampler album on Vanguard Records led him to be signed by the label.

He has had a long and steady career as a veteran Blues man. In the early 1990's he was signed by the Alligator label and made guest appearances on several albums, including a duet with Bonnie Raitt on her "Longing in Their Hearts" album and a stellar harmonica solo on "Suicide Blonde" by *INXS*.

Discography:
1966 - **Stand Back! Here Comes Charlie Musselwhite's Southside Band,** *Vanguard* // 1968 - **Louisiana Fog,** *Cherry Red* // 1968 - **Stone Blues,** *Vanguard* // 1968 - **Blues From Chicago,** *Cherry Red* // 1969 - **Memphis Tennessee,** *Mobile Fidelity* // 1969 - **Tennessee Woman,** *Vanguard* // 1971 - **Mylon,** *Cotillion* // 1974 - **Takin' My Time,** *Arhoolie* // 1974 - **Memphis Charlie,** *Arhoolie* // 1975 - **Leave the Blues to Us,** *Capitol* // 1975 - **Goin' Back Down South,** *Arhoolie* // 1977 - **Light of Your Shadow,** *Sussex* // 1978 - **Times are Getting Tougher Than Tough,** *Crystal Clear* // 1979 - **The Harmonica According To Charlie Musselwhite,** *Blind Pig* // 1982 - **Curtain Call,** *Red Lightnin'* // 1982 - **The Dynatones Featuring Charlie Musselwhite,** *War Bride* // 1984 - **Tell Me Where All the Good Times Gone,** *BRR* // 1985 - **Mellow-Dee,** *Cross Cut* // 1986 - **Cambridge Blues,** *Blue Horizon* // 1990 - **Ace of Harps,** *Alligator* // 1991 - **Signature,** *Alligator* // 1994 - **In My Time,** *Alligator* // 1996 - **Takin' Care of Business,** *Kent* // 1997 - **Rough News,** *Point Blank* // 1998 - **Curtain Call Cocktails,** *West Side* // 1999 - **Continental Drifter,** *Pointblank* // 2000 - **Up & Down the Highway Live: 1986,** *Indigo* // 2000 - **Best of the Vanguard Years,** *Vanguard* // **The Blues Never Die,** *Vanguard.*

Movies:
1999 - **Blues Brothers 2000.**

Bibliography:
Power Blues Harp, (with Phil Duncan), *Mel Bay Publications.*

Myers, Louis

Born: September 18, 1929 - Byhalia, MS
Died: September 5, 1994 - Chicago, IL

Blues guitar, harmonica player
Raised in a musical family, (his parents had worked with Charlie Patton, Washboard Sam, Blind Boy Fuller and others), Louis Myers was one of the cornerstones of Chicago-style Blues guitar playing.

He learned to play the guitar at eight and moved to Chicago, Myers soon became apart of the local Blues scene. While working with his brother Dave on guitar and Junior Wells on the harmonica, they formed *The Little Boys* around 1949. The group would soon be renamed *The Three Deuces, The Three Aces* then *The Four Aces* when drummer Fred Below joined them and finally just *The Aces.*

The Aces became one of the most popular back-up groups on the Chicago Blues scene and they would be featured on hundreds of recordings. During their career they worked with Little Walter, Muddy Waters, Big Bill Broonzy, Otis Spann, Luther Tucker, Otis Rush, Jimmy Rogers, Buddy Guy, Sunnyland Slim and a host of others.

Myers also would occasionally front the group and made a few records in his own right, many of which feature him playing the harmonica.

Discography:
1978 - **I'm a Southern Man,** *Testament* // 1983 - **Tell My Story Movin',** *Earwig* // 1992 - **Tell My Story Movin',** *Earwig* // 1996 - **Back Home To Clarksdale,** (with The Reunion Blues Band), *Icehouse.*

Myers, Sam

Born: February 19, 1936 - Laurel, MS

Blues singer, drums, harmonica player

Sam Myers began playing the harmonica at age seven and began working professionally in the Blues music field during the mid-1950's as a vocalist, drummer and harmonica player. He has played with Elmore James, Robert Miller, Lightnin' Hopkins, *The Mississippi Delta Blues Band* and others. Since 1982 he has been the lead vocalist and harmonica player for *Anson Funderburgh and The Rockets.* He favors playing the chromatic harmonica.

Discography: (also see - Anson Funderburgh and The Rockets)
1985 - **My Love is Here To Stay,** *Black Top* // 1997 - **That's What They Want,** (with Anson Funderburgh) // **Down Home in Mississippi,** *T.J.* // **Mississippi Delta Blues,** *T.J.* // **Mississippi Delta Blues Band,** *T.J.* // **Chromatic Style,** (with The Mississippi Delta Blues Band), *T.J.*

– N –

Nakamura, Tetsuya "Tex"
Latin Funk harmonica player
Tetsuya Nakamura replaced Lee Oskar in the group *War* in 1993 and has been playing with them ever since.

Discography: (see - War)

Nardella, Steve
Born: June 26, 1948 - Providence, RI

Blues singer, guitar, harmonica player
Steve Nardella has been working as a Blues musician since at least 1972. While doing most of his playing in the Michigan area, he made his recording debut backing Bobo Jenkins.

Discography:
1979 - **It's All Rock and Roll,** *Blind Pig* // 1993 - **Daddy Rollin' Stone,** *School Kids.*

Neal, Kenny
Born: October 14, 1957 - Baton Rouge, LA

Blues guitar, harmonica player
The son of Blues harmonica player Raful Neal, Kenny Neal plays the guitar as well as the harmonica. He began playing bass guitar in his father's band at age thirteen. He learned how to play the harmonica from Slim Harpo, who had given him his first harmonica at age three.

He played bass guitar behind Buddy Guy during the late 1970's and since then has fronted his own bands as well as guesting on albums by Tab Benoit, Eddie Kirkland, Lazy Lester and others.

Discography:
1987 - **Big News on the Bayou,** *Alligator* // 1988 - **Bio on the Bayou,** *King Snake* // 1989 - **Devil Child,** *Alligator* // 1991 - **Walking On Fire,** *Alligator* // 1993 - **Bayou Blood,** *Alligator* // 1994 - **Hoodoo Moon,** *Alligator* // 1997 - **Deluxe Edition,** *Alligator* // 1998 - **Blues Fallin' Down Like Rain,** *Telarc* // 2000 - **What You Got,** *Telarc.*

Neal, Raful
Born: June 6, 1936 - Baton Rouge, LA

Blues harmonica player
Raful Neal began playing the harmonica in 1950 after being taught the instrument by Ike Brown. During the early 1960's he toured with "Little" Eddie Lang and began recording on his own in 1968. His first group included Buddy Guy on guitar and when Guy left the group he was replaced by Lazy Lester.

Though he mostly stays in the Baton Rouge area, he occasionally travels to festivals and club dates. He has several children and grandchildren who have followed him into music, including his son Kenny, who is also a harmonica player and records for the Alligator label.

Discography:
1987 - **Louisiana Legend,** *Alligator* // 1991 - **I Been Mistreated,** *Ichiban* // 1998 - **Old Friends,** *Club Louisianne.*

Neckbrace
The neckbrace is a device used by many harmonica players that enables them to use their hands to play another instrument. The neckbrace holds the harmonica to the player's mouth, thereby leaving their hands available. The neckbrace is used most often by Folk, Country and Rock musicians.

Neill, Chris
Rock singer, harmonica player
Chris Neill was the featured harmonica player in the band *Stealers Wheel* from 1974 until 1978.

Discography: (with Stealers Wheel)
1974 - **Ferguslie Park,** *A&M* // 1975 - **Right or Wrong,** *A&M* // 1978 - **Stuck in the Middle with You,** *A&M* // 1978 - **The Best of Stealers Wheel,** *MFP.*

Nelson, "Chicago" Bob
Born: July 4, 1944 - Bogalusa, LA

Blues singer, harmonica player
Bob Nelson learned how to play the harmonica from his father, as well as getting instruction from Lazy Lester and Slim Harpo. He began playing in local bars in New Orleans during the late 1950's. After moving north to Gary, Indiana in 1959, he worked

as a sideman to Earl Hooker, JB Hutto, Howlin' Wolf, Muddy Waters, Slim Harpo and others.

During the mid-1960's he formed his own band, *The Chicago Bob Blues Band*. While touring extensively, he has worked with Johnny Shines, John Lee Hooker and *The Heartfixers*.

Discography:
1986 - **Cool On It,** (with The Heartfixers), *Landslide* // 1992 - **Hit and Run Lover,** *Wild Dog* // 1996 - **Back To Bogolusa,** *Kingsnake* // 1997 - **Just Your Fool,** (with The Shadows), **Highwater** // **Live,** (with The Heartfixers), *Landslide* // **The Heartfixers,** *Southland.*

The New Lost City Ramblers

Formed: 1958

Folk / Bluegrass band
The New Lost City Ramblers were one of the leading string bands of the early 1960's Folk Revival. They were co-founded and led by Mike Seeger, who played banjo and harmonica and is the brother of Folk music legend Pete Seeger.

See - Mike Seeger

Discography:
1958 - **The New Lost City Ramblers,** *Folkways* // 1959 - **The New Lost City Ramblers, Vol. 2,** *Folkways* // 1959 - **Songs from the Depression,** *Folkways* // 1959 - **Old Timey Songs for Children,** *Folkways* // 1961 - **Tom Paley, John Cohen and Mike Seeger Sing Songs of The New Lost City Ramblers,** *Folkways* // 1961 - **The New Lost City Ramblers, Vol. 3,** *Folkways* // 1961 - **The New Lost City Ramblers, Vol. 4,** *Folkways* // 1962 - **American Moonshine and Prohibition,** *Folkways* // 1963 - **The New Lost City Ramblers, Vol. 5,** *Folkways* // 1963 - **Gone To the Country,** *Folkways* // 1964 - **String Band Instrumentals,** *Folkways* // 1964 - **Old Timey Music** // 1965 - **Rural Delivery No. 1,** *Folkways* // 1966 - **Rememberance of Things To Come,** *Folkways* // 1968 - **Modern Times - Rural Songs From an Industrial Society,** *Folkways* // 1973 - **On the Great Divide,** *Folkways* // 1978 - **20 Years - Concert Performances 1958-1977,** *Flying Fish* // 1978 - **20th Anniversary Concert, Carnegie Hall,** *Flying Fish* // 1979 - **Twenty Years** // 1991 - **The Early Years (1958-1962),** *Folkways* // 1992 - **Vol. II, 1963-1973: Outstanding in Their Field,** *Folkways* // 1994 - **Old Time Music,** (with Cousin Emmy), *Vanguard* // 1997 - *There Ain't No Way Out, Folkways.*

The New World Harmonica Trio

Formed: 1995 - California

Harmonica trio
The New World Harmonica Trio was a band that featured the talents of Ron Kalina on lead chromatic, Michael Burton on chord

and Danny Wilson on Bass harmonica. The group was featured in the 1999 movie "Magnolia."

Discography:
The New World Harmonica Trio, *Kalinor* // **Time Was,** *Kalinor.*

Movies:
1999 - **Magnolia.**

The New York Dolls

Formed: 1971 - New York City, NY
Disbanded: 1977

Glam-Rock band
Based out of New York City, *The New York Dolls* were one of the first bands to hit it big in the Glam-Rock movement. The group featured David Johansen on lead vocals and harmonica.

See - David Johansen

Discography:
1973 - **New York Dolls,** *Mercury* // 1973 - **Seven Day Weekend,** *Receiver* // 1974 - **Too Much, Too Soon,** *Mercury* // 1981 - **Lipstick Killers,** *Combat* // 1984 - **Red Patent Leather,** *Fan Club* // 1985 - **After the Storm,** *Receiver* // 1992 - **Live in NYC ' 75,** *Receiver* // 1994 - **Rock & Roll,** *Mercury* // 1998 - **I'm a Human Being,** *Receiver* // 1999 - **Glam Rock Hits,** *Cleopatra* // 1999 - **The Glamorous Life Live,** *Big Ear* // 2000 - **Hard Night's Day,** *Norton.*

Newman, Charles

Born: 1915

Classical / Jazz harmonica player
Charles Newman grew up in Phoenix, Arizona and by 1934 he was doing radio work out of San Francisco. He began recording for the Decca label in 1938 and during his career he worked with Horace Heidt, Paul Whiteman, Fred Waring

and others. He was active well into his 70's.

The Nighthawks

Formed: 1972 - Washington, DC

Blues band

One of the east coast's leading Blues/Rock groups, *The Nighthawks* were co-founded by Harmonica player Mark Wenner and featured former *Wet Willie* harmonica player Jimmy Hall from 1985 until 1990.

See - Mark Wenner, Jimmy Hall

Discography:
1972 - **Rock and Roll,** *Varrick* // 1976 - **Open All Night,** *Mobile Fidelity* // 1976 - **Live 1976,** *Adelphi* // 1977 - **Jacks and Kings,** *Adelphi* // 1977 - **Live at the Psychedelly,** *Adelphi* // 1977 - **Side Pocket Shot,** *Adelphi* // 1977 - **Live,** *Genes* // 1980 - **The Nighthawks,** *Mercury* // 1981 - **Ten Years Live,** *Varrick* // 1981 - **Times Four,** *Adelphi* // 1983 - **Jacks and Kings Full House,** *Adelphi* // 1983 - **Rock and Roll,** *Varrick* // 1986 - **Live in Europe,** *Crosscut* // 1988 - **Back Track,** *Varrick* // 1988 - **The Best Of...,** *Genes* // 1989 - **Best of the Blues,** *Adelphi* // 1991 - **Trouble,** *Powerhouse* // 1991 - **Hard Living,** *Varrick* // 1993 - **Rock This House,** *Big Mo* // 1996 - P**ain and Paradise,** *Big Mo* // 1999 - **Still Wild,** *Platinum* // 2000 - **Citizen Wayne,** *Intuition* // **Hot Spot,** *Varrick* // **Best of the Rock, Hard Living.**

The Nitty Gritty Dirt Band

Formed: 1965 - Long Beach, CA

Country band

The Nitty Gritty Dirt Band is one of Country music's longest running groups. Though only having a small number of hits, such

as "Mr. Bojangles," they have enjoyed a long-standing cult status. Drummer Jimmie Fadden often doubles on the harmonica.

See - Jimmie Fadden

Discography:
1967 - **The Nitty Gritty Dirt Band,** *Liberty* // 1967 - **Ricochet,** *Liberty* // 1968 - **Pure Dirt,** *Liberty* // 1968 - **Rare Junk,** *Liberty* // 1968 - **Alive,** *Liberty* // 1969 - **Dead and Alive,** *Liberty* // 1970 - **Uncle Charlie and his Dog Teddy,** *Liberty* // 1972 - **All the Good Times,** *United Artists* // 1972 - **Will the Circle Be Unbroken,** *United Artists* // 1973 **Live,** *United Artists* // 1974 - **Stars and Stripes Forever,** *United Artists* // 1975 - **Dreams,** *United Artists* // 1976 - **Dirt, Silver and Gold,** *United Artists* // 1978 - **Dirt Band,** *United Artists* // 1979 - **An American Dream,** *United Artists* // 1980 - **Gold From Dirt,** *United Artists* // 1980 - **Make a Little Magic,** *United Artists* // 1981 - **Jealousy,** *United Artists* // 1983 - **Let's Go,** *United Artists* // 1984 - **Plain Dirt Fashion,** *Warner Brothers* // 1985 - **Partners, Brothers and Friends,** *Warner Brothers* // 1986 - **Early Dirt: 1967-1970,** *Decal* // 1987 - **Twenty Years of Dirt,** *Warner Brothers* // **Country Store: The Nitty Gritty Dirt Band,** *Country Store* // 1987 - **Hold On,** *Warner Brothers* // 1988 - **The Best Of..., Vol. 2,** *Atlantic* // 1988 - **Workin' Band,** *Warner Brothers* // 1989 - **More Great Dirt: The Best Of..., Vol. 2,** *Warner Brothers* // 1989 - **Will the Circle Be Unbroken, Vol. 2,** *Warner Brothers* // 1990 - **Rest of the Dream,** *MCA* // 1991 - **Live Two Five,** *Capitol* // 1992 - **Not Fade Away,** *Liberty* // 1992 - **The Real Nitty Gritty,** *CEMA* // 1994 - **Trials & Crosses,** *VP* // 1994 - **Acoustic,** *Liberty* // 1994 - **The Nitty Gritty Dirt Band - Roger McGuinn Live,** *Javelin* // 1997 - **The Christmas Album,** *Rising Tide,* 1998 - **Bang, Bang, Bang,** *MCA* // 2000 - **Super Hits,** *Warner Brothers.*

Movies:
1969 - **Paint Your Wagon.**

Nixon, Hammie

Born: January 22, 1908 - Brownsville, TN
Died: August 17, 1984 - Jackson, TN

Blues guitar, harmonica player

Hammie Nixon teamed up with Sleepy John Estes around 1924 and worked on and off as his harmonica player until Estes' death in 1977. Nixon learned to play the harmonica from Noah Lewis.

Discography:
1962 - **The Legend of Sleepy John Estes,** *Delmark* // 1976 - **Hammie Nixon** // 1984 - **Tappin' That Thing,** *High Water* // **Brownsville Blues,** *Delmark.*

No Strings Attached

Formed: June 1978 - Blacksburg, VA

Folk String Band

No Strings Attached is a string band from Virginia that mixes Jazz and World music into its sound. Co-founder Peter Hastings plays both diatonic and chromatic harmonicas with the group.

See - Peter Hastings

<u>Discography:</u>
1984 - **Isles of Langerhans,** *Turquoise* // 1985 - **Traditional Music of the Future,** *Turquoise* // 1986 - **Dulcimer Dimensions,** *Turquoise* // 1988 - **Take Five,** *Turquoise* // 1991 - **Coffee At Midnight,** *Turquoise* // 1992 - **Blue Roses,** *Turquoise* // 1996 - **Bellizona,** *Enessay Music.*

Norcia, "Sugar" Ray

Born: Westerley, RI

Blues / Rock singer, harmonica player

Sugar Ray Norcia is an east coast Blues/Rock harmonica player who began playing while in high school. He has performed with *Sugar Ray and The Bluetones, Ronnie Earl and The Broadcasters* and *Roomful of Blues* as well as playing on his own.

<u>Discography:</u> (with Roomful of Blues)
1980 - **Sugar Ray and The Bluetones,** *Baron* // 1989 - **Knockout,** *Varrick* // 1990 - **Don't Stand in My Way,** *Bullseye Blues* // 1994 - **Dance All Night,** *Bullseye Blues* // 1997 - **Under One Roof,** *Bullseye Blues* // 1998 - **Sweet and Swingin',** *Bullseye.*

Norris, Fate

Bluegrass banjo, harmonica player

Fate Norris played the banjo and harmonica with *Gid Tanner and his Skillet Lickers* from 1926 until the group was disbanded in 1931. They were one of the first old-time Country bands to ever record.

<u>Discography:</u> (see - The Skillet Lickers)

Novelle, Alex

Vaudeville harmonica player

Originally a member of *The Harmonica Rascals,* Alex Novelle pursued a solo career in the early 1940's using *The Stagg McMann Trio* as a back-up group.

Nulisch, Darrell

Born: September 14, 1952 - Dallas, TX

Blues singer, harmonica player

Darrell Nulisch co-founded the group *Anson Funderburgh and The Rockets* in 1978. After leaving that band in 1985 he played with *Ronnie Earl and The Broadcasters* for several years. In 1990 he formed his own back-up band, *Texas Heat,* and has been working with them ever since. He has also recorded with James Cotton, Hubert Sumlin, Otis Grand and others.

<u>Discography:</u> (also see - Anson Funderburgh and The Rockets)
1991 - **Business as Usual,** (with Texas Heat), *Blacktop* // 1996 - **Bluesoul, Higher Plane** // 1998 - **Whole Truth,** *Severn* // 2000 - **I Like It That Way,** *Severn* // **Thru the Years: A Retrospective,** (with Anson Funderburgh and The Rockets), *Blacktop.*

O'Brien, Johnny

Born: 1902
Died: 1991

Vaudeville harmonica player

Basing his career out of San Francisco, Johnny O'Brien organized *The Harmonica Hi-Hats* in 1937 from remnants of *The Harmonica Kings*. O'Brien played the diatonic harmonica and was one of the few players who mastered playing chromatic scales on the instrument.

After *The Harmonica Hi-Hats* disbanded in 1940, O'Brien continued in show business as a comedian and harmonica player. He joined up with Dave Doucette from 1968 to 1969 in *The Stereomonics* harmonica band.

Octave-Tuned Harmonicas

Octave tuned harmonicas are diatonic harmonicas built with a double set of reeds, the first being tuned to the standard diatonic scale, the second is tuned one octave higher, so that when a note is played, it also sounds the note one octave above it.

Odell, Mac

Real name: Odell McLeod
Born: May 31, 1916 - Roanoke, AL

Country singer-songwriter, guitar, harmonica player

Mac Odell began performing in the 1930's and became a regular on Chicago-area Country radio programs on WLS and WJJD during the late 1930's. He recorded dozens of sides over the next several years. He has worked primarily as a songwriter since the 1950's, but continues to perform on a limited basis.

Discography:

1961 - **Hymns for Country Folk**, *Audio Lab* // 1977 - **Be On Time**, *Folk Variety* // 1978 - **Wild Rose of the Mountain**, *Folk Variety* // 1978 - **Seven Seven Nashville Session**, *Folk Variety* // 1981 - **Austin, Texas Git Together**, *Folk Variety* // 1981 - **Early Radio**, *Old Homestead.*

Ollestad, Tollak

Born: Seward, AK

Jazz keyboards, harmonica player

Tollak Ollestad began playing the harmonica around the age of fifteen. He has since performed and recorded with Kenny Loggins, Dave Grusin, Christopher Cross, Sheena Easton, John Tesh, Al Jarreau, Don Henley and others.

Soundtracks:

Northern Exposure, TV // **Good Morning America,** TV // **Any Day Now,** TV // **The P.J.'s,** TV

Olson, Hans

Born: July 3, 1952 - San Bernardino, CA

Blues singer, guitar, harmonica player

Hans Olson began playing music at age twelve and was performing professionally by 1967. He did the harmonica playing for the television series "Evening Shade" and the mini-series "The Wild West." He works out of Phoenix, Arizona, mostly as an acoustic Blues act, while playing the harmonica on a neck-brace.

Discography:
1973 - **Western Winds,** *Joplin* // 1978 - **Blond Sun Album,** *Blond Sun* // 1980 - **Hans Olson Sings the Blues,** *Creamo* // 1981 - **The Aspen Tapes,** *Blond Sun* // 1986 - **Hans Olson - Solo,** *Blond Sun* // 1992 - **Where's the Grey?,** *Blond Sun* // 1992 - **Hans Olson,** *Sky Ranch* // 1995 - **Arizona Blues,** *Willing* // 1995 - **Kachina Blues,** *Blonde Sun* // 1996 - **Arizona,** *Blond Sun* // 1998 - **Other Sides,** *Willing.*

Television:
Evening Shade // **The Wild West** (mini-series).

Olson, Mark

Rock singer, guitar, keyboards, harmonica player

Mark Olson played several instruments, including the harmonica, with *The Jayhawks* from 1985 until 1995. He has also worked with *Rare Earth, Counting Crows* and John Hiatt.

Discography: (see - The Jayhawks)

Omar and The Howlers

Formed: Late 1970's - Austin, TX

Blues / Rock band

Omar and The Howlers is the band that was put together to back singer and harmonica player Omar Kent Dykes. While based out of Austin, Texas, the group has been a steady presence on the Blues charts since the 1980's. They have also featured harmonica player Gary Primich on three of their albums.

Discography:
1980 - **Big Leg Beat,** *Amazing* // 1984 - **I Told You So,** *Austin* // 1987 - **Hard Times in the Land of Plenty,** *Columbia* // 1991 - **Live at Paradiso,** *Bullseye* // 1992 - **Blues Bag,** *Bullseye* // 1992 - **Courts of Lulu,** *Bullseye* // 1995 - **Muddy Springs Road,** *Watermelon* // 1996 - **World Wide Open,** *Watermelon* // 1997 - **Southern Style,** *Watermelon* // 1997 - **Monkey Land,** *Discovery* // 1999 - **Swing Land,** *Black Top* // 2000 - **Live at the Opera House Austin, Texas,** *Phoenix Rising* // 2000 - **The Screamin' Cat,** *Provogue* // **Wall of Pride,** *Columbia.*

The Original Harmonica Band

Formed: 1976 - Los Angeles, CA

Vaudeville harmonica band

The Original Harmonica Band was a group that paid tribute to the early Vaudeville harmonica bands. Even featuring their own harmonica-playing midget, the band played around southern California and Las Vegas through the late 1980's.

Members of the group included Jimmy Curtale, Michael Burton, Bill McLean, Conley Day, Michael Scott, Felix Silla, Danny Welton, Eddie Gordon, Kevin Thompson, Don Powell, Gary Popenoe, Joe Gibb and others.

Oscher, Paul

Born: April 5, 1950 - Brooklyn, NY

Blues harmonica player

Paul Oscher began playing the harmonica at age twelve and was playing in New York's Blues clubs by the time he was fifteen. During the mid-1960's he became the first white harmonica player to hold the regular harmonica spot in Muddy Water's band.

After a few albums he left the group and not much was heard from him until the mid-1990's, when he released a new album of Blues music. Oscher has played and recorded with Victoria

Spivey, Johnny Young, *Savoy Brown*, Johnny Copeland, Eric Clapton, Keith Richards, Levon Helm, Big Bill Morganfield and Steve Guyger.

Discography:
1993 - **Rough Stuff,** *Lollipop* // 1996 - **Knockin' on the Devil's Door,** *Vice Roots* // 1997 - **The Deep Blues of Oscher,** *Blues Planet* // 2000 - **Living Legends Deep in the Blues,** *Blues Leaf* // **New York Really Has the Blues,** *Spivey.*

Oskar, Lee

Born: March 24, 1948 - Copenhagen, Denmark

Latin Funk harmonica player

Lee Oskar was raised in Copenhagen, Denmark and learned to play the harmonica at age six. After coming to America in 1966, he started playing the Los Angeles club scene. He began working with former *Animals* lead singer Eric Burdon, who brought him into the group, *Nightshift.* The resulting combination became the band *War.*

The group was an instant success, even though Burdon left shortly after he began working with them. They blended several types of ethnic music including Funk, Calypso, Latin and Jazz. Oskar's harmonica playing leant itself as an excellent accompaniment to the horn section.

Oskar recorded his first solo album in 1976 and in 1983, he began working with the Tombo Harmonica Company of Japan to produce Lee Oskar brand harmonicas. Although he played his last show with War in 1993, he still continues to perform occasionally with his former bandmates as *S.O.B.* and conducts

seminars on harmonica playing.

Discography:
1976 - **Lee Oskar,** *Avenue* // 1978 - **Before the Rain,** *Avenue* // 1980 - **My Road - Our Road,** *Avenue* // 1981 - **Anokoro,** *Nippon Columbia* // 1982 - **Friendly - Live in Japan,** *Nippon Columbia* // 1985 - **Touch the Future,** *Alpine/Luxeman* // 1997 - **You and I,** *Tokuma* // 1997 - **So Much in Love,** *Zebra* // 1997 - **Free,** *Avenue* // 1997 - **Live at the Pitt Inn,** *Avenue* // 1999 - **The Best of Lee Oskar,** *Rhino* // 2000 - **Romance,** *Oskar.*

Lee Oskar Harmonica Co.

Founded: 1983

Harmonica manufacturer
Headed by the former *War* harmonica player, the Lee Oskar Harmonica Company has its instruments manufactured by the Tombo Harmonica Company of Japan. They have pioneered the use of replaceable reed plates, alternate diatonic tunings as well as high and low tunings for diatonic harmonicas.

Overblowing / Overdrawing

Overblowing and overdrawing are the techniques of changing the airflow on a blow or draw note causing a note to sound that isn't built into the harmonica. These techniques enable players to achieve a full chromatic scale on a diatonic instrument.

On a "C" harmonica, overblows can be achieved on holes 1, 4, 5 and 6 and enable the harmonica player to play the E flats on 1 and 4, F sharp on 5 and B flat on the 6 hole. With overdraws a player can hit the C sharp on the 7 hole, the G sharp on the 9 and a C sharp on the 10 hole of the harmonica.

The Ozark Cowboys

Formed: 1950's

Country music band
The Ozark Cowboys was a trio that included harmonica player Onie Wheeler. After being heard by Grand Old Opry star Little Jimmie Dickens they went to Nashville to try to get a recording contract. Wheeler eventually got one for himself, but worked with the other two players as back-up musicians for most of the rest of his career.

See - Onie Wheeler

The Ozark Mountain Daredevils

Formed: 1971 - Springfield, MO

Country / Rock band
Originally based out of Springfield, Missouri, *The Ozark Mountain Daredevils* were leading exponents of Country/Rock during the early 1970's. Their first big hit, "If You Want To Get To Heaven," featured harmonica playing throughout. Lead

singer Steve Cash and guitarist Randle Chowning both played harmonica.

See - Steve Cash, Randle Chowning

Discography:
1973 - **Ozark Mountain Daredevils**, *A&M* // 1974 - **It'll Shine When it Shines**, *A&M* // 1975 - **The Car Over the** Lake, *A&M* // 1976 - **Men from Earth**, *A&M* // 1978 - **Don't Look Down**, *A&M* // 1978 - **It's Alive**, *A&M* // 1980 - **Ozark Mountain Daredevils**, *CBS* // 1983 - **The Best Of...**, *A&M* // 1989 - **Modern History**, *Conifer* // 1997 - **13**, *New Era* // 1997 - **Archive Alive**, *Archive* // 1997 - **Jackie Blue**, *Eclipse* // 1999 - **Concert Classics, Vol. 8**, *Renaissance*.

– P –

Paisley, Bob

Real name: James Robert Pailey
Born: March 14, 1931 - Ashe County, NC

Bluegrass guitar, mandolin, banjo, harmonica
Having played guitar and harmonica since his childhood, Bob Paisley played in *The Southern Mountain Boys* from 1964 until 1979, when he founded the group *Southern Grass*.

Discography:
1981 - **Bob Paisley and Southern Grass**, *Rounder* // 1981 - **Bluegrass**, *Rounder* // 1982 - **An Old Love Affair**, *Brandywine* // 1983 - **Pickin' in Holland**, *Strictly Country* // 1985 - **I Still Love You Yet**, *Mountain Laurel* // 1988 - **Home of Light and Love**, *Mountain Laurel* // 1992 - **No Vacancy**, *Brandywine* // 1997 - **Live in Holland**, *Strictly Country*.

Pankowitz, Victor

Also known as: Vic Pace
Died: January 13, 2000

Vaudeville harmonica player
As a boyhood friend of Alan "Blackie" Schackner, Victor Pankowitz is credited with having taught Schackner how to do tongue switching and other techniques on the harmonica. Pankowitz was a student at the Borrah Minevitch Harmonica Institute of America and a member of *The Philharmonicas* from 1935 to 1941. During the 1950's he played in Herb Shriner's harmonica orchestra.

Papparozzi, Robert

Born: October 14, 1952

Blues singer, harmonica player
Robert Papparozzi has been performing in the New York area since the late 1960's. As a session musician he has recorded and performed with *Culture Club*, Whitney Houston, Cyndi Lauper, Roberta Flack, Carole King, James Galway, Judy Collins and many others as well as doing commercials, soundtracks and appearing on Broadway in the musicals "Big River," "Shenandoah" and "The Will Rogers Follies." He performs and records as a Blues singer and harmonica player with *The Hudson River Rats*.

Discography:
1994 - **First Take**, *3 B's Music* // 1999 - **Get It While You Can**, *3 B's Music*.

Paris, Jon
Blues / Jazz harmonica player

While working primarily out of New York City, Jon Paris has recorded with Johnny Winter, Robert Gordon, Peter Green and others.

Discography:
1996 - **Rock the Universe,** *Fountainbleu.*

Parker, Herman "Little Junior"

Born: March 3,1927 - West Memphis, AR
Died: November 18, 1971 - Blue Island, IL

Blues singer, harmonica player
As a child, Junior Parker sang in local Gospel choirs around Clarksdale, Mississippi. In his early twenties he learned how to play the harmonica from Sonny Boy Williamson II (Rice Miller). Williamson eventually let Parker lead his local band when he went on the road.

By 1949 Parker was also playing with Howlin' Wolf and soon after with B.B. King. He began recording for the Sun label around 1953 and one of his songs, "Mystery Train," became a big hit for Elvis Presley.

Though never as big as he was in the 1950's, Parker continued to perform and record until his death from a brain tumor in 1971.

Discography:
1960 - **Driving Wheel,** *MCA/Duke //* 1961 - **Blues Consolidated,** *Duke //* 1964 - **Junior Parker,** *Bluesway //* 1967 - **Baby, Please,** *Mercury //* 1967 - **Like it Is,** *Mercury //* 1967 - **The Best Of...,** *MCA //* 1969 - **Honey-Drippin' Blues,** *Mercury //* 1969 - **Blues Man,** *Minit //* 1970 - **Outside Man,** *Capitol //* 1971 - **Dudes Doin' Business,** *Capitol //* 1971 - **100 Proof Black Magic,** *United Artists //* 1972 - **Blue Shadows Falling,** *Groove Merchant //* 1972 - **Good Things Don't Happen Every Day,** *Groove Merchant //* 1973 - **Sometime Tomorrow,** *Bluesway //* 1973 - **You Don't have to be Black,** *People //* 1973 - **I Tell Stories Sad and True,** *United Artists //* 1974 - **Blues for Mr. Crump,** *Polydor //* 1974 - **Love Ain't Nothing But Business,** *People //* 1976 - **The ABC Collection,** *ABC //* 1976 - **Love My Baby,** *Charly //* 1978 - **Legendary Sun Performers // Mystery Train,** *Rounder //* 1992 - **Junior's Blues, The Duke Recordings, Vol. One,** *MCA/Duke //* 1996 - **Mercury Recordings,** *Collectables //* 1998 - Backtracking - **The Duke Recordings, Volume 2,** *Duke //* 1998 - **I'm So Satisfied,** *Polygram //* 2000 - **Way Back Home,** *Connoisseur //* **Funny How Time Slips Away,** *Delta //* **Annie Get Your YoYo,** *MCA.*

Parsons, Gene

Born: September 4, 1944 - Los Angeles, CA

Country / Rock Multi-instrumentalist, including harmonica
Gene Parsons started playing music professionally in 1963. He joined The Byrds as a drummer in 1968 and stayed with them until 1972. Since then he has worked on a wide variety of projects on various instruments, including the harmonica. He has recorded with Arlo Guthrie, *The Everly Brothers,* Randy Newman, *The Flying Burrito Brothers* and more as well as devoting his time to solo projects.

Discography: (also see - The Byrds, The Flying Burrito Brothers)
1973 - **Kindling,** *Warner Brothers //* 1980 - **Melodies,** *Sierra //* 1992 - **The Kindling Collection,** *Sierra //* 1992 - **Birds of a Feather,** (with Meridian Green), *Sierra.*

Pattman, "Big Daddy" Neal

Born: January 10, 1926 - Madison County, GA

Blues singer, harmonica player
Neal Pattman learned how to play the harmonica at the age of nine from his father while growing up in rural Georgia. He began playing for tips as a teenager around Athens, Georgia, eventually settling in that town after taking a job as a dishwasher at the University there. After retiring from that job he devoted himself to playing full-time, touring and recording.

Discography:
1992 - **The Blues Ain't Left Yet,** *Global Village //* 1993 - **Drivin' South - Live at Lulu's //** 1997 - **Live in London,** *Erwin //* 1999 - **Prison Blues,** *Music Maker //* **Lightnin' Twist,** *High John.*

Paul, Les

Real name: Lester Polfus
Also known as: Rhubarb Red
Born: June 9, 1916 - Waukesha, WI

Pop guitar, harmonica player, inventor
Though known mostly for his guitars, his pioneering of multi-track recording and dozens of hit records with his *Les Paul Trio* and his wife Mary Ford, Les Paul's first musical instrument was the harmonica, which he learned to play in 1927. He performed with it during the early part of his career, usually playing with a neckbrace.

Paul's first professional job was playing guitar, harmonica and jug with *The Ozark Apple Knockers* in St. Louis and Chicago. He would later cut a few records as Rhubarb Red, playing guitar and harmonica.

Discography:
1947 - **Les Paul Trio,** *Laserlight //* 1958 - **16 Most Requested Songs,** *Capitol //* 1992 - **All-Time Greatest Hits,** *CEMA //* 1996 - **Radio Picks,** *Demand //* 1997 - **Love Songs by Les Paul and Mary Ford,** *Ranwood //* 1999 - **V-Disc Recordings,** *Collector's Choice //* **The Complete Decca Trios** (1936-1947), *MCA.*

Woody Paul

Real name: Dr. Paul Woodrow Chrisman
Born: August 23, 1949 - Nashville, TN

Country multi-instrumentalist, including harmonica
Woody Paul is a member of the Country comedy trio, *Riders in the Sky*. In addition to having his Ph.D. in theoretical plasma physics from M.I.T., he plays a variety of instruments, including the harmonica.

Discography: (see - Riders in the Sky)

Payton, Earlee

Born: November 24, 1923 - Pine Bluff, AR

Blues harmonica player
Earlee Payton began playing the harmonica around 1942, about the same time he moved to Chicago. By 1948 he was sitting in with local bands, including Muddy Waters' group. In 1954 he recorded his first record.

Though never as big a star as some of his peers, Payton has managed to keep active and has worked with Otis Rush, Freddy King and others.

Pedersen, Pete

Born: September 4, 1925 - Chicago, IL

Pop / Vaudeville harmonica player

Pete Pedersen grew up on the west side of Chicago and played in *The Harmonica Madcaps* with Al Fiore and Jerry Murad. After joining *The Harmonica Rascals* with Murad, he stayed with that group for several years until joining *The Don Henry Trio* with Don

Henry and Fuzzy Feldman. After that he worked for several years in a duo with Feldman called *The Harmonaires.*

Pedersen did most of the arranging for *The Harmonicats,* moved to Memphis, Tennessee in his later yearsand has worked as a producer and arranger ever since. He is still active to this day.

Discography:
1997 - **Groovin' High,** *Peter Buck Productions //* **Music and Memories,** (with Jim Watkins).

Peloquin, Mike

Born: 1960 - Champaign, IL

Blues saxophone, harmonica player
Mike Peloquin began playing the harmonica at the age of thirteen. He is now a session musician who has played harmonica for Mitch Woods, *Mr. Bungle,* Neal Schon, Tommy Castro and many others. In 1997 he won the Hohner World Harmonica Championship and released his first solo album in 2000.

Discography:
2000 - **House of Cards,** *Globe.*

Pie Plant Pete

Real name: Claud J. Moye
Also known as: Asparagus Joe, Jerry Wallace
Born: July 9, 1906 - Shawneetown, IL
Died: February 7, 1988

Country singer, guitar, harmonica player
Pie Plant Pete started playing the harmonica at age sixteen and favored the technique of playing the harmonica on a neckbrace while he played the guitar. He called this technique "The two-cylinder cob crusher."

He began working in radio on WLS in Chicago in 1927. There he teamed up with Bashful Harmonica Joe Troynan from 1936 until 1947 and continued performing intermittently until the late 1950's.

Discography:
1989 - **The Old-Time Country Music Collection,** *Cattle Germany.*

The Philharmonicas / The Philharmonica Trio

Formed: 1935 - New York City, NY
Disbanded: Mid-1940's

Vaudeville harmonica band
Organized in 1935 by Dave Macklin, an instructor from the Borrah Minevitch Harmonica Institute of America in New York City, *The Philharmonicas* was a band comprised of students from the school and they specialized in playing big band arrangements with their harmonicas.

Players in the group included Dave Macklin, Harry Halicki, Joe Jass, Charles Leighton, Frank Mitowski, Victor Pankowitz, Charles and Joe Pitello.

The band survived until the outbreak of World War Two. The Pitello Brothers and Harry Halicki joined the Coast Guard and continued performing as *The Philharmonica Trio*, later recording several records for the Columbia label.

Phillips, Bruce U. "Utah"

Born: 1935

Folk singer-songwriter, guitar, harmonica
Bruce "Utah" Phillips began playing music professionally after serving in the Korean War. His parents were labor leaders during the 1930's and Phillips used his music as a vehicle to express his social concerns. He played the harmonica on a neckbrace while playing the guitar. Phillips has largely retired from music since the 1990's, although he has recorded two albums with Ani DeFranco and had a tribute album dedicated to him.

Discography:
1969 - **El Capitan,** *Philo* // 1973 - **Good Though,** *Philo* // 1975 - **All Used Up,** *Philo* // 1984 - **We Have Fed You All for a Thousand Years,** *Philo* // 1991 - **I've Got To Know,** *Alcazar* // 1996 - **The Past Didn't Go Anywhere,** *Righteous Babe* // 1997 - **Loafer's Glory,** *Red House* // 1997 - **The Telling Takes Me Home,** *Philo* // 1999 - **Moscow Hold,** *Red House* // 1999 - **Fellow Workers,** (with Ani DiFranco), *Righteous Babe.*

Piazza, Rod

Born: December 18, 1947 - Riverside, CA

Blues harmonica player
Rod Piazza began his professional career in 1965 with *The Dirty Blues Band,* which lasted until 1968 when he teamed up as a duo with George "Harmonica" Smith. They worked together as *Bacon Fat* until Smith's death in 1982.

Piazza put together his new back-up group, *The Mighty Flyers,* in 1980 and has released a number of fine albums with them. He has also worked as a studio harmonica player, backing up Michelle Shocked, Johnny Dyer, Jimmy Rogers, Charlie Musselwhite, PeeWee Crayton and others.

Discography:
1967 - **The Dirty Blues Band,** *ABC/Bluesway* // 1968 - **Stone Dirt,** *ABC/Bluesway* // 1968 - **Bacon Fat,** (with George "Harmonica" Smith), *Blue Horizon* // 1970 - **Grease One for Me,** (with Bacon Fat), *Blue Horizon* // 1971 - **Tough Dude,** (with Bacon Fat), *Blue Horizon* // 1973 - **Rod Piazza Blues Man,** *LMI* // 1979 - **Chicago Flying Saucer Band,** *Gangster* // 1981 - **Radioactive Material** // 1981 - **The Mighty Flyers,** *Right Hemisphere* // 1982 - **Robot Woman II,** *Shanghai* // 1984 - **File Under Rock,** *Takoma* // 1985 - **From the**

Start to the Finnish // 1985 - **Feelin' Good with Jimmie Rogers,** *Blind Pig* // 1986 - **Harp Burn,** *Black Top* // 1988 - **So Glad to Have the Blues,** *Murray Brothers* // 1991 - **Blues in the Dark,** *Black Top* // 1992 - **The Essential Collection,** *Black Top* // 1992 - **Alphabet Blues,** *Black Top* // 1994 - **Live at B.B. King's Blues Club,** *Big Mo* // 1997 - **Tough and Tender,** *Tone-Cool* // 1997 - **California Blues,** *Black Top* // 1998 - **Vintage Live: 1975,** *Tone-Cool* // 1999 - **Here and Now,** *Tone-Cool.*

Video:
Blues Harp Experience.

Pigpen

Real name: Ron McKernan
Born: September 8, 1945 - San Bruno, CA
Died: March 8, 1973 - San Francisco, CA

Rock singer, organ, harmonica player
Ron "Pigpen" McKernan learned about Blues and R&B music from his father, who was a Blues disc jockey on a San Francisco area radio station. McKernan acquired his nickname "Pigpen" after the Peanuts cartoon character from his unkempt appearance.

During the early 1960's Pigpen teamed up with Jerry Garcia and other future members of *The Grateful Dead* to play in the band's early incarnations, including *Mother McCree's Uptown Jug Champions* and *The Warlocks.*

As *The Grateful Dead* drifted further in Psychedelic music and further away from its Blues roots, Pigpen performed less and less. He finally succumbed to liver damage caused by years of heavy drinking in 1973.

Discography: (see - The Grateful Dead)

Pitello, Charles

Vaudeville harmonica player

The brother of Joe Pitello, Charles Pitello played in *The Philharmonicas* from 1935 until 1941 and with *The Philharmonica Trio* during World War Two.

Pitello, Joe

Vaudeville harmonica player

The brother of Charles Pitello, Joe Pitello played in *The Philharmonicas* from 1935 until 1941 and with *The Philharmonica Trio* during World War Two.

Plant, Robert

Born: August 20, 1947 - Bromwich, England

Rock singer, harmonica player

Best known as the lead singer for the Heavy Metal Rock band *Led Zepplin*, Robert Plant occasionally plays the harmonica, both live and in the studio. He has also played harmonica on recordings by Alexis Korner and P.J. Proby.

Discography: (also see - Led Zepplin)
1982 - **Pictures at 11,** *Swan Song* // 1983 - **The Principle of Moments,** *Es Paranza* // 1984 - **Volume One,** (with The Honeydrippers), *Es Paranza* // 1985 - **Shaken 'n' Stirred,** *Es Paranza* // 1988 - **Now and Zen,** *Es Paranza* // 1990 - **Manic Nirvana,** *Es Paranza* // 1993 - **Fate of Nations,** *Es Paranza* // 1994 - **No Quarter: Jimmy Page and Robert Plant Unledded,** *Atlantic* // 1998 - **Walking Into Clarksdale,** *Atlantic.*

Pocket Piano

A nickname for the harmonica.

Pogson, Alan

Born: August 21, 1915

Vaudeville harmonica player

Alan Pogson played the third chromatic harmonica in *The Harmonica Hi-Hats* from 1937 until 1940 and switched to the chord harmonica when Sam Blanco left the group. He also played for *The Harmonica Rascals* around that time. Al Fiore credited Pogson with creating the distinctive chord harmonica arrangement for "Peg 'O' My Heart."

Polyphonia

A specialty harmonica built by M. Hohner, Inc. which allowed the player access to a full chromatic scale without using a slide mechanism. The polyphonia was used mostly for glissandos and other special effects.

Pope Pius XI

Real name: Ambrogio Damiano Achille Ratti
Born: May 31, 1857 - Desio, Italy
Died: February 10,1939 - The Vatican

Religious Leader

In the 1930's, the Hohner Harmonica Company built the world's most expensive harmonica for Pope Pius XI. The instrument was made out of gold and ivory and was encrusted with precious gems. Though it is unknown whether the Pope was a harmonica player, the harmonica remains as one of the treasures of The Vatican.

Popper, John

Born: March 29, 1967 - Cleveland, OH

Rock singer, harmonica player

John Popper began playing the harmonica after seeing Dan Aykroyd play in the movie, "The Blues Brothers." Mostly self-taught, Popper is the lead vocalist and harmonica player for the band *Blues Traveler*. He specializes in ultra-high speed leads during the group's long instrumental breaks.

Discography: (also see - Blues Traveler)
1999 - **Zygote,** *Interscope.*

Portnoy, Jerry

Born: November 25, 1943 - Evanston, IL

Blues harmonica player

Jerry Portnoy grew up in Chicago's Maxwell Street neighborhood, where his father owned a rug store. This brought him into contact with Chicago's Blues scene.

In 1974 he began playing with *The Muddy Waters Band*, where he appeared on several albums. After six years with Waters, Portnoy

139

and several members of Muddy's back-up band left to form *The Legendary Blues Band*. After six years of playing with that group, Portnoy left to work solo.

He co-founded the group *Ronnie Earl and The Broadcasters* in 1987 and stayed with them for two years. His present back-up band is called *The Streamliners*. He has performed with dozens of major artists including Duke Robillard, Bo Diddley, John Brim, Paul Rishell and Hubert Sumlin. He worked with Eric Clapton for about five years and appeared on his "From the Cradle" and "24 Nights" albums.

Discography: (also see - The Legendary Blues Band, Muddy Waters)
1991 - **Poison Kisses,** *Modern Blues* // 1995 - **Home Run Hitter,** *Indigo* // **Blues in a Dream,** *Indigo Records.*

Bibliography:
1997 - **Blues Harmonica Master Class,** *International Blues Management.*

Positions

Due to the fact that the diatonic harmonica can normally only play the major scale of the key that it's tuned for, many harmonica players resort to playing in different "Positions." Positions refer to playing a different key of harmonica than the key being played.

First Position or Straight Harp

This refers to playing the harmonica in the same key as the music that the harmonica player is trying to accompany. For instance, if the song is in the key of "C," the harmonica player uses a key of "C" harmonica.

First Position is generally used for melody playing, although many Folk players use the first position to play leads. It is also very handy to beginners for learning the rudiments of the harmonica's layout.

Second Position or Cross Harp or Blues Harp

The Second position is the practice of playing the harmonica five notes up from the music that the player is trying to accompany. This creates a "Blues scale" on the instrument and positions the accent notes of the Blues scale to be played on the draw holes of the harmonica, which enables the player to bend those notes for greater expression. For instance if the music is in the key of "C," the harmonica player would play a harmonica in the key of "F."

The Second position is widely used in the Blues, Folk, Country and Rock styles.

Third Position

Third position is widely used to accompany music in minor keys. If the music is in the key of "C minor," the harmonica player would use a harmonica in the key of "B flat."

This position is used mostly by Blues players to play on Blues songs in minor keys.

Fourth Position

An alternative to the third position, the fourth position also allows the harmonica player to accompany songs in minor keys. If the song is in the key of "C minor," the player would use a harmonica in the key of "E flat."

In addition to the positions mentioned above, many harmonica players have found that many, if not all, of the keys can be used to play different types of scales on the harmonica.

For music in the key of "C," these additional positions are:

5th Position - A Flat	6th Position - D Flat
7th Position - F Sharp	8th Position - B
9th Position - E	10th Position - A
11th Position - D	12th Position - G

Power, Brendan

Born: February 20, 1956 - Mombasa, Kenya

Celtic / Pop harmonica player

Brendan Power Grew up in New Zealand and moved to England in 1992. He has specialized in playing the traditional Irish music of his ancestors on the chromatic harmonica. He has recorded with Ray Charles, Shirley Bassey, Paul Young, Van Morrison and Sting as well as doing some of the music for the Irish dance spectacular "Riverdance."

Discography:
1984 - **Country Harmonica** // 1990 - **State of the Harp,** *Jayrem* // 1990 - **Harmonica Nights,** *Disky* // 1990 - **Licks N' Spits** // 1991 - **Digging In** // 1993 - **New Irish Harmonica,** *Green Linnet* // 1993 - **Harmonica,** *Jayrem* //

1995 - **Music From Riverdance**, *Greentrax* // 1995 - **Blow In** // 1996 - **Jig Jazz** // 1999 - **Dawn to Dusk**, *Jayrem* // 2000 - **Two Trains Running**, *Indigo* // 2000 - **Tanks Aloft: New Irish Harmonica Two** // 2000 - **Live in Ireland** // 2000 - **Two Trains Running**, *Indigo*.

Movies:
1999 - **Pushing Tin.**

Books:
Play Irish Music on the Blues Harp // **Play Irish Music on the Chromatic.**

Power, Duffy

Born: September 9, 1941

R&B singer, guitar, harmonica player
Duffy Power was a rather obscure R&B musician whose career reached its apex during the height of the British Invasion of the 1960's. He is best remembered for his back-up band that included Jack Bruce and John McLaughlin as well as for playing harmonica with Bert Jansch and Alexis Korner.

Discography:
1970 - **Innovations**, *Transatlantic* // 1973 - **Duffy Power**, *Spark* // 1976 - **Powerhouse**, *Buk* // 1986 - **Mary Open the Door**, *Rock Machine* // 1992 - **Blues Power**, *See for Miles* // 1992 - **Little Boy Blue**, *Edsel* // 1995 - **Just Say Blue**, *Retro*.

The Prairie Ramblers

Formed: 1930's - Kentucky
Disbanded: 1956

Country string band
The Prairie Ramblers were one of the regular bands on WLS radio from the 1930's until the 1950's and were also Gene Autry's first back-up band. Harmonica player Salty Holmes played with them from the early 1930's until 1937.

See - Salty Holmes

The Pretty Things

Formed: 1963 - Kent, England
Disbanded: 1971

Pop / Rock band
The Pretty Things started as a Blues-influenced Pop band during the British Invasion of the early 1960's. Bass guitar player John Stax also played the harmonica during the band's early days until 1966.

See - John Stax

Discography:
1965 - **The Pretty Things**, *Fontana* // 1965 - **Get the Picture?**, *Fontana* // 1965 - **Raining in My Heart**, *Fontana* // 1966 - **On Film**, *Fontana* // 1967 - **Don't Bring Me Down**, *Fontana* // 1968 - **Emotions**, *Fontana* // 1968 - **S.F. Sorrow**, *Edsel* // 1970 - **Parachute**, *Edsel* // 1973 - **Freeway Madness**, *Medice* // 1974 - **Silk Torpedo**, *Swan Song* // 1980 - **Cross Talk**, *Warner Brothers* // 1984 - **Live at the Heartbreak Hotel**, *Line* // 1987 - **Out of the Island**, *Inakustik* // 1991 - **Chicago Blues Tapes '91**, *Demon* // 1992 - **Get a Buzz: The Best of the Fontana Years**, *Fontana* // 1994 - **Wine, Women and Whiskey**, *Demon* // 2000 - **Latest Writs: Greatest Hits**, *Madfish*.

Pribojszki, Matyas "Matt"

Born: 1974 - Bekescsaba, Hungary

Blues singer, harmonica player

Matyas Pribojszki began playing the harmonica when he was fourteen. About a year later he heard his first American Blues records and dedicated himself to playing that style of harmoni-

141

ca. In 1995 he founded *The Blues Fools* and they have been touring Europe as well as releasing an album of their music. In 1997, Matyas won the harmonica championship at the Trossingen World Harmonica Festival.

Discography: (see - The Blues Fools)

Price, Topper

Southern Rock harmonica player

Topper Price is a harmonica player from Alabama who has played with Gregg Allman, Jimmy Hall, *The Subdudes, The Radiators, The Band* and Dickey Betts as well as playing and recording as a solo artist.

Discography:
1997 - **Long Way From Home,** *Vent.*

Priest, Steve

Born: February 23, 1950 - Middlesex, England

Rock singer, bass, harmonica player

Steve Priest played the bass guitar and harmonica as well as singing for the Rock band *Sweet* from the time it was formed in 1968 until they disbanded in 1980.

Discography: (see - Sweet)

Primich, Gary

Born: April 20, 1958 - Chicago, IL

Blues harmonica player

Gary Primich was raised in northwest Indiana and learned how to play the harmonica in Chicago's Blues scene before moving to Austin, Texas in the early 1980's. During the 1980's he front-

ed a band called *The Mannish Boys.*

Since going solo in 1990, Gary has recorded several albums as well as recording with *Omar and The Howlers,* Steve James, Tish Hinojosa, Jimmy Carl Black and Pat McLaughlin.

Discography:
1987 - **A L'il Dab'll Do Ya,** *Amazing* // 1988 - **Satellite Rock,** *Amazing* // 1991 - **Gary Primich,** *Amazing* // 1992 - **My Pleasure,** *Amazing* // 1993 - **Hot Harp Blues,** *Amazing* // 1994 - **Travelin' Mood,** *Flying Fish* // 1995 - **Mr. Freeze,** *Flying Fish* // 1996 - **Company Man,** *Black Top* // 1999 - **Botheration,** *Black Top.*

Movies:
1991 - **Ballad of a Sad Café.**

Bibliography:
Blues Harmonica - The Basics and Beyond.

Pryor, James "Snooky"

Born: September 15, 1921 - Lambert, MS

Blues harmonica player

"Snooky" Pryor grew up in Mississippi and was a boyhood friend of Bluesman Jimmy Rogers. He took up the harmonica and drums at age fourteen and was playing at local parties shortly thereafter. He moved to Helena, Arkansas in 1937 and then to Chicago in 1940.

After serving in the Army from 1942 to 1945 he returned to Chicago and began working with Floyd Jones, Johnny Young, Homesick James, John Lee "Sonny Boy Williamson, Big Bill Broonzy, Memphis Minnie and others. He is considered to be one of the pioneers of early amplified harmonica, since he played through public address systems as early as World War Two.

He began recording in 1948, mostly as a sideman, but also as the lead artist for several labels. After dropping out of music for several years he returned and has remained somewhat active ever since, both in the studio and on stage.

Discography:
1973 - **Do It If You Want**, *Bluesway* // 1974 - **Homesick James and Snooky Pryor**, *Caroline* // 1980 - **Snooky and Moody**, *Flyright* // 1984 - **Shake Your Boogie**, *Big Bear* // 1987 - **Snooky**, *Blind Pig* // 1992 - **Too Cool To Move**, *Antone's* // 1992 - **Snooky Pryor**, *Paula* // 1994 - **In This Mess Up to My Chest**, *Antone's* // 1997 - **Mind Your Own Business**, *Antone's* // 1997 - **Snooky Pryor and the Country Blues**, *Sequel* // 1999 - **Can't Stop Blowin'**, *Electro-Fi* // 1999 - **Shake My Hand**, *Blind Pig* // 2000 - **Double Shot**, *Electro-Fi* // **Back To the Country**, (with Johnny Shines), *Blind Pig* // **Real Fine Boogie**, *Flyright* // **Hand Me Down Blues**, *Relic*.

Psallmelodikon

An early 19th century name for the harmonica, the Psallmelodikon was invented around 1828 and featured valves as a way to single out the reeds.

Puckett, Holland "Si"

Also known as: Harvey Watson
Born: July 15, 1899 - Patrick County, VA
Died: July 28, 1934

Country singer, guitar, harmonica player
Holland "Si" Puckett spent most of his life around Mount Airy, North Carolina. After developing an early talent on the guitar and harmonica, he cut several sides for the Gennett label during 1927 and 1928. His musical career came to an abrupt end when he received several fatal knife wounds in a card game.

Pugh, "Forest City" Joe

Born: July 10, 1926 - Hughes, AR
Died: April 3, 1960 - Horseshoe Lake, AR

Blues singer, piano, guitar, harmonica player
"Forest City" Joe Pugh began playing music professionally while still in his teens growing up in rural Arkansas. While traveling extensively, he managed to work with Big Joe Williams, Willie Cobbs, Howlin' Wolf, Sonny Boy Williamson II (Rice Miller) and others.

He began recording for the Aristocrat label in 1949 and worked steadily until his death in a car accident in 1960.

Puleo, Johnny

Born: 1913
Died: 1983

Vaudeville harmonica player

The inspiration for Borrah Minevitch's *Harmonica Rascals*, Johnny Puleo combined comedy with harmonica playing and was the main attraction of the group. Whether he was a dwarf, a midget or the victim of rickets as a child is open to speculation. Whatever the reason, Minevitch used Puleo's shortness as the basis for much of *The Harmonica Rascals* onstage antics.

Minevitch first saw Puleo in a talent contest in 1927 and immediately saw the possibilities for a Vaudeville harmonica band. He signed Puleo to a lifetime contract, paying only a small fraction of what Puleo was worth.

Exploited by Minevitch, Puleo tried to form his own band in Washington D.C. around 1942. Minevitch, however, got a court injunction barring him from playing anywhere other than with *The Harmonica Rascals* and Puleo was soon back performing with the *Rascals*.

Puleo was finally released from his nearly slave-like conditions in 1955 when Minevitch was killed by his wife's lover. Puleo immediately formed *Johnny Puleo and his Harmonica Gang* with Eddie Gordon, Dominic Sgro, Tony Sgro, Frank Marquis, JoJo DeFluvio, Carl Ford, Les McGann, Gene DeMase and Dave Doucette. They played together until Puleo retired from show business in 1973. Although he made nearly a dozen movies during the 1930's and 40's with *The Harmonica Rascals*, Puleo didn't make his screen debut until the 1956 movie "Trapeze."

Discography: (see - Johnny Puleo's Harmonica Gang)
Movies: (also see - The Harmonica Rascals)
1956 - **Trapeze.**

– Q –

Quinn, Derek

Born: May 24, 1942 - Manchester, England

British Rock guitar, harmonica

Derek Quinn played the guitar and harmonica for the early 1960's British Invasion band, *Freddie and the Dreamers* as well as playing with Jim Capaldi, Viv Stanshall and others.

Discography: (see - Freddie and the Dreamers)

The Quintones

Formed: 1942 - Chicago, IL
Disbanded: 1944

Vaudeville harmonica band

Organized around 1942 by Jimmy Mulcay, *The Quintones* featured Jerry Murad, Al Fiore, Don Les, Ronny Salzman and vocalist Barbara Engels. After playing the vaudeville and nightclub circuit for about two years, the group was pared down to a trio when Salzman and Engels left to get married.

The remaining trio changed its name to *The Harmonicats*.

– R –

Rachell, James "Yank"

Born: March 16, 1910 - Brownsville, TN
Died: April 9, 1997 - Indianapolis, IN

Blues mandolin, guitar, harmonica

"Yank" Rachell began playing music at age eight. He learned to play the mandolin from an uncle of his and over the next few years he took up guitar and harmonica as well. By the time he was in his 20's he was working with Hambone Willie Newbern, John Lee "Sonny Boy" Williamson, Big Joe Williams and Sleepy John Estes.

Estes and Rachell worked together with harmonica player Hammie Nixon on and off until Estes died in the mid-1960's. Rachell specialized in the mandolin while Hammie Nixon took care of most of the harmonica playing. Rachell also made some recordings with John Lee "Sonny Boy" Williamson during the 1930's and with Gus Cannon in the 1960's.

Discography:
1964 - **Yank Rachell,** *Blue Goose* // 1986 - **Complete Recorded Works Vol. 1 & 2,** *Wolf* // 1986 - **Mandolin Blues,** *Delmark* // 1986 - **Blues Mandolin Man,** *Blind Pig* // 1987 - **Chicago Style,** *Delmark* // 1996 - **Pig Trader Blues,** *Slippery Noodle* // 1998 - **Too Hot for the Devil,** *Flat Rock* // 1999 - **Yank Rachell: The Blue Goose Album,** *Random Chance.*

Raines, Annie

Born: July 3, 1969 - Beverly, MA

Blues singer, harmonica player

Annie Raines began playing the harmonica at age of seventeen and within a year she was playing around Boston's Blues scene. Since 1993 she has teamed up with Blues guitarist Paul Rishell,

played in John Sebastian's *J-Band*, been on National Public Radio's "Prairie Home Companion" program andplayed on Susan Tedeschi's first two albums as well as recording several albums with Paul Rishell.

Discography:
1993 - **Swear To Tell the Truth,** *Tone-Cool* // 1996 - **I Want You To Know,** *Tone Cool* // 1999 - **Moving to the Country,** *Tone-Cool.*

Ramsey, Pat

Born: 1953 - Shreveport, LA

Blues harmonica player

Pat Ramsey began playing the harmonica at age seventeen and was playing professionally by the time he was twenty. He has appeared on several Johnny Winter albums as well as recording two solo albums.

Discography:
1999 - **Live at the Grand,** *Rampat* // **It's About Time,** *Rampat.*

Raney, Wayne

Born: August 17, 1921 - Wolf Bayou, AR
Died: January 23, 1993

Country harmonica player

Wayne Raney learned how to play the harmonica at age five by listening to Lonnie Glosson perform on the radio during the late 1920's. By 1934 he was performing on the radio and even recorded for the Bluebird label.

In 1936 he started playing with Lonnie Glosson and the two worked together as a team on and off for the next twenty-five years as a harmonica duet, occasionally working with *The Delmore Brothers,* a guitar duo.

During the 1940's Raney sold harmonicas by mail order by promoting them on his radio broadcasts. He claimed to have sold over a million instruments a year during his peak.

In 1954 Raney began playing back-up for Country music star Lefty Frizzell and in 1958 he founded his own record labels, RimRock and Poorboy Records. After Stax Records bought out his label in 1974 he retired.

Discography:
1958 - **Songs from the Hills,** *King* // 1960 - **Wayne Raney and the Raney Family,** *Starday* // 1964 - **Don't Try to Be What You Ain't,** *Starday* // 1960's - **We Need a Lot More Jesus** // 1970 - **Pardon** // 1970 - **Tear Down the Mountains,** *Rimrock* // 1970 - **Gathering in the Sky,** *Rimrock* // 1984 - **The Delmore Brothers and Wayne Raney:**

When They Let the Hammer Down, *Bear Family* // 1986 - **Real Hot Boogie,** *Charly* // **More Hot Boogie,** *Charly.*

Bibliography:
1990 - **Life Has Not Been a Bed of Roses.**

Raphael, Mickey

Born: 1951 - Dallas, Texas

Country harmonica player

Mickey Raphael learned how to play the harmonica as a teenager and got some lessons on the instrument from Don Brooks. He started playing with Willie Nelson in 1973 and has been the regular harmonica player with him ever since.

Raphael has also worked as a session musician behind Emmylou Harris, Leon Russell, Kenny Wayne Shepherd, Jerry Jeff Walker, Elton John, *The Beach Boys, Blue Oyster Cult, The Allman Brothers, Motley Crue, the Chieftans* and many others.

Discography: (solo)
1988 - **Hand To Mouth,** (with Paul Butterfield), *Arno.*

Movies:
1980 - **Honeysuckle Rose** // 1984 - **Songwriter.**

The Red Fox Chasers

Formed: 1927
Disbanded: 1930's

Country band

The Red Fox Chasers were formed as a partnership between A.P. Thompson and harmonica player Bob Cranford. One of the more popular string bands of the late 1920's, they recorded for the Gennet label in the late 1920's.

See - Bob Cranford

Discography:
1967 - **The Red Fox Chasers,** (1928-1930), *County.*

Reed, Jimmy

Born: September 6, 1925 - Dunleith, MS
Died: August 29, 1976 - Oakland, CA

Blues singer, guitar, harmonica player
After learning how to play the harmonica from his father, Jimmy Reed developed one of the most distinctive styles in Blues harmonica playing by concentrating on the high-end blow notes to play leads.

He moved to the Chicago area in 1943 and soon teamed up with guitarist and harmonica player Eddie Taylor, who gave him some lessons on how to play the harmonica. They worked out of Gary, Indiana as a trio with Reed playing the guitar with the harmonica on a neckbrace.

In 1953 they signed to the VeeJay label in Chicago and had a long series of hits, including "Big Boss Man," Bright Lights, Big City and a whole series of others. Between 1957 and 1963 he had twelve songs on the R&B charts.

Troubled by epilepsy and chronic drinking problems, Reed continued performing until his death in 1976.

Discography:
1958 - **I'm Jimmy Reed,** *VeeJay* // 1959 - **Rockin' with Reed,** *VeeJay* // 1960 - **Found Love,** *VeeJay* // 1960 - **Now Appearing,** *VeeJay* // 1961 - **At Carnegie Hall,** *VeeJay* // 1962 - **Just Jimmy Reed,** *VeeJay* // 1962 - **The Best of Jimmy Reed,** *VeeJay* // 1962 - **Wailin' the Blues,** *Tradition* // 1963 - **Preachin' the Blues,** *Stateside* // 1963 - **T'ain't No Big Thing...But He Is!,** *VeeJay* // 1963 - **The Best of the Blues,** *VeeJay* // 1963 - **The 12-String Guitar Blues,** *VeeJay* // 1964 - **More of the Best of Jimmy Reed,** *VeeJay* // 1964 - **Jimmy Reed at Soul City,** *VeeJay* // 1965 - **Jimmy Reed,** *Flyright* // 1965 - **The Legend, the Man,** *VeeJay* // 1967 - **The New Jimmy Reed Album,** *Bluesway* // 1967 - **Soulin',** *Bluesway* // 1968 - **Big Boss Man,** *Bluesway* // 1969 - **Down in Virginia,** *Bluesway* // 1970 - **The Soulful Sound of Jimmy Reed,** *Upfront* // 1970 - **As Jimmy Is,** *Roker* // 1971 - **Let the Bossman Speak!,** *Blues On Blues* // 1973 - **I Ain't From Chicago,** *Bluesway* // 1973 - **The Ultimate Jimmy Reed,** *Bluesway* // 1976 - **Blues is My Business,** *VeeJay* // 1976 - **Cold Chills,** *Antilles* // 1977 - **The Best Of...,** *GNP* // 1980 - **Jimmy Reed is Back,** *Roots* // 1980 - **Hard Walkin' Hanna,** *Versatile* // 1980 - **Shame, Shame, Shame,** *Charly* // 1981 - **High and Lonesome,** *Charly* // 1985 - **Upside Your Head,** *Charly* // 1988 - **Got Me Dizzy,** *Charly* // 1988 - **Bright Lights, Big City,** *Chameleon* // 1989 - **Ride 'em On Down,** *Charly* // 1989 - **Heartaches and Troubles,** *MCA* // 1992 - **Greatest Hits,** *Hollywood* // 1993 - **Speak the Lyrics to Me, Mama Reed,** *VeeJay* // 1994 - **Jimmy Reed, Vol. 1 & 2,** *Ronn* // 1995 - **Classic Recordings,** *Tomato* // 1996 - **Cry Before I Go,** *Drive Archive* // 1996 - **Big Legged Woman,** *Collectables* // 1996 - **Rockin' with Reed,** *Eclipse* // 1996 - **Honest I Do and Other Classics,** *Intercontinent* // 1997 - **Upside the Wall,** *Dove* // 1997 - **Lost in the Shuffle,** *32 Jazz* // 1998 - **His Greatest Recordings,** *Aim* // 1998 - **Masters,** *Cleopatra* // 2000 - **20 Classic Tracks,** *Cleopatra* // 2000 - **Blues Masters, the Very Best Of...,** *Rhino* // **Something Else,** *Sunset* // **Blues Series: Paula Records,** *Adventures* // **New Jimmy Reed,** *HMV* // **Roots of the Blues,** *Kent* // **Soul Greats,** *Upfront* // **I'm the Man Down There,** *Charly* // **Compact Command Performances,** *Motown.*

Reeds

Reeds are thin metal slats that produce the notes on the harmonica. They are fixed at one end to the reedplate and the other end is gapped slightly away from the reedplate. Air is blown or drawn across the reed, causing it to vibrate and produce a musical tone.

The Regan Harmonica Co.
Harmonica manufacturing company
The George P. Regan Harmonica Company operated in northern California from the mid-1930's until the Hohner company began re-exporting harmonicas to the United States after World War Two.

Reilly, Tommy

Born: August 21, 1919 - Guelph, Ontario, Canada
Died: September 25, 2000 - England

Classical harmonica soloist
Tommy Reilly's father was a Canadian harmonica bandleader and wrote several books on how to play the harmonica. Tommy began playing in 1935 and performed in his father's band.

The Reilly family moved to England in 1935 and Tommy spent several years during World War Two in German prison camps after being caught in enemy territory. He used the time to practice his harmonica playing and became so adept at the instrument that his guards regularly supplied him with instruments.

After returning to England in 1945, he embarked on a career as a Pop and Classical harmonica soloist and began recording on the *Parlaphone* label in 1951. He played mostly Pop music until the 1970's, when he shifted his focus to a mostly Classical repertoire.

During his career he played with Bing Crosby, Barbara Streisand, Marlene Dietriech and others as well as having several Classical works composed specifically for him by such composers as Michael Spivakovsky, Graham Whettam, Gordon Jacob, Karl Heinz Koper, James Moody, Vilem Tausky, Robert Farnon, Fried Walter, Joseph Kosma and others.

Discography:
1978 - **Harmonica Recital,** *London* // 1986 - Serenade, *Chandos* // 1987 - **British Folk Songs,** *Chandos* // 1988 - **Works for Harmonica and Orchestra,** *Chandos* // 1988 - **Thanks for the Memory,** *Chandos* // 1990 - **Jacob: Divertimento, Etc.,** *Chandos* // 1991 - **Serenade, Vol. 2,** *Chandos* // 1994 - **Tommy Reilly Plays Harmonica Concertos,** *Chandos* // 1994 - **Herrmann: "Night Digger,"** *LXCD* // 1995 - **Walton, Grainger, Smetna, Borodin, Arnold,** *BBC Radio Classics* // **Andre Gagnon: Romantique,** *STR-CD* // **Tommy Reilly with Academy of St. Martin-In-the Field, Sir Neville Marriner** // **Tommy Reilly with Skaina Kanga.**

Relf, Keith

Born: March 22, 1943 - London, England
Died: May 14, 1976 - London, England

Blues / Rock singer, harmonica player
Keith was the lead vocalist and harmonica player for *The Yardbirds,* one of the top Blues-influenced bands from the British Invasion of the early 1960's. Relf was heavily influenced by Chicago Blues harmonica players and the group even backed up Sonny Boy Williamson II (Rice Miller) on one of his European tours.

After *The Yardbirds* broke up in the late 1960's, Relf was briefly part of a Folk music duo called *Together,* the band Reign and then helped to found the group *Renaissance,* where he sang and played harmonica on their first few albums. Relf died in 1976 after being electrocuted while playing the guitar.

Discography: (also see - The Yardbirds)
1969 - **Renaissance,** (with Renaissance), *Elektra* // 1971 - **Illusion,** (with Renaissance), *Island* // 1972 - **Prologue,** (with Renaissance), *One Way* // 1973 - **Ashes are Burning,** (with Renaissance), *One Way* // 1974 - **Turn of the Cards,** (with Renaissance), *Repertoire* // 1975 - **Scheherazade & Other Stories,** (with Renaissance), *Repertoire* // 1976 - **Live at Carnegie Hall,** (with Renaissance), *Repertoire* // 1995 - **De Capo,** (with Renaissance), *Repertoire.*

Rhythm Willie

Real name: William Hood
Born: September 15, 19(10)?

Blues harmonica player
Virtually nothing is known about the life of Rhythm Willie except that he was a Blues harmonica player who recorded during the 1930's and 40's in the Chicago area and had an exceptionally large range of styles and techniques on the harmonica.

Richter System

Introduced by a Bohemian named Richter, the Richter System brought blow and draw reed plates to the harmonica around 1825. He arranged the notes in such a way that the blow notes would play the major chord of the diatonic scale and the draw notes would play the dominant seventh, thus making it difficult to play a sour note. This is still the reed configuration most common in harmonicas today.

Riddle, Jimmie

Born: September 3, 1918 - Dyersburg, TN
Died: December 10, 1982

Country harmonica player
Jimmie Riddle started playing the harmonica at age four and by the time he was sixteen he was playing in bands around Memphis, Tennessee. He preferred using a chromatic harmonica to play Country music.

He did his first recordings with *The Swift Jewel Cowboys* in 1939 and in 1943 he became the regular harmonica player with Roy Acuff's *Smokey Mountain Boys.* He played with Acuff for most of his career.

As a Nashville studio player he backed up Johnny Horton, Red Foley, Jim Reeves, Jimmy Dean and a host of others. He also recorded two solo albums. During the 1970's he became a regular on the "Hee Haw" television series, often working with Jackie Phelps.

Discography:
1964 - **Country Harmonica,** *Cumberland Records* // 1964 - **Country Music Cannonball with The Swift Jewel Cowboys,** *Starday* // 1967 - **Let's Go,** *Briar* // 1980 - **Chuck Wagon Swing,** (with The Swift Jewel Cowboys), *String.*

Movies:
1943 - **Sing, Neighbor, Sing.**

Riddles, Nat

Born: February 4, 1952 - New York City, NY
Died: August 11, 1991 - Richmond, VA

Blues harmonica player
Nat Riddles was a Blues harmonica player who worked primarily out of New York City. He played and recorded with Larry Johnson, Screamin' Jay Hawkins, Bill Dicey and other Blues greats as well as giving lessons to Adam Gussow.

Riders in the Sky

Formed: 1977 - Nashville, TN

Country band
Based out of Nashville, Tennessee, *Riders in the Sky* is a trio whose sound and style harkens back to the singing cowboy movies of the 1930's. They've recorded several albums as well as being featured on National Public Radio, The Nashville Network, The Grand Old Opry and their own show on CBS television.

Multi-instrumentalist Woody Paul sings and plays the harmonica.

See - Woody Paul

<u>Discography:</u>
1979 - **Three on the Trail,** *Rounder* // 1980 - **Cowboy Jubilee,** *Rounder* // 1981 - **Prairie Serenade,** *Rounder* // 1982 - **Weeds and Water,** *Rounder* // 1983 - **Live,** *Rounder* // 1984 - **Saddle Pals,** *Rounder* // 1986 - **New Trails,** *Rounder* // 1987 - **The Cowboy Way,** *MCA* // 1987 - **Best of the West,** *Rounder* // 1987 - **Best of the West Rides Again,** *Rounder* // 1988 - **Riders Radio Theater,** *MCA* // 1988 - **Riders Go Commercial,** *MCA* // 1990 - **Horse Opera,** *MCA* // 1991 - **Harmony Ranch,** *Columbia* // 1992 - **Saturday Morning with Riders in the Sky,** *MCA* // 1992 - **Merry Christmas From Harmony Ranch,** *Columbia* // 1992 - **Live,** *Rounder* // 1994 - **Cowboys in Love,** *Columbia* // 1994 - **Always Drink Upstream from the Herd** // 1996 - **Cowboy Songs,** *Easydisc* // 1996 - **Public Cowboy #1: The Music of Gene Autry,** *Rounder* // 1998 - **Yodel the Cowboy Way,** *Easydisc* // 1998 - **Great Big Western Howdy from Riders in the Sky,** *Rounder* // 1999 - **Christmas the Cowboy Way,** *Rounder* // 2000 - **Woody's Roundup,** *Walt Disney.*

<u>Movies:</u>
1985 - **Sweet Dreams.**

Riley, Billy Lee

Born: October 5, 1933 - Pocahantas, AR

Rockabilly guitar, piano, harmonica player

Billy Lee Riley learned how to play the harmonica from local black farm workers while growing up in Arkansas. After being signed by Sam Phillips, Riley started recording for the Sun label in 1955. As a Rockabilly artist he had hits with "Flying Saucer Rock and Roll" and "Red Hot." During his time with the Sun label he also played as a sideman with Roy Orbison, Jerry Lee Lewis, Johnny Cash and Charlie Rich.

After moving to Los Angeles in 1962, he worked with Dean Martin, Herb Alpert, *The Beach Boys,* Ricky Nelson, Pearl Bailey and others. He quit music in the 1970's, made a minor comeback in 1979 and returned to music full-time in the late 1990's.

<u>Discography:</u>
1964 - **Big Harmonica Special,** *Mercury* // 1965 - **Harmonica Beatlemania,** *Mercury* // 1965 - **Whiskey-A-Go- Go Presents,** *Mercury* // 1966 - **In Action,** *GNP* // 1966 - **Funk Harmonica,** *Crescendo* // 1968 - **Twist and Shout!,** *Cowboy Carl* // 1977 - **Billy Lee Riley,** *Charly* // 1978 - **Legendary Sun Performers,** *Charly* // 1978 - **Sun Sounds Special,** *Charly* // 1990 - **Classic Recordings,** *Bear Family* // 1994 - **Blue Collar Blues,** *High Tone* // 1995 - **Rockin' Fifties,** *Icehouse* // 1997 - **Hot Damn!,** *Capricorn* // 1999 - **Red Hot: the Best Of...,** *Collectables* // 2000 - **Shade Tree Blues,** *Icehouse* // **Southern Soul,** *Mojo.*

Ringenberg, Jason

Born: November 22, 1958 - Kewanee, IL

Rock singer, guitar, harmonica player
Jason Ringenberg was the founder and leader of *Jason and The Scorchers,* the leading proponents of the "Cow Punk" style of Rock music. Ringenberg plays harmonica as well as being a lead vocalist, guitar player and a songwriter.

<u>Discography:</u> (also see - Jason and The Scorchers)
1991 - **One Foot in the Honky Tonk,** *Liberty* // 2000 - **A Pocketful of Soul,** *Courageous Chicken.*

Ripps, Don
Vaudeville harmonica player
Don Ripps played in *The Harmonica Rascals* and also in *The Cappy Barra Harmonica Ensemble* as a bass harmonica player from 1935 until 1941, when he left the group to get married.

Robbins, Pro
Vaudeville harmonica player
Pro Robbins played the bass harmonica in the second unit (New York Based), of *The Cappy Barra Harmonica Ensemble* from 1940 through 1944. He also played the bass harmonica for *The Three Harpers* after World War two until the group disbanded.

Roberts, Kenny

Real name: George Kingsbury
Born: October 14, 1926 - Lenoir City, TN

Country singer-songwriter, guitar, harmonica player
Kenny Roberts learned the guitar, fiddle and harmonica as a child and began his professional career as a musician after win-

ning a talent competition when he was thirteen years old.

Very popular in both radio and recordings during the 1940's and 50's, he specialized in the yodeling form of singing. He has maintained his career to this day.

Discography:
1965 - **Indian Love Call**, *Starday* // 1966 - **Yodelin' Kenny Roberts Sings Country Songs**, *Coral Masters* // 1969 - **Country Music Singing Sensation**, *Starday* // 1967 - **The Incredible Kenny Roberts**, *Starday* // 1969 - **Country Music Singing Sensation**, *Starday* // 1970 - **Jealous Heart**, *Starday* // 1971 - **I Never See Maggie Alone**, *Nashville* // 1971 - **Yodelin' with Kenny Roberts**, *Point* // 1972 - **Tribute To Elton Britt** // 1978 - **Feelings of Love** // 1981 - **Then and Now**, *Longhorn* // 1988 - **Just Call Me Country** // 1991 - **You're My Kind of People** // 1994 - **Traditional Country**, *Music Room* // 1996 - **Jumpin' & Yodelin'**, *Bear Family* // 2000 - **Out West the West Winds Blow**, *Vogue*.

Robinson, Edward
Classical composer

Edward Robinson wrote "Chiimark Suite for Harmonica and Orchestra" in 1940 and "Gay Head Dance for Harmonica and Orchestra" in 1941 for John Sebastian, Sr.

Robinson, LC "Good Rockin'"

Real name: Louis Charles Robinson
Born: May 15, 1915 - Brenham, TX
Died: September 26, 1976 - Berkeley, CA

Blues guitar, violin, harmonica player
Since his father was a harmonica player, Louis Robinson learned to play the instrument, as well as guitar and fiddle, while growing up in Texas. By the late 1920's he was playing at parties and dances with his brother. In the 1930's he toured with carnivals and black music revues and made his first radio appearance with *The Three Hot Brown Boys*.

During the 1940's he worked with Johnny Otis and even made his first recordings with his brother, A.C. Over the next thirty years he would record and perform regularly, including with Muddy Waters in 1971, until his death from a heart attack in 1976.

Discography:
1971 - **Ups and Downs**, *Arhoolie* // 1974 - **House Cleanin' Blues** // 1997 - **Mojo in My Hand**, *Arhoolie*.

Robinson, Stan
Vaudeville harmonica player
Stan Robinson was a black multi-instrumentalist and bandleader of the 1930's who specialized in playing the polyphonia.

Robinson, Tad
Born: June 24, 1956 - New York City, NY
Blues singer, harmonica player

Tad Robinson is a singer and harmonica player who has worked with *Dave Spector and The Bluebirds, Big Shoulders, Floyd McDaniel* and others, in addition recording two albums of his own and appearing on several compilation albums.

Discography:
1994 - **One to Infinity**, *Delmark* // 1998 - **Last Go Round**, *Delmark*.

Movies:
1992 - **Under Siege.**

Rock Harmonica
Though the harmonica played an enormous role in Country and Blues music, Rock's two primary sources, it was not really popular in Rock music until the British Invasion of the early 1960's.

Led by *The Beatles*, nearly every British band had at least one member who could play the harmonica. In America Rock harmonica did not really catch on until Folk music influenced it and white Blues enthusiasts started drifting into the Rock scene.

With the exception of a few players, like Robert Plant of *Led Zepplin* and Magic Dick of *The J. Geils Band*, the Heavy Metal / Hard Rock scene of the 1970's and 80's virtually ignored the harmonica and it wasn't until the late 1980's, with groups like *Timbuk 3* and *Blues Traveler*, that the Alternative music movement really started to re-introduce the harmonica into Rock music.

Roddy, Ted

Born: May 2, 1952 - Corpus Christi, TX

Country / Rock singer-songwriter, harmonica player

Ted Roddy began playing the harmonica while attending junior high school in Corpus Christi, Texas. He formed his first band in Dallas in the late 1970's. Since moving to Austin in the mid-1980's, Roddy has had a fairly successful career as a singer-songwriter as well as playing harmonica with Sue Foley, Jimmie Dale Gilmore, Jello Biafra, Candye Kane, Hal Ketchum and many others.

Discography:
1995 - **Full Circle**, *Hightone* // 2000 - **Tear Time**, *The Music Room*.

Rodgers, Andy

Also known as: The Midnight Cowboy
Born: March 14, 1922 - Liberty, MS

Blues singer, guitar, harmonica player

Andy Rodgers got his first guitar from his boyhood friend, Bo Diddley and learned how to play the harmonica from both Sonny Boy Williamsons, who used to visit his mother's house. He began performing professionally at age eleven

He settled in California during the 1940's and over the years worked at a variety of jobs, including as a cowboy, where he got his nickname, "The Midnight Cowboy," and his distinctive style of dress.

He's recently been playing on the Blues festival scene and has recorded two albums.

Discography:
1993 - **Freight Train Blues**, *Snowflake* // 1995 - **Chicken**

Thief Blues, *Snowflake*.

Rogers, Jimmy

Real name: James A. Lane
Born: June 3, 1924 - Ruleville, MS
Died: December 19, 1997 - Chicago, IL

Blues guitar, piano, harmonica player

Like many Blues guitarists, Jimmy Rogers began by playing the harmonica, which he learned when he was eight years old. After moving to Chicago in 1941, he became a mainstay in the city's Blues scene, where he worked with John Lee "Sonny Boy" Williamson, Sunnyland Slim, Big Bill Broonzy and others.

During his career he worked as a sideman to Muddy Waters, Howlin' Wolf, Mighty Joe Young, Johnny Littlejohn and others as well as recording on his own. He also featured harmonica players Walter Horton and Little Walter in his bands.

Discography:
1950's - **Chicago Bound**, *Chess* // 1971 - **Gold Tailed Bird**, *Shelter* // 1973 - **Sloppy Drunk Nice**, *Black and Blue* // 1974 - **That's All Right**, *Chess* // 1976 - **Living with the Blues**, *Vogue* // 1979 - **Jimmy Rogers and Left Hand Frank** // 1982 - **Live: Jimmy Rogers**, *JSP* // 1982 - **Chicago Blues**, *Capitol* // 1985 - **Feelin' Good**, *Murray Brothers* // 1985 - **Dirty Dozens** // 1989 - **That's All Right**, *Charly* // 1990 - **Ludella**, *Antone's* // 1990 - **Jimmy Rogers Sings the Blues**, *Shelter* // 1991 - **Walking By Myself**, *Huub* // 1993 - **With Ronnie Earl and The Broadcasters** // 1993 - **Hard Working Man**, *Charly* // 1994 - **Bluebird**, *Analogue* // 1995 - **Chicago Blues Masters, Vol. 2**, *Capitol* // 1997 - **The Complete Chess Recordings**, *MCA/Chess* // 1998 - **Blues Blues Blues**, *Atlantic* // **Jimmy Rogers**, *Chess* // **Left Me with a Broken Heart**, *Vogue*.

The Rolling Stones

Formed: 1962 - London, England

British Rock band

Second only to The Beatles in popularity, The Rolling Stones have been performing and recording steadily since the early 1960's. Arising from the *Blues Incorporated* scene, they've featured harmonica players Mick Jagger and Brian Jones as co-founders as well as using Chicago harmonica ace, Sugar Blue, as a sideman for several of their albums.

See - Mick Jagger, Brian Jones

Discography:
1964 - **The Rolling Stones**, *London* // 1964 - 12X5, *London* // 1965 - **The Rolling Stones Now!**, *London* // 1965 - **December's Children**, *London* // 1965 - **Out of Our Heads**, *London* // 1966 - **Aftermath**, *London* // 1966 - **Big Hits: High Tide and Green Grass**, *London* // 1966 - **Got Live if You Want it**, *London* // 1967 - **Between the**

Buttons, *London* // 1967 - **Flowers**, *London* // 1967 - **Their Satanic Majestie's Request**, *London* // 1968 - **Beggar's Banquet**, *London* // 1969 - **Through the Past Darkly**, *London* // 1969 - **Let it Bleed**, *London* // 1970 - **Get Your Ya-Ya's Out**, *London* // 1971 - **Sticky Fingers**, *Rolling Stones* // 1971 - **Hot Rocks**, *London* // 1972 - **Exile On Main Street**, *Rolling Stones* // 1972 - **More Hot Rocks**, *London* // 1973 - **Goat's Head Soup**, *Rolling Stones* // 1974 - **It's Only Rock and Roll**, *Rolling Stones* // 1975 - **Metamorphosis**, *ABKCO* // 1975 - **Made in the Shade**, *Rolling Stones* // 1976 - **Black and Blue**, *Rolling Stones* // 1977 - **Love You Live**, *Rolling Stones* // 1978 - **Some Girls**, *Rolling Stones* // 1980 - **Emotional Rescue**, *Rolling Stones* // 1981 - **Sucking in the Seventies**, *Rolling Stones* // 1981 - **Tattoo You**, *Rolling Stones* // 1982 - **Still Life**, *Rolling Stones* // 1982 - **In Concert**, *Polydor* // 1983 - **Undercover**, *Virgin* // 1984 - **Rewind**, *Rolling Stones* // 1986 - **Dirty Work**, *Rolling Stones* // 1989 - **Singles Collection**, *ABKCO* // 1989 - **Steel Wheels**, *Rolling Stones* // 1991 - **Flashpoint**, *Rolling Stones* // 1994 - **Voodoo Lounge**, *Rolling Stones* // 1995 - **Stripped**, *Virgin* // 1996 - **The Rolling Stones Rock and Roll Circus**, *ABKCO* // 1997 - **Bridges To Babylon**, *Virgin* // 1998 - **No Security**, *Virgin*.

Roper, Skid

Real name: Richard Banke
Born: October 19, 1954 - National City, CA

Rock percussion, mandolin, harmonica player
As the musical partner of Rock comedian Mojo Nixon, Skid Roper has been a presence in Rock music since the mid-1980's in addition to recording some albums of his own.

Discography:
1985 - **Mojo Nixon and Skid Roper**, *RBI/Enigma* // 1986 - **Frenzy**, *Restless* // 1987 - **Bo-Day-Shus!!**, *Enigma* // 1989 - **Trails Plowed Under**, *Enigma* // 1989 - **Root, Hog or Die**, *Enigma* // 1990 - **Unlimited Everything**, *Enigma* // 1991 - **Lydia's Café**, *Enigma*.

Rosenberg, Susan

Born: 1959 - Connecticut

Pop / Jazz harmonica player
Susan Rosenberg began playing the harmonica at age seven and later studied with Robert Bonfiglio, Cham-Ber Huang and Charles Leighton. She has performed with Harry Connick Jr., Les Paul and others. In 1999 she founded Mega Mouth Records, where she released an album of her own material as well as an album of Classical music by Charles Leighton.

Discography:
1999 - **Angel with a Harp**, *Mega Mouth*.

Ross, George

Real name: George Popolizio
Born: August 10, 1916 - New Haven, CT

Vaudeville harmonica player
George Ross began his career in show business as a member of *The Checker Harmonica Band*. During most of the 1930's he was a member of *The Harmonica Rascals* and was also a member of *The Three B's* with Eddie Goldstein and Harry Bee. He worked for several years with his wife, Ruth, as a harmonica duet.

Ross, Dr. Isiah

Real name: Charles Isiah Ross
Born: October 21, 1925 - Tunica, MS
Died: May 28, 1993 - Flint, MI

Blues singer, guitar, drums, harmonica player
Dr. Isiah Ross probably learned how to play the harmonica from his father at about the age of six. He was playing at parties and church functions by the time he was nine and was working professionally by the late 1930's.

After serving in the U.S. Army during World War Two, he returned to Mississippi and began working steadily in music. He started playing on the radio in 1949 and did his first recordings in 1951. Over the years he worked with several back-up bands and also worked as a one-man band.

After moving to Flint, Michigan in 1954, he played around the midwest until his death in 1993.

Discography:
1954 - **Boogie Disease**, *Arhoolie* // 1965 - **Call the Doctor**, *Testament* // 1966 - **Flying Eagle** // 1971 - **I'd Rather Be an Old Woman's Baby**, *Fortune* // 1972 - Dr. Ross, the Harmonica Boss, *Fortune* // 1974 - **Jivin' the Blues**, *Big Bear* // 1975 - **Live at Montreux**, *Atlantic* // 1981 - **His Earliest**

Recordings, *Arhoolie* // 1994 - **I Want All My Friends to Know,** *JSP* // 1998 - **One Man Band,** *Takoma/Ace.*

On Video:
2000 - **The Last Concert, the Doc Ross Fund.**

Ross, Sammy
Vaudeville harmonica player

Sammy Ross was one of the midgets that Borrah Minevitch used to replace Johnny Puleo in various units of *The Harmonica Rascals*, both on stage and in two of their movies.

Movies: (also see: The Harmonica Rascals)
1965 - **The War Lord** // 1994 - *Trading Mom.*

Ruffo, "Steamin'" Stan
Born: June 16, 1951 - Los Angeles, CA

Blues saxophone, harmonica player

Stan Ruffo began playing the saxophone at age eleven and the harmonica at age 28. In his mid-30's he started to play professionally. While working primarily out of central California, Ruffo has recorded two albums as well as appearing on several compilation recordings and with John Ussery.

Discography:
1993 - **Live at the Bastille,** *Stan Ruffo Productions* // **Blues On Tap,** *Sho' Nuff.*

Rush, Bobby
Born: November 10, 1931

Blues / Soul singer, harmonica player

Bobby Rush has been a steady performer in Blues clubs and at festivals for over 45 years. He had his first hit record in 1971 with the song "Chicken Heads." He has slowly developed a worldwide audience with his bawdy Blues shows.

Discography:
1979 - **Rush Hour,** *Philadelphia* // 1990 - **A Man Can Give it Out, But He Can't Take it,** *La Jam* // 1991 - **I Ain't Studdin' You,** *Urgent* // 1992 - **Handy Man,** *Urgent* // 1992 - **Instant Replays: The Hits,** *Ichiban* // 1995, **She's a Good Un, It's Allright,** *Ronn* // 1996 - **Sue,** *La Jam* // 1996 - **Wearing it Out,** *La Jam* // 1996 - **Gotta Have Mercy,** *La Jam* // 1996 - **One Monkey Don't Stop No Show,** *Waldoxy* // 1997 - **Lovin' a Big Fat Woman,** *Waldoxy* // 1997 - **It's Allright, Vol. 2,** *Ronn* // 1997 - **What's Good for the Goose is Good for the Gander,** *La Jam* // 1998 - **Southern Soul,** *Cannonball* // 1999 - **The Best of Bobby Rush,** *La Jam* // 2000 - **Hoochie Man,** *Waldoxy.*

Rush, Otis

Born: April 29, 1934 - Philadelphia, MS

Blues singer, guitar, harmonica player

As with many of the great Blues guitarists, Otis Rush can also play the harmonica. After moving to Chicago in 1948, Rush has proven himself as a leading Blues guitarist and singer.

Discography:

1958 - **Otis Rush and Magic Sam**, *Flyright* // 1958 - **1956-1958: His Cobra Recordings**, *Flyright* // 1960 - **Door To Door** (with Albert King), *Chess* // 1964 - **Chicago - the Blues - Today!** // 1968 - **This One's a Good Un**, *Blue Horizon* // 1969 - **Mourning in Morning**, *Atlantic* // 1972 - **Blues Masters, Vol. 2**, *Blue Horizon* // 1975 - **Cold Day in Hell**, *Delmark* // 1976 - **Right Place, Wrong Time**, *Hightone* // 1977 - **Lost in the Blues**, *Alligator* // 1977 - **Live in Europe**, *Evidence* // 1978 - **So Many Roads**, *Delmark* // 1978 - **Troubles, Troubles** // 1979 - **Screamin' and Cryin'**, *Evidence* // 1980 - **Groanin' the Blues**, *Flyright* // 1980 - **Other Takes 1956/58**, *Flyright* // 1985 - **Tops**, *Blind Pig* // 1993 - **Double Trouble**, *Charly* // 1994 - **Ain't Enough Comin' In**, This Way Up // 1994 - **This Way**, *Mercury* // 1994 - **Live in Japan 1986**, *Castle* // 1996 - **Blues Interaction**, *Sequel* // 1996 - **Live and Lonesome**, *Genes* // 1998 - **Any Place I'm Goin'**, *House of Blues*. // 2000 - **Good 'Uns**, *Westside* // **Chicago Blues**, *Blue Horizon* // **Live at the Chicago Blues Festival**, *Intermedia* // **Classic Recordings**, *Charly*.

Russo, William

Born: June 25, 1928 - Chicago, IL

Classical composer

During the late 1960's, William Russo composed "Three Pieces for Blues Band and Symphony Orchestra" and "Street Music for Harmonica & Orchestra" for harmonica player Corky Siegel.

Recording Availability:

1973 - **William Russo - Leonard Bernstein**, (soloist - Corky Siegel), *Deutsche Grammophon* // 1981 - **Bernstein: Symphonic Dances**, (soloist - Corky Siegel), *Deutsche Grammophon* // **Gershwin, Russo, Joplin and Others**, (soloist - Corky Siegel), *Deutsche Grammophon*.

Ruth, Peter "Madcat"

Born: April 2, 1949 - Evanston, IL

Blues harmonica player

Peter "Madcat" Ruth grew up in the Chicago area where he learned how to play the harmonica by listening to the city's many great Blues players and even took some lessons from Big Walter Horton.

He made the acquaintance of the family of Jazz legend Dave

Brubeck. Ruth toured and recorded several albums with Brubeck and family. Since striking out for a solo career in the 1980's, Madcat's been a fixture on the club and festival circuit ever since. He has recorded with *Blackfoot*, Rory Block, *Gemini* and several others. He teamed up with guitarist Shari Kane in 1978 and the two have performed as a duo since that time.

Discography:

1982 - **Madcat Live at Nature's Table, Vol. 1 & 2**, *Beancake* // 1984 - **Madcat Gone Solo**, *Beancake* // 1993 - **Key To the Highway**, *SKR* // 1988 - **Madcat's Pressure Cooker Live at the Pig**, *Beancake* // 1998 - **Harmonicology**, *Beancake* // 1999 - **Up Against the Wall**, *Hit Records* // 2000 - **Madcat and the Cats Live at the Ark**, *Beancake* // 2000 - **Triple Play Live**, *Beancake* // **Mostly for Kids**, *Beancake* // **More Kid's Stuff**, *Beancake* // **Pressure Cooker**, *Beancake*.

Rye, Steve

Died: July 19, 1992 - England

Blues / Rock harmonica player

Steve Rye played the harmonica and sang for *The Groundhogs*, a British Blues band formed in 1963. The group recorded two albums as a Blues Band, (including one as a back-up band for John Lee Hooker), before pursuing a harder Rock sound. Rye left the group after the Blues albums were recorded. He occasionally appeared as a guest artist on a variety of projects, including making appearances on albums by *The Brunning Hall Sunflower Blues Band*, Jo Ann Kelly, Dave Kelly and others.

Discography: (see - The Groundhogs)

– S –

Saffire: The Uppity Blues Women

Formed: 1984 - Virginia

Blues Trio

Saffire is a Blues trio from Virginia that plays traditional styles Blues, mainly about women's issues. The group features Gaye Adegbalola on vocals, guitar and harmonica.

See - Gaye Adegbalola

<u>Discography:</u>
1990 - **Saffire: The Uppity Blues Women,** *Alligator //* 1991 - **Hot Flash,** *Alligator //* 1992 - **Broadcasting,** *Alligator //* 1994 - **Old, New, Borrowed and Blue,** *Alligator //* 1996 - **Cleaning House,** *Alligator //* 1998 - **Live and Uppity,** *Alligator //* **The Middle Aged Blues,** *Saffire.*

Salgado, Curtis

Born: February 4, 1954 - Everett, WA

Blues singer, harmonica player

Curtis Salgado is a Blues harmonica player from the Pacific northwest who has been performing professionally since 1975. He was the model upon which John Belushi based his character in *The Blues Brothers.* He played with Robert Cray on four of his albums, with *Roomful of Blues,* as well as performing on his own.

<u>Discography:</u>
1991 - **Curtis Salgado and The Stilettos,** *JRS //* 1995 - **More Than You Can Chew,** *Rhythm Safari //* 1997 - **Hit It 'n Quit It,** *Lucky //* 1999 - **Wiggle Out of This,** *Shanachie //*

Live at the Roadhouse, *Criminal.*

Samples, Alvin "Junior"

Born August 10, 1926 - Cumming, GA
Died: November 13, 1983 - Cumming, GA

Country comedian, harmonica player

Junior Samples began his career in show business at age forty, after having a novelty hit with a comedic monologue. He was a regular cast member on the "Hee-Haw" television series for fourteen years. Although known primarily as a comedian, Samples could also play the harmonica.

<u>Discography:</u>
1967 - **The World of Junior Samples,** *Chart //* 1968 - **Bull Sessions at Bull's Gap,** *Chart //* 1970 - **That's a Hee Haw,** *Chart //* 1971 - **The Best Of...,** *Chart.*

Santana, Andy

Blues harmonica player

Andy Santana is a Blues harmonica player who works out of the San Francisco Bay area. He has performed and recorded with Jimmy Rogers, Luther Tucker, Willie Dixon, Angela Strehli, Sista Monica and others.

Sasone, Jumpin' Johnny

Born: 1956 - Orange, New Jersey

Zydeco / Blues accordion, harmonica player

While working primarily out of New Orleans, "Jumpin'" Johnny Sasone has been performing and recording for several years. He began playing music at age eight and picked up the harmonica in his teens. He worked as the vocalist and harmonica player for *Ronnie Earl and The Broadcasters* during the late 1980's. He has since released several solo albums.

Discography:
1991 - **Mr. Good Thing,** *King Snake* // 1997 - **Crescent City Moon,** *Bullseye Blues* // 1999 - **Watermelon Patch,** *Bullseye Blues* // **Where Y'at?,** *Shortstack.*

Satan and Adam

Formed: 1986 - New York City, NY
Disbanded: 1999

Blues duo

Satan and Adam were a Harlem-based Blues duo consisting of guitarist/drummer Sterling "Mr. Satan" Magee and harmonica player Adam Gussow.

They began their career as street musicians and were signed to the Flying Fish label after making a cameo appearance in *U2's* movie, "Rattle and Hum." They continued working as street musicians as well as making club and festival appearances through the end of the 1990's, when Magee's health deteriorated.

See - Adam Gussow

Discography:
1991 - **Harlem Blues,** *Flying Fish* // 1993 - **Mother Mojo,** *Flying Fish* // 1996 - **Living on the River,** *Rave On.*

Movies:
1988 - **Rattle and Hum.**

Sayles, Charlie

Born: January 4, 1948 - Woburn, MA

Blues harmonica player

After serving in the Vietnam War, Charlie Sayles taught himself to play the harmonica. He was discovered working as a street musician in New York City in 1976 and has enjoyed a sporadically successful career ever since.

Discography:
1976 - **The Raw Harmonica Blues of Charlie Sayles,** *Dusty Road* // 1990 - **Night Ain't Right,** *JSP* // 1995 - **I Got Something to Say,** *JSP* // 1999 - **Union Mission Blues** // 2000 - **Hip Guy - The Best of the JSP Sessions,** *JSP.*

Bibliography:
1976 - **How To Play the Harmonica,** *Smithsonian.*

Scarlett, Will

Folk / Blues harmonica player
Will Scarlett played the harmonica for the group *Hot Tuna* from 1969 until 1971. He has also recorded with David Bromberg, Jerry Garcia & David Grisman, Country Joe McDonald and others.

Discography: (see - Hot Tuna)

Schackner, Alan "Blackie"

Born: September 1, 1917

Pop / Vaudeville harmonica player

While growing up in New York City, Alan "Blackie" Schackner was boyhood friends with Victor Pankowitz, who taught him the technique of tongue switching. Schackner earned the nickname "Blackie" from his dark complexion.

He started his professional career in the early 1930's by playing with Murray Lane's *Harmonica Scamps* and was once featured in "Ripley's Believe It or Not" for playing the "Hora Staccatto" in 90 seconds. After World War Two he worked in lounges as a soloist. He did some of the music for the film "Portrait of Jennie" and composed the hit song, "The Happy Cobbler." In addition to that he was a soloist behind Kate Smith, Arthur Godfrey, Kim Carnes and Gene Kelly.

Schackner has worked as an arranger and composer and has written several instruction books for the harmonica. He was named SPAH's "Harmonica Player of the Year" in 1999.

Discography:
Best of the Light Classics // Music for Listening.

Bibliography:
Complete Book of Chromatic & Diatonic State of the Art Repairs // Everything You Wanted to Know About the Chromatic Harmonica // Everything You Wanted to Know About the Blues Harp and Marine Band // 25 Popular Tunes for the One Inch - 4 Hole Harmonica.

Movies:
1948 - **Portrait of Jennie.**

Scheckter, Sam

Born: 1913
Died: December 18, 1995

Vaudeville harmonica player
Sam Scheckter learned to play the harmonica while growing up in Philadelphia. He was a member of Carl Freed's *Harmonica Harlequins*, where he played the second chromatic harmonica from 1934 to 1935.

He joined *The Cappy Barra Harmonica Ensemble* in 1935. He played the chord harmonica and switched to the second chromatic harmonica when Mike Chimes joined the group. He is considered to one of the earliest full-time chord harmonica players. Scheckter stayed with *Cappy Barra* until 1940, but never returned to music as a full-time profession.

Schirra, Wally

March 12, 1923 - Hackensack, NJ

Astronaut
As an astronaut on the Gemini IV mission, Wally Schirra smuggled a Hohner "Little Lady" harmonica on board and played "Jingle Bells" on it on December 16, 1965, thus making the harmonica the very first musical instrument to be played in outer space.

The M. Hohner company later issued a Wally Schirra model harmonica. The original instrument he played in outer space may be seen at the National Air and Space Museum in Washington D.C.

Schwartz, Lenny
Vaudeville harmonica player
Lenny Schwartz played the second chromatic harmonica in

Johnny O'Brien's *Harmonica Hi-Hats* from 1937 until 1940.

Scott, Cyril

Born: September 27, 1879
Died: December 31, 1970

Classical Composer
Cyril Scott wrote "Serenade for Piano and Harmonica" for Larry Adler in 1936.

The Scratch Band

Formed: 1980

Country Band
The Scratch Band backs up Country music star Don Williams and features Danny Flowers on the harmonica. They have recorded one album featuring Danny Flowers as the lead artist.

See - Danny Flowers

Discography: (see - Danny Flowers)

Sebastian, John

Real name: John Sebastian Pugliese
Born: 1914
Died: 1980

Classical harmonica soloist

The son of a wealthy banking family from Philadelphia, John Sebastian Pugliese won a city harmonica championship at age sixteen and also played in Albert Hoxie's harmonica band. After studying art in Italy, he decided to pursue a career as a Classical harmonica soloist.

Unlike most Classical soloists, Sebastian decided to avoid playing any Pop material, instead specializing in Baroque music. In addition to adapting Classical works to the harmonica, several composers wrote pieces especially for him, including Edward Robinson, George Kleinsinger, Norman Dello Joio, Walter Anderson, Henry Cowell, Alan Hovhaness, Heitor Villa-Lobos, Alexander Tcherepnin, Luciano Chailly, Frank Lewin and others.

His son, John B. Sebastian, Jr. also became a harmonica player and led the group *The Lovin' Spoonful*.

Discography:
A Harmonica Recital, *Deutsche Grammophon* // **Harmonica and Saxophone Concertos By Villa-Lobos, Et Al,** *Urania*.

Sebastian, John B., Jr.

Born: March 17, 1944 - New York City, NY

Folk singer-songwriter, guitar, harmonica player

The son of Classical harmonica soloist John Sebastian, John B. Sebastian, Jr. began working in the Jug band and Folk music scene of the early 1960's. He was a member of *The Mugwumps* with Denny Doherty, Mama Cass Elliott and Zal Yanosky. He founded the Folk/Rock band *The Lovin' Spoonful* in 1965 and wrote most of their big hits, including "Do You Believe in Magic?," "Summer in the City," "Day Dream" and a host of others.

The group broke up in 1968 following a drug bust and Sebastian decided to pursue a solo career. After a terrific performance at the Woodstock music festival, he recorded several albums and even had a big hit with the theme song from the television series "Welcome Back, Kotter." He has released solo albums on a regular basis ever since.

In addition to his career as a singer-songwriter, Sebastian has shown that he can hold his own on the harmonica. He did guest shots on *Crosby, Stills, Nash and Young's* "Déjà vu" and "Roadhouse Blues" by *The Doors*. He also co-wrote a course in Blues harmonica with Paul Butterfield.

Discography: (also see - The Lovin' Spoonful)
1970 - **John B. Sebastian,** *MGM* // 1970 - **John Sebastian Live,** *MGM* // 1971 - **Cheapo Cheapo Production Presents The Real Live John Sebastian,** *Reprise* // 1971 - **The Four of Us,** *Reprise* // 1974 - **The Tarzana Kid,** *Reprise* // 1976 - **Welcome Back,** *Reprise* // 1989 - **The Best Of...,** *Rhino* // 1993 - **Tar Beach,** *Shanachie* // 1996 - **I Want My Roots,** (with Annie Raines), *Musicmasters* // 1996 - **King Biscuit Flower Hour,** *King Biscuit* // 1999 - **Chasin' Gus' Ghost,** *Hollywood* // 2000 - **Live,** *EMI-Capitol*.

Film:
1966 - **You're a Big Boy Now** // 1966 - **What's Up Tiger Lily?.**

Bibliography:
1982 - **Blues Harmonica,** (with Paul Butterfield) // 1996 - **John Sebastian Teaches Blues Harmonica,** (video, book, CD) // **J.B.'s Harmonica,** (fiction).

Seeger, Mike

Born: August 15, 1933 - New York City, NY

Bluegrass banjo, harmonica player

The son of Folk music scholar Charles Seeger and brother of Folk musicians Pete and Peggy Seeger, Mike Seeger was a co-founder and banjo player for *The New Lost City Ramblers* from the mid-1950's through it's many incarnations.

In addition to playing the banjo, Seeger sings and plays the harmonica. He has recorded several albums over the years, both solo and with friends and family members.

Discography: (also see - The New Lost City Ramblers)
1957 - **American Folk Songs,** *Folkways* // 1960 - **Indian Summer,** *Folkways* // 1962 - **Old Time Country Music,** *Folkways* // 1963 - **Sings and Plays Autoharp,** *Folkways* // 1964 - **Hello Stranger,** *Vanguard* // 1966 - **Mike and Peggy Seeger,** *Argo* // 1966 - **Tipple, Loom and Rail,** *Folkways* // 1967 - **Music from the True Vine,** *Mercury* // 1968 - **Strange Creek Singers** // 1988 - **Fresh Old Time String Band Music,** *Rounder* // 1989 - **American Folk Songs for Christmas,** *Rounder* // 1992 - **Animal Folk Songs for Children,** *Rounder* // 1994 - **Third Annual Farewell Reunion Concert,** *Rounder* // 1994 - **Fret n' Fiddle,** *Rounder* // 1996 - **Way Down in North Carolina,** *Rounder* // 1998 - **Southern Banjo Sounds,** *Smithsonian/Folkways* // **American Folk Songs for Children,** (with Peggy Seeger), *Rounder*.

Semien, Sidney

Also known as: Good Rockin' Sidney
Born: April 9, 1938 - Lebeau, LA
Died: February 2, 1998 - Lake Charles, LA

Blues / Zydeco guitar, harmonica player
Sidney Semien started performing and recording Zydeco music in 1953 and made his first recordings for the Carl label in 1957. Best known as a guitarist, he could also play the harmonica.

Discography:
1975 - **They Call Me Rockin'**, *Flyright* // 1985 - **Boogie, Blues 'n' Zydeco**, *Maison de Soul* // 1985 - **My Toot Toot**, *Epic* // 1987 - **Creole**, *ZPC* // 1987 - **Crowned Prince of Zydeco**, *Maison de Soul* // 1987 - **A Celebration Holiday**, *ZBC* // 1987 - **Give Me a Good Time Woman**, *Maison de Soul* // 1987 - **A Holiday Celebration**, *ZBC* // 1987 - **Hot Steppin'**, *ZBC* // 1987 - **My Zydeco Shoes Got the Zydeco Blues**, *Maison de Soul* // 1988 - **Live with the Blues**, *JSP* // 1990 - **Original My Toot Toot**, *Sony* // 1993 - **Mais Yeah Chere!**, *Maison de Soul* // 1996 - **Zydeco is Fun**, *Maison de Soul* // **Squeeze That Thing**, *ZBC* // **Joy To the South**, *Bally Hoo* // **Creole: Talk of the Town**, *ZBC*.

The Sgro Brothers

Born: Wellsville, OH

Vaudeville harmonica players

Brothers Tony and Dominic Sgro played in *Johnny Puleo's Harmonica Gang* and also with the harmonica band assembled by Herb Shriner in the 1950's. They currently perform as a harmonica duo.

Discography:
2000 - **Sgro Brothers 2000** // **Hooked On Harmonicas** // **Harmonica High** // **Harmonica Heaven** // **A Touch of Italy** // **Festival Time** // **Harmonica Swing** // **Pop Classics, Vol. 1** // **Gospel Classics**.

Shade, Will

Also known as: Son Brimmer
Born: February 5, 1898 - Memphis, TN
Died: September 18, 1966 - Memphis TN

Jug band harmonica player
Will Shade took up the harmonica as a teenager after over-strenuous labor left him unable to do hard work. By his late teens he was performing with Furry Lewis, Charlie Burse, Will Weldon, Jab Jones and others who would soon become members of *The Memphis Jug Band*.

One of the most influential of the 1920's Jug band leaders, Will Shade's *Memphis Jug Band* recorded 73 sides for various labels between 1927 and 1934. Not only did Shade play the harmonica, but the group also featured Furry Lewis and a young Walter Horton on the instrument.

Shade continued playing solo and with Gus Cannon, Memphis Minnie and others well into the early 1960's.

Discography: (see - The Memphis Jug Band)

Shaw, Tom

Born: March 4, 1908 - Breham, TX
Died: February 24, 1977 - San Diego, CA

Blues guitar, harmonica player
Tom Shaw was taught to play the harmonica by his father when he was nine years old. By the time he was in his teens he was playing on the streets for tips and in the 1920's he worked with Blind Lemon Jefferson

He moved to California in 1934 and for the rest of his life he performed only sporadically.

Discography:
1972 - **Blind Lemon's Buddy**, *Blue Goose* // 1974 - **Born in Texas**, *Testament*.

Shelby, James "Son"

Born: 1927 - Jasper, TX

Blues guitar, harmonica player
Born blind, Son Shelby learned how to play the harmonica from his father as a child. He worked primarily for tips for most of his career, but did record an album for the Swoon label in 1972.

Sheng

Originating in China about 3,000 years ago, the Sheng is thought to be one of the first free-reeded instruments and is a direct ancestor of the harmonica. The principle of the free-reeded instrument spread across Asia, with regional differences arising. Other Asian free-reeded instruments include the Khaen (Thailand), the Kobing, (Philippines), the Klui (Thailand), the Hnyin (Burma), the Saeng-Whaeng (Korea) and the Sho (Japan).

The first Shengs were brought to Europe during the later part of the 18th century. Shortly afterwards, organ makers were experimenting with new free-reeded instruments. Organ makers trying to build a western version of the Sheng built the first harmonicas.

Short, JD

Also known as: Jelly Jaw
Born: December 26, 1902 - Port Gibson, MS
Died: October 21, 1962 - St. Louis, MO

Blues multi-instrumentalist, including harmonica
JD Short began his musical career playing at parties when he was seventeen years old. After moving to St. Louis in 1923, he began recording for the Paramount label. He also worked as a clarinet player in Jazz bands through the 1930's.

After World War Two he began working as a one-man band and incorporated the harmonica into his act. He occasionally worked with his cousin, Big Joe Williams.

Discography:
1962 - **Legacy of the Blues, Vol. 8,** *GNP Crescendo* // 1963 - **Blues from the Mississippi Delta,** *Folkways* // 1965 - **Stavin' Chain Blues,** (with Big Joe Williams), *Delmark* // **St. Louis Blues,** *Wolf* // **JD Short: 1930-33,** *Wolf* // **St. Louis Country Blues,** *Document.*

Shriner, Herb

Born: May 29, 1918 - Toledo, OH
Died: April 23, 1970

Vaudeville humorist, harmonica player
Herb Shriner began his career as a radio harmonica player nicknamed "Harmonica Herb" during the 1930's. One evening after his lips got too tired to continue playing, he started doing a comedic monologue to cover up dead air space. He was an instant success and was soon a top radio comedian.

He never gave up the harmonica, but he incorporated it into his act using several trick harmonicas to get laughs. He also made a few serious harmonica recordings and played with such greats as Charles Leighton, Alan "Blackie" Schackner, Mike Chimes, Victor Pankowitz, Cham-Ber Huang, Dave Doucette, Don Henry, Frank Mitowski, the Sgro Brothers and Alan Pogson.

His popularity was such that the M. Hohner Company issued several Herb Shriner model harmonicas.

Discography:
1955 - **Herb Shriner On Stage,** *Columbia.*

Shu, Eddie

Real name: Edward Shulman
Born: August 18, 1918 - Brooklyn, NY
Died: July 4, 1986 - Tampa, FL

Jazz saxophone, clarinet, harmonica player

Though usually listed in Jazz encyclopedias as a tenor saxophone player, Eddie Shu began his musical career as a harmonica player in 1935, while playing in *The Cappy Barra Harmonica Ensemble.* During World War Two he did a harmonica duet act with Stan Harper.

After the war he mostly played the saxophone and performed with George Shearing, Buddy Rich, Lionel Hampton and Louis Armstrong. He also played the harmonica with *The Gene Krupa Trio* from 1954 until 1958. During the 1970's he did free-lance work in New York City.

Discography:
1949 - **New Stars - New Sounds, Vol. 1,** *Mercer* // 1955 - **Eddie Shu,** *Bethlehem.*

Siegel, Mark "Corky"

Born: October 24, 1943 - Chicago, IL

Blues / Classical singer, piano, harmonica player
Corky Siegel began working with Blues guitarist Jim Schwall as a Blues duo in 1965. After adding a bass guitarist and a drummer, they became leading proponents, along with Paul Butterfield and Charlie Musselwhite, of the white Blues revival of the late 1960's.

Vanguard Records signed the band in 1965 and they recorded five albums for the label. During this period composer William Russo saw the group and wrote "Three Pieces for Blues Band and Orchestra" for them. The band recorded several more albums before dissolving in 1975.

Siegel has since pursued a solo career as well as appearing on albums by Bonnie Koloc, *Big Twist and The Mellow Fellows* and John Prine. A reunion concert of *The Siegel-Schwall Band* led to a renewed interest in Corky's career as a performer. His interest in blending Classical forms with Blues music has led him to work with Chamber Blues, a four-piece chamber music group with a percussionist. He still occasionally performs with *The Siegel-Schwall Band*.

Discography:
1966 - **The Siegel-Schwall Band**, *Vanguard* // 1967 - **Say Siegel-Schwall**, *Vanguard* // 1968 - **Shake!**, *Vanguard* // 1970 - **Siegel-Schwall 70**, *Vanguard* // 1971 - **Siegel-Schwall Band**, *Wooden Nickel* // 1972 - **Sleepy Hollow**, *Wooden Nickel* // 1973 - **953 West**, *Wooden Nickel* // 1973 - **Three Pieces for Blues Band and Orchestra**, *Deutsche Grammophon* // 1974 - **Live Last Summer**, *Wooden Nickel* // 1974 - **RIP Siegel-Schwall**, *Wooden Nickel* // 1974 - **The Best Of...**, *Vanguard* // 1974 - **Corky Siegel**, *Dharma* // 1988 - **Siegel-Schwall Reunion**, *Alligator* // 1991 - **Where We Walked**, *Vanguard* // 1994 - **Chamber Blues**, *Alligator* // 1998 - **Complimentary Colors**, *Gadfly* // 1999 - **Solo Flight 1975-1980**, *Gadfly* // 1999 **The Siegel Schwall Band - The Very Best of the Wooden Nickel Years (1971 - 1974)**, *Varese*.

Simmons, Malcolm "Little Mack"

Born: January 25, 1934 - Twist, AR
Died: October 24, 2000 - Chicago, IL

Blues singer, harmonica player

"Little Mack" Simmons learned how to play the harmonica while growing up on a farm in Arkansas. He began playing at local parties while he was still in his teens. He moved to St. Louis in 1952 and was exposed to urban Blues and worked with Robert Nighthawk.

After moving to Chicago in 1954, he quickly became a regular in the city's thriving Blues scene and recorded his first records in 1959. Over the years he performed and recorded on a regular basis, although he slowed down due to ill health in the later part of the 1990's.

Discography:
1994 - **Come Back To Me Baby**, *Wolf* // 1997 - **High and Lonesome**, *St. George* // 1997 - **Little Mack is Back**, *Electro-Fi* // 1998 - **Somewhere Down the Line**, *Electro-Fi* // 1999 - **The P.M./Simmons Collection**, *Electro-Fi*.

Simpson-Smith, Judy

Pop / Vaudeville harmonica player

Judy Simpson-Smith began playing the harmonica in 1977 and was soon competing on the instrument at several international competitions. She married was to Al Smith in December of 1985 and the two formed a musical partnership. Judy plays the lead chromatic, diatonic, bass and chord harmonicas in *The Harmonica Hotshots*. She was named SPAH's harmonica player of the year in 1985.

Singer, Randy

Born: February 13, 1957

Studio harmonica player

Randy Singer is a studio harmonica player who has worked with Julio Inglesias, Garth Brooks, Tanya Tucker, *Blondie* and many others as well as doing the harmonica work for ads and soundtracks.

by playing with Jimmy Rogers, Koko Taylor, John Primer, Bernard Allison, Larry Garner, H-Bomb Ferguson, *The Kinsey Report* and others as well as releasing two albums of his own music.

Discography:
1996 - **Bone To Pick with You,** *Tongue n Groove* // 1999 - Shoulder To the Wind, *Tongue n Groove.*

Sky, Patrick

Born: October 2, 1940 - College Park, GA

Folk singer-songwriter, guitar, banjo, harmonica

A part of the 1960's Folk music scene, Patrick Sky's career has

The Skillet Lickers

Formed: 1924 -Atlanta, GA
Disbanded: 1931

Country band
One of Country music's early popular string bands, *Gid Tanner* and *The Skillet Lickers* featured Fate Norris on the banjo and harmonica. They began recording for the Columbia label in 1926 and cut 88 sides over the next several years.

See - Fate Norris

Discography:
1970 - **Gid Tanner** // 1973 - **Gid Tanner and his Skillet Lickers** // 1975 - **Gid Tanner and his Skillet Lickers, Vol. 2** // 1977 - **Kickapoo Medicine Show** // 1981 - **A Day at the County Fair** // 1980's - **A Corn Licker Still in Georgia** // 1996 - **Old Time Fiddle Tunes and Songs,** *County* // 2000 - **Skillet Lickers, Vol. 1-6,** *Document* // 2000 - **Complete Recorded Works: 1930-1934, Vol. 5,** *Document.*

Skoller, Matthew

Born: August 3, 1962 - Canton, NY

Blues harmonica player
Since moving to Chicago in 1987, Matthew Skoller has made a name for himself as a blues harmonica player and band leader

been marked by both his artistic integrity and controversy. Sky began playing music professionally in Greenwich Village where he played guitar and harmonica and was making records by 1965. Sky also played with Buffy Sainte-Marie from 1964 to 1967.

As his career developed, his songs began hitting hard at America's social and political problems. His album, "Songs That Made America Famous" was held from release for over two years, which stalled Sky's career. He has persevered and continues to perform and record on a regular basis.

Discography:

1965 - **Singer-Songwriter**, *Elektra* // 1965 - **Patrick Sky**, *Vanguard* // 1966 - **A Harvest of Gentle Clang**, *Vanguard* // 1968 - **Reality is Bad Enough**, *Verve* // 1969 - **Photographs**, *Verve* // 1972 - **Songs That Made America Famous**, *Adelphi* // 1976 - **Two Steps Forward One Step Back**, *Leviathan* // 1985 - **Through a Window**, *Shanachie*.

TV Slim (see - Oscar Wills)

Smith, Al
Pop / Vaudeville harmonica player

Al Smith was a member of *The Harmonica Rascals* from 1953 to 1955, then worked with various harmonica bands from that point forward. He currently works with his wife, Judy Smith playing chord, bass and chromatic harmonicas as *The Harmonica Hotshots*. He was named SPAH's harmonica player of the year in 1994.

Smith Gary
Blues harmonica player

Gary Smith grew up in San Jose, California and began playing the harmonica in the late 1960's. He received some lessons on the instrument from Charlie Musselwhite. His first Blues band was formed in 1969 and included Robben and Pat Ford.

Since forming his own band in the early 1970's, he's been a mainstay in the San Francisco Bay area's Blues scene. He has also put out a video on Blues harmonica technique.

Discography: (also see - The Ford Blues Band)
1974 - *Gary Smith's Blues Band, Messaround* // 1976 - **Blue Bay**, *Flying Saucer* // 1991 - **Up the Line**, *Messaround* // 1996 - **Gary Smith & John Stevens**, *Ecstatic Peace*.

Video:
Amplified Blues Harp De-Mystified, *Mountain Top Video*.

Smith, George "Harmonica

Also known as: Little Walter Jr., The Harmonica King
Real name: Allen George Smith
Born: April 22, 1924 - Helena, AR
Died: October 2, 1983 - Los Angeles, CA

Blues harmonica player

George "Harmonica" Smith was as famous for a generation of young harmonica players that he influenced as he was for his actual playing. He learned how to play the harmonica when he was four years old from his mother. By his early teens he was playing at local parties and dances around Cairo, Illinois.

He began hoboing during the late 1930's and he didn't settle in Chicago until 1951. He began playing with Muddy Waters around 1954, but moved to Kansas City later the same year. He did his first recordings for the RPM label at that time.

Over the next few years he traveled extensively, performing and recording everywhere he went. He worked with Muddy Waters, Otis Spann, Otis Rush, Champion Jack Dupree, Big Mama Willie Mae Thornton and a host of others.

By the end of the 1950's he had settled in the San Francisco Bay area and was working in the local Blues scene. By the late 1960's he was acting as a mentor to a generation of young harmonica players including Kim Wilson, James Harman, William Clarke and Rod Piazza, with whom he formed the band *Bacon Fat* in the 1970's. The two performed together until Smith's death in 1983.

Discography: (also see - Muddy Waters)
1956 - **Oopin' Doopin' Doopin'**, *Ace* // 1968 - **Tribute to Little Walter**, *World Pacific* // 1969 - **Blues with a Feeling** // 1970 - **Arkansas Trap**, *Deram* // 1970 - **No More Time for Jive**, *Blue Horizon* // 1970 - **Grease One for Me**, (with Bacon Fat), *Blue Horizon* // 1971 - **Tough Dude**, (with Bacon Fat), *Blue Horizon* // 1973 - **George Smith of the Blues**, *Crosscut* // 1979 - **Blowin' the Blues**, *P-Vine* // 1983 - **Boogie'n with George**, *Murray Brothers* // 1991 - **Harmonica Ace**, *Virgin* // 1991 - **Little George Smith**, *Ace* // 1998 - **Now You Can Talk About Me**, *Blind Pig* // **George Smith**, *Dobre* // **George Smith**, *Shoe* // **Elke**

162

Blues, Vol. 1&2, *Wolf.*

Smith, Manny

Born: January 16, 1921 - Pennsylvania

Vaudeville harmonica player
Manny Smith played the chord harmonica in *The Stagg McMann Trio* from the late 1930's until the early 1950's.

Discography: (see - The Stagg McMann Trio)

Smith, Mark E.

Born: March 5, 1957 - Manchester, England

Rock singer, keyboards, harmonica player
Mark E. Smith is the founder and leader of the Alternative Rock band, *The Fall.* In addition to singing and playing the keyboards, he also plays the harmonica.

Discography: (see - The Fall)

Smith, "Whispering" Moses

Born: January 25, 1932 - Union Church, MS
Died: April 19, 1984 - Baton Rouge, LA

Blues singer, harmonica player
Moses "Whispering" Smith started playing the harmonica at age fourteen and spent most of his early adulthood playing at local parties and dances around Mississippi. During the late 1950's he started playing with Lightnin' Hopkins.

Although he worked steadily as a journeyman Blues player, he didn't start recording until 1963, when he signed with the Excello label. He recorded and performed on a regular basis until his death in 1984.

Discography:
1971 - **Over Easy**, *Excello* // 1984 - **Louisiana Blues** // **Authentic R&B**, *Stateside* // **The Excello Story**, *Blue Horizon* // **The Excello Years**, *Excello* // **Montreaux Blues Festival**, *Excello* // **Rooster Crowed for Day**, *Flyright* // **Swamp Blues**, *Blue Horizon* // **25 Years with The Blues**, *Blues Unlimited.*

Smith, Russell

Born: June 17, 1949 - Lafayette, TN

Country / Rock singer, guitar, harmonica player
Russell Smith played guitar and harmonica for the Country/Rock group, *The Amazing Rhythm Aces.* Since the group broke up in the early 1980's, Smith has worked as a songwriter and released several solo albums.

Discography: (also see - The Amazing Rhythm Aces)
1978 - **Russell Smith**, *Capitol* // 1989 - **This Little Town**, *Epic.*

Smith, "Shakin"

Born: August 26, 1950
Blues harmonica player

Shakin' Smith began playing the harmonica when he was five years old. He began going to Blues bars and working with various harmonica greats like Howlin' Wolf, Jimmy Reed and Junior Wells while he was still a teenager. Forming his own band in 1969, Smith has been a staple of the upstate New York Blues scene and released his first album in 2000 featuring Robert Jr. Lockwood on guitar.

Discography:
2000 - **Wizard of the Harmonica**, *Shakin Smith.*

Smith, "Little" Willie
Blues harmonica player
"Little" Willie Smith was the Blues harmonica player who sat in on the recording of "Diddy Wah Diddy" by Bo Diddley in 1958. Very little has been heard from him since that time.

The Smiths

Formed: 1982 -Manchester, England
Disbanded: 1987

Alternative Rock band
A cutting-edge Alternative Rock band of the 1980's, *The Smiths* featured guitarist Johnny Marr playing the harmonica on many of their songs.

See - Johnny Marr

Discography:
1984 - **The Smiths**, *Sire* // 1984 - **Hatfull of Hollow**, *Sire* // 1985 - **Meat is Murder**, *Sire* // 1986 - **The Queen is Dead**, *Sire* // 1987 - **Strangeways Here We Come**, *Sire* // 1987 - **Louder Than Bombs**, *Sire* // 1987 - **The World Won't**

Listen, *Rough Trade* // 1988 - **The Peel Sessions**, *Dutch East Indies* // 1988 - **Rank**, *Sire* // 1992 - **The Best, Vol. 1&2**, *Sire* // 1995 - **Singles**, *Reprise*.

The Smokey Mountain Boys
Country-Western band
The Smokey Mountain Boys were Country music star Roy Acuff's back-up band and included Jimmie Riddle in the 1940's and Larry McNeely during the late 1960's playing the harmonica.

See - Jimmie Riddle, Larry McNeely

Snow, Charles
Vaudeville harmonica band leader
Charles Snow was a Vaudeville harmonica bandleader whose group, *The Broadway Pirates*, backed up one-legged dancer Charles Bennington during the late 1920's and early 30's.

Snow, Hank
Real name: Clarence Eugene Snow
Born: May 9, 1914 - Brooklyn, Nova Scotia, Canada
Died: December 20, 1999 - Madison, TN

Country singer-songwriter, guitar, harmonica player
Heavily influenced by the recordings of Vernon Dalhart, Hank Snow grew up in Nova Scotia and developed his harmonica playing while working on Arctic fishing boats.

Snow started recording for the Bluebird label in 1936 and over the next few decades he recorded over 840 songs. He began performing at the Grand Old Opry in 1950 and remained active until his death in the late 1990's.

Discography:
1956 - **Country Classics**, *RCA* // 1961 - **Biggest Country Hits**, *RCA* // 1982 - **20 of the Best**, *RCA* // 1988 - **The Singing Ranger: 1949-1953**, *Bear Family* // 1990 - **The Singing Ranger, Vol. 2**, *Bear Family* // 1991 - **The Thesaurus Transcriptions**, *Bear Family* // 1994 - **The Singing Ranger, Vol. 3**, *Bear Family* // 1994 - **Yodeling Ranger (1936-1947)**, *Bear Family* // 1997 - **The Essential Hank Snow**, *RCA* // 1998 - **Best of the Best**, *King* // 1998 - **I've Been Everywhere**, *BMG Special* // 1999 - **Yodeling Ranger: Young Hank Snow 1936-1943**, *Bear Family* // 2000 - **Hall of Fame: 1979**, *King* // 2000 - **Blues for My Eyes**, *Jasmine*.

Bibliography:
1994 - **The Hank Snow Story**, *University of Illinois Press*.

The Society for the Preservation and Advancement of the Harmonica (SPAH)
Formed in 1962 by harmonica enthusiasts in the Detroit, Michigan area, SPAH is a national club devoted to the harmonica and it's players. SPAH publishes a quarterly newsletter, "Harmonica Happenings" and hosts an annual convention. The club helps to foster local harmonica clubs and festivals in the United States and around the world.

Solomon, Phil
Vaudeville harmonica player
Phil Solomon played the chord harmonica in Carl Freed's *Harmonica Harlequins* and *The Cappy Barra Harmonica Ensemble* during the 1930's.

Sonnen, Fred
Harmonica band leader
Fred Sonnen led *The Baltimore Harmonica Band*, which included both Adler brothers, Larry and Jerry, during the 1920's.

Sonnier, Jo-El
Born: October 2, 1946 - Rayne, LA

Cajun singer-songwriter, accordion, harmonica
Jo-el Sonnier began playing music at age six and recorded his first album by the time he was thirteen. His specialty is the Cajun music of his native Louisiana, although he tends to blend it with Rock and Country stylings.

During the 1970's he played around California, playing mostly Country Music. After returning to Louisiana in 1979, he started focusing on his native Cajun music. He has performed with Dolly Parton, Elvis Costello, Emmylou Harris, Albert Lee, Johnny Cash and Steve Winwood.

Sonnier's main instrument is the accordion, but he also doubles on the harmonica.

Discography:
1975 - **Cajun Life**, *Rounder* // 1979 - *Cajun Valentine*, *Goldband* // 1979 - **Hurricane Avory**, *Goldband* // 1979 - **Scene Today in Cajun Music**, *Goldband* // 1987 - **Come On Joe**, *RCA* // 1990 - **Have a Little Faith**, *RCA* // 1991 - **Tears of Joy**, *Capitol* // 1992 - **Hello Happiness Again**, *Liberty* // 1992 - **The Complete Mercury Sessions**, *Mercury* // 1994 - **Cajun Roots**, *Rounder* // 1996 - **Cajun Young Blood**, *Ace* // 1996 - **Live in Canada**, *Stony Plain* // 1997 - **Cajun Pride**, *Rounder* // 1998 - **Here To Stay**, *Intersound* // 1999 - **Cajun Blood**, *Sonnier* // 2000 - **Cajun Valentino**, *Goldband*.

Son Volt
Formed: 1994

Rock Band
Son Volt is the Alternative Country / Rock band that was put together by Jay Farrar after *Uncle Tupelo* broke up. Farrar plays guitar, mandolin and harmonica in the group as well as singing and writing most of the band's material.

See - Jay Farrar

Discography:
1995 - **Trace,** *Warner Brothers* // 1997 - **Straightaways,** *Warner Brothers* // 1998 - **Wide Swing Tremelo,** *Warner Brothers.*

The Sons of the Blues

Formed: 1978 - Chicago, IL

Blues band

The Sons of the Blues derived their name from the fact that the group's original line-up included sons of Chicago Blues masters Willie Dixon and Carey Bell. The band features Billy Branch on the harmonica.

See - Billy Branch

Discography:
1982 - **Live Recorded,** *L&R* // 1983 - **Where's the Money?,** *Red Beans* // **Romancing the Blue Stone,** (with The Chi-Town Hustlers), *Blue Phoenix.*

Sorin, Ron
Rock harmonica player

Ron played the harmonica for the Chicago-based Rock group *Big Shoulders* during the late 1980's.

Discography: (see - Big Shoulders)

Sousa, John Philip

Born: November 6, 1854 - Washington, DC
Died: March 6, 1932 - Reading, PA

Marching band leader

John Philip Sousa wrote "The Harmonica Wizard March" for Albert Hoxies's harmonica band in the 1930's.

Southern Grass

Formed: 1979 - North Carolina

Bluegrass band

Southern Grass is a band that specializes in playing Bluegrass music. It was founded by Bob Paisley who plays the harmonica as well as several stringed instruments.

See - Bob Paisley

Discography:
1981 - **Bob Paisley and Southern Grass,** *Rounder* // 1982 - **An Old Love Affair,** *Brandywine* // 1983 - **Pickin' in Holland,** *Strictly* // 1985 - **I Still Love You Yet,** *Mountain Laurel* // 1988 - **Home of Light and Love,** *Mountain Laurel* // 1992 - **No Vacancy,** *Brandywine.*

Southside Johnny and The Asbury Jukes

Formed: 1974 - Asbury Park, NJ

Rock band

Paralleling the career of friend and fellow New Jersian, Bruce Springsteen, *Southside Johnny and The Asbury Jukes* have enjoyed moderate chart success during the past two decades. The group is led by harmonica player and vocalist "Southside" Johnny Lyon.

See - Southside Johnny Lyon

Discography:
1976 - **Live at the Bottom Line,** *Epic* // 1976 - **I Don't Want To Go Home,** *Epic* // 1977 - **This Time It's for Real,** *Legacy* // 1978 - **Hearts of Stone,** *Epic* // 1979 - **Havin' a Party with Southside Johnny,** *Epic* // 1979 - **The Jukes,** *Mercury* // 1980 - **Love is a Sacrifice,** *Mercury* // 1981 - **Reach Out and Touch the Sky,** *Mercury* // 1983 - **Trash It Up! Live,** *Mirage* // 1984 - **In the Heat,** *Atco* // 1986 - **At Least We Got Shoes,** *Atlantic* // 1988 - **Slow Dance,** *A&M* // 1991 - **Better Days,** *Impact* // 1993 - **The Best Of...,** *Legacy* // 1993 - **All I Want is Everything,** *Rhino* // 1996 - **Rockin' with The Jukes,** *Sony* // 1997 - **Spittin' Fire,** *Grapevine* // 1998 - **Restless Heart,** *Rebound* // 2000 - **Live at the Paradise Theatre Boston,** *Phoenix Media* // 2000 - **Messin' with the Blues** // **Ruff Stuff.**

Spann, Otis

Born: March 21, 1930 - Jackson, MS
Died: April 24, 1970 - Chicago, IL

Blues piano, organ, harmonica player

Best known as the piano cornerstone of the Chess Records Blues stable of the 1950's, Otis Spann, like many of his label mates, could also play the harmonica.

Discography:

1960 - **Otis Spann is the Blues,** *Candid* // 1960 - **Complete Candid Sessions - Otis Spann/Lightnin' Hopkins,** *Mosaic* // 1960 - **Walking the Blues,** *Candid* // 1963 - **Blues is Where Iit's At,** *Beat Goes On* // 1963 - **Portrait in Blues,** *Storyville* // 1963 - **Piano Blues,** *Storyville* // 1963 - **Otis Spann,** *Storyville* // 1964 - **Chicago Blues,** *Testament* // 1967 - **Nobody Knows My Troubles,** *Polydor* // 1968 - **Bottom of the Blues,** *Bluesway* // 1968 - **Raw Blues,** *London* // 1969 - **Cracked Spanner Head,** *Deram* // 1969 - **The Blues Never Die,** *Original Blues Classics* // 1970 - **Cryin' Time,** *Vanguard* // 1970 - **Sweet Giant of the Blues,** *Blues Time* // 1970 - **Otis Spann,** *Everest* // 1970 - **The Everlasting Blues,** *Spivey* // 1972 - **Walking the Blues,** *Candid* // 1973 - **Heart Heavy with Trouble,** *Bluesway* // 1974 - **Blues Rocks,** *Blues Time* // 1974 - **Cry Before I Go,** *Bluesway* // 1983 - **Candid Spann, Vol. 1,** *Candid* // 1983 - **Nobody Knows Chicago Like I Do,** *Charly* // 1984 - **Rarest,** *JSP* // 1984 - **Take Me Back Home** // 1991 - **This is the Blues,** *Huub* // 1991 - **Blues Masters, Vol. 10,** *Storyville* // 1993 - **The Biggest Thing Since Colossus,** *Blue Horizon* // 1993 - **Blues of Otis Spann...Plus,** *See for Miles* // 1994 - **Otis Spann's Chicago Blues,** *Testament* // 1995 - **Down To Earth,** *MCA* // 1996 - **Good Morning, Mr. Blues,** *Storyville.*// 1997 - **Live the Life,** (with Muddy Waters), *Testament* // 1999 - **The Best of the Vanguard Years,** *Vanguard* // 2000 - **Last Call,** *Mr. Cat Music.*

Spencer, W.C.

Blues singer, guitar, drums, harmonica player

W.C. Spencer works as a one-man Blues band, mostly on the east coast. He began playing music at the age of ten and plays foot-pedal bass, drums, guitar and harmonica at the same time.

Discography:
1997 - **Bluescat,** *Catscan* // 1998 - **Over Time,** *Catscan.*

Sperling, Sam

Vaudeville harmonica player
Sam Sperling played harmonica in *The Cappy Barra Harmonica Ensemble* from 1935 to 1940.

Spivakovsky, Michael

Born: 1919
Died: 1983

Classical composer
Michael Spivakovsky wrote "Concerto for Harmonica and Orchestra" in 1951 for Tommy Reilly.

Recording Availability:
1977 - **Reilly Plays Villa-Lobos, Spivakovsky, Arnold and Others,** *Chandos* // 1994 - **Tommy Reilly Plays Harmonica Concertos,** *Chandos.*

Springsteen, Bruce

Born: September 23, 1949 - Freehold, NJ

Rock singer-songwriter, guitar, harmonica player
Since his emergence in the Rock music scene in the mid-1970's, Bruce Springsteen has dominated the charts as a singer-songwriter. Heavily influenced by Folk musicians like Woody Guthrie and Bob Dylan, Springsteen usually plays the harmonica on a neckbrace.

Discography:
1975 - **Greetings From Asbury Park, N.J.,** *Columbia* // 1973 - **The Wild, the Innocent and the E Street Shuffle,** *Columbia* // 1975 - **Born To Run,** *Columbia* // 1978 - **Darkness at the Edge of Town,** *Columbia* // 1980 - **The River,** *Columbia* // 1982 - **Nebraska,** *Columbia* // 1984 - **Born in the USA,** *Columbia* // 1986 - **Live 1975-1985,** *Columbia* // 1987 - **Tunnel of Love,** *Columbia* // 1992 - **Human Touch,** *Columbia* // 1992 - **Lucky Town,** *Columbia* // 1993 - **In Concert / MTV Unplugged,** *Columbia* // 1995 - **Greatest Hits,** *Columbia* // 1996 - **The Ghost of Tom Joad,** *Columbia* // 1999 - **Eighteen Tracks,** *Sony.*

Sprott, Horace

Born: February 2, 18(90?) - Sprott, AL

Blues singer, guitar, harmonica player
After serving time on a prison farm in Montgomery, Alabama, Horace Sprott played the guitar and harmonica at local parties and dances from the mid-1920's until the mid-1950's. He recorded for the Folkways label in 1954 and appeared on CBS television in 1956.

Discography:

1955 - **Music from the South, Vol. 2, 3 & 4: Horace Sprott,** *Folkways.*

Stackhouse, Houston

Born: September 28, 1910 - Wesson, MS
Died: September 23, 1980 - Houston, TX

Blues guitar, mandolin, harmonica player
Houston Stackhouse learned how to play the guitar from Tommy Johnson during the 1920's and also picked up the harmonica along the way. During the course of his career he performed with Robert Nighthawk, Jimmie Rogers, Sonny Boy Williamson II (Rice Miller), Little Walter, Peck Curtis and a host of other Blues greats.

He began working in radio around 1946, but did not start recording until 1967. He remained active well into the 1970's.

Discography:
1968 - **Mississippi Delta Blues, Vol. 1** // 1994 - **Cryin' Won't Help You,** *Genes* // 1997 - **Big Road Blues,** *Wolf //* **Houston Stackhouse, 1910-1980,** *Wolf.*

Stafford, Jim

Born: January 16, 1944 - Eloise, FL

Country multi-instrumentalist including harmonica
After moving to Nashville in 1962, Jim Stafford tried his hand as a musician and songwriter. He had a series of novelty hits in the mid-1970's including "Spiders and Snakes" and "My Girl Bill." He plays the harmonica as well as several other instruments.

Discography:
1973 - **Jim Stafford,** *MGM* // 1974 - **Spiders and Snakes,** *MGM* // 1975 - **Not Just Another Pretty Foot,** *MGM* // 1994 - **The Ultimate Jim Stafford,** *Bransounds* // 1995 - **Greatest Hits,** *Curb* // 1998 - **The Best Of...,** *PSM.*

The Stagg McMann Trio

Formed: 1936 - Lancaster, PA
Disbanded: 1951

Vaudeville harmonica band
Formed in 1936, *The Stagg McMann Trio* derived its name from parts of the names of its three players: Paul Steigerwald (bass harmonica), Hugh McCaskey (chromatic harmonica) and Manny Smith (chord harmonica). Originally from Lancaster, Pennsylvania, the three got together in a large church basement harmonica band.

After high school they moved to New York City where they played amateur nights specializing in Jazz and Popular music and they were eventually hired to back up ex-*Harmonica Rascal* Alex Novelle.

After Novelle was drafted in 1940 they continued working as a trio for a short time until World War Two interrupted their careers. After the war they resumed playing steadily and recorded an album in 1950. The group split up shortly after its release.

See - Paul Steigerwald, Hugh McCaskey, Manny Smith
Discography:
1950 - **The Legendary Stagg McMann Trio.**

Stax, John

Real name: John Fullegar
Born: April 6, 1944 - London, England

Rock bass, harmonica player
John Stax played the bass guitar and harmonica for the Blues influenced British Rock band, *The Pretty Things,* from 1963 until 1967.

Discography: (see - The Pretty Things)

Steigerwald, Paul

Vaudeville harmonica player
Paul Steigerwald played the bass harmonica for *The Stagg McMann Trio* from the mid-1930's until 1951.

Discography: (see - Stagg McMann)

The Stereomonics

Formed: 1968 - Las Vegas, NV
Disbanded: 1969

Harmonica band
Formed by Dave Doucette, *The Stereomonics* featured Eddie Gordon on the chord harmonica and even included Johnny O'Brien for a while.

Stevens, Mike

Born: October 9, 1957

Bluegrass harmonica player
Mike Stevens is a Canadian harmonica player who specializes in Bluegrass music. He has been playing since he was fifteen years old and has appeared at The Grand Old Opry on numerous occasions. He has performed with *Jim & Jesse*, Roy Acuff, Bill Monroe and countless others.

Discography:
1975 - **Set the Spirit Free,** *Novus* // 1975 - **Light Up the Night,** *Novus* // 1990 - **Mike Stevens, Harmonica,** *Stevens* // 1993 - **Blowin' Up a Storm,** *Pinecastle* // 1994 - **Life's Railway To Heaven,** *Stevens* // 1995 - **Colin's Cross,** *MSM* // 1998 - **Joy,** *Malaco* // 1998 - **Normally Anomaly,** *MSM.*

Bibliography:
1997 - **Bluegrass Harmonica,** *Centerstream.*

Stewart, Jimmy

Born: May 20, 1908 - Indiana, PA
Died: July 3, 1997 - Hollywood, CA

Actor

The legendary Hollywood actor Jimmy Stewart learned how to play the harmonica for his role in the 1941 film, "Pot 'O' Gold." He was coached by harmonica virtuoso Jerry Adler, who actually did the harmonica playing for the movie's soundtrack.

Stewart continued playing the instrument after completing the picture and even took it with him on some bombing missions he flew in World War Two.

Stewart, Rod

Born: January 10, 1945 - London, England

Rock singer, harmonica player

Though known primarily as a lead vocalist, Rod Stewart also played harmonica with *Jimmy Howell and The Five Dimensions* during the mid-1960's and allegedly made his recording debut playing the harmonica on Millie Small's "My Boy Lollipop." He also spent some time as the lead vocalist and harmonica player for the bands, *Long John Baldry and his Hoochie Coochie Men* and *Steampacket*.

Stidham, Arbee

Born: February 9, 1917 - DeValls Bluff, AR

Blues singer, saxophone, guitar, harmonica player

From a musical family, (his father played in *The Jimmie Lunceford Band*, his uncle played in *The Memphis Jug Band*), Arbee Stidham began playing music professionally while still in his early teens. By the time he was thirteen he was playing behind Bessie Smith. Later he traveled to Arkansas where he made radio appearances and worked the local clubs.

He started recording in the late 1940's and remained active for several decades, primarily as a singer and guitar player, until he retired from music in 1974.

Discography:
1961 - **Tired of Wandering,** *Bluesville* // 1961 - **Arbee's Blues,** *Smithsonian* // 1972 - **Time for Blues,** *Mainstream* // 1973 - **There's Always Tomorrow / Bring the Blues Back,** *Smithsonian* // 1982 - **My Heart Belongs To You,** *Crown Prince.*

Stone, Sly

Real name: Sylvester Stewart
Born: March 15, 1944 - Dallas, TX

Funk singer, keyboards, harmonica player

Sly Stone was the founder of one of the most influential Rock/Funk groups of the late 1960's, *Sly and the Family Stone*. Besides being one of the few integrated bands of the period, their music fused Soul, Pop and Rock into their unique sound.

Stone began singing Gospel at age four in the San Francisco Bay area and recorded his first record at age sixteen. While working as a disc jockey, he began putting his new band together around 1967.

Their music was instantly successful and they had several big hits with songs like "Stand!," "I Want To Take You Higher," "Dance To the Music" and several others.

Stone's career slowed down in the mid-1970's, although he has made several attempts at a comeback since then.

Discography:
1967 - **A Whole New Thing,** *Epic* // 1968 - **M'Lady,** *Direction* // 1968 - **Dance To the Music,** *Epic* // 1968 - **Life,** *Epic* // 1968 - **Stand!,** *Epic* // 1970 - **Greatest Hits,** *Epic* // 1971 - **There's a Riot Going On,** *Epic* // 1973 - **Fresh,** *Epic* //

1974 - **Small Talk**, *Epic* // 1975 - **High on You**, *Epic* // 1975 - **High Energy**, *Epic* // 1976 - **Heard You Missed Me, Well I'm Back**, *Epic* // 1979 - **Ten Years Too Soon**, *Epic* // 1979 - **Back on the Right Track**, *Warner Brothers* // 1981 - **Anthology**, *Epic* // 1983 - **Ain't But the One Way**, *Warner Brothers* // 1994 - **Precious Stone**, *Ace* // 1998 - **Masters**, *Cleopatra* // 1998 - **Dance To the Music**, *Magnum* // 1999 - **Backtracks**, *Renaissance* // 1999 - **In the Still of the Night**, *Magnum* // 2000 - **My Only Love**, *CRG*.

Stoneman, Ernest "Pop"

Born: May 25, 1893 - Iron Ridge, VA
Died: June 14, 1968

Country autoharp, harmonica player

A major proponent of the autoharp, Ernest "Pop" Stoneman was the patriarch of a large musical family. The best known for his playing of the autoharp, he played several instruments including the harmonica.

Discography:

1957 - **Old Time Tunes of the South**, *Folkways* // 1959 - **Cool Cowboy**, *Capitol* // 1968 - **Ernest V. Stoneman and his Dixie Mountaineers**, *Historical* // 1975 - **Ernest V. Stoneman and The Blue Ridge Corn Shuckers**, *Rounder* // 1980 - **Round the Heart of Old Galax**, *County* // 1982 - **A Rare Find!**, *Stonehouse* // 1986 - **Ernest V. Stoneman with Family and Friends**, *Old Homestead* // 1991 - **Sinking of the Titanic, Vol. III**, *Old Homestead* // 1996 - **Edison Recordings - 1928**, *County*.

Stovepipe No. 1

Real name: Sam Jones

Blues singer, stovepipe, harmonica player

From Cincinnati, Sam Jones was a Blues musician who played a stovepipe, (similar in style to a jug), during the 1920's. He often partnered with Blues guitar and harmonica player David Crockett.

Discography:

1988 - **Stovepipe No. 1 and David Crockett**, *Document*.

Stowers, Freeman

Blues harmonica player

Freeman Stowers recorded four sides for the Gennett label in 1929. Billed as "The Cotton Belt Porter," he specialized in doing train imitations on the harmonica.

Discography:

Sinners and Saints, *Document*.

Straight Harp

Another name for the first diatonic position, straight harp refers to the harmonica player playing in the same key as the music they are accompanying.

See - Positions

Strehli, Angela

Born: November 22, 1945 - Lubbock, TX

Blues singer-songwriter, bass, harmonica player

Known primarily as a singer and songwriter, Angela Strehli began on the harmonica and bass guitar before becoming a full-time vocalist. While doing most of her work around the Austin, Texas area, she was the first artist to record for the Antone's label. In addition to her own recordings, Strehli has worked with Marcia Ball, Sue Foley, Joe Louis Walker, Lou Ann Barton and others.

Discography:

1987 - **Soul Shake**, *Antone's* // 1990 - **Dreams Come True**, *Antone's* // 1994 - **Blonde and Blue**, *Rounder* // 1998 - **Deja Blue**, *House of Blues*.

The Strnad Brothers

Harmonica band

A harmonica trio from the Detroit area, *The Strnad Brothers* consists of brothers Don, Frank and George. They also manufacture Strnad harmonica microphones.

Strong, Henry

Born: September 1, 1928 - West memphis, AR
Died: June 3, 1954 - Chicago, IL

Blues harmonica player

Henry Strong was a Blues harmonica player who played in Muddy Water's band, replacing Walter Horton in 1952, until he was stabbed to death in 1954.

Sun, Joe

Real name: Joe Paulson
Born: September 25, 1943 - Rochester, MN

Country singer-songwriter, guitar, harmonica player

Joe Sun began to play guitar and harmonica while attending college. He has worked as a Country/Folk singer-songwriter ever since. While he hasn't achieved great commercial success, he has managed to garner the respect of such luminaries as Bob Dylan, Jimmy Buffett, Steve Goodman, Kris Kristopherson, John Prine and others.

Discography:

1979 - **Old Flames (Can't Hold a Candle To You)**, *Ovation* // 1980 - **Out of Your Mind**, *Ovation* // 1981 - **Livin' On Honky Tonkin' No More**, *Elektra* // 1983 - **The Best Of...**, *Elektra* // 1984 - **Joe Sun with Shotgun**, *Intercord* // 1986 - **The Sun Never Sets**, *Sonet* // 1988 - **Twilight Zone**, *Dixie Frog* // 1989 - **Hank Bogart Still Lives**, *Dixie Frog* // 1991 -

Out on the Road, *Dixie Frog* // 1992 - **Dixie and Me,** *Crazy* // 1993 - **Some Old Memories,** *Crazy.*

Supertramp

Formed: 1969 - England

Rock band

One of the top Art-Rock groups of the 1970's, Supertramp had enormous success with such songs as "Take the Long Way Home," "The Logical Song" and several others, many of which featured keyboard player and vocalist Rick Davies playing the harmonica.

See - Rick Davies

Discography:

1970 - **Supertramp,** *A&M* // 1971 - **Indelibly Stamped,** *A&M* // 1973 - **Extremes,** *Deram* // 1974 - **Crime of the Century,** *A&M* // 1975 - **Crisis? What Crisis?,** *A&M* // 1977 - **Even in the Quietest Moments,** *A&M* // 1979 - **Breakfast in America,** *A&M* // 1980 - **Paris,** *A&M* // 1982 - **Famous Last Words,** *A&M* // 1985 - **Brother Where You Bound,** *A&M* // 1986 - **The Autobiography of Supertramp,** *A&M* // 1987 - **Free as a Bird,** *A&M* // 1987 - **Classics, Vol. 9,** *A&M* // 1988 - **Supertramp Live 88,** *A&M* // 1992 - **The Very Best Of,** *A&M* // 1997 - **Some Things Never Change,** *Chrysalis.*

Sweet

Formed: 1968 - London, England
Disbanded: 1982

Rock Band

Sweet was an English Rock band that had several hits in the mid-1970's, including "Fox on the Run," "Ballroom Blitz" and "Love is Like Oxygen." Their bass guitar player, Steve Priest, also played the harmonica.

See - Steve Priest

Discography:

1971 - **Funny How Sweet CoCo Can Be,** *RCA* // 1972 - **Biggest Hits,** *RCA* // 1973 - **Sweet,** *Razor & Tie* // 1974 - **Sweet Fanny Adams,** *RCA* // 1974 - **Desolation Boulevard,** *Capitol* // 1975 - **Strung Up,** *RCA* // 1976 - **Give Us A Wink,** *Capitol* // 1977 - **Off the Record,** *Capitol* // 1978 - **Level Headed,** *Capitol* // 1978 - **Short & Sweet,** *Capitol* // 1979 - **Cut Above the Rest,** *Capitol* // 1980 - **VI,** *Capitol* // 1980 - **Water's Edge,** *Capitol* // 1982 - **Identity Crisis,** *Polydor* // 1983 - **Sweet's Golden Greats** // 1984 - **Sweet 16 - It's, It's the Sweet's Hits** // 1987 - **Hard Centres - The Rock Years** // 1989 - **The Collection** // 1989 - **Live at the Marquee,** *Maze* // 1989 - **Blockbusters** // 1992 - **The Best Of...,** *Capitol* // 1993 - **Ballroom Blitz - Live 1973,** *Dojo* // 1994 - **A,** *Aim* // 1994 - **Live for Today,** *Receiver* // 1994 - **Rock and Roll Disgrace,** *Receiver* // 1995 - **Private Collection,** *Receiver* // 1996 - **Solid Gold Action,** *Receiver* // 1997 - **Electric Landlady,** *Receiver* // 1997 - **Golden Hits,** *Intercontinent* // 1997 - **Archive,** *Rialto* // 1998 - **Best of Sweet,** *Cema* // 1999 - **Blockbuster Alternative Takes,** *Cleopatra* // 1999 - **Greatest Hits Remixed,** *Cleopatra* // **Land of Hope and Glory,** *Receiver.*

– T –

Tankersley, Ray

Born: March 22, 1921

Vaudeville harmonica player

A one-time member of *The Harmonica Rascals* during the 1930's and 40's, Ray Tankersley also played in Johnny Puleo's secret harmonica band in 1942. After leaving *The Harmonica Rascals* he worked for the George P. Regan Harmonica Company during World War Two.

Tannenbaum, Chaim

Folk banjo, harmonica player

Chaim Tannenbaum has played with Loudon Wainwright III and *Kate and Anna McGarrigle* for several years and has appeared on many of their albums.

Tate, Douglas

Born: October 28, 1934 - Yarm-ot-Tees, Yorkshire, England

Classical harmonica player, writer, harmonica builder

Douglas Tate won the British Harmonica Championship several times as well as winning the World Championship Chromatic Solo prize in 1967 and several prizes in the diatonic solo category. He built custom chromatic harmonicas for Tommy Reilly and Larry Adler, later working with designer Bobbie Giordano to develop the Renaissance model harmonica. In 2000 he was elected President of SPAH, the first non-American to hold that post.

Bibliography:

2000 - **Play the Harmonica Well,** *Hal Leonard* // 2000 - **Make Your Harmonica Work Better,** *Hal Leonard.*

Tausky, Vilem

Classical composer

Vilem Tausky wrote "Concerto for Harmonica and Orchestra" for Tommy Reilly.

Recording Availability:
1976 - **Tommy Reilly Performs Vaughan-Williams, Tausky, Moody and Others,** (Tommy Reilly - Soloist), *Chandos.*

Taylor, Earl

Born: June 17, 1929 - Rosehill, VA
Died: January 28, 1984

Bluegrass singer-songwriter, mandolin, guitar, harmonica player

Earl Taylor took up the harmonica at age twelve and started playing professionally when he was seventeen. He began recording in 1955, the same year that he put together his group, *The Stoney Mountain Boys Bluegrass Band.* They were the first Bluegrass group to ever play at Carnegie Hall.

Equally adept at several stringed instruments as well as the harmonica, Earl Taylor continued playing well into the mid-1970's.

Discography:
1959 - **Folk Songs from the Bluegrass,** *United Artists* // 1963 - **Bluegrass Taylor-Made,** *Capitol* // 1968 - **Bluegrass Favorites,** *Rural Rhythm* // 1971 - **Bluegrass Favorites, Vol. 2&3,** *Rural Rhythm* // 1974 - **The Bluegrass Touch,** *Vetco* // 1976 - **Body and Soul,** *Vetco.*

Taylor, Greg "Fingers"

June 3, 1952 - Wichita, Kansas

Blues / Rock harmonica player

Greg "Fingers" Taylor began playing piano at the age of eight and was playing in Rock bands by the time he was thirteen. Later picking up the harmonica, he moved to Mississippi, where he made the acquaintance of "Mississippi" Fred McDowell and other Blues musicians. It was while attending the University of Southern Mississippi that he first played with up and coming musician Jimmy Buffett.

Taylor was an active member of Jimmy Buffett's Coral Reefer Band from 1974 to 2000. He has also worked with *The Eagles,* Emmylou Harris, Jimmy Hall, Sam Lay, Little Milton, Jerry Jeff Walker, James Taylor and others as well as recording several albums as a solo artist.

Discography:
1992 - **New Fingerprints,** *Appaloosa* // 1996 - **Harpoon Man,** *Appaloosa* // 1997 - **Old Rock 'n' Roller,** *Ripete* // 1998 - **Hotel Maids, Highways & Honky Tonks,** *Monkeybeat* // 2000 - **Real Good Time: The Blues Side of Greg "Fingers" Taylor** // 2000 - **Back To the Blues,** *Monkeybeat* // **Chest Pains,** *MCA.*

Taylor, "Little" Johnny

Born: February 11, 1943 - Memphis, TN

Gospel / Blues singer, harmonica player

Often confused with a fellow Gospel artist who also goes by the same name, "Little" Johnny Taylor has been singing Gospel music since the early 1950's, in addition to performing with other Blues artists, including Johnny Otis. Taylor also plays the harmonica.

Discography:
1963 - **Little Johnny Taylor,** *Galaxy* // 1970 - **Everybody Knows My Good Thing,** *Ronn* // 1973 - **Open House,** *Ronn* // 1974 - **Super Taylors,** *Ronn* // 1979 - **Little Johnny Taylor,** *Ronn* // 1980 - **As Long as I Don't See You,** *Charly* // 1981 - **I Should Been a Preacher,** *Red Lightning'* // 1988 - **Stuck in the Mud,** *Ichiban* // 1988 - **Part Time Love,** *Ace* // 1989 - **Ugly Man,** *Ichiban* // 1997 - **You're Looking Good,** *Nasha* // **Galaxy Years,** *Ace* // **Greatest Hits,** *Fantasy.*

Tcherepnin, Alexander

Born: January 20, 1899 - St. Petersburg, Russia
Died: September 29, 1977 - Paris, France

Classical composer

Alexander Tcherepnin wrote "Concerto for Harmonica and Orchestra" in 1953 for John Sebastian, Sr.

Available recordings:
Harmonica and Saxophone Concertos By Villa-Lobos, Et Al, *Urania.*

Terry, Doc

Born: 1921 - Sunflower, MS

Blues harmonica player

Doc Terry began playing the harmonica during the early 1930's.

After serving in the U.S. Army during World War Two, he returned to the East St. Louis area to play in the local Blues scene. He recorded on his own DTP label in the early 1970's.

Terry, Sonny

Real name: Saunders Terrell
Born: October 24, 1911 - Greensboro, GA
Died: March 11, 1986 - Mineola, NY

Blues singer, harmonica player

One of the greatest of the Country/Blues harmonica players, Sonny Terry's career spanned over five decades and influenced a generation of harmonica players that followed him. After learning how to play the harmonica from his father and heavily influenced by the playing of Deford Bailey, Sonny played the instrument in earnest after losing the sight in both eyes in two separate childhood accidents.

His career started as a street performer in North Carolina when he was eighteen years old. He moved to Durham, N.C., where he teamed up with Blind Boy Fuller and in 1938 they began recording together. The recordings were heard by John Hammond, who brought Sonny up to New York City to perform at his "Spirituals To Swing" concert.

When Fuller died in 1940, Sonny teamed up with Blues guitarist Brownie McGhee. They came to New York City and roomed with Leadbelly, who introduced them to Woody Guthrie. They teamed up together for awhile as *The Headline Singers*. During the 1940's Terry recorded with Guthrie, McGhee, Cisco Houston, Buddy Moss and Champion Jack Dupree as well as playing harmonica in the Broadway production of "Finian's Rainbow."

From the 1950's on he worked as a duo with Brownie McGhee, performing and recording regularly. The two were even part of the Broadway production of "Cat on a Hot Tin Roof."

In the 1960's, the pair began working in movies beginning in 1963 with a concert appearance in the movie "Festival." The team of Sonny Terry and Brownie McGhee would stay together until just before Terry died in 1986, although the two never did get along personally.

Discography:
1952 - **Climbin' Up**, *Savoy* // 1958 - **Harmonica and Vocal Solos** // 1958 - **Sonny Terry's New Sound**, *Smithsonian* // 1958 - **Brownie McGhee and Sonny Terry**, *Smithsonian* // 1958 - **Sing**, *Smithsonian/Folkways* // 1959 - **On the Road** // 1960 - **Just a Closer Walk with Thee**, *Original Blues Classics* // 1960 - **Blues in a Story**, *World Pacific* // 1960 - **Back To New Orleans**, *Fantasy* // 1960 - **Sonny's Story**, *Original Blues Classics* // 1961 - **Brownie's Blues**, *Original Blues Classics* // 1961 - **Sonny and Brownie at Sugar Hill**, *Original Blues Classics* // 1961 - **Down Home Blues**, *Sharp* // 1961 - **Hootin' and Hollerin'**, *Choice* // 1961 - **The Sound of America**, *Choice* // 1961 - **Work Songs Play Songs**, *Choice*

// 1962 - **Blues All Round My Head**, *Bluesville* // 1963 - **Blues in My Soul**, *Bluesville* // 1963 - **Sonny Terry and Lightnin' Hopkins**, *Bluesville* // 1963 - **Get Togeteher**, *Verve* // 1963 - **Guitar Highway**, *Verve* // 1963 - **Washboard Band Country Dance Music** // 1963 - **Live at the Second Fret**, *Bluesville* // 1963 - **Sonny is King**, *Original Blues Classics* // 1965 - **Lightnin', Sonny & Brownie**, *Society* // 1965 - **At the Bunkhouse**, *Smash* // 1966 - **Blues is My Companion**, *Verve* // 1969 - **In London**, *Marble Arch* // 1969 - **Long Way From Home**, *Bluesway* // 1969 - **Sonny Terry and Woodie Guthrie**, *Ember* // 1969 - **Where the Blues Began**, *Fontana* // 1972 - **Shouts and Blues**, *America* // 1973 - **I Couldn't Believe My Eyes**, *See for Miles* // 1974 - **Hometown Blues**, *Mainstream* // 1976 - **Black Night Road**, *Tomato* // 1976 - **Chain Gang Blues**, *Collectables* // 1976 - **Sonny Terry's Washboard Band**, *Smithsonian* // 1978 - **Midnight Special**, *Fantasy* // 1984 - **Whoopin'**, *Alligator* // 1986 - **Old Town Blues, Vol. 1** // 1987 - **Toughest Terry and Baddest Brown** // 1987 - **Sonny Terry**, *Collectables* // 1987 - **Blowin' the Fuses: Golden Classics**, *Collectables* // 1989 - **Sonny and Brownie**, *A&M/Mobile Fidelity* // 1990 - **California Blues**, *Fantasy* // 1991 - **Sonny Terry and Brownie McGhee**, *Original Blues Classics* // 1991 - **The Folkways Years, 1944-63**, *Smithsonian/Folkways* // 1994 - **Po' Boys**, *Drive Archive* // 1994 - **The 1958 London Sessions**, *Collectables* // 1994 - **Sonny Terry / Brownie McGhee / Big Bill Broonzy**, *Castle* // 1995 - **Conversation with the River**, *World Network* // 1995 - **Sonny Terry**, *Capitol* // 1995 - **Whoopin' the Blues: The Capitol Recordings, 1947-1950**, *Capitol* // 1995 - **Wizard of the Harmonica**, *Storyville* // 1996 - **The Original**, *Collector's* // 1997 - **Going It Alone**, *Blues Alliance* // 1998 - **Live at the Penelope Café**, *Just a Memory* // 1999 - **Backwater Blues**, *Fantasy* // 1999 - **Real Blues**, *Emporio* // 2000 - **Shake Down**, *Catfish* // 2000 - **Absolutely the Best**, *Fuel 2000* // 2000 - **Complete Recorded Works, 1938-1955**, *Document* // **1944-55**, *Travelin' Man* // **The Complete Brownie McGhee**, *Columbia/Legacy* // **Blues Masters, Vol. 5**, *Storyville* // **Mr. Brownie and Mr. Terry: The Bluesville Years**, *Prestige* // **Sonny Terry and his Mouth Organ**, *Stinson*.

Movies:
1963 - **Festival** // 1969 - **Whoopin' the Blues** // 1971 - **Cisco Pike** // 1972 - **Playing the Thing** // 1972 - **Buck and the Preacher** // 1972 - **Book of Numbers** // 1973 - **Blues for a Black Film** // 1975 - **Sincerely the Blues** // 1976 - **Leadbelly** // 1979 - **The Jerk** // 1986 - **Crossroads** // 1997 - **Red River Blues**, (video), *Vestapol* // 1997 - **Whoopin' the Blues**, (video), *Vestapol*.

Bibliography:
1975 - **Harp Styles of Sonny Terry by Kent Cooper and Fred Palmer** - *Oak Publications* // 1995 - **A Source Book for Sonny Terry Licks by Tom Ball** - *Hal Leonard Publishing*.

Thacker, George

Bluegrass harmonica player

George Thacker is a Bluegrass harmonica player who began playing at age thirteen and has appeared at the Grand Old Opry.

Discography:

1996 - **Blazing a New Trail,** *Pinecastle.*

Thei, W.

Harmonica manufacturer

W. Thei of Vienna was an early manufacturer of harmonicas from the 1830's to the 1880's.

Them

Formed: 1963 - Belfast, Ireland
Disbanded: 1966

Irish Rock band

Them was one of the few Irish bands to take part in the British Invasion of the early 1960's. They scored hits with songs like "Gloria," "Here Comes the Night" and others. They were led by Van Morrison who sang and played harmonica.

See - Van Morrison

Discography:

1965 - **Angry Young Them,** *Decca //* 1965 - **Them,** *Decca //* 1965 - **Here Comes the Night,** *Parrot //* 1966 - **Them Again,** *Decca //* 1972 - **Them,** *Decca //* 1977 - **The Story of Them,** *London //* 1998 - **The Story of Them Featuring Van Morrison,** *Deram / Polygram.*

Thielemans, Jean "Toots"

Born: April 29, 1922 - Brussels, Belgium

Jazz guitar, harmonica player

One of the greatest of the jazz harmonica players, Jean "Toots" Thielemans began playing the harmonica at age seventeen after seeing Larry Adler play in a movie. He also took up the guitar at age twenty.

He came to America on vacation in 1947. While playing at a Jazz jam session in New York City, he was heard by agent Billy Shaw. Toots sent Shaw some demos which Shaw played for Benny Goodman. Goodman hired Thielemans to play with him on a European tour in 1950.

Thielemans moved to America permanently in 1951 and played with Dinah Washington and Charlie Parker. He joined *The George Shearing Quintet* in 1952. He has been recording and performing heavily ever since. Over the course of his career he has performed with Peggy Lee, Ella Fitzgerald, Quincy Jones, Billy Joel, Julian Lennon, Bill Evans, Oscar Peterson and dozens of others. He has also done an extensive amount of Hollywood soundtrack work.

Discography:

1955 - **The Sound,** *Columbia //* 1957 - **Man Bites Harmonica,** *Original Jazz Classics //* 1958 - **On Stage,** (with George Shearing) // 1958 - **Toots Thielemans and his Orchestra //** 1958 - **Time Out for Toots,** *Decca //* 1959 - **The Toots Thielemans Quartet //** 1959 - **The Soul of Toots Thielemans,** *Doctor Jazz //* 1960 - **Toots Thielemans with Kurt Edelhagen and his Orchestra //** 1961 - **The Toots Thielemans Trio //** 1961 - **Toots Thielemans and Arne Domnerus //** 1962 - **Toots Thielemans and Dick Hyman //** 1962 - **The Whistler and his Guitar,** *ABC //* 1965 - **Toots Thielemans,** *Paramount //* 1967 - **Contrasts,** *Command //* 1968 - **Toots Thielemans with Herbie Hancock //** 1969 - **Toots Thielemans with Orchestra //** 1970 - **A Taste of Toots //** 1972 - **Toots and Svend,** *Sonet //* 1974 - Live, *Polydor //* 1974 - **The Silver Collection,** *Verve //* 1974 - **Images,** *Candid //* 1974 - **Captured Live,** *Choice //* 1974 - **Toots Thielemans and Friends //** 1974 - **Toots Thielemans Captured Alive,** *Polydor //* 1975 - **The Oscar Peterson Big Six At Montreux //** 1975 - **Live Two,** *Inner City //* 1976 - **Old Friends //** 1976 - **Live Three //** 1979 - **Slow Motion //** 1980 - **Dizzy Gillespie At Montreux //** 1980 - **A Jazz Hour with...Toots Thielemans,** *Airegin //* 1980 - **Live in the Netherlands,** *Pablo //* 1981 - **Jean "Toots" Thielemans Live! //** 1981 - **Nice to Meet You //** 1984 - **Autumn Leaves,** *Soul Note //* 1985 - **Chiko's Bar //** 1985 - **Your Precious Love //** 1986 - **Just Friends,** *Jazzline //* 1986 - **Do Not Leave Me,** *Stash/Milan //* 1987 - **Apple Dimple,** *Denon //* 1987 - **Aquarela Do Brazil,** *Verve //* 1988 - **Trust Your Heart,** *Concord Jazz //* 1989 - **Footprints,** *EmArcy //* 1989 - **In Tokyo,** *Denon //* 1991 - **For My Lady,** *EmArcy //* 1992 - **The Brazil Project,** *Private Music //* 1993 -

The Brazil Project, Volume 2, *Private Music* // 1933 - **Martial Solal,** *Erato* // 1994 - **East Coast, West Coast,** *Private Music* // 1994 - **Harmonica Jazz,** *Tristar* // 1995 - **Bringing it Together,** (with Stephane Grappelli), *Cymekob* // 1995 - **Concerto for Harmonica,** *TCB* // 1996 - **Two Generations,** *Limetree* // 1996 - **Verve Jazz Masters 59,** *Verve* // 1998 - **Chez Toots,** *Private Music* // 2000 - **Toots Thielemans,** *Giants of Jazz* // 2000 - **The Live Takes, Vol. 1,** *Narada* // **Yesterday & Today,** *Gazell* // **Personalidade,** *Verve* // **Guitars and Strings and Things,** *Command.*

Movies:
1964 - **The Pawnbroker** // 1969 - **Midnight Cowboy** // 1971 - **The Anderson Tapes** // 1971 - **Brother John** // 1972 - **The Getaway** // 1973 - **Cinderella Liberty** // 1974 - **Sugarland Express** // 1978 - **The Wiz** // 1990 - **Funny About Love** // 1995 - **French Kiss** // TV - **Sesame Street.**

Thomas, Henry "Ragtime Texas"

Born 1874 - Big Sandy, TX

Blues singer, guitar, quills, harmonica player
Henry "Ragtime Texas" Thomas was one of the earliest known Blues musicians. Virtually nothing is known about his personal life or his music except for a handful of recordings he did for the Vocalion label in 1927. These included songs like "Fishin' Blues," "Don't Ease Me In," later covered by *The Grateful Dead* and "Bulldoze Blues," the latter was covered almost note-for-note by the band *Canned Heat* as "Going Up the Country."

In addition to guitar and panpipes, (also known as "quills"), Thomas could also play the harmonica, although he never recorded with it.

Discography:
1989 - **Texas Worried Blues,** *Yazoo* // 1991 - **Sings the Texas Blues,** *Origin* // 2000 - **Complete Recorded Works,** *Document.*

Kid Thomas - (see Lou Watts)

Thomas, Ray

Born: December 29, 1941 - Worchestershire, England

Rock singer, bass, flute, harmonica player
Ray Thomas was one of the original members of *The Moody Blues*, dating back to when the band was an R&B band as part of the British Invasion. He occasionally contributed harmonica as well as bass guitar, flute and vocals. Thomas also recorded with Sleepy John Estes and *The Graeme Edge Band.*

Discography: (also see - The Moody Blues)
1975 - **From Mighty Oaks,** *Polydor* // 1976 - **Hopes, Wishes and Dreams,** *Threshold.*

Thompson, Ernest

Born: 1892 - Forsyth County NC
Died: 1961

Country singer, guitar, harmonica player
Like fellow North Carolinian Sonny Terry, Ernest Thompson lost his sight as a teenager. He took up music and played for tips on the streets of Winston-Salem and other local towns as well as performing at local dances and schools. Thompson recorded 34 sides for the Columbia label in 1924.

Thompson, Hank

Born: September 3, 1925 - Waco, TX

Country singer-songwriter, guitar, harmonica
Hank Thompson learned how to play the harmonica as a child while growing up in Texas. After winning several talent contests as a teenager, he switched to guitar after seeing Gene Autry.

He began performing on the radio in 1942, but soon joined the Navy for the duration of World War Two. After the war he went to Princeton and the University of Texas, but was back to working on the radio in 1947. He started recording for Capitol Records in 1948 and had records on the charts almost every year from 1952 to 1982. He is still active to this day.

Discography:
1953 - **Songs of the Brazos Valley,** *Capitol* // 1955 - **North of the Rio Grande,** *Capitol* // 1956 - **New Recordings of All Time Hits,** *Capitol* // 1956 - **Favorite Waltzes,** *Capitol* // 1957 - **Hank Thompson Favorites** // 1957 - **Hank!,** *Capitol* // 1958 - **Dance Ranch,** *Capitol* // 1959 - **Songs for Rounders,** *Capitol* // 1960 - **Most of All,** *Capitol* // 1960 - **This Broken Heart of Mine,** *Capitol* // 1961 - **An Old Love Affair,** *Capitol* // 1961 - **At the Golden Nugget,** *Capitol* // 1961 - **A Six Pack To Go,** *Dot* // 1962 - **No. 1 Country and Western Band,** *Capitol* // 1962 - **Live at the Cherokee Frontier Days in Wyoming,** *Capitol* // 1963 - **Live at the State Fair of Texas,** *Capitol* // 1964 - **It's Christmas Time with Hank,** *Capitol* // 1965 - **Breakin' in Another Heart,** *Capitol* // 1965 - **The Luckiest Heartache in Town,** *Capitol* // 1966 - **Breakin' the Rules,** *Capitol* // 1966 - **Where is the Circus** (and Other Heart Breakin' Hits) // 1967 - **A Gold Standard Collection** // 1967 - **The Countrypolitan Sound of Hank Thompson's Brazos Valley Boys,** *Warner Brothers* // 1967 - **Just an Old Flame,** *Capitol* // 1968 - **Country Blues** // 1968 - **Hank Thompson Sings the Gold Standards** // 1968 - **On Tap, In the Can or in the Bottle,** *Dot* // 1968 - **Country Blues,** *Tower* // 1969 - **Smokey the Bar,** *Dot* // 1969 - **Salutes Oklahoma,** *Dot* // 1970 - **The Instrumental Sound of Hank Thompson's Brazos Valley Boys** // 1971 - **Next Time I Fall in Love, (I Won't),** *Dot* // 1972 - **25th Anniversary Album** // 1972 - **Cab Driver: A Salute to the Mills Brothers,** *Dot* // 1973

- **1000 and One Nighters,** *Churchill* // 1973 - **Kindly Keep It Country,** *Dot* // 1974 - **Movin' On** // 1975 - **Hank Thompson Sings the Hits of Nat King Cole** // 1976 - **Back in the Swing of Things** // 1977 - **The Thompson Touch** // 1977 - **Country Comes to Carnegie Hall** // 1977 - **Doin' My Thing** // 1978 - **Brand New Hank** // 1980 - **The Best of the Best Of...,** *Gusto* // 1980 - **Take Me Back To Texas,** *MCA* // 1986 - **Hank Thompson** // 1987 - **Greatest Hits, Volumes 1&2,** *Step One* // 1988 - **Here's to Country Music,** *Step One* // 1996 - **The Best of Hank Thompson: 1966-79,** *Varese* // 1996 - **Vintage,** *Capitol* // 1996 - **Hank Thompson and his Brazos Valley Boys,** *Bear Family* // 1997 - **Real Thing,** *Curb* // 1998 - **Sounds of the Brazos Valley,** *Bear Valley* // 1999 - **Hankworld: the Unissued World Transcriptions,** *Bloodshot* // 1999 - **Country Music Hall of Fame 1989,** *King* // 2000 - **Seven Decades,** *Hightone.*

Thompson, Les
Jazz harmonica player
Les Thompson is a Jazz harmonica player who has worked with Al Jarraeu, Tom Waits, *Hall and Oates* and Jaye P. Morgan.

Discography:
1952 - **Gene Norman Presents "Just Jazz,"** *RCA* // 1953 - **Les Thompson,** *Victor.*

Thornbury, James
Blues singer, guitar, harmonica player

James Thornbury played harmonica with the group *Canned Heat* from 1984 until 1987.

Discography: (see - Canned Heat)

Thornton, "Big Mama" Willie Mae
Born: December 11, 1926 - Montgomery, AL
Died: July 25, 1984 - Los Angeles, CA

Blues singer, harmonica player
Known mostly as a Blues singer, "Big Mama" Willie Mae Thornton began her musical career during the late 1930's. She began recording for the E&W label in 1951. Among her hits were "Hound Dog," which was a huge hit for Elvis Presley and "Ball and Chain," which was covered by Janis Joplin.

Occasionally playing the harmonica, she performed and recorded with James Cotton, Muddy Waters, Junior Parker, Johnny Otis, George "Harmonica" Smith, Walter Horton and a host of others. She remained active until her death in 1984.

Discography:
1966 - **In Europe,** *Arhoolie* // 1967 - **Chicago Blues,** *Arhoolie* // 1967 - **Big Mama the Queen At Monterey,** *MCA* // 1968 - **Ball and Chain,** *Arhoolie* // 1969 - **Stronger Than Dirt,** *Mercury* // 1970 - **Maybe,** *Roulette* // 1970 - **The Way it Is,** *Mercury* // 1971 - **She's Back,** *Backbeat* // 1973 - **Saved,** *Pentagram* // 1975 - **Jail,** *Vanguard* // 1975 - **Sassy Mama,** *Vanguard* // 1978 - **Mama's Pride,** *Vanguard* // 1990 - **The Original Hound Dog,** *Ace* // 1991 - **They Call Me Big Mama,** *MCA* // 1992 - **Hound Dog: the Peacock Recordings,** *MCA* // 1994 - **The Rising Sun Collection,** *Just a Memory* // 2000 - **The Complete Vanguard Recordings,** *Vanguard* // **Quit Snoopin' Round My Door,** *Ace* // **Big Mama with the Chicago Blues Band,** *Arhoolie.*

The Three Harpers
Formed: Late 1930's

Vaudeville harmonica band
The Three Harpers were a harmonica trio that performed in Vaudeville from the mid-1930's until sometime after World War Two. They were formed by Stan Harper, who played the lead chromatic harmonica and also included Pro Robbins on the bass harmonica and Pete Delisante on the chord harmonica.

Timbuk 3
Formed: 1984 - Madison, WI
Disbanded: 1995

New-Wave duo
Formed by the husband and wife team of Pat and Barbara K. McDonald, *Timbuk 3* used the unusual gimmick of performing as duet accompanied by the pre-taped rhythm section played on a boom box. Originally teaming up in Madison, Wisconsin and eventually settling in Austin, Texas, the pair had several hits from their first album, "Greetings From Timbuk 3," including "The Future's So Bright."

Both of them played the harmonica as well as guitar and other instruments.

See - Barbara K. McDonald, Pat McDonald

Discography:
1986 - **Greetings From Timbuk 3**, *IRS* // 1988 - **Eden Alley**, *IRS* // 1989 - **Edge of Alliance**, *IRS* // 1991 - **Big Shot in the Dark**, *IRS* // 1992 - **The Best Of...**, *IRS* // 1993 - **Espace Orano**, *Watermelon* // 1995 - **A Hundred Lovers**, *High Street* // 1995 - **Back To Back**, *EMI-Capitol*.

Tin Sandwich

A nickname for the harmonica.

Tippin, Aaron

Born: July 3, 1958 - Pensacola, FL

Country singer-songwriter, guitar, harmonica
Aaron Tippin began playing music at age ten and was performing professionally by the mid-1980's. He began recording for the RCA label in 1990. In addition to being an accomplished singer-songwriter, he also plays the guitar and harmonica.

Discography:
1990 - **You've Got To Stand for Something**, *RCA* // 1992 - **Read Between the Lines**, *RCA* // 1993 - **Call of the Wild**, *RCA* // 1994 - **Lookin' Back at Myself**, *RCA* // 1995 - **Tool Box**, *RCA* // 1997 - **Greatest Hits and Then Some**, *RCA* // 1998 - **What This Country Needs**, *Hollywood* // 1998 - **Super Hits**, *RCA* // 1998 - **The Essential**, *RCA* // 2000 - **People Like Us**, *Lyric Street*.

The Tombo Harmonica Co.

Harmonica manufacturer
Located in Tokyo, Japan, the Tombo Harmonica Company has been manufacturing harmonicas for over 80 years. In 1984 they started building harmonicas for the Lee Oskar Company.

Tongue Blocking

Tongue blocking is the technique where the player uses their tongue in addition to their lips to block out the hole that they wish to play. One big advantage to playing this way is that the player has the ability to switch their tongue to various positions in the hole that is formed by the lips, thereby giving the player the chance to switch right, left or in the center and split the airflow in and out of the instrument.

Also see - Blocking

Tremolo Tuning

These are diatonic harmonicas built with a double set of reeds, slightly detuned, to produce a tremolo or wavering tone effect.

Troynan, "Bashful Harmonica" Joe

Born: March 25, 1913 - Pleasant City, OH

Country harmonica player

Bashful Harmonica Joe Troynan worked as the musical partner of Pie Plant Pete from 1936 until 1947.

Discography:
1989 - **The Old Time Country Music Collection**, *Cattle Country*.

Turk, Mike

Born: July 28, 1951 - The Bronx, NY

Blues / Jazz harmonica player

Mike Turk began playing the harmonica in his early teens while growing up in the Bronx. Equally adept at both diatonic and chromatic instruments, he has forged a name for himself, recording several solo albums and doing movie soundtracks. He has also performed and recorded with *The Temptations*, Jerry Lee Lewis, Marvin Hamlisch, Van Dyke Parks, *The Boston Jazz Ensemble* and others.

Discography:
1974 - **Bears Taste Fine**, *Mill City* // 1992 - **Harmonica Salad**, *Tin Sandwich* // 1996 - **Turk's Works**, *Tin Sandwich* // 1999 - **A Little Taste of Cannonball**, *Organic*.

Movies:
1990 - **Dick Tracy** // 1991 - **City of Hope** // 1996 - **Lonestar**.

Tyler, Steven

Born: March 26, 1948 - New York City, NY

Rock singer, harmonica player
As the lead singer for the Rock band *Aerosmith*, Steven Tyler occasionally plays the harmonica.

Discography: (see - Aerosmith)

U2

Formed: 1978 -Dublin, Ireland

Rock Band

U2 is an Irish Rock band that has been a leader in the alternative music scene since the 1980's. The lead singer, Bono, also plays the harmonica on stage and in the studio

See - Bono

<u>Discography:</u>

1980 - Boy, *Island* // 1981 - **October,** *Island* // 1983 - **War,** *Island* // 1983 - **Under a Blood Red Sky,** *Island* // 1984 - **Unforgettable Fire,** *Island* // 1985 - **Wide Awake in America,** *Island* // 1987 - **Joshua Tree,** *Island* // 1988 - **Rattle and Hum,** *Island* // 1991 - **Achtung Baby,** *Island* // 1993 - **Zooropa,** *Island* // 1997 - **Pop,** *Island* // 1998 - **Best of 1980-1990 / B Sides,** *Polygram* // 2000 - **All That You Can't Leave Behind,** *Polygram.*

<u>Movies:</u>

1980 - **Rattle and Hum.**

Uncle Henry's Original Kentucky Mountaineers

Formed: 1928 - Louisville, KY
Disbanded: 1952

Country string band

One of the more popular bands to emerge from Louisville, Kentucky in the 1920's and 30's, *Uncle Henry's Original Kentucky Mountaineers* blended string band music with comedy. During the 1930's the group featured Curly Bradshaw on the harmonica.

See - Curly Bradshaw

Uncle Tupelo

Formed: 1987 - Belleville, IL
Disbanded: 1993

Alternative Country / Rock band

Co-founded by songwriters Jay Farrar and Jeff Tweedy, *Uncle Tupelo* was one of the bands that pioneered the resurgence of Country/Rock in the late 1980's and early 90's. The group featured Jay Farrar playing the guitar, mandolin and the harmonica.

See - Jay Farrar

<u>Discography:</u>

1990 - **No Depression,** *Rockville* // 1991 - **Still Feel Gone,** *Rockville* // 1992 - **March 16-20, 1992,** *Rockville* // 1993 - **Anodyne,** *Sire.*

U.S. Presidents

There have been at least seven U.S. Presidents who are known to have played the harmonica. They are:

<u>Abraham Lincoln</u> (1809-1865) According to Carl Sandburg's biography, Lincoln played the harmonica at one of his debates with Stephen Douglass.

<u>Theodore Roosevelt</u> (1858-1919) In addition to leading the Rough Riders during the Spanish-American War and winning the Nobel Peace Prize, Teddy Roosevelt also enjoyed playing the harmonica.

<u>Woodrow Wilson</u> (1856-1924) Usually perceived as something of a highbrow, Woodrow Wilson was a harmonica enthusiast.

<u>Warren G. Harding</u> (1865-1923) During his short administration Warren G. Harding kept a collection of harmonicas in the White House.

<u>Calvin Coolidge</u> (1872 - 1933) "Silent" Calvin Coolidge is said to have entertained White House visitors with his harmonica playing.

<u>Dwight D. Eisenhower</u> (1890-1969) The winning general of World War Two, Dwight D. Eisenhower was also a harmonica player.

<u>Ronald Reagan</u> (1911-) The great communicator learned to play "Red River Valley" on the harmonica while recuperating from his assassination attempt in 1981.

Valves (see - Windsavers)

Vaughan-Williams, Ralph

Born: October 12, 1872 - Down Ampney, England
Died: August 26, 1958 - London, England

Classical Composer

Ralph Vaughan-Williams composed "Romance for Harmonica, Strings and Piano in D Flat" for Larry Adler in 1951.

<u>Recordings:</u>

1977 - **Vaughan-Williams, Tausky, Moody, Jacob,** (Tommy Reilly - soloist), *Chandos* // 1994 - **Romances,** (Robert Bonfiglio - soloist), *High Harmony* // 1999 - **Fantasia on Greensleeves,** *Decca* // **Vaughan-Williams: Greensleeves, Folk Song Suite, Etc.,** (Tommy Reilly - soloist), *London.*

Verwey, Jan

Born: July 24, 1936 - Vlissingen, the Netherlands

Jazz harmonica player
Jan Verwey is a Jazz harmonica player from the Netherlands who has worked with Bill Goodwin, Denise Jannah, Colette Wickenhagen and others as well as recording several albums of his own.

Discography:
1982 - **Watch What Happens** // 1986 - **Golden Collection** // 1990 - **The Dutch Collection** / 1992 - **You Must Believe in Spring, Timeless** // 1996 - **The Miles Davis Project,** *Wilibrod Jazz.*

Vibrato

Vibrato is a regular oscillating of the volume or tone of the harmonica. This can be achieved by a number of methods including moving the hands to control the volume, opening and constricting the throat or by moving the tongue inside the mouth while playing. Vibrato can greatly enhance the expressive quality of the harmonica.

Villa-Lobos, Heitor

Born: March 5, 1887 - Rio de Janeiro, Brazil
Died: November 17, 1959 - Rio de Janeiro, Brazil

Classical Composer
Heitor Villa-Lobos wrote "Concerto for Harmonica, W. 524" in 1956 for John Sebastian, Sr.

Recording Availability:
1988 - **Bonfiglio Performs Villa-Lobos: Bachianas Brasileiras No. 5,** *RCA* // 1989 - **Harmonica and Saxophone Concertos By Villa-Lobos, Et Al,** (John Sebastian - soloist), *Urania* // 1994 - **Tommy Reilly Plays Harmonica Concertos,** (Tommy Reilly - soloist), *Chandos.*

Vincent, Monroe

Also known as: Polka Dot Slim, Mr. Calhoun
Born: December 9, 1919 - Woodville, MS
Died: 1982

Blues singer, drums, harmonica player
Monroe Vincent played the harmonica from his early childhood and began playing professionally after serving in the U.S. Army during World War Two. After settling in New Orleans around 1954, he worked as a street musician for tips. Then he moved to Baton Rouge in 1958 where he occasionally worked with Blues guitarist Lightnin' Slim.

He began recording for a variety of labels using several different names including Vince Monroe, Mr. Calhoun and Polka Dot Slim in the late 1950's and early 60's. He moved to the west coast in the 1970's.

Discography:
1976 - **Gonna Head for Home // Real Blues from New Orleans,** *Bandy.*

Vint, Mo

Pop / Vaudeville harmonica player
Mo Vint worked in a duet with former *Harmonicat* Don Les, playing chord harmonica and foot pedal bass until Les' death in 1995. He was also a part of *The Reeds* harmonica band, which featured Bernie Bray. Vint continues to perform as a solo artist.

Discography: (also see - Don Les, Bernie Bray)
Mo Vint Does Big Band // Mo Goes Country // Mo Swings // Just Me // Mo Sings the Oldies.

Von Schmidt, Eric

Born: May 29, 1930 - Westport, CT

Folk singer-songwriter, guitar, harmonica player
Eric Von Schmidt began working as a Folk/Blues singer-songwriter during the late 1950's. He was active in the Folk music scene that prospered at that time in Cambridge, Massachusetts. He also served as an early influence on Bob Dylan, who was making his start on the East coast during the early 60's.

He was fairly inactive as a musician from the 1970's until the mid-1990's, although he did write a comprehensive history of the Cambridge music scene that was published in the late 1970's. He sometimes works with Paul Geremia on guitar and harmonica.

Discography:
1961 - **Rolf Cahn and Eric Von Schmidt,** *Folkways* // 1964 - **Folk Blues,** *Folkways* // 1965 - **Eric Von Schmidt Sings,** *Folkways* // 1970 - **Who Knocked the Brains Out of the Sky?,** *Smash/Mercury* // 1972 - **Second Right Third Row,** *Polydor* // 1977 - **The Cruel Family,** *Philo* // 1995 - **Baby, Let Me Lay it on You,** *Gazell.*

Bibliography:
1979 - **Baby Let Me Follow You Down,** *AnchorPress/Doubleday.*

Wakefield, Frank

Born: June 26, 1934 - Emery Gap, TN

Country multi-instrumentalist, including harmonica

Frank Wakefield began playing harmonica at age 6 and was performing professionally by the time he was 16. Known primarily as a mandolin player, (He taught David Grisman,) he also wrote the song "Different Drum" which became Linda Ronstadt's first big hit.

Discography:

1964 - **Red Allen and Frank Wakefield - Bluegrass,** *Folkways* // 1971 - **The Frank Wakefield Band,** *Rounder* // 1974 - **Pistol Packin' Mama,** *Round* // 1978 - **Frank Wakefield and The Good Ol' Boys,** *Flying Fish* // 1993 - **She's No Angel,** *Relix* // 1993 - **Frank Wakefield and Dave Nelson and The Good Old Boys,** *Grateful Dead* // 1994 - **Kitchen Tapes,** *Acoustic Discs* // **Blues Stay Away from Me,** *Takoma* // **Frank Wakefield,** *Flying Fish* // **Frank Wakefield with Country Cooking,** *Rounder.*

Wakely, Jimmy

Real name: James Clarence Wakely
Born: February 16, 1914 - Mineola, AR
Died: September, 23, 1982 - Mission Hills, CA

Country multi-instrumentalist including harmonica

Jimmy Wakely worked throughout his early adulthood as a part-time musician in the Oklahoma City area. Afteroving to California in 1940, he worked on Gene Autry's "Melody ranch" radio show and began cutting records almost immediately thereafter.

Wakely started doing movies during the 1940's, mostly as a singing cowboy. He had a string of hits from the mid-1940's through the mid-1950's, including "Bushel and a Peck," a duet he recorded with Margaret Whiting.

He continued recording and performing through the 1970's.

Discography:

1954 - **Christmas on the Range,** *Capitol* // 1954 - **Songs of the West,** *Capitol* // 1956 - **Santa Fe Trail,** *Decca* // 1957 - **Enter Rest and Pray,** *Decca* // 1959 - **Country Million Sellers,** *Shasta* // 1959 - **Merry Christmas,** *Shasta* // 1960's - **Lonesome Star Guitar Man** // 1960 - **Jimmy Wakely Sings,** *Shasta* // 1966 - **Slipping Around,** *Dot* // 1966 - **Christmas with Jimmy Wakely,** *Dot* // 1967 - **I'll Never Slip Around Again,** *Pickwick/Hilltop* // 1968 - **Show Me the Way** // 1969 - **Here's Jimmy Wakely,** *Vocalion* // 1969 - **Heart Aches,** *Decca* // 1969 - **A Cowboy Serenade,** *Tops* // 1970 - **Now and Then,** *Decca* // 1970 - **Big Country Songs,** *Vocalion* // 1971 - **Jimmy Wakely Country,** *Shasta* // 1973 - **Blue Shadows,** *Coral* // 1973 - **Jimmy Wakely Family Show,** *Shasta* // 1974 - **Jimmy Wakely On Stage,** *Shasta* // 1974 - **The Wakely Way with Country Hits** // 1975 - **The Gentle Touch** // 1975 - **The Jimmy Wakely CBS Radio Show,** *Shasta* // 1975 - **The Singing Cowboy,** *Shasta* // 1975 - **Western Swing and Pretty Things,** *Shasta* // 1976 - **An Old Fashioned Christmas** // 1976 - **A Tribute to Bob Wills** // 1976 - **Precious Memories** // 1977 - **Moments to Remember** // 1977 - **Reflections** // 1980 - **The Early Transcriptions,** *Danny* // 1996 - **Beautiful Brown Eyes,** *Richmond* // 1998 - **Jimmy Wakely Collector's Edition,** *Simitar* // 2000 - **Christmas Collection,** *Varese* // 2000 - **The Very Best Of...,** *Varese* // **Four Walls,** *MCA* // **Vintage Collections,** *Capitol.*

Walden, John "White Boy"

Born: October 23, 1948 - London, England

Blues singer, harmonica player

John Walden has been playing the harmonica since he was eight years old. Since getting into the Blues at age thirteen, he has been playing professionally for over thirty years. He was a medal winner at the 1996 European Harmonica Festival.

Discography:

1997 - **John Walden's Blues Band,** *JWBB.*

Walker, Phillip

Born: February 11, 1937 - Welsh, LA

Blues guitar, piano, harmonica player

Known primarily as a guitar player, Phillip Walker began playing at the age of thirteen and was sitting in with local Bluesmen by the time he was fifteen. Around that time he started recording as a sideman and eventually worked with several of the early greats of Rock and Roll, including Lloyd Price, Fats Domino, Etta James, Jimmy Reed, Little Richard and a host of others.

He finally recorded on his own in the late 1960's and has maintained a steady career ever since.

Discography:

1973 - **Blues,** *Hightone* // 1977 - **Someday You'll Have These Blues,** *Hightone* // 1979 - **All Night Long They Play the Blues** // 1980 - **Blues Show Live from the Pit Inn,** *Ypuityeru* // 1982 - **From L.A. To L.A.,** *Rounder* // 1984 - **Tough as I Want to Be,** *Rounder* // 1990 - **Mr. Fulbright's Blues, Volume 1** // 1990 - **The Bottom of the Top,** *Hightone* // 1992 - **Big Blues from Texas,** *JSP* // 1995 - **Working Girl Blues,** *Black Top* // 1998 - **I Got a Sweet Tooth,** *Black Top.*

Wall, Chris

Born: Newport Beach, CA

Country singer-songwriter, guitar, harmonica player
From a musical family, Chris Wall has been a singer-songwriter since the mid-1980's. After being seen performing by Jerry Jeff Walker, he was signed to the Rykodisc label. Wall also plays guitar and harmonica.

Discography:
1991 - **No Sweat,** *Rykodisc* // 1991 - **Honky Tonk Heart,** *Rykodisc* // 1998 - **Tainted Angel,** *Cold Spring* // 1998 - **Any Saturday Night in Texas - Live,** *Cold Spring* // 1999 - **Cowboy Nation,** *Cold Spring.*

Little Walter - (see Walter Jacobs)

Walton, Wade

Born: October 10, 1923 - Lombardy, MS
Died: January 10, 2000 - Clarksdale, MS

Blues singer, guitar, harmonica player
Best known as a musical barber, Wade Walton cut the hair of some of the greatest Bluesmen in history from his barbershop in Clarksdale, Mississippi. Big John Wrencher died in Walton's chair and the bottle of whiskey that Big John was drinking at the time was enshrined in the shop for many years.

Walton is also a Bluesman in his own right. Beginning at age twelve he was singing and dancing with his brother in minstrel shows. During the 1940's and 50's he worked in *The Kings of Rhythm* with Ike Turner. He did some recording in the 1960's, appeared in several documentaries, but chose not to leave Clarksdale, thus limiting his career. He appeared at local Blues festivals and remained active at his barbershop until his death in 2000.

Discography:
1962 - **The Blues of Wade Walton: Shake 'em On Down,** *Bluesville.*

Movies:
1970 - **Blues Like Showers of Rain** // 1974 - **Mississippi Delta Blues** // **Give My Poor Heart Ease: Mississippi Delta Bluesmen.**

War

Formed: 1969 - Long Beach, CA

Latin Funk band
Originally known as *Nightshift, War* came into the musical spotlight when they were joined by ex-*Animals* lead singer, Eric Burdon and Danish harmonica player, Lee Oskar. After two albums, Burdon left and the group created a presence of it's own.

Together they created a distinctive Latin-Funk sound and had a number of hits, including "Low Rider," "Cisco Kid," "Why Can't We Be Friends," "Summer" and many more, all of which featured Oskar's distinctive harmonica playing.

Lee Oskar left the group during the late 1970's to pursue a solo career and to sell his own line of harmonicas. His place as the harmonica player has recently been taken over by Tetsuya "Tex" Nakamura, though Oskar occasionally sits in with the band.

See - Lee Oskar, Tetsuya Nakamura

Discography:
1970 - **Eric Burdon Declares War,** *MGM* // 1970 - **The Black Man's Burdon,** *MGM* // 1971 - **War,** *United Artists* // 1971 - **All Day Music,** *United Artists* // 1972 - **The World is a Ghetto,** *United Artists* // 1973 - **Deliver the Word,** *United Artists* // 1974 - **War Live!,** *United Artists* // 1974 - **Radio Free War,** *United Artists* // 1975 - **Why Can't We Be Friends?,** *United Artists* // 1976 - **Love is All Around,** *ABC* // 1976 - **Greatest Hits,** *United Artists* // 1977 - **Platinum,** *Untited Artists* // 1977 - **Platinum Jazz,** *Blue Note* // 1977 - **Galaxy,** *MCA* // 1978 - **Youngblood,** *United Artists* // 1979 - **The Music Band 1&2,** *MCA* // 1980 - **The Music Band - Live** // 1982 - **Outlaw,** *RCA* // 1983 - **Life (is So Strange),** *RCA* // 1991 - **The Best of War and More,** *Rhino* // 1994 - **Peace Sign,** *Avenue* // 1994 - **Best of The Music Band,** *MCA* // 1994 - **Anthology,** *Rhino* // 1996 - **The Best of War and More Vol. 2,** *Rhino* // 1999 - **Grooves and Messages: Greatest Hits,** *Rhino.*

Muddy Waters

Real name: McKinley Morganfield
Born: April 4, 1915 - Rolling Fork, MS
Died: April 30, 1983 - Downers Grove, IL

Blues singer, guitar harmonica player
The great patriarch of Chicago Blues, Muddy Waters grew up in rural Mississippi. He started out by playing the harmonica at age nine and even performed locally on the instrument. After switching over to guitar at age seventeen he never returned to playing the harmonica, preferring to let others play it for him.

He was first recorded in 1941 by folklorist Alan Lomax. Waters moved to Chicago in 1943, switched to electric guitar and quickly became the leading player of the Chicago-style of electric Blues music until his death in 1983.

The list of harmonica players who were in his bands reads like a Who's Who of Blues harmonica and they included Little Walter, Walter Horton, Henry Strong, Carey Bell, George "Harmonica" Smith, James Cotton, Paul Butterfield, Mojo Buford, Jerry Portnoy, Junior Wells and Paul Oscher.

Discography:
1947-55 - **Back in the Early Days,** *Syndicate Chapter* // 1955-58 - **Good News,** *Syndicate Chapter* // 1956 - **Mississippi Blues,** *London* // 1958 - **The Best of Muddy Waters,** *Ches*

// 1960 - **Muddy Waters at Newport**, *MCA/Chess* // 1963 - **Folk Festival of the Blues**, *MCA* // 1964 - **Folksinger**, *Chess* // 1964 - **Muddy Waters Sings Big Bill Broonzy**, *MCA/Chess* // 1965-68 - **Live, 1965-68**, *CFPC* // 1965 - **The Real Folk Blues**, *MCA/Chess* // 1965 - **Muddy Waters with Little Walter**, *Vogue* // 1966 - **The Blues Man**, *Polydor* // 1966 - **Down on Stovall's Plantation**, *Testament* // 1966 - **Muddy, Brass and Blues**, *Chess* // 1967 - **Mud in Your Ear**, *Muse* // 1967 - **Blues From Big Bill's Copacabana**, *MCA/Chess* // 1967 - **More Real Folk Blues**, *MCA/Chess* // 1968 - **Live in Paris: 1968**, *French Concerts* // 1968 - **Sail On**, *Chess* // 1968 - **Super Super Blues Band**, *MCA/Chess* // 1968 - **Electric Mud**, *MCA* // 1968 - **Super Blues**, *MCA/Chess* // 1969 - **After the Rain**, *Chess* // 1970 - **They Call Me Muddy Waters**, *MCA/Chess* // 1970 - **Vintage Mud**, *Sunnyland* // 1970 - **They Call Me Muddy Waters**, *Chess* // 1971 - **McKinley Morganfield AKA Muddy Waters**, *Chess* // 1971 - **The London Muddy Waters Sessions**, *MCA/Chess* // 1971 - **Live at Mister Kelly's**, *MCA/Chess* // 1974 - **Live in Antibes, 1974**, *French Concerts* // 1974 - **"Unk" in Funk**, *Chess* // 1974 - **Muddy and the Wolf**, *MCA/Chess* // 1974 - **London Revisited**, *Chess* // 1975 - **The Muddy Waters Woodstock Album**, *Chess* // 1976 - **Unreleased in the West**, *Moon* // 1976 - **Live in Switzerland, 1976 - Vol. 1**, *Landscape* // 1976 - **Live at the Jazz Jamboree**, *Poljazz* // 1977 - **Hard Again**, *Blue Sky* // 1978 - **I'm Ready**, *Blue Sky* // 1979 - **Muddy "Mississippi" Waters: Live**, *Blue Sky* // 1980 - **Chicago 5 Golden Years**, *Chess* // 1981 - **King Bee**, *Blue Sky* // 1982 - **Rolling Stone**, *Chess* // 1984 - **Rare and Unissued**, *MCA/Chess* // 1987 - **Fathers and Sons**, *Vogue* // 1987 - **The Best Of...**, *MCA/Chess* // 1989 - **Trouble No More/Singles (1955-1959)**, *MCA/Chess* // 1990 - **The Chess Box**, *MCA/Chess* // 1991 - **Can't Get No More Grindin'**, *MCA/Chess* // 1992 - **The Complete Muddy Waters 1947-1967**, *Charly* // 1992 - **Blue Skies**, *Columbia/Legacy* // 1993 - **Live in 1958**, *MW* // 1992 - **Mannish Boy**, *Sound* // 1992 - **She Moves Me**, *Roots* // 1993 - **The Complete Plantation Recordings**, *MCA/Chess* // 1994 - **One More Mile**, *MCA/Chess* // 1995 - **Live at Newport**, *Charly* // 1995 - **Goodbye Newport Blues**, *Blue Moon* // 1995 - **Collaboration**, *Rhino* // 1996 - **Baby, Please Don't Go**, *Vogue* // 1997 - **His Best 1947-1955**, *MCA/Chess* // 1997 - **Paris, 1972**, *Pablo* // 1997 - **Featuring Dizzy Gillespie**, *Laserlight* // 1997 - **Hoochie Coochie Man**, *Laserlight* // 1997 - **Blues Legend**, *MCA* // 1998 - **His Best 1956-1964**, *MCA/Chess* // 1998 - **King of the Electric Blues**, *Epic* // 1998 - **Goin' Way Back**, *Just a Memory* // 1998 - **Gold Collection, Fine Tune** // 1999 - **The Best Of..., 20th Century Masters**, *MCA* // 1999 - **The Lost Tapes**, *Blind Pig* // 2000 - **Country Blues**, *Catfish* // 2000 - **Rollin' Stone: The Golden Anniversary**, *MCA* // 2000 - **Back to Back**, *Edeltone* // 2000 - **Got My Mojo Working**, *Legend* // 2000 - **Mojo**, *Music Club* // 2000 - **Ol' Man Mud**, *Arpeggio Blues* // **Rollin' and Tumblin'**, *Charly* // **Mississippi Rollin' Stone**, *Magnum* // **Sweet Home Chicago**, *Intermedia* // **The Warsaw Sessions, Vol. 1 & 2**, *Kicking Mule* // **First Recording Sessions 1941-1946**, *Document*.

Movies:
1960 - **The Subterraneans** // 1970 - **The Blues is Alive and Well in Chicago** // 1970 - **Chicago Blues** // 1971 - **Dynamite Chicken** // 1974 - **Street Music** // 1974 - **Mandingo** // 1978 - **The Last Waltz**.

On Video:
2000 - **In Concert: 1971**, *Shanachie* // 2000 - **Got My Mojo Working**, *Shanachie*.

Watson, Doc

Real name: Arthel Watson
Born March 2, 1923 - Deep Gap, NC

Country guitar, banjo, harmonica player

Though he is known primarily for his flat-picking style of guitar, Doc Watson began playing music on the harmonica and received a new one every year for Christmas while growing up. He often plays the harmonica on a neckbrace.

Discography:
1961 - **Old Time Music at Clarence Ashley's, Vol. 1 & 2**, *Folkways* // 1963 - **Doc Watson and Family**, *Folkways* // 1964 - **Doc Watson**, *Vanguard* // 1964 - **Treasures Untold**, *Vanguard* // 1965 - **Doc Watson and Son**, *Vanguard* // 1966 - **Home Again**, *Vanguard* // 1966 - **Southbound**, *Vanguard* // 1967 - **Ballads from Deep Gap**, *Vanguard* // 1967 - **Old Timey Concert**, *Vanguard* // 1968 - **Good Deal**, *Vanguard* //

1968 - **Doc Watson in Nashville**, *Vanguard* // 1971 - **Doc Watson On Stage Featuring Merle Watson**, *Vanguard* // 1972 - **Two Days in November**, *Sugar Hill* // 1972 - **Elementary Doc Watson**, *Flying Fish* // 1973 - **Then and Now**, *Sugar Hill* // 1975 - **Memories**, *Sugar Hill* // 1977 - **The Watson Family Tradition**, *Rounder* // 1979 - **Look Away**, *United Artists* // 1979 - **Live and Pickin'**, *United Artists* // 1981 - **Red Rocking Chair**, *Flying Fish* // 1982 - **A Folk and Country Legend** // 1983 - **Doc and Merle Watson's Guitar Album**, *Flying Fish* // 1984 - **In the Pines** // 1984 - **Riding the Midnight Train**, *Sugar Hill* // 1984 - **Down South**, *Sugar Hill* // 1985 - **Pickin' the Blues**, *Flying Fish* // 1988 - **Portrait**, *Sugar Hill* // 1988 - **The Essential Doc Watson**, *Vanguard* // 1990 - **On Praying Ground**, *Sugar Hill* // 1991 - **My Dear Old Southern Home**, *Sugar Hill* // 1992 - **Remembering Merle**, *Sugar Hill* // 1994 - **Songs from the Southern Mountains**, *Sugar Hill* // 1995 - **Docabilly**, *Sugar Hill* // 1995 - **The Original Folkways Recordings, 1960-1962**, *Smithsonian* // 1995 - **The Vanguard Years**, *Vanguard* // 1996 - **Watson Country**, *Flying Fish* // 1997 - **Doc & Dawg**, *Acoustic Disc* // 1998 - **Home Sweet Home**, *Sugar Hill* // 1999 - **Third Generation Blues**, *Sugar Hill* // 1999 - **The Best of Doc Watson: 1964-1968**, *Vanguard* // 2000 - **Foundation: Doc Watson Guitar Instrumental Collection**, *Sugar Hill* // **Sings Songs for Little Pickers**, *Alacazam!* // **At Folk City**, *Rounder* // **Favorites**, *EMI*.

Watson, El

Country harmonica player

El Watson was an old-time Country harmonica player from Tennessee who recorded for the Victor label in 1927.

Discography:
1992 - **Great Harp Players (1927-1936)**, *Document*.

Watson, Johnny "Jimmy"

Also known as: Daddy Stovepipe, Sunny Jim
Born: April 12, 1867 - Mobile, AL
Died: November 1, 1963 - Chicago, IL

Blues guitar, jug, kazoo, harmonica player

Born and raised in Mobile, Alabama, Johnny Watson, also known as "Daddy Stovepipe," began his musical career around 1910 by performing in minstrel shows. He did some recordings during the 1920's, both solo and also with fellow Bluesman, Whistlin' Pete.

He spent most of the rest of his life working as a street musician and did some recordings just before his death in 1963.

Discography:
1961 - **Blues From Maxwell Street** // 1986 - **Harmonicas Unlimited** // **Alabama: Black Country Dance Bands**, *Document*.

Watts, Lou

Also known as: Tommy Lewis, Kid Thomas
Born: June 20, 1934 - Sturgis, MS
Died: April 13, 1970 - Beverly Hills, CA

Blues drums, harmonica player

After moving to Chicago in 1941, Lou Watts learned how to play the harmonica from "Little" Willie Smith and began playing in Blues bars during the late 1940's. He frequently sat in with Little Walter, Muddy Waters, Elmore James, Bo Diddley and others.

Watts' career came to an abrupt end in 1970. He was involved in a car accident that killed a small boy. Watts was cleared of the manslaughter charge, but the boy's father shot Watts dead shortly afterward.

Webber, Saul

Vaudeville harmonica player

Saul Webber played in Carl Freed's *Harmonica Lads* from 1935 until the outbreak of World War Two.

Webster, Katie

Real name: Katheryn Jewel Thorne
Born: September 9, 1939 - Houston, TX
Died: September 5, 1999 - League City, TX

Blues singer, piano, harmonica player

Best known as a Blues piano player and singer, Katie Webster began her professional career in Dallas, Texas around 1957 and played in Jack Ruby's nightclub. She moved to Louisiana in 1959 and became the house piano player for Jay Miller's recording studio and recorded with Lazy Lester, Lonesome Sundown, Slim Harpo, Lightnin' Slim, Otis Redding and others. In 1964 she became Otis Redding's regular piano player, a position she held until Redding's death in 1967.

During the mid-1970's her career took an upswing as she began performing and recording as a solo artist. She recorded several albums for the Arhoolie and Alligator labels.

Discography:
1977 - **Whooee Sweet Daddy**, *Flyright* // 1979 - **Katie Webster Has the Blues** // 1980's - **You Can Dig it** // 1980's - **Live and Well** // 1987 - **I Know That's Right**, *Arhoolie* // 1988 - **The Many Faces of Katie Webster** // 1988 - **Swamp Boogie Queen**, *Alligator* // 1990 - **Two-Fisted Mama!**, *Alligator* // 1991 - **Katie Webster**, *Paula* // 1991 - **No Foolin'**, *Alligator* // 1999 - **Deluxe Edition**, *Alligator* // **Pounds of Blues**, *Charly*.

Weiser, Glenn

Born: May 1, 1952 - Ridgewood, NJ

Blues / Celtic guitar, harmonica player, writer

Glenn Weiser began playing the guitar at the age of sixteen and took up the harmonica three years later. As a performer, he has performed with Buddy Guy, Junior Wells, Koko Taylor and others. As a writer he has written three books for the harmonica as well as writing dozens of articles for various publications.

Bibliography:
Blues and Rock Harmonica, *Centerstream* // **Masters of Blues Harp,** *Hal Leonard* // **Irish and American Fiddle Tunes for the Harmonica,** *Centerstream*.

Weiss, Christian
Harmonica manufacturer
Christian Weiss was a 19th century manufacturer of harmonicas and partner with his cousin Christian Messner. Their factory in Trossingen, Germany was building harmonicas as early as 1827. According to legend, Matthias Hohner learned the secrets of making harmonicas after taking a tour of their facility.

Their company continued to make harmonicas until 1928, when they were bought out by M. Hohner, Inc.

Wells, Junior
Real name: Amos Blakemore
Born: December 9, 1934 - Memphis, TN
Died: January 15, 1998 - Chicago, IL

Blues singer, harmonica player
While growing up in Memphis, Tennessee, Junior Wells taught himself to play the harmonica with some coaching by Junior Parker and was playing on the streets for tips by the time he was seven. His family moved to Chicago when he was twelve and he was already playing in the city's Blues bars when he was fourteen.

An immediate hit on the local Blues circuit, Wells performed with Tampa Red, Big Maceo, Sunnyland Slim, Muddy Waters and a host of others. By the end of the 1940's he had grouped up with Dave and Louis Myers and Fred Below as *The Aces*. When Little Walter decided to leave Muddy Waters' band to go solo, Wells took over as Muddy's harmonica player and Walter took on *The Aces* as his back-up band.

Wells worked as a Muddy Waters' harmonica player over the next few years and recorded his first solo album in 1965. He quickly became a Chicago Blues institution. He worked closely with guitarist Buddy Guy as well as guest starring with a variety of music's biggest stars, including Bonnie Raitt, *The Rolling Stones* and Van Morrison.

In late 1997 he slipped into a coma and passed away in January of 1998.

Discography:
1965 - **Hoodoo Man Blues,** *Delmark* // 1966 - **It's My Life, Baby,** *Vanguard* // 1966 - **On Tap,** *Delmark* // 1968 - **You're Tuff Enough,** *Blue Rock* // 1968 - **Comin' At You,** *Vanguard* // 1969 - **Southside Blues Jam,** *Delmark* // 1969 - **Live at the Golden Bear,** *Blue Rock* // 1970 - **Buddy and The Juniors** // 1971 - **In My Younger Years,** *Red Lightnin'* // 1972 - **Buddy Guy and Junior Wells Play the Blues,** *Atlantic* // 1973 - **I Was Walking Through the Woods,** *Chess* // 1977 - **Live at Montreux,** *Evidence* // 1977 - **Blues Hit the Big Town,** *Delmark* // 1979 - **Got to Use Your Head,** *Blues Ball* // 1979 - **Pleading the Blues,** *Isabel* // 1970's - **Blues with a Beat,** *Delmark* // 1982 - **Drinkin' TNT 'n' Smokin' Dynamite,** *Blind Pig* // 1986 - **Messin' with the Kid,** *Paula* // 1986 - **Universal Rock,** *Flyright* // 1986 - **Chiefly Wells,** *Flyright* // 1990 - **Harp Attack!,** (with Carey Bell, Billy Branch and James Cotton), *Alligator* // 1991 - **1957-1966,** *Paula* // 1991 - **Alone and Acoustic,** *Alligator* // 1992 - **Undisputed Godfather of the Blues,** *GBW* // 1993 - **Better Off with the Blues,** *Telarc* // 1995 - **Everybody's Getting Some,** *Telarc* // 1996 - **Come on This House,** *Telarc* // 1997 - **Junior Wells Live at Legends,** *Telarc* 1998 - **Keep On Steppin': The Best Of...,** *Telarc* // 1998 - **Best of the Vanguard Years,** *Vanguard* // 1999 - **Junior Well and Friends,** *Charly*.

Movies:
1970 - **Chicago Blues** // 1998 - **Blues Brothers 2000.**

Video:
Junior Wells Teaches Blues Harmonica, *Hot Licks Video*.

Weltman, Sandy
Born: June 9, 1956 - St. Louis, MO

Jazz banjo, harmonica player
Originally a banjo player, Sandy Weltman began playing the harmonica in the late 1970's. Sandy studied with Howard Levy and integrates overblows as well as bending into his playing. In

1991 he won second place in two categories at the World Harmonica Competition. In addition to the more traditional forms of Jazz that he has played through the years, Sandy also plays Klezmer-style harmonica.

Discography:
1998 - **New World Harmonica Jazz,** *Wildstone* // **Escape Velocity,** (with The Sandroids), *Wildstone.*

Welton, Danny
Pop / Vaudeville harmonica player

The son of a Vaudeville performer, Danny Welton began playing the harmonica at age of three and was playing in his father's band by the time he was five. He began appearing in movies at

the of twelve and has been performing as a harmonica soloist ever since that time, working with orchestras, on cruise ships and in lounges

Discography:
1996 - **The Naked Sea Suite** // 1998 - **Summer in San Francisco,** *Danwell* // 1998 - **Hot Harmonica,** *Danwell* // **Are You Lonesome Tonight?** // **Harmonica Hijinx.**

Movies:
1949 - **Mr. Soft Touch** // 1950 - **Hoe Down** // 1950 - **Military Academy** // 1950 - **A Life of Her Own** // 1950 - **Emergency Wedding** // 1952 - **Meet Danny Wilson** // 1954 - **The Wild One** // 1954 - **Bamboo Prison** // 1963 - **Captain Newman, MD.**

Wenner, Mark
Born: November 2, 1948 - Washington, DC

Blues harmonica player

Lead singer and harmonica player Mark Wenner help found the Blues / Rock group, *The Nighthawks* in 1972 and has been playing with the band since that time. He has also appeared on albums by Greg Kihn, Archie Edwards, Bob Margolin and others as well as recording two albums of solo material.

Discography: (also see - The Nighthawks)
1989 - **Nothin' But the Devil,** *Powerhouse* // 2000 - **Runs Good, Needs Paint,** *Right on Rhythm.*

Weston, John
Born: December 12, 1927 - Brinkley, AR

Blues singer, harmonica player
Although he's played the harmonica for most of his life, John Weston didn't start playing professionally until Willie Cobbs

urged him to play in the mid-1970's. Weston began playing his first solo gigs in the early 1980's and had his first record out in 1992.

Discography:
1992 - **So Doggone Blue,** *Fat Possum* // 1997 - **Got To Deal with the Blues,** *Midnight Creep* // 1997 - **I'm Doing the Best I Can,** *Appaloosa* // 2000 - **Blues At Daybreak,** *Wilco.*

Wet Willie

Formed: 1970
Disbanded: 1980

Southern Rock band

As one of the leading proponents of the 1970's Country / Rock sound, *Wet Willie* incorporated a strong influence of R&B and Blues into it's music. They were fronted by lead singer and saxophone player Jimmy Hall, who also played the harmonica. Their biggest hit, "Keep On Smiling" featured Hall playing a harmonica solo.

See - Jimmy Hall

Discography:
1971 - **Wet Willie,** *Capricorn* // 1972 - **Wet Willie II,** *Capricorn* // 1973 - **Drippin' Wet,** *Capricorn* // 1974 - **Keep On Smilin',** *Capricorn* // 1975 - **Dixie Rock,** *Capricorn* // 1976 - **The Wetter the Better,** *Capricorn* // 1977 - **Left Coast Live,** *Capricorn* // 1977 - **Greatest Hits,** *Capricorn* // 1978 - **Manorism,** *Epic* // 1979 - **Which One's Willie,** *Epic* // 1994 - **The Best of Willie,** *Polydor* // **Country Side of Life,** *Polygram.*

Wheatstone, Sir Charles

Born: February 6, 1802 - Gloucester, England
Died: 1875

Inventor

Sir Charles Wheatstone invented the concertina as well as other free-reeded instruments. He is often credited by some English historians as having invented the harmonica in 1828.

Wheeler, "Big" Golden

Born: December 15, 1929 - Beaconton, GA
Died: July 20, 1998 - Chicago, IL

Blues harmonica player

Golden Wheeler picked up the harmonica after hearing Buster Brown on the radio. Afteroming to Chicago in the 1950's, he made the acquaintance of Muddy Waters and Little Walter and began playing in the city's Blues bars. He formed his first band in 1956, recorded his first album in 1993 for the Delmark label and was usually backed by the band, *The Ice Cream Men.*

Discography:
1990 - **Chicago Blues Session, Vol. 14,** (with A.C. Reed), *Wolf* // 1993 - **Big Wheeler's Bone Orchard,** *Delmark* // 1997 - **Jump In,** *Delmark.*

Wheeler, Onie

Born: November 10, 1921 - Senath, MO
Died: May 26, 1984

Country singer, harmonica player

Onie Wheeler got into music professionally after winning a talent contest while serving in the armed forces during World War Two. After the war he performed on several radio stations in Missouri and Arkansas and was signed by the Okeh label in 1953.

During the 1950's he worked with Elvis Presley, Jerry Lee Lewis, Carl Perkins, Billy Lee Riley and even recorded solo for the Sun label. He recorded steadily through the 1960's and joined Roy Acuff's band in 1965, playing with Acuff as well as recording and playing with his own group until he died on stage in 1984.

Discography:
1973 - **John's Been Shuckin' My Corn,** *Onie* // 1991 - **Onie's Bop,** *Bear Family.*

Whettam, Graham
Classical Composer

Graham Whettam wrote "Concerto Scherzoso for Harmonica and Orchestra" in 1951 for Larry Adler, "Fantasy for Harmonica and Orchestra" in 1953 for Tommy Reilly and "Second Concerto for Harmonica and Orchestra" in 1961 for Tommy Reilly.

White, Buck

Real name: H.S. White
Born: December 13, 1930 - Oklahoma

Country multi-instrumentalist including harmonica
Buck White has been playing music professionally since 1947 and is known mostly for his piano playing and singing. In addition to recording with Jerry Douglas, David Grisman, Emmylou Harris, Kathy Mattea, Guy Clark and others, he performs with his wife and daughters as *The Whites* and as *Buck White and The Down Home Folks*. His daughter is married to Country music star Rick Skaggs.

Discography:
1972 - **Buck White and The Down Home Folks,** *County* // 1977 - **Live at the Old Time Pickin' Parlor,** *County* // 1977 - **That Down Home Feeling,** *Runner* // 1978 - **Poor Folks Pleasure,** *Sugar Hill* // 1979 - **More Pretty Girls Than One,** *Sugar Hill* // 1983 - **Old Familiar Feeling** // 1984 - **Forever You** // 1985 - **Whole New World** // 1986 - **Greatest Hits,** *MCA/Curb* // 1988 - **Doing It By the Book,** *Word* // 1995 - **Poor Folks Pleasure,** *Koch* // 1996 - **Give a Little Back,** *Rock Bottom* // 2000 - **A Lifetime in the Morning,** *Ceili Music.*

White, Booker T. "Bukka"

Born: November 12, 1906 - Houston, MS
Died: February 26, 1977 - Memphis, TN

Blues singer, guitar, piano, harmonica player
"Bukka" White began in music early, after learning to play the guitar from his father when he was nine years old and piano at eleven. He began working professionally in music in 1921 in the St. Louis area.

In addition to music, White also worked as a baseball player and professional boxer during the 1930's. He served time for assault on a Mississippi prison farm from 1937 to 1939. It was there that he made his first recordings for the Library of Congress in 1939. After getting out of prison he played with Jack Kelly in various Jug bands and recorded for the Vocalion label in 1940.

He served a term in the Navy during World War Two and returned to music after the war. He became a favorite on the Folk circuit and remained active until his death in 1977. He is also famous for teaching his cousin, B.B. King, how to play Blues guitar.

Discography:
1960-63 - **Sky Songs, Vol. 1 & 2,** *Arhoolie* // 1968 - **Memphis Hot Shots,** *Blue Horizon* // 1969 - **Bukka White (37/40),** *Columbia* // 1970 - **Parchman Farm,** *Columbia* // 1972 - **Blues Master, Vol. 4,** *Blue Horizon* // 1972 - **Baton Rouge Mosby Street,** *Blues Beacon* // 1976 - **The Complete Sessions 1930-1940,** *Travelin' Man* // 1989 - **Three Shades of Blues,** *Biograph* // 1991 - **Legacy of the Blues, Volume One,** *GNP Crescendo* // 1993 - **Shake 'Em On Down,** *ROIR* // 1994 - **1963 Isn't 1962,** *Genes* // 1994 - **The Complete Bukka White,** *Columbia* // 1995 - **Good Gin Blues,** *Drive* // 1996 - **Big Daddy,** *Biograph* // 1999 - **On the Road Again,** (with Furry Lewis), *Adelphi/Genes* // 1998 - **Mississippi Blues,** *Takoma/Ace* // **Aberdeen Mississippi Blues,** *Travelin' Man* // **Tennessee Blues,** *Wolf.*

Films:
1972 - **Blues Under the Skin** // 1976 - **Cocksuckers Blues** // **Along Old Man River** // **Booker T. Washington White: Bukka White.**

White, "Schoolboy" Cleve

Born: June 10, 1928 - Baton Rouge, LA

Blues guitar, harmonica player
"Schoolboy" Cleve White taught himself how to play the harmonica at age six and was performing with local groups by the mid-1940's around Baton Rouge, Louisiana. He recorded with Lightnin' Slim in 1954 and also recorded as a solo artist on the Ace label during the late 1950's.

White worked steadily in the Blues through the 1960's. He moved to Los Angeles in 1969 and retired from music for several years. He resurfaced as a musician in the 1970's, where he played in the San Francisco Bay area and performed until the early 1980's, when he retired permanently from music.

White, Tony Joe

Born: July 23, 1943 - Goodwill, LA

Country / Rock singer-songwriter, guitar, harmonica
Tony Joe White is probably best known for his hit song "Polk Salad Annie" and for having written Brook Benton's big hit "Rainy Night in Georgia." He began playing music at age sixteen, worked with several bands over the next few years and finally rose to national prominence during the late 1960's. He continues writing and performing to this day.

Discography:
1968 - **Black and White,** *Monument* // 1968 - **...Continued,** *Monument* // 1970 - **Tony Joe,** *Monument* // 1971 - **Tony Joe White,** *Warner Brothers* // 1972 - **The Train I'm On,** *Warner Brothers* // 1973 - **Home Made Ice Cream,** *Warner Brothers* // 1973 - **Two Originals,** *WEA* // 1977 - **Eyes, 20th Century** // 1977 - **Tony Joe White,** *20th Century* // 1980 - **Real Thing,** *Casablanca* // 1983 - **Dangerous,** *Columbia* // 1984 - **Roosevelt and Ira Lee** // 1990 - **Live!** // 1992 - **Closer To the Truth** // 1993 - **The Path of a Decent Groove** // 1993 - **The Best Of...,** *Warner Brothers* // 1995 - **Lake Placid Blues,** *Remark* // 1998 - **One Hot July,** *Polygram.*

Whitter, Henry

Born: April 6, 1892 - Grayson County, VA
Died: November 10, 1941 - Morganton, NC

Country singer, harmonica player

Henry Whitter was one of the very first Country harmonica players to record. His career began by providing entertainment for his fellow cotton mill workers in North Carolina. After traveling to New York City in the early 1920's, he recorded several sides for the Okeh label starting in 1923. One of the songs, "Wreck of the Old 97," was recorded shortly after by Vernon Dalhart and became Country music's first million selling record. Whitter also made the very first recording of the song, "Tom Dooley."

He also worked during the 1920's as a duet with fiddler G.B. Grayson. After Grayson died in a car crash in 1930, Whitter's career rapidly declined and he finally succumbed to diabetes in 1941.

Discography:

1976 - **Going Down Lee Highway** // 1999 - **1928-1930 Recordings**, *County* // 2000 - **Complete Recorded Works**, *Document* // **Grayson and Whitter, Complete Works**, *Old Homestead* // **Grayson and Whitter**, *Country*.

The Who

Formed: 1964 - London, England

British Rock band

The Who has been one of Rock and Roll's top bands since the mid-1960's. Their lead singer, Roger Daltry, occasionally plays the harmonica.

See - Roger Daltry

Discography:

1965 - **My Generation**, *Decca* // 1966 - **Happy Jack**, *Decca* // 1967 - **The Who Sell Out**, *Decca* // 1968 - **Magic Bus**, *Decca* // 1969 - **Tommy**, *Decca* // 1970 - **Live at Leeds**, *Decca* // 1971 - **Who's Next**, *Decca* // 1971 - **Meaty, Beaty, Big and Bouncy**, *Decca* // 1973 - **Quadrophenia**, *MCA* // 1974 - **Odds and Sods**, *MCA* // 1975 - **The Who By Numbers**, *MCA* // 1978 - **Who Are You**, *MCA* // 1979 - **The Kids Are Allright**, *MCA* // 1981 - **Face Dances**, *Warner Brothers* // 1982 - **It's Hard**, *Warner Brothers* // 1983 - **Who's Greatest Hits**, *MCA* // 1984 - **Who's Last**, *MCA* // 1985 - **Who's Missing**, *MCA* // 1987 - **Two's Missing**, *MCA* // 1988 - **Who's Better, Who's Best**, *MCA* // 1990 - **Join Together**, *MCA* // 1994 - **The Who: Thirty Years of Maximum R&B**, *MCA* // 2000 - **The BBC Sessions**, *MCA*.

Wiggins, "Harmonica" Phil

Born: May 8, 1954 - Washington, DC

Blues harmonica player

Phil Wiggins began playing the harmonica when he was a high school student growing up in Virginia. He joined up with Blues guitarist John Cephas in 1976 and the two have been working together as an acoustic Blues duo ever since. Wiggins has also played harmonica with Ann Rabson, *Sweet Honey in the Rock*, Mason Daring and others.

Discography: (see - Cephas & Wiggins)

Wilkins, Joe Willie

Born: January 7, 1923 - Davenport, MS
Died: March 28, 1979 - Memphis, TN

Blues guitar, harmonica player

Joe Willie Wilkins taught himself how to play the harmonica as a child growing up in rural Mississippi. He began performing in his father's band at local dances when he was ten.

He started traveling at age twelve and over the next few years he worked with Sonny Boy Williamson II (Rice Miller), Robert Jr. Lockwood, Willie Love, Willie Nix and a host of others. He made frequent appearances on the radio starting in the mid-1940's and recorded as a sideman for Arthur Crudup, Joe Hill Louis, Big Joe Williams, Roosevelt Sykes, B.B. King and several others.

He continued to work steadily until his death in 1979.

Discography:

1991 - **Goin' in Your Direction.**

Williams, Arthur

Born: July 8, 1937 - Tunica, MS

Blues harmonica player

Arthur Williams began playing harmonica at about age ten while growing up in the Chicago area. Over the years he's played with Muddy Waters, Eddie Taylor, Willie Mabon, Sam Carr and Frank Frost, with whom he recorded an album in 1964. He currently lives and works in the St. Louis area.

Discography:
1999 - **Harpin' On It**, *Fedora* // 2000 - **Ain't Goin' Down**, *Fedora*.

Williams, Doc

Real name: Andrew Smik, Jr.
Born: June 26, 1914 - Cleveland OH

Country singer, guitar, harmonica player
"Doc" Williams grew up outside of Pittsburgh, Pennsylvania and has been playing music professionally since 1934. In 1946 he teamed up with his wife Chickie and the pair have been a popular Country music act ever since.

Discography:
1962 - **25th Anniversary Album**, *Wheeling* // 1966 - **Wheeling Back to Wheeling**, *Wheeling* // 1969 - **Favorites Old and New**, *Wheeling* // 1972 - **The Doc Williams Show**, *Wheeling* // 1974 - **Lonely**, *Doxx* // 1978 - **The Doc Williams Collection (1951-1957)**, *Cattle Germany* // 1990 - **Doc and Chickie Williams: Collectors Series #3**, *Wheeling* // **Sings Country and Western**, *Wheeling* // **Williams Family Sacred Album**, *Wheeling* // **Daddy's Little Angel**, *Wheeling* // **From Out of the Beautiful Hills of West Virginia**, *Wheeling* // **Doc and Chickie Together**, *Wheeling* // **Reminiscing**, *Wheeling* // **The Three of Us**, *Wheeling* // **We've Come a Long Way Together**, *Wheeling*.

Williams, Hank Jr.

Real name: Randall Hank Williams
Born: May 26, 1949 - Shreveport, LA

Country singer-songwriter, guitar, harmonica player
The son of Country music legend Hank Williams, Hank Williams Jr. has been performing professionally since he was eight years old and has maintained a very steady presence on the Country music charts. He can play a number of instruments, including the harmonica.

Discography:
1976 - **Fourteen Greatest Hits**, *MGM* // 1979 - **Family Tradition**, *Warner* // 1980 - **Habits Old & New**, *Warner* // 1981 - **The Pressure is On**, *Warner* // 1981 - **Rowdy**, *Warner* // 1982 - **High Notes**, *Warner* // 1983 - **Strong Stuff**, *Warner* // 1983 - **Man of Steel**, *Warner* // 1985 - **Greatest Hits, Vol. 2**, *Warner/Curb* // 1989 - **Greatest Hits III**, *Warner/Curb* // 1991 - **The Best Of...**, *Curb* // 1995 - **American Legends: The Best of the Early Years**, *PSM* // 1995 - **Gospel Favorites**, *Rebound* // 1995 - **20 Hits Special Collection**, *Curb* // 1999 - **All-Time Greatest Hits**, *Curb* // 2000 - **Bocephus Box Set**, *Curb*.

Williams, "Big" Joe

Born: October 16, 1903 - Crawford, MS
Died: December 17, 1982 - Macon, MS

Blues guitar, accordion, harmonica player
Best known as a 9-string guitar player, "Big" Joe Williams began playing music at age five and left home to work as a traveling musician by the time he was twelve. During the 1920's and 30's he played with *The Rabbit Foot Minstrel*, *The Birmingham Jug Band*, Little Brother Montgomery and Bogus Blind Ben Covington. He made his first recordings in 1921.

He worked steadily through most of his life and served as a major influence on various Folk and Blues musicians. He was one of the first musicians to hire Muddy Waters and in 1962 he featured a young Bob Dylan playing harmonica on one of his albums.

Discography:
1947 - **Big Joe Williams and Sonny Boy Williamson**, *Blues Classics* // 1958 - **Piney Woods Blues**, *Delmark* // 1960 - **Tough Times**, *Arhoolie* // 1961 - **Walking Blues**, *Fantasy* // 1961 - **Nine String Guitar Blues**, *Delmark* // 1961 - **Blues on Highway 49**, *Delmark* // 1961 - **Walking Blues**, *Fantasy* // 1963 - **Blues for 9 Strings**, *Bluesville* // 1964 - **Back to the Country**, *Testament* // 1964 - **Studio Blues**, *Bluesville* // 1964 - **Back to the Country**, *Testament* // 1964 - **Big Joe Williams at Folk City**, *Prestige* // 1965 - **Early Recordings, 1935-41**, *Mamlish* // 1966 - **Classic Delta Blues**, *Milestone* // 1966 - **Stavin' Chain Blues**, *Delmark* // 1967 - **Hell Bound and Heaven Sent**, *Smithsonian/Folkways* // 1969 - **Hand Me Down My Old Walking Stick**, *World Pacific* // 1969 - **Thinking of What They Done to Me**, (with Charlie Musselwhite), *Arhoolie* // 1970 - **Big Crawlin' Snake**, *RCA* // 1972 - **Blues From Mississippi**, *Storyville* // 1972 - **Big Joe Williams**, *Storyville* // 1974 - **Live 1974** - *Wolf* // 1974 - **Legacy of the Blues, Vol. 6**, *GNP Crescendo* // 1974 - **Ramblin' Wandering Blues**, *Storyville* // 1975 - **Don't Your Plums Look Mellow**, *Bluesway* // 1978 - **Back To the Roots**, *Ornament* // 1980 - **Big Joe Williams**, *L&R* // 1988 - **Malvina, My Sweet Woman**, *Oldie Blues* // 1990 - **Shake Your Boogie**, *Arhoolie* // 1991 - **Delta Blues: 1951**, *Trumpet* // 1991 - **Complete Works, Vol. 1&2, (1935-49)**, *Document* // 1993 - **Blues from the Southside**, *Pilz* // 1996 - **Wild Cow Blues**, *Magnum* // 1996 - **Mississippi's Big Joe Williams and his Nine-String Guitar**, *Smithsonian /Folkways* // 1996 - **Have Mercy**, *Tradition* // 1998 - **No More Whiskey**, *Evidence* // 1998 - **These are My Blues**, *Testament* // 1999 - **Goin' Back to Crawford**, *Arhoolie* // 1999 - **Crawlin' King Snake**, *Catfish* // 2000 - **Big Joe Williams and Friends**, *Cleopatra* // 2000 - **The Legend at His Best**, *Collectables*.

Williams, Joe "Jody"

Also known as: Little Papa Joe
Born: February 3, 1935 - Mobile, AL

Blues singer, guitar, drums, piano, harmonica

"Jody" Williams is best remembered as being a major creative force in Chicago Blues guitar during the 1950's and early 60's. He was raised in Chicago from the time he was six years old and his first instrument was the harmonica. As a boyhood friend of Bo Diddley, the two learned guitar together and Bo Diddley later featured Williams on several of his early recordings, including "Who Do You Love."

Williams was in great demand and recorded with Billy Boy Arnold, Jimmy Rogers, Muddy Waters, Otis Spann and B.B. King. During the mid-1960's Williams took up electronics and has been working in that field ever since. In 2000 he began playing in Chicago Blues clubs again.

Discography:
1977 - **Leading Brand**, *Red Lightnin'*.

Williams, Robin

Real name: Robin Williams Murphy III
Born: March 16, 1949

Folk singer-songwriter, guitar, harmonica player

Though he is best known as a guitar player, Robin Williams can also play a little harmonica. He and his wife Linda have been working regularly since 1975 with Garrison Keillor on his "Prairie Home Companion" radio program on National Public Radio. They have recorded several albums, not only as a duet, but also with *The Hopeful Gospel Quartet* and as *Robin and Linda Williams and Their Fine Group*.

Discography:
1981 - **Harmony**, *June Appeal* // 1984 - **Close as We Can Get**, *Flying Fish* // 1985 - **Nine Til Midnight**, *Flying Fish* // 1988 - **All Broken Hearts are the Same**, *Sugar Hill* // 1990 - **The Rhythm of Love**, *Sugar Hill* // 1992 - **Garrison Keillor and The Hopeful Gospel Quartet** // 1993 - Live in Holland, *Strictly Country Holland* // 1993 - **Turn Toward Tomorrow**, *Sugar Hill* // 1994 - **Robin & Linda Williams & The Fine Group**, *Sugar Hill* // 1995 - **Good News**, *Sugar Hill* // 1996 - **Sugar for Sugar**, *Sugar Hill* // 1998 - **Devil of a Dream**, *Sugar Hill* // 2000 - **In the Company of Strangers**, *Sugar Hill*.

Williams, Tex

Real name: Sollie Paul Williams
Born: August 23, 1917 - Ramsey, IL
Died: October 11, 1985 - Newhall, CA

Country Singer, multi-instrumentalist including harmonica

Tex Williams was a Country musician who began playing at age five and was performing on the radio by the time he was thirteen. He made a number of short films during the 1940's and signed to Capitol Records in 1946. His recording of "Smoke! Smoke! Smoke!" became the first million selling record for Capitol and Williams enjoyed moderate success until his death from lung cancer in 1985.

Discography:
1955 - **Dance-O-Rama-Tex**, *Decca* // 1958 - **Tex Williams' Best**, *Camden* // 1960 - **Smoke! Smoke! Smoke!**, *Capitol* // 1962 - **Country Music Time**, *Decca* // 1963 - **Tex Williams in Las Vegas**, *Liberty* // 1966 - **Tex Williams**, *Sunset* // 1966 - **Two Sides of Tex Williams**, *Boone* // 1966 - **The Voice of Authority** // 1966 - **The Voice of Authority**, *Imperial* // 1971 - **A Man Called Tex**, *Monument* // 1974 - **Those Lazy Hazy Days**, *Granite* // 1978 - **14 All-Time Country Hits** // 1981 - **Tex Williams and California Express**, *Garu* // 1996 - **Vintage Collections Series**, *Capitol* // 1997 - **On the Air (1947-49)**, *Country Routes* // 2000 - **The Very Best Of...**, *Varese*.

Williamson, John Lee "Sonny Boy"

Born: March 30, 1914 - Jackson, TN
Died: June 1, 1948 - Chicago, IL

Blues harmonica player

One of the most influential of the early Chicago Blues harmonica players, John Lee "Sonny Boy" Williamson began playing harmonica at age five, while growing up in rural Tennessee. By his mid-teens he was working as a traveling musician and accompanying Yank Rachell, Sleepy John Estes and Sunnyland Slim. He made his first records in Aurora, Illinois for the Bluebird label in 1937.

He quickly became one of the most popular harmonica players in the Chicago area. He worked with Big Bill Broonzy, Big Joe Williams, Lazy Bill Lucas, Baby Face Leroy and even helped Muddy Waters get his first paying gig in Chicago. His popularity was such that when Rice Miller began his radio show in Helena, Arkansas, he decided to use the name "Sonny Boy Williamson" to help increase his popularity, although this has led to a lot of confusion for historians. Williamson also gave harmonica lessons to a young Billy Boy Arnold.

Williamson's life came to an abrupt end on June 1, 1948. While returning from playing a show at Chicago's Plantation Club, he was mugged and stabbed in the head with an ice pick.

Discography:
1964 - **Big Bill and Sonny Boy** // 1990 - **Throw a Boogie Woogie**, *RCA* // 1991 - **Complete Recorded Works, Volumes 1-5**, *Document* // 1995 - **Sugar Mama**, *Indigo* // 1997 - **The Bluebird Recordings**, *RCA* // **Sonny Boy Williamson, Vol. 1: 1937-39**, *Qualiton*.

Williamson, "Sonny Boy II"

Real name: Alex "Rice" Miller
Born: December 5, (1897?) - Glendora, MS
Died: May 25, 1965 - Helena, MS

Blues singer-songwriter, harmonica player

Rice Miller taught himself to play the harmonica at age five and was playing for tips at local parties by the time he was nine. By his early 20's he was traveling all over the south, by playing harmonica to make a living. By the 1930's he was beginning to get noticed and worked with Sunnyland Slim, Elmore James, Big Boy Crudup, Robert Johnson, Robert Jr. Lockwood, B.B. King and many other Blues greats. He even taught his brother-in-law, Howlin' Wolf, how to play the harmonica.

In 1941 he and Lockwood landed a job playing on a mid-day radio show for the King Biscuit Flour Company. The show was a huge success and created a new name for Miller. The station's manager, wanting to cash in on the popularity of John Lee "Sonny Boy" Williamson's records, decided to bill Miller as "Sonny Boy Williamson." Miller stuck with the name and even insisted in later years that he was the original "Sonny Boy."

He started recording prolifically in the early 1950's and signed with to the Chess label in 1955. He became and stayed one of the most popular Blues performers for the rest of his life. In 1963 he toured Europe and recorded with *The Yardbirds* and *The Animals*. After returning from England, he began wearing Edwardian suits and bowler hats. Before his death he returned to his home in Helena, Arkansas and revived his headlining on the King Biscuit Time radio program.

Discography:
1959 - **Down and Out Blues**, *MCA/Chess* // 1962 - **Portraits in Blues**, *Storyville* // 1963 - **Sonny Boy and Memphis Slim**, *Vogue* // 1964 - **With the Yardbirds and the Animals**, *Optimum* // 1964 - **Help Me**, *Chess* // 1965 - **In Memorium**, *Chess* // 1965 - **This is My Story**, *Chess* // 1965 - **The Blues of Sonny Boy Williamson**, *Storyville* // 1965 - **The Real Folk Blues**, *MCA/Chess* // 1966 - **Don't Send Me No Flowers**, *Charly* // 1967 - **The Original**, *Blues Classics* // 1967 - **More Real Folk Blues**, *MCA/Chess* // 1968 - **One Way Out**, *MCA/Chess* // 1969 - **Bummer Road**, *MCA/Chess* // 1973 - **In Paris: Sonny Boy Williamson and Memphis Slim**, *GRP Crescendo* // 1975 - **Jam Session**, *Charly* // 1979 - **Don't Make a Mistake**, *Blues Ball* // 1979 - **Bye Bye Bird**, *Blues Night* // 1980 - **Sonny Boy Williamson & Big Joe Williams**, *Vine* // 1989 - **King Biscuit Time**, *Arhoolie* // 1989 - **Clownin' with the World**, *Trumpet* // 1991 - **The Chess Years**, *Charly* // 1991 - **Don't Start Me Talkin'**, *Huub* // 1992 - **Keep it to Ourselves**, *Alligator* // 1993 - **The Essential Sonny Boy Williamson**, *MCA/Chess* // 1994 - **Trumpet Masters Vol. 5: from the Bottom**, *Collectables* // 1994 - **Goin' in Your Direction**, *Trumpet* // 1995 - **In Europe with Clapton, Dixon and Spann**, *Evidence* // 1995 - **Rainy Day Blues**, *Drive* // 1997 - **His Best**, *MCA/Chess* // 1999 - **Live in England**, *Charly* // 1999 - **Baby Please Don't Go**, *Nostalgia* // 1999 - **American Blues Legend**, *Charly* // 1999 - **Shotgun Blues**, *Catfish* // 2000 - **Bring Another Half Pint**, *Recall* // **Live in London with Eric Clapton**, *L&R* // **Rare Sonny Boy Williamson**, *RCA* // **Boppin' with Sonny**, *Magnum* // **Work with Me**, *Chess* // **Stop Crying**, *Chess* // **The Best Of...**, *Chess* // **Solo Harmonica**, (with Walter Horton), *Document.*

Willing, Foy

Real name: Foy Wilingham
Born: 1915 - Bosque County, TX
Died: June 24, 1978

Country singer, guitar harmonica player

Foy Willing began playing harmonica as a child and learned how to play the guitar later. He began playing professionally around Waco, Texas as a teenager and by 1933 was performing on the radio in New York City. He helped to form *The Riders of the Purple Sage* in the 1940's. The group backed up Roy Rogers for several years until they disbanded in 1952. Willing continued to perform sporadically until his death in 1978.

Discography:
1950 - **Riders of the Purple Sage**, *Varsity* // 1958 - Cowboy, *Roulette* // 1962 - **The New Sound of American Folk**, *Jubilee* // 1992 - **Foy Willing and The New Riders of the Purple Sage**, *ASWT* // 1998 - **Collector's Edition**, *Similar.*

Willis, Aaron "Little Sun"

Also known as: Little Sonny
Born: October 6, 1932 - Greensboro, AL

Blues singer, guitar, harmonica player

Aaron Willis began his career in music singing Gospel music in church choirs while in his teens. After moving to Detroit in 1954, he began playing the harmonica while working as a photographer in the city's Blues bars. He received some instruction on the harmonica from Sonny Boy Williamson II (Rice Miller) and adopted his stage name from him.

in 1956 he formed his own band and was recording two years later. After a few singles he stopped recording and would not return to the studio until 1969. He has been recording and performing steadily ever since.

Discography:
1970 - **New King of the Blues Harmonica,** *Stax //* 1974 - **Hard Goin' Up,** *Enterprise //* 1980 - **Black and Blue,** *Stax //* 1992 - **Sonny Side Up,** *Glynn //* 1995 - **Ann Arbor Blues & Jazz Festival, Vol. 2,** *Schoolkids //* 1996 - **Blues with a Feeling,** *Sequel.*

Willis, Bruce

Born: March 19, 1955 - Germany

Actor

Before embarking on his career as an actor, Bruce Willis played saxophone and harmonica in an R&B band called *Loose Goose.* He returned to music for a brief time in 1987 with a couple of Soul/Blues albums where he sang and played harmonica. He has also guest starred on albums by Brian Setzer and Robert Kraft.

Discography:
1987 - **The Return of Bruno,** *Razor & Tie //* 1989 - **If It Don't Kill You, It Just Makes You Stronger,** *Motown //* 2000 - **Millenium Series,** *Polygram.*

Wills, Oscar

Also known as: TV Slim
Born: February 10, 1916 - Houston, TX
Died: October 21, 1969 - Kingman, AZ

Blues guitar, harmonica player

Oscar Wills began playing both the guitar and harmonica while in his teens and worked for a while playing juke joints and local dances around Houston, Texas. By the late 1930's he stopped playing music and did not revive his career until he moved to Louisiana in the 1950's.

He began recording for the Cliff label in 1957 and had a few minor hits. During the 1960's Wills mainly worked in his own TV repair shop in Los Angeles and made only a few sporadic appearances as a musician. It was while returning from playing a show in Chicago that he was killed in a fatal car accident.

Discography:
1957 - **Flat Foot Sam,** *Moonshine.*

Wilson, Al "Blind Owl"

Born: July 4, 1943 - Boston, MA
Died: September 3, 1970 - Topanga, CA

Blues singer, guitar, harmonica player

Al Wilson originally entered the Blues field as an historian and record collector. He played harmonica and guitar on recordings by Son House and John Lee Hooker in the early 1960's.

In the mid-1960's he teamed up fellow Blues enthusiast Bob Hite to form the band, *Canned Heat.* Wilson stayed with the group as a vocalist, guitar and harmonica player until his death from drug related causes in 1970.

Discography: (see - Canned Heat)

Wilson, Chris

Born: September 10, 1952

Rock singer, guitar, harmonica player

Chris Wilson replaced Roy Loney in the band, *The Flamin' Groovies* in 1971. Wilson sang, played guitar and harmonica with the group until 1983. in addition to recording several solo albums, he has played harmonica on recordings by *Crowded House, The Barracudas,* and others.

Discography: (also see - The Flamin' Groovies)
1994 - **Randon Centuries,** *Marilyn //* 1994 - **Chris Wilson & the Sneetches,** *Marilyn //* 1995 - **Back on the Barbary,** *Marilyn.*

Wilson, Danny

Born: October 25, 1935

Vaudeville / Jazz harmonica player

Danny Wilson began playing violin at the age of seven. He started playing the harmonica when he was 35. After gravitating to the bass harmonica, Wilson was one of many players who substituted in *The Harmonicats*. He has also played in *The New World Harmonica Trio* and currently plays with *The Dave McKelvey Trio*. In 1986 Danny Wilson was awarded the SPAH "Harmonica Player of the Year" award.

Discography: (see - Ron Kalina, Dave McKelvey)

Wilson, Harding "Hop"

Born: April 27, 1921 - Grapeland, TX
Died: August 27, 1975 - Houston, TX

Blues steel guitar, harmonica player

Best known as one of the few steel guitar players in Blues music, Harding Wilson learned to play the harmonica while growing up in Texas. He got his nickname "Hop" from his childhood use of the word 'harp' for harmonica.

After serving in the Army and working several years outside of music, he began playing professionally in 1956 and enjoyed a fairly successful career in Blues until his death in 1975.

Discography:

1986 - **Blues with Friends**, *Goldband* // 1988 - **Steel Guitar Flash!**, *Ace* // 1989 - **Rockin' Blues Party**, *Charly* // 1993 - **Houston Ghetto Blues**, *Bullseye Blues*.

Wilson, Kim

Born: January 6, 1951 - Detroit, MI

Blues / Rock vocals, harmonica player

As singer, harmonica player and front man for *The Fabulous Thunderbirds*, Kim Wilson has put together an impressive body of work that has reaped both critical acclaim and a high degree of success for any Blues harmonica player.

Wilson was born in Detroit, but moved to Los Angeles in 1960. It was there that he made the acquaintance of George "Harmonica" Smith, who taught him to play Blues harmonica. After moving to Minnesota, Wilson played in the group *The Aces of Straights and Shuffles,* which was managed by Willie Dixon. On a trip to Austin, Texas, Wilson sat in on a jam session with a young Stevie Ray Vaughan. Stevie's brother Jimmie heard the jam and invited Wilson to move down to Texas to play in a new band he was forming call *The Fabulous Thunderbirds*.

The group has managed to garnered an enormous amount of commercial success for a Blues / Rock band and in spite of a few personnel shifts in recent years, continues to perform and record to this day. Wilson has also pursued a solo career by recording several albums, in addition to playing the harmonica on albums by Lou Ann Barton, Albert Collins, Ronnie Earl, Lightnin' Hopkins, Sue Foley, Steve Freund, Eric Johnson, B.B. King, Pinetop Perkins, Bonnie Raitt, Jimmy Rogers, Santana, Paul Simon, Katie Webster and others.

Discography:

1993 - **Tigerman**, *Antones* // 1994 - **That's Life**, *Antone's* // 1997 - **My Blues**, *Blue Collar* // 1997 - **Will the Circle Be Unbroken**, *Black Magic* // **Kim Wilson**, *Antone's* // **High Water**, *Private Music*.

Windsavers (or Valves)

Windsavers are small, flexible flaps that cover the slot on the reedplate opposite from the reed that is being played. Usual made of a plastic material, windsavers block the air from blowing through the opposite reed from the one that is being played, thus saving wind.

Wiseman, Bob

Folk / Rock keyboards, vocals, harmonica

Keyboard player Bob Wiseman has been working with the Folk / Rock band *Blue Rodeo* for several years as well as recording as a solo artist. In addition to playing the keyboards, Wiseman occasionally fills in on the harmonica.

Discography: (also see - Blue Rodeo)

1990 - **Bob Wiseman Sings Wrench Turtle: In Her Dream,** *Risqué Disque / Atlantic* // 1991 - **Presented by Lake Michigan Soda,** *WEA* // 1993 - **City of Wood,** *WEA* // 1994 - **In By Of,** *Bare None* // 1994 - **Beware of Bob,** *Sabre Toque* // 1995 - **Accidentally Acquired Beliefs,** *WEA* // 1997 - **More Work Songs from the Planet of the Apes,** *GFC.*

Wonder, Stevie

Real name: Steveland Judkins Morris
Born: May 13, 1950 - Saginaw, MI

Soul singer-songwriter, multi-instrumentalist, including harmonica

Easily the best known and most influential of the harmonica players in the field of Soul music, Stevie Wonder has been recording and performing since he was twelve years old. Blinded shortly after he was born, he started playing music early as a child, first on the piano, then on the drums and harmonica.

Wonder started playing the harmonica on a Hohner Little Lady harmonica that was given to him as a gift. About a year later, an uncle gave him his first chromatic, which he quickly mastered. In 1961 he was discovered by Berry Gordy of Motown Records, who immediately signed him to the label. After his first three singles failed to achieve any reasonable sales, Motown decided to release a live cut of Wonder's called "Fingertips, Part Two," a harmonica instrumental which became an instant success.

Since that time, Stevie Wonder has been a regular hit machine and has become a music industry unto himself. In addition to his regular recordings, many of which feature Wonder playing the harmonica, he's played harmonica with *The Eurythmics, The Chilites, The Manhattan Transfer,* Elton John, Dionne Warwick, Quincy Jones, Chaka Khan, Dizzy Gillespie, Paul McCartney, Michael Jackson and many others.

Discography:

1963 - **Little Stevie Wonder: 12 Year Old Genius,** *Motown* // 1963 - **Tribute To Uncle Ray,** *Motown* // 1963 - **The Jazz Soul of Little Stevie,** *Motown* // 1963 - **Stevie Wonder,** *Motown* // 1963 - **Workout Stevie, Workout,** *Motown* // 1964 - **With a Song in My Heart,** *Motown* // 1965 - **Steveie at the Beach,** *Motown* // 1966 - **Up-Tight (Everything's Allright),** *Motown* // 1966 - **Down To Earth,** *Motown* // 1967 - **I Was Made to Love Her,** *Motown* // 1967 - **Someday at Christmas,** *Motown* // 1968 - **Greatest Hits,** *Motown* // 1968 - **Alfie,** *Motown* // 1968 - **For Once in My Life,** *Motown* // 1969 - **My Cherie Amour,** *Motown* // 1969 - **Eivets Rednow,** *Motown* // 1970 - **Stevie Wonder Live,** *Motown* // 1970 - **Signed, Sealed & Delivered,** *Motown* // 1970 - **Live at the Talk of the Town,** *Motown* // 1971 - **Where I'm Coming From,** *Motown* // 1971 - **Stevie Wonder's Greatest Hits, Vol. 2,** *Motown* // 1972 - **Music of My Mind,** *Motown* // 1972 - **Talking Book,** *Motown* // 1973 - **Innervisions,** *Motown* // 1974 - **Fulfillingness' First Finale,** *Motown* // 1976 - **Songs in the Key of Life,** *Motown* // 1976 - **Portrait,** *EMI* // 1977 - **Looking Back,** *Motown* // 1979 - **Journey Through the Secret Life of Plants,** *Motown* // 1980 - **Hotter Than July,** *Motown* // 1982 - **Stevie Wonder's Original Musiquarium I,** *Motown* // 1984 - **The Woman in Red,** *Motown* // 1985 - **In Square Circle,** *Motown* // 1985 - **Love Songs,** *Motown* // 1987 - **Characters,** *Motown* // 1991 - **Music from the Movie Jungle Fever,** *Motown* // 1994 - *Motown* **Legends: I Was Made To Love Her,** *Polygram* // 1995 - **Conversation Peace,** *Motown* // 1995 - **Natural Wonder,** *Motown* // 2000 - **At the Close of the Century,** *Motown.*

Wood, Britt

Vaudeville comedian, harmonica player

Britt Wood was a Vaudeville comedian of the 1920's and 30's who incorporated harmonica into his act.

Woods, Johnny

Born: November 1, 1917
Died: 1990

Blues bass guitar, harmonica player

Johnny Woods was a Blues harmonica player from Mississippi who recorded with Ernie Johnson and Shawn Pittman as well as recording an album of his own material.

Discography:

1984 - **The Blues of Johnny Woods,** *Swingmaster.*

Wrencher, "Big" John

Also known as: One-arm John
Born: February 12, 1923 - Sunflower, MS
Died: July 15, 1977 - Clarksdale, MS

Blues singer, harmonica player

John Wrencher taught himself how to play the harmonica while growing up in rural Mississippi. He left home when he was 24 years old to hobo around the country while supporting himself by playing harmonica.

Over the next several years he would make his home in Detroit and St. Louis and traveled extensively to play the Blues. It was during one of his trips in 1958 that he was involved in a car accident that took off his left arm.

In 1962 he settled in Chicago and instantly became a fixture at the Maxwell Street Market, where he played for tips. Over the years he performed and recorded with Baby Boy Warren, Little George Jackson, Johnny Young, Pat Rushin, Eddie Taylor and a host of others.

It was on a trip back to his home in 1977 that he suffered a fatal heart attack while stopping in at Wade Walton's barbershop in Clarksdale, Mississippi.

Discography:
1974 - **Big John's Boogie**, *Big Bear* // 1978 - **Maxwell Street Alley Blues**, *Blue Sting* // 1994 - **The Chicago String Band**, *Testament* // **Memphis To Maxwell**, *Jawes*.

– Y –

Yaney, Clyde "Skeets"

Born: June 16, 1912 - Mitchell, IN

Country singer-songwriter, guitar, harmonica
"Skeets" Yaney began his career by winning a talent contest at age six for "Best Entertainer in Southern Indiana," for his singing and harmonica playing act. He later teamed up with accordion player Frankie Taylor as *Skeets and Taylor* during the 1930's and 40's.

He became known primarily for his yodeling and was named National Yodeling Champion seven times. During his career he recorded for the Columbia, MGM and Town & Country labels. He retired in the late 1970's.

The Yardbirds

Form: 1963 - London, England
Disbanded: 1967

English Blues / Rock band
The Yardbirds were probably one of the more influential of the English Blues / Rock bands, who produced guitarists Eric Clapton, Jeff Beck and Jimmy Page. In 1963 the group performed and recorded with Sonny Boy Williamson II (Rice Miller). The band was fronted by singer-harmonica player Keith Relf. Their early play list featured many Chicago Blues standards.

See - Keith Relf

Discography:
1964 - **Five Live Yardbirds**, *Rhino* // 1965 - **Having a Rave-Up with the Yardbirds**, *Epic* // 1965 - **For Your Love**, *Epic* // 1966 - **Over Under Sideways Down**, *Epic* // 1966 - **The Yardbirds**, *Columbia* // 1966 - **Roger the Engineer**, *Edsel* // 1966 - **The Yardbirds with Sonny Boy Williamson**, *Mercury* // 1967 - **Blow-Up**, *MGM* // 1968 - **Little Games**, *EMI* // 1971 - **Live Yardbirds Featuring Jimmy Page**, *Epic* // 1986 - **Greatest Hits Vol. 1 1964-1966**, *Rhino* // 1991 - **On the Air**, *Band of Joy* // 1991 - **Vol. 1 - Smokestack Lightning**, *Sony* // 1991 - **Blues, Backtracks and Shapes of Things**, *Sony* // 1992 - **The**

Yardbirds Little Games Sessions & More, *EMI* // 1995 - **Clapton's Cradle: The Early Yardbirds**, *Evidence* // 1997 - **Live at the BBC**, *Warner Archive* // 1999 - **Live at the Crawdaddy**, *Repertoire* // 1999 - **BBC Sessions**, *Repertoire*.

Movies:
1966 - **Blow Up**.

York, David "Rock Bottom"

Blues singer, harmonica player

David "Rock Bottom" York is a Blues harmonica player who has been playing professionally since the late 1970's and has cut several solo albums as well as working with Roy Bookbinder, *The Silver King Band*, Diamond Tooth Mary and others.

Discography:
1991 - **Family Place**, *Verrat* // 1993 - **Harmaniac**, *Danger Zone* // 1995 - **Too Many Bad Habits**, *Double Trouble* // 1997 - **Tone**, *Tricknology* // 1999 - **Shake Your Boogie Leg**, *New Moon Blues*.

York, George

Born: February 17, 1910 - Louisa, KY
Died: July 1974

Country singer-songwriter, guitar, harmonica
George York teamed up with his brother, Leslie, in the 1930's to form The York Brothers. They began recording in 1939 and had a regional hit with "Hamtramck Mama." They signed to the Decca label in 1941.

Their musical careers were sidetracked when they enlisted in the navy after the outbreak of World war Two. After the war they joined the Grand Old Opry and signed with the King label. They left the Opry in 1950, but continued working in radio and doing live performances until the late 1950's.

Discography:
1958 - **The York Brothers, Vol. 1**, *King* // 1958 - **The York Brothers, Vol. II**, *King* // 1963 - **16 Greatest Country Songs**, *King* // 1987 - **Early Favorites**, *Old Homestead* // 200 - **Detroit in the 40's & 50's, Vol. 1**, *Collector*.

York, Rusty

Real name: Charles Edward York
Born: May 24, 1935 - Harlan County, KY

Country/Bluegrass/Rockabilly multi-instrumentalist, including harmonica

Rusty York began playing music professionally as a banjo picker in the early 1950's. After a brief foray into Rockabilly in the late 1950's, he returned to Bluegrass. He founded Jewell Records in 1961 and has run it ever since, occasionally recording and performing.

Discography:

1960 - **Rusty York and the Kentucky Mountain Boys,** *Bluegrass Special //* 1968 - **Bluegrass Gospel Songs,** *Rural Rhythm //* 1973 - **Dueling Banjos,** *QCA //* 1981 - **Rock N' Memories,** *Jewel.*

Young, Johnny

Born: January1, 1918 - Vicksburg, MS
Died: April 18, 1974 - Chicago, IL

Blues guitar, mandolin, harmonica

Johnny Young probably learned to play the harmonica from his mother, Nellie, and certainly learned to play guitar and mandolin from his uncle, Anthony Williams. Johnny played in the area of Rolling Fork, Mississippi during his teens and worked with Robert Nighthawk, Sleepy John Estes and Hammie Nixon before moving to Chicago in 1940.

From the 1940's through the 1960's he worked with John Lee "Sonny Boy" Williamson, Muddy Waters, Snooky Pryor, Floyd Jones, Memphis Slim, Howlin' Wolf, Sunnyland Slim and others. He started making records in 1947.

Although his recording activity was mostly inactive from the early 1950's until the mid-60's, he was a mainstay in the Chicago Blues scene and was well known as one of the few mandolin players in Urban Blues. During later years he worked with Walter Horton and Otis Spann and remained active until his death from a heart attack in 1974.

Discography:

1966 - **Johnny Young and his Friends,** *Testament //* 1965 - **Johnny Young and his Chicago Blues Band,** *Arhoolie //* 1967 - **Chicago/Blues/Today, Vol. 3,** *Vanguard //* 1969 - **Fat Mandolin,** *Blue Horizon //* 1972 - **Blues master No. 9,** *Blue Horizon //* 1973 - **I Can't Keep My Foot from Jumping,** *Bluesway //* 1974 - **Chicago Boogie //** 1993 - **Chicago Blues,** (with James Cotton and Walter Horton), *Arhoolie.*

Movies:

1963 - **And This is Free.**

Young, Neil

Born: November 12, 1945 - Toronto, Canada

Folk / Rock singer-songwriter, guitar, harmonica

In a career spanning more than four decades, Neil Young has managed to work in most forms of modern music including Rock, New Wave, Blues, Punk, Folk and Country. He is probably the most influential songwriter in the American Folk music scene after Bob Dylan and like Dylan, he plays the harmonica on a neckbrace.

After learning to play guitar and harmonica in his teens, he played in several bands in his native Toronto. Soon after moving to Los Angeles in the mid-1960's, he was playing the group *Buffalo Springfield,* which also featured Stephen Stills. After leaving the band in 1968 to pursue a highly successful solo career, Neil Young also spent time working with *Crosby, Stills, Nash and Young* during the early 1970's and in subsequent reunions.

He has continued to maintain a high output of recorded material through the years and has a tendency to experiment in a number of different styles.

Discography: (also see - Buffalo Springfield)
With Crosby, Stills, Nash and Young:

1970 - **Déjà Vu,** *Atlantic //* 1971 - **Four Way Street,** *Atlantic //* 1974 - **So Far,** *Atlantic //* 1988 - **American Dream,** *Atlantic.*

Solo:

1969 - **Neil Young,** *Reprise //* 1969 - **Everybody Knows This is Nowhere,** *Reprise //* 1970 - **After the Gold Rush,** *Reprise //* 1972 - **Harvest,** *Reprise //* 1972 - **Journey Through the Past,** *Reprise //* 1973 - **Time Fades Away,** *Reprise //* 1974 - **On the Beach,** *Reprise //* 1975 - **Tonight's the Night,** *Reprise //* 1975 - **Zuma,** *Reprise //* 1976 - **Long May You Run,** *Reprise //* 1977 - **American Stars and Bars,** *Reprise //* 1978 - **Decade,** *Reprise //* 1978 - **Comes a Time,** *Reprise //* 1979 - **Rust Never Sleeps,** *Reprise //* 1979 - **Live Rust,** *Reprise //* 1980 - **Where the Buffalo Roam,** *MCA //* 1980 - **Hawks and Doves,** *Reprise //* 1981 - **Re-Ac-Tor,** *Reprise //* 1982 - **Trans,** *Geffen //* 1983 - **Everybody's Rockin',** *Geffen //* 1985 - **Old Ways,** *Geffen //* 1986 - **Landing on Water,** *Geffen //* 1987 - **Life,** *Geffen //* 1987 - **This Note's for You,** *Geffen //* 1987 - **The Best Of...,** *Warner Brothers //* 1989 - **Freedom,** *Geffen //* 1989 - **Eldorado,** *Reprise //* 1990 - **Ragged Glory,** *Geffen //* 1991 - **Arc,** *Geffen //* 1991 - **Weld,** *Geffen //* 1992 - **Harvest Moon,** *Geffen //* 1993 - **Lucky Thirteen,** *Geffen //* 1993 - **Excursions Into Alien Territory,** *Geffen //* 1993 - **Unplugged,** *Reprise //* 1994 - **Sleeps with Angels,** *Reprise //* 1995 - **Mirror Ball,** *Reprise //* 1995 - **"Gold" Anniversary Edition,** *Warner Brothers //* 1996 - **Dead Man,** *Vapor //* 1996 - **Broken Arrow,** *Reprise //* 1997 - **Year of the Horse,** *Warner Brothers //* 2000 - **Silver and Gold,** *Warner Brothers.*

– Z –

Z., Jimmy

Real name: Jimmy Zavala

Rock harmonica player

Jimmy Z has made a career as a studio harmonica player with artists like Eric Burdon, Carole King, Rick Springfield, Edgar Winter, Rod Stewart, *Tom Petty and The Heartbreakers* and many more. His harmonica solo on the song "Missionary Man" by the *Eurythmics* is a classic Rock harmonica piece.

Discography:
1988 - **Anytime...Anyplace!,** *IRS //* 1991 - **Muzical Madness,** *Ruthless.*

Zaremba, Peter

Born: September 16, 1954 - Maspeth, NY

Alternative Rock singer, keyboards, harmonica player

Peter Zaremba was one of the leaders of the Alternative Rock band The Fleshtones. In addition to playing the keyboards and singing, Zaremba also played harmonica. He has also played with *? and The Mysterians, Sam the Sham & The Pharoahs* and others.

Discography: (also see - The Fleshtones)
1986 - **Spread the Word,** *Moving Target.*

Selected Bibliography

Books:

Adler, Larry - *It Ain't necessarily So,* New York, NY: Grove Press, 1984.

Adler, Larry - *Me and My Big Mouth,* Blake Publishing, 1994.

Baggelaar, Kristin and Milton, Donald - *Folk Music: More Than Just a Song,* New York, NY: Thomas Y. Crowell Company, 1976.

Ball, Tom - *A Sourcebook for Sonny Terry Licks,* Anaheim Hills, CA: Centerstream Publishing, 1995.

Barnard, Russell - *The Comprehensive Country Music Encyclopedia,* New York, NY: Random House, 1994.

Barrett, David - *Mel Bay's Complete Classic Chicago Blues Harp,* Pacific, MO: Mel Bay Publications, 1995.

Burbank, Richard - *Twentieth Century Music,* New York, NY: Facts On File Publications, 1984.

Charters, Samuel - *The Bluesmakers,* New York, NY: De Capo Press, 1991.

Clarke, Donald, ed. - *The Penguin Encyclopedia of Popular Music,* London, England: Viking, 1989.

Cohn, Lawrence - *Nothing But the Blues,* New York, NY: Abbeville Press, 1993.

Cooper, Kent and Terry, Sonny - *Harp Styles of Sonny Terry,* New York, NY: Hyperion Publishing, 1995.

Davis, Francis - *The History of the Blues,* New York, NY: Hyperion Publishing, 1995.

Dearling, Robert, ed. - *The Illustrated Encyclopedia of Musical Instruments,* New York, NY: Schirmer Books, 1996.

Duncan, Phil - *Chromatic Harmonica Method,* Pacific, MO: Mel Bay Publications, 1983.

Duncan, Phil - *Mel Bay's Complete Harmonica Book,* Pacific, MO:

Mel Bay Publications, 1992.

Erlewine, Michael, Bogdanov, Vladimir, Woodstra, Chris and Koda, Eds. - *The All Music Guide to the Blues,* San Francisco, CA: Milton Freeman Books, 1996.

Erlewine, Michael, Bogdanov, Vladimir, Woodstra, Chris, Erlewine, Stephen Thomas, Eds. - *The All Music Guide To Country,* San Francisco, CA: Miller Freeman Books, 1997.

Feather, Leonard - *The Encyclopedia of Jazz,* New York, NY: Horizon Press, 1960.

Field, Kim - *Harmonicas, Harps and Heavy Breathers,* New York, NY: Fireside Press, 1993. Second edition - Cooper Square Publishing, 2000.

Freidel, Frank - *Our Country's Presidents,* Washington, DC: National Geographic Society, 1983.

Gindick, Jon - *The Natural Blues and Country Harmonica,* Hollywood, CA: Crossharp Press, 1986.

Glover, Tony "Little Sun" - *Blues Harp,* New York, NY: Oak Publications, 1965.

Haffner, Martin and Wagner, Christoph - *Made in America, Played in the USA,* Trossingen, Germany: Harmonikamuseum, 1993.

Harp, David - *Instant Chromatic Harmonica,* Montpelier, VT: Musical i Press, 1991.

Harris, Sheldon - *The Blues Who's Who,* New Rochelle, NY: Arlington House, 1979.

Hitchcock, H. Wiley and Sadie, Stanley, eds. - *The New Grove Dictionary of American Music,* New York, NY: Grove's Dictionaries of Music, 1986.

Hood, Phil, Ed. - *Artists of American Folk Music,* New York, NY: William Morrow, 1986.

Katz, Ephraim - *The Film Encyclopedia*, New York, NY: Harper Collins Publishers, 1994.

Kernfield, Barry - *The New Grove Encyclopedia of Jazz*, London, England: Macmillan Press, 1988.

Kingsbury, Paul, Ed. - *The Encyclopedia of Country Music*, New York, NY: Oxford University Press, 1998.

Kingsbury, Paul - *The Grand Old Opry History of Country Music*, New York, NY: Random House, 1995.

Hupferburg, Hubert - *The Book of Classical Music Lists*, New York, NY: Facts On File Publications, 1985.

Larkin, Colin, ed. - *The Guinness Encyclopedia of Popular Music*, London, England: Guinness Publishing, 1995.

Lawless, Ray - *Folksingers and Folksongs in America*, New York, NY: Duell, Sloan and Pierce, 1960.

Leighton, Hal - *How To Play the Harmonica for Fun and Profit*, Borden Publishing, 1978.

Lissauer, Robert - *Lissauer's Encyclopedia of Popular Music in America: 1888 to the Present*, New York, NY: Facts On File Publications, 1996.

Lloyd, Norman - *The Golden Encyclopedia of Music*, New York, NY: Western Publishing, 1968.

Lomax, Alan - *The Land Where Blues Began*, New York, NY: Pantheon Books, 1993.

Marcuse, Sybil - *Musical Instruments: A Comprehensive Dictionary*, Garden City, NY: Doubleday & Company, 1964.

Marsh, David and Stein, Kevin - *The Book of Rock Lists*, Dell Publishing, 1982.

McCloud, Barry - *Definitive Country, New York*, NY: Perigree Books, 1995.

Millard, Bob - *Country Music, New York*, NY: Harper Collins, 1993.

Miller, Jim, ed. - *The Rolling Stone Illustrated History of Rock and Roll*, New York, NY: Random House, 1980.

Milne, Tom - *Time Out Film Guide*, New York, NY: Penguin Books, 1993.

Morgan, Tommy - *Chromatic Harmonica*, Van Nuys, CA: Alfred Publishing, 1987.

Morton, Brian and Collins, Pamela, eds. - *Contemporary Composers*, Chicago, IL: St. James Press, 1992.

Morton, David C., Wolfe, Charles K. - *Deford Bailey: A Black Star in Early Country Music*, University of Tennessee Press, 1993.

Musselwhite, Charlie and Phil Duncan - *Power Blues Harp*, Pacific, MO: Mel Bay Publications, 1990.

Palmer, Robert - *Deep Blues*, New York, NY: Penguin Books, 1981.

Rees, Dafydd and Crampton, Luke - *DK Encyclopedia of Rock Stars*, New York, NY: DK Publishing, 1996.

Romanowski, Pat and George-Warren, Holly, eds. - *The Rolling Stone Encyclopedia of Rock and Roll*, New York, NY: Simon and Schuster, 1995.

Sadie, Stanley, ed. - *The New Grove Dictionary of Music and Musicians*, Washington, DC: Groves Dictionaries, 1980.

Sandburg, Carl - *Abraham Lincoln, the Prairie Years*, New York, NY: Harcourt, Brace & Co., 1926.

Santelli, Robert - *The Big Book of Blues*, New York, NY: Penguin Books, 1993.

Scott, Frank - *The Down Home Guide to the Blues*, Pennington, NJ: A Capella Books, 1991.

Sebastian, John - *An Introduction to Chromatic Harmonica*, Hicksville, NY: M. Hohner, Inc., 1972.

Shatzkin, Mike, ed. - *The Ballplayers*, New York, NY: Arbor House, William Morrow, 1990.

Slide, Anthony - *The Vaudevillians*, Westport, CT: Arlington House, 1981.

Sonnier, Austin, Jr. - *A Guide to the Blues*, Westport, CT: Greenwich Press, 1994.

Stambler, Irwin and Landon, Grelun - *The Encyclopedia of Folk, Country and Western Music*, New York, NY: St. Martin's Press, 1983.

Stevens, Mike - *Bluegrass Harmonica*, Anaheim Hills, CA: Centerstream Publishing, 1997.

Strong, Martin C. - *The Great Rock Discography*, Edinburgh, Scotland: Canongate Publishing Ltd.

Von Schmidt, Eric and Rooney, Jim - *Baby Let Me Follow You Down*, New York, NY: Anchor Press/Doubleday, 1979.

Walker, John, ed. - *Halliwell's Film Guide 1996* - New York, NY: Harper Collins Publishing, 1995.

Walters, Neal, Mansfield, Brian - *Music Hound Folk: the Essential Album Guide*, Detroit, MI: Invisible Ink Press, 1998.

Wolff, Rick, ed. - *The Baseball Encyclopedia*, New York, NY: Macmillan Publishing, 1990.

Wynn, Ron, ed. - *The All Music Guide to Jazz*, San Francisco, CA: Miller Freeman Books, 1994.

York, William - *Who's Who in Rock Music*, New York, NY: Scribner Publishing, 1982.

Periodicals:

American Harmonica Newsletter, Various Issues.

The Atlantic, Jan. 1982 - "The Harmonica in America" by Fred Nadis.

Billboard, July 9, 1983 - "Grand Old Opry Veterans Remember Deford Bailey" by Edward Morris.

Blues Access, Various issues.

Blues Revue, Various issues.

Buddy Guy's Legends Bluesletter, Various issues.

The Chicago Tribune, Various issues.

Country Living, May 1989 - "All Tuned Up" by Johnnye Montgomery.

Down Beat, Various issues.

Easy Reeding, Various issues.

Entertainment Weekly, July 11, 1997 - "Harmonica Convergence" by Tom Sinclair.

The Harmonica Educator, Various issues.

Harmonica Happenings, Various issues.

Harmonica Information Press, Various issues.

Living Blues, Various issues.

Pioneer Press, Various issues.

R&B Juke Box (UK), Various issues.

Smithsonian, November 1995 - "Harmonicas Are…," by Rudolph Chelminski.

Brochures and Pamphlets:
The Art of Playing Hohner Chromatic Harmonicas, New York, NY: M. Hohner, Inc., 1937.

A Brief History of the Hohner Marine Band Harmonica, M. Hohner, Inc., 1996.

Chromatic Harmonica Course, Chicago, IL Wm. Kratt Co., M.M. Cole Publishing House, 1933.

Easy Reeding, Richmond, VA: M. Hohner, Inc., 1996.

The Harmonica in Fiction:
McCloskey, Robert, *Lentil,* New York, NY: Viking Press, 1940.

Sebastian, John B., *J.B.'s Harmonica,* San Diego, CA: Harcourt-Brace-Jananovich Publishing, 1993.

Service, Robert, *The Song of the Mouth Organ,* (Poem).

Steig, William, *Zeke Peppin,* New York, NY: Harper Collins Publishing, 1994.

Steinbeck, John, *The Grapes of Wrath,* (Chapter 23), New York, NY: 1939.

Internet:
Literally thousands of websites have been consulted during the research and development of this book. Due to the vast number of sites and to the fact that many sites change addresses from time to time, it would be impossible to accurately list even a small percentage of them.

If you have internet access, my best advice is to get into one of the many search engines that are available and use the word "Harmonica" or any one of it's nicknames and let the computer take you through the tens of thousands of choices that are available.

Harmonica Clubs

Harmonica clubs are an excellent way to meet and play with other harmonica enthusiasts. There are quite a few in the U.S. and around the world. Most will meet on a fairly regular basis as well as sponsor special events and publish newsletters throughout the year.

SPAH (The Society for the Preservation and Advancement of the Harmonica)
PO Box 865
Troy, MI 48099

All Japan Harmonica Federation
2-37-22, Nishi-Nippori, Arakawa-ku
Tokyo, Japan 116

Bay Area Harmonicas
1001 Woodside Ave.
Essexville, MI 48732

Buckeye State Harmonica Club
1991 West 3rd St.
Columbus, OH 43212

Cambridge Harmonica Orchestra
7 Hatch Rd. - Box 699
Truro, MA 02666-0699

Capitol District Harmonica Club
40 Woodside Dr.
Scotia, NY 12302

Capitol Harmonica Club
1123 Cameron Rd.
Alexandria, VA 22308

Cardinal State Harmonica Club
2229 Russet Leaf Lane
Virginia Beach, VA 22308

Catstown Harmonica Club
Trambrugweg 51
5707 XZ Helmond, The Netherlands

City of Palms, Seniors Harmonica Band
1895 N. Tamiami Tr., C-12
N. Ft. Myers, FL 33903

Club Harmonica de Quebec
2632-B Rue Clement
Charlesbourg, QC, Canada G1H-7B1

Deutscher Harmonika Verband e. V.
Postfach 1150
D-73635 Trossingen, Germany

Dutch Harmonica Association (NOVAM)
PO Box 224
4600 AE Bergen op Zoom, The Netherlands

Federation Internationale de l' Harmonica (FIH)
Hohnerstrasse 8
D-78647 Trossingen, Germany

Federation of International Harmonica in Japan
2-7-4, Iwamoto-Cho, Chiyoda-Ku
C/O Moridaira Inst. Co., Ltd.
Tokyo, 101, Japan

Firehouse Harmonica Club
900 N. Broad St. #4409
Brooksville, FL 34601-6338

Floridacats Harmonica Club
900 N. Broad St., #4409
Brooksville, FL 34601-6338

Fort Myers Florida Harmonica Club
7761 Twin Eagle Ln.
Ft. Myers, FL 33912-1863

France Harmonica Association
118, Avenue Jean-Jaures, Appt 220
75019 Paris, France

Garden City Harmonica Club
29146 Sheridan
Garden City, MI 48135

Garden State Harmonica Club
PO Box 28
New Milford, NJ 07646

Gateway Harmonica Club (GHC)
14650 Baratton Drive
Florissant, MO 63034

Golden Oldies Harmonica Band
16699 Bagley Rd., Tri City Senior Center
Middleburg Hts., OH 44130

Grand Rapids Harmonica Club
1587 Mullins NW
Grand Rapids, MI 49504

Harmonica Aficionados Society
21B Smith Street
Singapore 058935

Harmonica Band of Towerpoint
4860 East Main St., B-94
Mesa, AZ 85205

Harmonica Collectors International
P.O. Box 6081
Chesterfield, MO 63006-6081

Harmonica Institute, Mouth Organ House
Shahu College Road, 13, State Bank Colony #2
Pune, MAH 411009, MAH, India 411009

Harmonica Organization of Texas (HOOT)
2363 Gus Thomasson Rd.
Dallas, TX 75228

Harmonicas of Alabama
429 Hickory St.
Birmingham, AL 35206

Harmonicas of Michigan (HOM)
826 Troywood
Troy, MI 48083

Harmonicas Tableau
#306 - 7107 Elbow Dr. S.W.
Calgary, Canada T2V-1J8

The Harmonichords
8745 E. SW 92nd Place
Ocala, FL 34481

Harmonicas of Louisville
516 Dale Ave.
Louisville, KY 40214

Hawaii Society of Harmonica Players (HSHP)
3840 Claudine St.
Honolulu, HI 98616

Hudson Valley Harmonicas
151 California Rd.
Yorktown Hts., NY 10598

Indiana Harmonica Club
PO Box 567
New Palestine, IN 46163

International Harmonica Organization (IHO)
144 Windham Rd., Springbourne, Bournemouth,
Dorset, England BH1-4RA

The Jacks and Jills
1945 Ridgeview Rd., Upper Arlington Sr. Center
Upper Arlington, OH 43221

Japan Harmonica Art Association
3-37-6-202, Ikegami, Ohta-Ku
Tokyo, 146, Japan

Kansas City Harmonicateers Harmonica Club
3024 North 47th St.
Kansas City, KS 66104-2442

Kansas City Metro Harmonica Society
PO Box 3883
Shawnee, KS 66203

Kent Chromatics
6 Gresham Close
Bexley, Kent, UK DA5-1EW

Korea Harmonica Association
302 Mi Dong B/L, 195-1 Nak Won Dong, Jong ro gu
Seoul, Korea

Lake Wheeler Harmonica Club
6013 Brack Penny Rd.
Raliegh, NC 27603

Lincoln Park Harmonica Club
1671 Mill St.
Lincoln Park, MI 48146

Long Island Harmonica Club
PO Box 118
East Meadow, NY 11554-0118

Los Angeles Regional Harmonica Association (LAHRA)
1731 Barry Ave., #212
Los Angeles, CA 90025

Macomb County Harmonica Club (MCHC)
8123 Virginia Park
Centerline, MI 48015

Malaysia Harmonica Association
Jalan Masjid India, 50100, Suite 9, 14th Floor
Semua House
Kuala Lumpur, West Malaysia

Melody Harmonica Society
Apt. Block 143, Jalan Bukit Merah, #09-1136
Rep. of Singapore 160143

Miami Valley Harmonica Club
3454 Folk Ream Rd., PO Box 1
Springfield, OH 45502-9619

Mile High Harmonica Club
1800 Swadley St.
Lakewood, CO 80215

Million Dollar Harmonica Club
Box 62, RR1, Ludingtonville Rd.
Holmes, NY 12531

Milwaukee Harmonica Club
4964 N. Larkin St.
Milwaukee, WI 53217-6044

Monte Vista Harmonica Club
8865 E. Baseline Rd.
Mesa, AZ 85208

National Harmonica League
Rivendell - High St., Shirrell Heath
Southhampton, Hampshire, England SO32-2JN

Nutmeg State Harmonica Club
161 Kennedy Drive
Bridgeport, CT 06606

Olympus Harmonica Club
950 East 3300 South
Salt Lake City, UT 84106

Omaha Metro Area Harmonica Arts (OMAHA)
4535 Manchester
Omaha, NE 68152

Paso Del Norte Harmonica Club
1088 Thunderbird
El Paso, TX 79912

Penang Harmonica Workshop
25, Jalan Concord 15, 11200 Tanjung Bungah
Penang, Malaysia

Point Pleasant Harmonica Club
2408 Beech St.
Point Pleasant, NJ 08742-3617

Rose City Harmonica Club
4431 Bonnymede
Jackson, MI 49201

Rubber Capitol Harmonica Club
270 E. Wilbeth Rd.
C/O St. Peter's Episcopal Church
Akron, OH 44301

Santa Clara Valley Harmonica Club
3380 Cork Oak Way
Palo Alto, CA 94303-4138

Schweitzerische Mundharmonica (SMI)
Gemeindehausstr. 13, Interessen Gemeinschaft
CH-6010 Kriens, Switzerland

Senior Reeds Harmonica Club
1701 N. Franklin
Dearborn, MI 48128-1027

Shelby Harmonica Players Society (SHARPS)
PO Box 1991
Alabaster, AL 35007

South Florida Harmonica Club
10400 NW 30th Court, #408
Sunrise, FL 33322-2028

Southern Michigan Harmonica Association
PO Box 173
East Leroy, MI 49051-0174

Steel Valley Harmonica Club
PO Box 333
McDonald, OH 44437

Sunparlor Harmonica Club
1427 Stuart
LaSalle, Ontario, Canada N9J-1Y5

Tampa Bay Harmonica Club
2831 Lake Saxon Dr.
Land O' Lakes, FL 34639-6620

Twin City Harmonica Society
3629 - 37th Ave. South
Minneapolis, MN 55406

Union Harmonica Band
1050 Jeanette c/o Union Recreation Dept.
Union, NJ 07083

Valley Harpers of Virginia
583 Cresthaven Ct.
Front Royal, VA 22630-2328

Western Pennsylvania Harmonica Society
320 Dinnerbell Rd.
Butler, PA 16002

Windy City Harmonica Club
PO Box 24
Westmont, IL 60559-0024

Wolverine Harmonica Club
10377 Verona Rd.
Battle Creek, MI 49017

Woodstock Harmonica Association
PO Box 275
Harbord, 2096 NSW, Australia

Wynmoor Harmonica Club
4301 Martinique Circle, A-1
Coconut Creek, FL 33066-1450

Y.O.H. Harmonica Club
P.O. Box 2130
Peekskill, NY 10566

Yellow Pine Enhancement Society Harmonica Contest
P.O. Box 23
Yellowpine, ID 83677-0023

Harmonica Instruction

Because of an almost total lack of accredited, formal training available in the U.S. for the harmonica, players have had to rely on word of mouth, books, tapes or videos to learn how to play their instruments. Many of these materials can.be purchased through local music stores, directly from harmonica companies or from several mail-order companies that specialize in the harmonica. I suggest that you contact them and request a catalog of the materials they have available.

Alfred Publishing
PO Box 17878
Anaheim, CA 92807

Arby Publishing House
PO Box 221092
Newhall, CA 91322-1092

Blues Harmonica Masterclass
PO Box 523
Waltham, MA 02254

Centerstream Publishing
16380 Roscoe Blvd.
Van Nuys, CA 91410-0003

Cross Harp Press
20965 Waveview
Topanga, CA 90292

Harmonica Music Publishing Co.
PO Box 671
Hermosa Beach, CA 90254-0671

Homespun Tapes
PO Box 694
Woodstock, NY 12498

Mel Bay Publications
#4 Industrial Dr.
Pacific, MO 63069

Mountain Top Productions
7 West 41st Ave.
San Mateo, CA 94403

Musical I Press
PO Box 3400
Middlesex, VT 05602

The Music Tree
Harmonica Master Class
17470 Monterey Rd.
Morgan Hill, CA 95037

Simpson & Smith
2398 Southern Rd.
Richfield, OH 44286

Steelman & Associates, Inc.
7249 Winchester Rd.
New market, AL 35761

Tatanka Publishing
PO Box 4104
Arlington Hts, IL 60006-4104

Turtle Bay School of Music
244 E. 52nd St.
New York, NY

Harmonica Magazines

There are several fine publications devoted exclusively to the harmonica. They provide a wealth of information related to the harmonica in every issue. Many harmonica clubs also publish regular newsletters. Here are a few:

American Harmonica Associates Newsletter
(Published monthly and is usually filled with information on nearly aspect of the harmonica.)
104 Highland Ave.
Battle Creek, MI 49015-3272

Easy Reeding
(Published roughly about three times a year and covers topics related to the M. Hohner Harmonica Company and it's endorsees)
M. Hohner, Inc.
1000 Technology Park Drive
Glen Allen, VA 23060

Harmonica Happenings
(SPAH's quarterly newsletter)
PO Box 865
Troy, MI 48099-8865

Harmonica Information Press
(Published sporadically by harmonica master Winslow Yerxa, this magazine is chock full of useful information)
203 14th Ave.
San Francisco, CA 94118

Harmonica World
(Published Bi-monthly by the National Harmonica League)
Victor Brooks
Walnut Cottage
10, Bonegate Rd.
Brighouse, West Yorkshire, U.K.

The Harmonica Educator
(Published quarterly and geared towards a more scholarly approach to the harmonica.)
Mr. Richard Smith
PO Box 340
North Hampton, OH 45349-0340

Harmonica Player
(German publication by Didi Neumann)
Agnes-Bernauer-Strasse 256
81241 Munchen, Germany

Harmonica Mail-Order Companies

Mail order and Internet catalogs can be an excellent source for harmonicas and harmonica-related materials. The selection and prices are usually better than their retail counterparts. Here are a few of the companies that are excellent mail-order and on-line resources.

Coast To Coast Music
PO Box 1857
Ellicott City, MD 21041-1857

Elderly Instruments
1100 N. Washington
Lansing, MI 48901

F&R Farrell Co.
PO Box 133
Harrisburg, OH 43126-0133

Harp Depot
PO Box 567
New Palestine, IN 46163

Joe's Virtual Music Store
7369 N. 46th St.
Augusta, MI 49012

Kevin's Harps
210 Farnsworth Ave.
Bordentown, NJ 08505

Lark in the Morning
PO Box 1176
Mendocino, CA 95460

Norman's Harmonica Centre
1 Links Close, Caister-On-Sea
Norfolk, England NR30 5DD

Harmonica Manufacturers

Blue Moon Harmonicas
261 Marvel Drive
Lancaster, OH 43130

Frank Huang International
176-3 Central Ave.
Farmingdale, NY 11735

Hering S/A Brinquedos E. Instuentos Musicals
Rua Ari Barroso
685 Galpao C/D - B. Salto do Norte, CEP: 80065-130
Blumenau - Santa Catarina, Brazil 0473

Hering USA
25 SE 2nd Ave. - Suite 435
Miami, FL 33131

M. Hohner, Inc.
100 Technology Park Dr.
Glen Allen, VA 23060

Matth. Hohner AG
Postfach 1260
D-78636 Trossingen, Germany

Harmonica Import
Weltmeister Harmonicas
641 East 1250 North
Nephi, UT 84648

Huang Harmonicas
C/O Insignia International
12A Seabro Ave.
N. Amityville, NY 11701

Ilus Harmonica Design
Renaissance Harmonicas
1950 North Point Blvd. #606
Tallahassee, FL 32308-4179

101 Products, Inc.
8736 Lion St.
Rancho Cucamonga, CA 91730

Lee Oskar Harmonicas
PO Box 1120
Duvall, WA 98019

Suzuki Corporation
PO Box 261030
San Diego, CA 92126-9877

Tombo Musical Instruments Co., Ltd.
2-37-22 Nishi-Nippori, Arakawa-Ku
Tokyo 116, JAPAN

Weltmeister Import Canada
498 St. Johns Rd.
Toronto, ONT, Canada M6S 2L5

Various Artist Recordings

Baton Rouge Harmonica, *Flyright.* This collection features recordings by Jimmy Anderson, Lazy Lester, Slim Harpo, Sylvester Buckley and Jimmy Dotson.

Best of the Central NY Harmonica Blowoff 1996-1998, *Poverty.* This collection features highlights from the annual Harmonica Blow-off and features ten cuts by various players, including Tom Townsley, Doug Jay, Matt Tarbell, Bernie Clarke, Pete McMahon, Ted Hennessey and Gary Primich.

Blow By Blow, *Sundown.* This collection features Junior Wells, Jerry McCain, Andy Belvin, Sammy Lewis, Eddie Hope and Charles Walker.

Blow It Till You Like It, *Charly* or *Sun Records.* This collection features Walter Horton, Joe Hill Louis, Woodrow Wilson Adams, Dr. Isiah Ross, Houston Boines, Hot Shot Love and Willie Nix.

Blowin' the Blues - Best of the Great Harp Players, Vanguard. This collection features Junior Wells, James Cotton, Big Walter Horton, Charlie Musselwhite, Corky Siegel, Paul Butterfield and more.

Blues Harmonica Spotlight, *Blacktop Records.* This collection features James Harman, Darrell Nulisch, Sam Myers, Rod Piazza, Lee McBride, Sugar Ray Norcia and Kim Wilson.

Blues Harp Greats, *Easydisc.* This collection features James Cotton, Carey Bell, Magic Dick, Annie Raines, Clarence Butler, Mark Hummel, George "Mojo" Buford, Charlie Sayles, Billy Boy Arnold, Paul Butterfield and Steve Bell.

Blues Harp Hotshots, *Easydisc.* This collection features Lee McBee, Sugar Ray Norcia, James Harman, Rod Piazza, Charlie Sayles, Sam Myers, Clarence Butler, Carey Bell, Jordan Patterson and Randy McAllister.

Blues Harp Power, *Easydisc.* This collection features James Cotton, Sugar Ray Norcia, Louisiana Red, Rod Piazza, Jumpin' Johnny Sasone, William Clarke, Sam Myers, Johnny Hoy, Darrell Nulisch and Lee McBee.

Blues Masters, Volume 4: Harmonica Classics, *Rhino Records.* This collection features Little Walter, Jimmy Reed, James Cotton, Sonny Boy Williamson II, Junior Wells, Paul Butterfield, Lazy Lester, Jerry McCain, Howlin' Wolf, Billy Boy Arnold, Big John Wrencher, Walter Horton, Snooky Pryor, Hot Shot Love, George "Harmonica" Smith, Slim Harpo, Kim Wilson and Charlie Musselwhite.

Blues Masters, Volume 16: More Harmonica Classics, *Rhino.* This collection features Sonny Boy Williamson, Little Walter, Magic Dick, Junior Wells, Sonny Terry, Gary Primich, James Cotton, Jimmy Reed, Paul Butterfield, Lazy Lester, Papa Alexander Lightfoot, Dr. Isiah Ross, William Clarke, Slim Harpo and Howlin' Wolf.

A Celebration of Blues, Great Blues Harp, *CBL.* This Collection features James Cotton, Sugar Blue, Charlie Musselwhite, Junior Wells, Walter Horton, Billy Branch, King Biscuit Boy, Sugar Ray Norcia, Kim Wilson and Magic Dick.

Chicago Blues Harmonicas, *Paula.* This collections features Baby Face Leroy, Snooky Pryor, John Lee Henley, Little Willie Foster, Louis Myers, Sonny Boy Williamson II and Walter Horton.

Chicago Blues Harmonica, *Wolf.* This collection features Snooky Pryor, James Cotton, Lester Davenport, Golden Wheeler, Dusty Brown, Little Mack Simmons, Birmingham Jones and Billy Branch.

Deep Harmonica Blues, *Excello.* This collection features Little Sonny, Jerry McCain, Ole Sonny Boy, Baby Boy Warren, Lightnin' Slim, Slim Harpo, Lazy Lester, Whispering Smith, Jimmy Anderson, Jolly George and Sonny Boy Williamson II.

Devil in the Woodpile, *Indigo.* This collection features Deford Bailey, Palmer McAbee, Bullet Williams, Freeman Stowers, Robert Cooksey, Jaybird Coleman, Will Shade, Noah Lewis, Blues Birdhead, Jed Davenport, Alfred Lewis, Hammie Nixon, Jazz Gillum, Sonny Terry and John Lee "Sonny Boy" Williamson.

Down Home Harp, *Testament.* This collection features Big Walter Horton, Little Walter Jacobs, Johnny Young, Robert Nighthawk, Billy Boy Arnold, James "Bat" Robinson, Cool Venson, Big John Wrencher, Harmonica Slim, Willie Lee Harris, John Lee Henley and others.

Essential Blues Harmonica, *House of Blues.* This collection features Charlie Musselwhite, Frank Frost, Magic Dick, Sonny Boy Williamson II, William Clarke, Billy Boy Arnold, Sugar Ray Norcia, Little Sonny, Paul deLay, James Cotton, Little Walter, Junior Wells, Willie Cobbs, Sonny Terry, Rod Piazza, Little Sammy Davis, Snooky Pryor, Jimmy Reed, Jazz Gillum, Kim Wilson, Howlin' Wolf, Carey Bell, George "Harmonica" Smith, Walter Horton, Sugar Blue, John Lee "Sonny Boy" Williamson, Raful Neal, Louis Myers and The Aces, Kenny Neal, Leon Brooks and Junior Parker.

Excello Harmonica Blues Variety, *AVI/Excello.* This Collection features Jimmy Anderson, Lazy Lester, Jerry McCain, Baby Boy Warren, Sonny Boy Williamson II, Little Sonny, Whispering Smith and Ole Sonny Boy.

Good Time Blues, *Columbia/Legacy.* This collection features Will Shade, Buddy Moss, Sonny Terry, Robert Lee McCoy and Jordan Webb.

Got Harp if You Want It, *Blue Rock-it.* This Collection features Rick Estrin, Charlie Musselwhite, William Clarke, Mark Ford, Mark Hummel, Andy Just and several others.

Great Harp Players (1927-30), *Document.* This collection features Francis and Sowell, El Watson, Palmer McAbee, Freeman Stowers, Blues Birdhead, Ollis Martin, George "Bullet" Williams, Ellis Williams, Smith & Harper and Alfred Lewis.

Hard Times: L.A. Blues Anthology, *BMA.* This collection features Smokey Wilson, Curtis Jack Griffin, Johnny Dyer, George "Harmonica Smith and Alex Schultz. Produced by William Clarke.

Harmonica Blues, *Yazoo.* This collection features Jaybird Coleman, Freeman Stowers, Alfred Lewis, Deford Bailey, Bobby Leecan and Robert Cooksey, Jazz Gillum, Chuck Darling, Robert Hill and others.

Harmonica Blues, *Wolf.* This collection features Smith and Harper, George Clarke, Rhythm Willie and Eddie Kelly.

The Harmonica Blues, *Storyville.* This collection features European recordings by Sonny Terry, Dr. Isiah Ross, Hammie Nixon and Sonny Boy Williamson II.

Harmonica Blues Kings, *Delmark.* This collection features Big Walter Horton and Alfred "Blues King" Harris.

Harmonica Masters, *Yazoo.* This collection features Deford Bailey, Palmer McAbee, Noah Lewis, Dr. Humphrey Bate, Jed Davenport, Gwen Foster, Herman Crook, Jaybird Coleman, Salty Holmes, Freeman Stowers and others.

Harmonicas Unlimited, Volumes 1&2, *Document.* This collection features Elder R. Wilson, Eddie Mapp, James Moore, Ellis Williams, William McCoy, Blind Roger Hays and Daddy Stovepipe.

Harp Attack!, *Alligator.* This recording is a four-way jam between Billy Branch, Carey Bell, James Cotton and Junior Wells.

Harpbeat of the Swamp, *Kingsnake.* This collection features Lazy Lester, Chicago Bob Nelson, Raful Neal, Jumpin' Johnny Sasone and others.

Harp Blowers, (1925-1936), *Document.* This collection features John Henry Howard, Deford Bailey, D.H. "Bert" Bilbro and

George Clarke.

Harps, Jugs, Washboards and Kazoos, *RST.* This collection features The Five Harmaniacs, The Salty Dog Four, The Scorpion Washboard Band and Rhythm Willie and His Gang.

Heavy Duty Harpin', *M. Hohner, Inc.* This collection includes Charlie McCoy, The Harmonicats, Pete Pedersen, Peter "Madcat" Ruth, The Cambridge Harmonica Orchestra, Toots Thielemans, Deford Bailey, Richard Hayman, Andy Just, Kirk "Jelly Roll" Johnson and Steve Morrell.

Heavy Harp, *Rollin' and Tumblin'.* This collection features Billy Branch, Sam Myers, Rodney Hatfield, Jim Rosen, Jay Miller, Joe Pinkerton and Lamont Gillespie.

House Rockin' & Hip Shakin' Vol. 4: Bayou Blues Harp, Hip-O. This collection includes Lazy Lester, Slim Harpo, Schoolboy Cleve, Jerry McCain, Silas Hogan, Whispering Smith, Little Sonny and more.

Juicy Harmonica, *Sundown.* This collection features Eddie Burns, Jerry McCain, Chicago Sunny Boy (Joe Hill Louis), Sonny Boy Williamson, Sonny Terry, Model T Slim, Jesse "Mule" Thomas and Sir Arthur.

Low Blows: An Anthology of Chicago Harmonica Blues, *Rooster.* This collection includes Walter Horton, Carey Bell, Mojo Buford, Big Leon Brooks, Good Rockin' Charles, Big John Wrencher and others.

Lowdown Memphis Harmonica Jam, *Nighthawk.* This colllection features Hot Shot Love, Joe Hill Louis, J.D. Horton, Walter Horton and Willie Nix.

Memphis Harmonica Kings, *Matchbox.* This collection features Noah Lewis and Jed Davenport.

Memphis Harp and Jug Blowers (1927-1936), *Document.* This collection features Jed Davenport, The Memphis Jug Band, Minnie Wallace and Little Buddy Doyle.

Pieces of Eight, *Making Tracks.* This collection features Jimmy Powers, Lisa & Preston Sturges, Tetsuya Nakamura, Iron Man Mike Curtis, Stanley Behrens, Kelly Rucker, Chris Hansen, David McKelvey, Ron Thompson, Larry David, Steve Kruse and Preston Smith being backed by LeRoi Sorgo's band.

Suckin' and Blowin', *Sundown.* This collection features George "Harmonica" Smith, Jerry McCain, Papa Alexander Lightfoot, Cousin Leroy, Long Gone Miles, John Lee "Sonny Boy" Williamson, Ole Sonny Boy and Sonny Terry.

Sun Records Harmonica Classics, *Rounder.* This collection features Walter Horton, Joe Hill Louis and Doctor Isiah Ross.

Superharps, *Red Lightnin'.* This collection features 1967 recordings of Little Walter with Muddy Waters and 1977 recordings of Billy Boy Arnold.

Superharps, *Telarc.* This recording is a four-way jam between James Cotton, Billy Branch, Charlie Musselwhite and Sugar Ray Norcia.

A Taste of Harp, *Moonshine.* This collection features Big John Wrencher, Tommy Louis, Big Jay McNeely and Ace Holder.

Texas Harmonica Greats, *Collectables.* This collection features Johnny Winter, Billy Bizor, Juke Boy Bonner, Sonny Boy Williamson II, Loudmouth Johnson, Gary Sapone, Paul Christensen, Jay Jay Johnson and Sonny Boy Terry.

Texas Harmonica Rumble, Vol. 1 & 2, *Fan Club.* These collections feature Mark Hummel, Jumpin' Johnny Sasone, Ron Sorin, Little Hatch, Big Al Blake and Ted Roddy.

This is Blues Harmonica, *Delmark Records.* This collection features Junior Wells, Carey Bell, Hammie Nixon, Little Walter, Big Walter Horton, Billy Boy Arnold, Billy Branch, Jimmy Burns, Lynwood Slim, Kim Wilson, Lester Davenport, Louis Myers, "Big" Golden Wheeler and others.

Three Harp Boogie, *Rhino Records.* A three-way jam featuring Billy Boy Arnold, Paul Butterfield and James Cotton.

West Coast Wailers, *Double Trouble.* This collection features Mick Martin, Dave Wellhausen, Chris "Hammer" Smith, Doug Jay and Steamin' Stan Ruffo.

Yokohama 95, *Japanese Import.* This collection features highlights from the 1995 Yokohama Harmonica Festival in Japan, including performances by Larry Adler, Charlie McCoy, Don Les with Mo Vint, Pete Pedersen and several outstanding Japanese harmonica players.

Photo Credits

Gaye Adegbalola: Photo by Susan Bacchieri, Courtesy of Gaye Adegbalola // Jerry Adler: Photo Courtesy of Jerry Adler // Larry Adler: Photo Courtesy of M. Hohner, Inc. // Red Archibald: Photo by Donna Loeffler, Courtesy of M. Hohner, Inc. // Deford Bailey: Photo Courtesy of M. Hohner, Inc. // Richard Bain: Photo Courtesy of Richard Bain // Steve Baker: Photo Courtesy of Steve Baker // Tom Ball: Photo By Mark Mosrie, Courtesy of Tom Ball // David Barrett: Photo Courtesy of David Barrett // Bob & Chris Bauer: Photo Courtesy of Bob Bauer // Harry Bee: Photo Courtesy of Harry Bee // Carey Bell: Photo by Brett Littlehales, Courtesy of Blind Pig Records // Dan Bellini: Photo Courtesy of Howard and The White Boys // Duster Bennett: Photo Courtesy of M. Hohner, Inc. // Donald Black: Photo Courtesy of Donald Black // Bud Boblink: Photo Courtesy of Bud Boblink // Robert Bonfiglio: Photo Courtesy of Robert Bonfiglio // Don Brooks: Photo Courtesy of M. Hohner, Inc. // Norton Buffalo: Photo by Pat Johnson, Courtesy of Norton Buffalo // Mojo Buford: Photo Courtesy of M. Hohner, Inc. // Jens Bunge: Photo by Marianne Hamann, Courtesy of Jens Bunge // Wild Child Butler: Photo by Marc Norburg, Courtesy of Live Earth Management // Paul Butterfield: Photo Courtesy of M. Hohner, Inc. // Mike Caldwell: Photo Courtesy of M. Hohner, Inc. // Johnny Cash: Photo Courtesy of M. Hohner, Inc. // Steve Cash: Photo Courtesy of M. Hohner, Inc. // William Clarke: Photo by Marc PoHempner, courtesy of M. Hohner, Inc. // Willie Cobbs: Photo Courtesy of M. Hohner, Inc. // Bob Corritore: Photo by Szabo, Courtesy of Bob Corritore // James Cotton: Photo Courtesy of M. Hohner, Inc. // Morris Cummings: Photo By Steve Roberts, Courtesy of M. Hohner, Inc. // "Ironman" Mike Curtis: Photo Courtesy of Mike Curtis // Art Daane: Photo Courtesy of Art Daane // Lester Davenport: Photo Courtesy of M. Hohner, Inc. // Guy Davis: Photo by C. Taylor Crothers, Photo Courtesy Red House Records // Little Sammy Davis: Photo Courtesy of M. Hohner, Inc. // Bruno De Filippi: Photo By: Ricardo Schwamenthal, Courtesy of Bruno De Filippi // Paul deLay: Photo by Ross Hamilton, Courtesy of Evidence Records // Lou Delin: Photo Courtesy of Lou Delin // Carlos Del Junco: Photo Courtesy of Carlos Del Junco // Leo Diamond: Photo Courtesy of M. Hohner, Inc. // Magic Dick: Photo Courtesy of M. Hohner, Inc. // Donovan: Photo Courtesy of M. Hohner, Inc. // Dave Doucette: Photo Courtesy of M. Hohner, Inc. // Sherman Doucette: Photo courtesy of Sherman Doucette // Mr. Downchild: Photo Courtesy of Mr. Downchild // Mark Dufresne: Photo Courtesy of Mark Dufresne // Little Arthur Duncan: Photo by Susan Greenburg, Courtesy of Delmark Records // Johnnie Dyer: Photo by Artline Studio, Courtesy of M. Hohner, Inc. // Bob Dylan: Photo Courtesy of M. Hohner, Inc. // Jonathan Edwards: Photo Courtesy of M. Hohner, Inc. // Rick Estrin: Photo by Kent Lacin, Courtesy of M. Hohner, Inc. // Jimmie Fadden: Photo Courtesy of M. Hohner, Inc. // George Fields: Photo Courtesy of George Fields // Mark Ford: Photo Courtesy of Blue Rock'It Records // Lee Fortier: Photo Courtesy of Fine as Wine Records // William Galison: Photo Courtesy of M. Hohner, Inc. // Geneva Red: Photo by Deone Jahnke, Courtesy of Ourkives Music // Jon Gindick: Photo Courtesy of Jon Gindick // Tony Glover: Photo Courtesy of M. Hohner, Inc. // Eddie Gordon: Photo Courtesy of Eddie Gordon // Mark Graham: Photo Courtesy of M. Hohner, Inc. // Buddy Greene: Photo Courtesy of Buddy Greene // Studebaker John Grimaldi: Photo by Gary Hannabarger, Courtesy of Blind Pig Records // Sigmund Groven: Photo Courtesy of Sigmund Groven // Dennis Gruenling: Photo Courtesy of Dennis Gruenling // Steve Guyger: Photo by Randy Santos, Courtesy of Severn Records // Tom Hall: Photo Courtesy of Tom Hall // John Paul Hammond: Photo Courtesy of M. Hohner, Inc. // James Harman: Photo Courtesy of Cannonball Records // Harmonica Hotshots: Photo Courtesy of Al Smith // Harmonica Rascals: Photos Courtesy of Ray Tankersley // Harmonica Slim: Photo Courtesy of M. Hohner, Inc. // The Harmonicats: Photo Courtesy of M. Hohner, Inc. // Stan Harper: Photo Courtesy of Stan Harper // Richard Hayman: Photo Courtesy of M. Hohner, Inc. // Patrick Hazell: Photo Courtesy of Patrick Hazell // Jia-Yi He: Photo courtesy of Jia-Yi He // Bob Hite: Photo Courtesy of M. Hohner, Inc. // Clint Hoover, Photo Courtesy of Clint Hoover // Walter Horton: Photo Courtesy of M. Hohner, Inc. // Johnny Hoy: Photo by Barbara Hoy, Courtesy of Tone-Cool Records // Cham-Ber Huang: Photo Courtesy of Cham-Ber Huang // Mark Hummel: Photo by Evie Quarles, Courtesy of Mark Hummel // Richard Hunter: Photo Courtesy of Richard Hunter // Little Walter Jacobs: Photo Courtesy of M. Hohner, Inc. // Kirk "Jelly Roll" Johnson: Photo Courtesy of Kirk Johnson // Brian Jones: Photo Courtesy of M. Hohner, Inc. // Johnny "Yarddog" Jones: Photo Courtesy of M. Hohner, Inc. // Mindy Jostyn: Photo Courtesy of Mindy Jostyn // Andy Just: Photo Courtesy of Blue Rock'It Records // Ron Kalina: Photo Courtesy of Ron Kalina // King Biscuit Boy: Photo Courtesy of M. Hohner, Inc. // King's Harmonica Quintet: Photo Courtesy of The King's Harmonica Quintet // Mick Kinsella: Photo Courtesy of Mick Kinsella // John Koerner: Photo Courtesy of M. Hohner, Inc. // Pierre LaCocque: Photo by Alain Richard, Courtesy of Michel LaCocoque // Charles Leighton: Photo Courtesy of Charles Leighton // John Lennon: Photo Courtesy of M. Hohner, Inc. // Howard Levy: Photo Courtesy of Howard Levy // John "Juke" Logan: Photo Courtesy of M. Hohner, Inc. // Larry Logan: Photo Courtesy of Larry Logan // Mel Lyman: Photo Courtesy of M. Hohner, Inc. // Johnny Lyon: Photo by Michael Tamborrino, Courtesy of M. Hohner, Inc. // Taj Mahal: Photo by Jef Jaisun, Courtesy of M. Hohner, Inc. // Darrell Mansfield: Photo Courtesy of Darrell Mansfield // Mike Markowitz: Photo by John-Ward Leighton, Courtesy of Blind Pig Records // Johnny Mars: Photo Courtesy of M. Hohner,

Index

C

J

N

O

P

Q

R

Walker, Jerry Jeff 26, 145, 171, 180

Walker, Phillip 179

Wall, Chris 180

Walter, Fried 37, 146

Walton, Wade 180, 194

War 18, 69, 128, 134, 180

Waters 6, 7, 11, 15, 19, 25, 26, 27, 29, 31, 33, 38, 39, 49, 72, 78, 81, 85, 86, 87, 90, 93, 94, 101, 102, 105, 121, 126, 127, 129, 137, 139, 140, 149, 150, 162, 166, 175, 180, 181, 182, 183, 185, 188, 189, 195, 206

Watson, Doc 62, 181, 182, 208

Watson, El 182, 205

Watson, Johnny "Jimmy" 182

Watts, Lou 174, 182

Weaver, Curley 53, 118, 125

Webber, Saul 36, 62, 75, 182

Webster, Katie 182, 192

Weiser, Glenn 182, 183

Weiss, Christian 5, 82, 118, 183

Wells, Junior 7, 19, 25, 40, 85, 90, 93, 124, 127, 163, 180, 183, 204, 205, 206, 208

Weltman, Sandy 91, 183, 208

Welton, Danny 133, 184, 208

Wenner, Mark 130, 184, 208

Weston, John 184, 185

Wet Willie 73, 130, 185

Wheatstone, Sir Charles 185

Wheeler, "Big" Golden 185, 205, 206, 208

Wheeler, Onie 134, 185

Whettam, Graham 8, 37, 146, 185

White, Booker T. "Bukka" 104, 186

White, Buck 186

White, "Schoolboy" Cleve 186

White, Tony Joe 186

Whitter, Henry 187

The Who 43, 187

Wiggins, Phil 34, 187, 208

Wilkins, Joe Willie 39, 187

Williams, Arthur 187

Williams, "Big Joe" 38, 40, 54, 55, 81, 83, 84, 92, 126, 143, 144, 159, 187, 188, 189

Williams, Doc 188

Williams, George "Bullet" 38, 205

Williams, Hank Jr. 188

Williams, Joe "Jody" 189

Williams, Robin 189

Williams, Tex 189

Williamson, John Lee "Sonny Boy" 12, 26, 39, 78, 81, 83, 119, 144, 150, 188, 189, 190, 205, 206

Williamson, Sonny Boy II (Rice Miller) 7, 15, 25, 29, 30, 51, 63, 84, 85, 90, 102, 104, 105, 114, 119, 136, 142, 143, 144, 147, 167, 187, 190, 191, 194, 195, 204, 205, 206, 208

Willing, Foy 190

Willis, Aaron "Little Sun" 191

Willis, Bruce 191

Wills, Oscar 162, 191

Wilson, Al "Blind Owl" 32, 82, 191, 208

Wilson, Chris 59, 191

Wilson, Danny 3, 16, 77, 95, 117, 129, 184, 192, 208

Wilson, Harding "Hop" 192

Wilson, Kim 57, 107, 162, 192, 204, 205, 206, 208

Wilson, Woodrow 177

Wiseman, Bob 22, 193

Wonder, Stevie 29, 193

Wood, Britt 193

Woods, Johnny 193

Wrencher, "Big" John 180, 193, 204, 205, 206

Y

Yaney, Clyde "Skeets" 194

The Yardbirds 6, 12, 20, 147, 190, 194

York, David "Rock Bottom" 194

York, George 194

York, Rusty 195

Young, Johnny 11, 33, 55, 134, 142, 194, 195, 205

Young, Neil 15, 28, 54, 61, 195

Z

Z., Jimmy 196

Zaremba, Peter 196

About the Author

Peter Krampert is a free-lance writer and harmonica player from the Chicago area. He has contributed articles to numerous publications including *Easy Reeding Magazine, The American Harmonica Newsmagazine* as well as writing a Daily Almanac for five web-based harmonica news groups. He has played harmonica for about 25 years in nearly every style of music and has performed with the bands *Uncle Buffalo, Wishbone Jones and The Last Band on Earth.* He currently resides in the Chicago area with his lovely wife, Donna.

The Encyclopedia of the Harmonica is an ongoing project and is subject to future editions with additions and revisions. We welcome your comments, tips and suggestions. Please send any comments to:

Peter Krampert
Tatanka Publishing
PO Box 4104
Arlington Hts., IL USA 60006-4104

or visit: www.eharmonica.net